Frommer's®

SO-BFB-891

Ottawa
2nd Edition

by Louise Dearden

Here's what the critics say about Frommer's:

"Amazingly easy to use. Very portable, very complete."

— Booklist

"Detailed, accurate, and easy-to-read information for all price ranges."
— Glamour Magazine

"Hotel information is close to encyclopedic."

— Des Moines Sunday Register

"Frommer's Guides have a way of giving you a real feel for a place."
— Knight Ridder Newspapers

WILEY

John Wiley & Sons Canada, Ltd.

About the Author

Canadian writer **Louise Dearden** has been an enthusiastic traveler since her first trip to Europe as a child. She spent 15 years zigzagging across the U.K., interspersed with numerous visits to Western Europe, before settling back in her native Ontario in 1990. In addition to her travel writing exploits, Louise writes for corporate clients, magazines, newspapers, and a conference publishing company. She has recently completed her first work of historical fiction.

Published by:

John Wiley & Sons Canada, Ltd.

6045 Freemont Blvd.
Mississauga, ON L5R 1L1

Library and Archives Canada Cataloguing in Publication

Dearden, Louise
        Frommer's Ottawa / Louise Dearden. — 2nd ed.

Includes index.
ISBN-13 978-0-470-83667-9
ISBN-10 0-470-83667-9

1. Ottawa (Ont.)—Guidebooks. I. Title. II. Title: Complete guide to Ottawa.

FC3096.18.D419 2005   917.13'84045   C2005-902296-5

General Manager: Robert Harris
Editor: Robert Hickey
Project Manager: Elizabeth McCurdy
Project Coordinator: Pamela Vokey
Publishing Services Director: Karen Bryan
Publishing Services Manager: Ian Koo
Cartographer: Mapping Specialists
Text Layout: Pat Loi

Front cover photo: © Bill Brooks/Masterfile
Back cover photo: © The Canadian Press

Special Sales

For reseller information, including discounts and premium sales, please call our sales department: Tel: (416)646-7992. For press review copies, author interviews, or other publicity information, please contact our marketing department: Tel: (416)646-4584; Fax: (416)236-4448.

Manufactured in Canada
5   4   3   2   1

Contents

List of Maps

Acknowledgments

My sincere thanks to editor Robert Hickey for his professionalism and valuable guidance throughout this project. Thanks are also due to copy editor extraordinaire Kelli Howey and the folks at Mapping Specialists. A special thank you to my husband and children for their continuing patience and tolerance over the years in dealing with a spouse and parent who works in a home office.

— Louise Dearden

An Invitation to the Reader

In researching this book, we discovered many wonderful places — hotels, restaurants, shops, and more. We're sure you'll find others. Please tell us about them, so we can share the information with your fellow travelers in upcoming editions. If you were disappointed with a recommendation, we'd love to know that, too. Please write to:

Frommer's Ottawa, 2nd edition

John Wiley & Sons Canada, Ltd. • 6045 Freemont Blvd • Mississauga, ON L5R 4J3

An Additional Note

Please be advised that travel information is subject to change at any time — and this is especially true of prices. We therefore suggest that you write or call ahead for confirmation when making your travel plans. The authors, editors, and publisher cannot be held responsible for the experiences of readers while traveling. Your safety is important to us, however, so we encourage you to stay alert and be aware of your surroundings. Keep a close eye on cameras, purses, and wallets, all favorite targets of thieves and pickpockets.

Frommer's Star Ratings, Icons & Abbreviations

Every hotel, restaurant, and attraction listing in this guide has been ranked for quality, value, service, amenities, and special features using a **star-rating system.** In country, state, and regional guides, we also rate towns and regions to help you narrow down your choices and budget your time accordingly. Hotels and restaurants are rated on a scale of zero (recommended) to three stars (exceptional). Attractions, shopping, nightlife, towns, and regions are rated according to the following scale: zero stars (recommended), one star (highly recommended), two stars (very highly recommended), and three stars (must-see).

In addition to the star-rating system, we also use **seven feature icons** that point you to the great deals, in-the-know advice, and unique experiences that separate travelers from tourists. Throughout the book, look for:

Finds	Special finds — those places only insiders know about
Fun Fact	Fun facts — details that make travelers more informed and their trips more fun
Kids	Best bets for kids and advice for the whole family
Moments	Special moments — those experiences that memories are made of
Overrated	Places or experiences not worth your time or money
Tips	Insider tips — great ways to save time and money
Value	Great values — where to get the best deals

The following **abbreviations** are used for credit cards:

| AE American Express | DISC Discover | V Visa |
| DC Diners Club | MC MasterCard | |

Frommers.com

Now that you have the guidebook to a great trip, visit our website at **www.frommers.com** for travel information on more than 3,000 destinations. With features updated regularly, we give you instant access to the most current trip-planning information available. At Frommers.com, you'll also find the best prices on airfares, accommodations, and car rentals — and you can even book travel online through our travel booking partners. At Frommers.com, you'll also find the following:

- Online updates to our most popular guidebooks
- Vacation sweepstakes and contest giveaways
- Newsletter highlighting the hottest travel trends
- Online travel message boards with featured travel discussions

What's New in Ottawa

As Canada's capital city, Ottawa is constantly in the spotlight. Thankfully, many of the best reasons to visit Ottawa — the national museums, annual festivals, abundant greenspace and waterways, bicultural nature of the community, and the city's charming ability to be both sophisticated and informal — never seem to alter. But no city ever sits still, and since the first edition of this guide was published Ottawa has had its share of changes that are of interest to tourists. So read on, and catch up with what's new in Canada's capital.

PLANNING YOUR TRIP If you plan to fly to Ottawa, your arrival will be a much more pleasant experience now that the new passenger terminal is open. It's easy to navigate, spacious, and has plenty of shops and services in the public areas and in the departure zone (after passing through security). In addition to **Air Canada** (www.air canada.com), the major carrier serving Ottawa, there are a number of smaller domestic airlines and several major U.S. airlines, including American Airlines. **Zoom Airlines Inc.** (www.fly zoom.ca) is a recently established discount carrier flying direct to Ottawa from Glasgow and London (Gatwick).

ACCOMMODATIONS The biggest news on the hotel front has to be the opening of the posh **Brookstreet Resort** (525 Legget Dr. *C* **613/271-1800**) in the heart of west-end Ottawa's high-tech community, commonly known as Silicon Valley North. The resort features The Marshes, an 18-hole championship Robert Trent Jones II public golf course, complete with GPS-equipped golf carts. In spring 2005 The MarchWood, a European par 3 course, was added. In the hotel, full spa and health club facilities are on offer, and guest rooms offer boutique-hotel styling and comfort. The hotel restaurant, **Perspectives,** has won a number of major awards. Several properties in downtown Ottawa have completed major renovations to the tune of several million dollars, including **The Lord Elgin, Minto Place Suite Hotel, Holiday Inn & Suites** (formerly Ramada Hotel & Suites Ottawa), and **Travelodge Hotel & Convention Centre, Ottawa West,** which features a new Wet & Wild Waterpark with rooms overlooking the indoor pool area. **Novotel Ottawa** has renovated and upgraded two guest-room floors, which now offer such luxuries as duvets and 32-inch wall-mounted LCD TVs. The **University of Ottawa** is now offering summer accommodation in its recently completed 2-bedroom-apartment residences, which are exceptional value. In terms of amenities, most hotels now offer in-room high-speed Internet access — increasingly wireless, and often complimentary.

DINING My favorite new discovery is **The Urban Pear,** 151 Second Ave. *C* **613/569-9305.** Sparks Street Mall is constantly challenged to attract business after the white-collar, sensible-shoe crowd has left for the day, and one of the bright spots that is determined to make a difference is **L'Ange** (109B Sparks St. *C* **613/232-8777**).

A relative newcomer, **Luxe Bistro** (47 York St. ℂ **613/241-8805**) has made an impression on young and monied clientele. **Zoe's Lounge,** at the Fairmont Château Laurier Hotel, has extended its delicious and authentic English afternoon tea menu to include a special Canadian tea and champagne tea. Other notable new reviews in this guide — for not necessarily new restaurants — include **Signatures** (453 Laurier Ave. E. ℂ **613/236-2499**), **ARC Lounge & Restaurant** (140 Slater St. ℂ **613/238-2888**), and **L'Argoät** (39A rue Laval, Gatineau (Hull Sector) ℂ **819/771-6170**). Sadly, L'Amuse Gueule has closed its bistro, after having moved from the Glebe to Wellington Street West a couple of years ago, although they are still operating the catering business. To my delight, however, I was introduced to two establishments in the same gourmet-to-go vein: **A Culinary Conspiracy** (541 Rideau St. ℂ **613/241-3126**) and **Epicuria Fine Food Store and Catering** (419 Mackay St. ℂ **613/745-7356**).

ATTRACTIONS The top news story is the opening of the new **Canadian War Musuem** (1 Vimy Place ℂ **800/555-5621**), which held its opening ceremonies on May 8, 2005, the 60th anniversary of VE (Victory in Europe) Day and the 125th anniversary of the Canadian War Museum. Built on LeBreton Flats, a greenspace area about 2km (1.25 miles) west of Parliament Hill, the Museum is a must-see destination for its stunning architecture, its creative vision of presenting the human story of Canada's role in conflicts and war, and its state-of-the-art exhibits.

The Centre Block of the Parliament Buildings, with its famous Peace Tower, was finally cleared of its scaffolding and shrouds when the laborious cleaning of the exterior was completed. It now stands proud and clear, but the **Library of Parliament,** with its glorious 16-sided dome hewn from Nepean sandstone and supported outside by flying buttresses, has been closed to the public since 2002. The extensive conservation and restoration project is scheduled to be completed in 2005. A major five-year renovation project began in 2004 at the **Canadian Museum of Nature** (240 McLeod St. ℂ **800/263-4433**). The museum is open during this period, but exhibitions will close in their turn as the work progresses. Open in 2005 are Birds in Canada, Mammals in Canada, Creepy Critters Gallery, Animals in Nature Gallery, and the Plant Gallery & Nature's Pharmacy; the earth gallery and dinosaur gallery are closed. A new fossil gallery, containing two true-to-life dioramas and life-size dinosaur models, is scheduled to open in 2006. Ottawa resurrected its **CFL (Canadian Football League) team** in the 2002 season, dubbing it the **Ottawa Renegades,** following the demise of the Ottawa Rough Riders at the end of the 1996 season. The Renegades play at Frank Clair Stadium in Lansdowne Park. The city's lacrosse team, the Ottawa Rebels, has ceased operation.

EXPLORING THE REGION **LaFlêche Caves,** in Val-des-Monts, Quebec, has added an **aerial adventure park** to its site, consisting of an impressive 82 bridges suspended from the tops of the trees in the forests of the Laurentians.

The Best of Ottawa

Canadians are proud of their capital city, with good reason. Ottawa lies in a magnificent natural setting on the south shore of the Ottawa River, with the picturesque rolling hills of the Outaouais region as a backdrop. The Parliament Buildings perch graciously on the escarpment, their architectural grandeur on display for all to admire. Ottawa's location on the border of predominantly English-speaking Ontario and French-speaking Quebec symbolizes the importance of the relationship between the two cultures.

Ottawa's appeal lies in its charming blend of sophistication and informality. Businessmen in somber wool overcoats clutch briefcases as they skate to work on the Rideau Canal. Sleek black limousines ferry foreign dignitaries to their engagements, in-line skaters and cyclists darting around them. Rows of tulips stand like sentries wearing multi-colored tunics, while students and tourists lounge on the grass, soaking up the spring sun. National museums feature world-class exhibits with entrance fees that the man in the street can afford to pay. Throughout the year, the region fizzes and sizzles with festivals and events to entertain the whole family.

I first experienced Ottawa as a guest at the biggest, most exuberant birthday party I'd ever attended. Thousands of party-goers flooded the streets, decked out in the red and white of the Canadian flag, but the atmosphere was benevolent and relaxed. As I wound my way through the crowds, I exchanged smiles and greetings with strangers, spontaneous gestures spurred by nothing more than a common nationality. I remember the day as a blur of pageantry, ceremony, music, and dancing, punctuated by a grand finale of fireworks exploding in the night sky. Celebrating Canada Day in the nation's capital sparked an affection for Ottawa that has only strengthened over the past ten years.

For a time, I was fortunate enough to live close to the city. Suddenly, I felt more like a resident than a tourist. I began to shop, explore, and dine in Ottawa on a regular basis and grew to appreciate the city more and more as I discovered its many treasures. I have marveled at the national museums, slept comfortably in hotels and B&Bs, been intrigued by heritage attractions, been entertained by world-class performers, tasted superb cuisine, shopped beyond my budget, walked the network of pathways, cruised the Ottawa River, and hiked through the autumn leaves. I'm not a native Ottawan, so I may be accused of looking at the city through tourist-tinted glasses, but I find Ottawa to be bursting with attractions and activities. I hope that you do too.

1 The Best of Ottawa Experiences

- **Celebrate Canada's Birthday:** Spend Canada Day (July 1) in the nation's capital — there's no experience quite like it. Head downtown and prepare for a full day of uniquely Canadian celebrations. Start the day with the ceremony of the Changing of the Guard.

Watch the Canadian flag rise above the Peace Tower on Parliament Hill, chat with the friendly Mounties mingling with the crowds (don't forget to ask if they'll pose for a photo), and take in a free concert. Have your face painted or tattooed (temporarily) in red and white, wave a paper flag, and buy a hat or T-shirt with a Canadian symbol to blend in with the throngs of people wandering the streets. In the evening, cast your eyes skyward for the best fireworks display of the year. See chapter 2, page 23.

- **Skate on the Rideau Canal:** Even if you live in a part of the country where ice-skating is a winter activity, it likely takes place at a community rink, where you end up skating around . . . and around . . . and around. An hour or two of that is enough to make anyone hang up their blades for good. But in Ottawa, you can experience the world's ultimate skating rink — the Rideau Canal — which offers almost 8km (5 miles) of wide-open space and ever-changing scenery. Warm-up huts are stationed along the way, where you can sip a hot chocolate or munch on a Beaver Tail pastry. Skate and sled rentals are available. See chapter 7, page 170.

- **Enjoy the Waterways:** Ottawa's history is deeply tied to the waterways in the region, and the scenic Ottawa River, Rideau River, and Rideau Canal make a major contribution to the beauty of the city. You can watch the locks in operation, take a cruise on the Ottawa River or the Rideau Canal, rent a paddleboat, canoe, or kayak on Dow's Lake, picnic on the city's riverbanks, sizzle on a sandy beach, or ride the white water of the Ottawa River northwest of the city. See chapter 6, page 123, and chapter 10, page 220.

- **Marvel at the Museums:** At a minimum, set aside half a day to spend at either the **Canadian Museum of Civilization** or the new **Canadian War Museum.** These stunning buildings are home to world-class museum exhibits. At the Canadian Museum of Civilization, life-size renderings of the social, cultural, and material history of Canada since the landing of the first Europeans in A.D. 1000 will captivate even the most reluctant museum-goer. The majestic Grand Hall displays more than 40 gigantic totem poles from the Pacific Northwest. A hands-on Children's Museum, which invites children to experience the fascinating cultural mosaic of the world we live in, is housed within the complex. The **Canadian War Museum,** which opened in May 2005, is a spectacular facility, with architecture that is simply awe-inspiring. The permanent galleries have made full use of leading-edge museum-design theories and techniques to bring to life Canada's role in conflicts and war, emphasizing how military events have affected Canadians at a personal, national, and international level. Allow time to also visit the special exhibitions, war art gallery, Memorial Hall, and Regeneration Hall. Expect to be emotionally moved and intellectually engaged. See chapter 6, page 119.

- **Play in the Snow at Winterlude:** This annual winter festival, held during the first three weekends of February, is filled with snow, ice, and loads of fun. Downtown Ottawa and Gatineau are transformed into winter wonderlands filled with gigantic snow sculptures, glittering ice sculptures, and a Snowflake Kingdom especially for kids. The Snowbowl, a new outdoor entertainment venue, features a variety of performances including music, skating demonstrations, and more. Winterlude activities are based at three main sites: the Rideau Canal Skateway (major access points are Rideau Street downtown, Fifth Avenue and Lansdowne Park in the Glebe, and Dow's Lake), Confederation Park, and Jacques-Cartier Park in Gatineau. See chapter 2, page 20.

• **Sink Your Teeth into a Beaver Tail:** Visit the original stand in the ByWard Market for this famous fast-food treat, which was first served in 1978 and now enjoys a huge following. But don't worry — there are no real furry creatures involved. Beaver Tails are flat, deep-fried pastries shaped like a beaver tail. Choose drizzled chocolate, cinnamon and sugar, garlic, cheese, or other toppings. Don't count the calories; you can easily burn up a Beaver Tail or two by skating on the canal or biking on the scenic pathways. See chapter 5, page 95.

• **View the Parliament Buildings and the Ottawa Skyline:** From the Alexandra Bridge, Jacques-Cartier Park in Gatineau, and the pathways along the north shore of the Ottawa River, you'll get a breathtaking view of the Parliament Buildings and the Ottawa skyline. The view from the Capital Infocentre on Wellington Street facing toward the front of Parliament Hill is one of the most photographed in Ottawa. See chapter 3, page 55.

• **Ride to the Top of the Peace Tower:** When you've taken in the grace and majesty of the exterior of the Parliament Buildings, hop in the elevator and ride up to the observation deck at the top of the Peace Tower. Built between 1919 and 1927, the 92-m (302-ft.) tower is a memorial to the more than 60,000 Canadian soldiers who lost their lives during World War I. The glass-enclosed observation deck offers magnificent views in all directions. See chapter 6, page 113.

• **Stroll the ByWard Market:** The ByWard Market district has something for everyone, from funky shops to swank restaurants, outdoor cafes, and an authentic farmers' market with excellent-quality fresh produce and flowers. The place bustles with activity and bubbles with personality. See chapter 6, page 136.

• **Shop in the Glebe:** This fashionable shopping district stretches along Bank Street between the Queensway and the Rideau Canal. Most retailers are independent and the merchandise is good quality. It's well worth spending a morning or afternoon strolling up one side of the street and down the other. See chapter 8, page 173.

• **Tiptoe through the Tulips:** Visit Ottawa in mid-May and you'll be dazzled by literally millions of tulips blooming throughout the capital region. Commissioner's Park, alongside Dow's Lake, features an orchestrated display of tulip beds with more than 300,000 blooms. Many of the events of the Canadian Tulip Festival take place in Major's Hill Park, northeast of the Parliament Buildings and behind the Fairmont Château Laurier Hotel. Ottawa's festival of tulips began with a gift of several thousand bulbs from the Dutch royal family after World War II. Since then, the tulips of Ottawa have grown to represent international friendship and the arrival of spring in Canada. See chapter 2, page 21.

• **Be Dazzled by the Autumn Leaves:** Gatineau Park, a wilderness area covering 361 sq. km (141 sq.

miles) in Quebec's Gatineau Hills, is a short drive from downtown Ottawa. It's beautiful in all seasons, but the abundance of deciduous trees makes it especially colorful in the fall. There are many hiking trails to suit a variety of ages and fitness levels. Maps are available. See chapter 10, page 208.

2 Best Hotel Bets

• **Best Historic Hotel:** The elegant Edwardian **Fairmont Château Laurier** (1 Rideau St. © **800/441-1414** or 613/241-1414) is a most admirably preserved and maintained property, both the exterior and interior. If you're looking for tradition, luxury, and attentive service, this is the place to stay. The extensive health club and pool area, added in 1929, superbly demonstrate Art Deco design. The Château Laurier's fairytale-castle appearance, refined interior, and exceptionally well-trained staff compel me to also bestow upon it, with great pleasure, the **Best Romantic Hotel** designation.

• **Most Stylish Stay: ARC the.hotel** (140 Slater St. © **800/699-2516** or 613/238-2888) scoops the award in this category. A sophisticated blend of luxury and efficiency is the hallmark of this upscale boutique hotel. Striving to anticipate and meet the needs of frequent travelers, ARC the.hotel provides a relaxing retreat from the demands of the everyday world. There really is no hotel experience quite like it.

• **Best for Families:** With so many Ottawa hotels competing for the family leisure market, family packages and facilities for children abound at many downtown properties, so it's not easy to choose a single property as the best of the bunch. For many years, the **Delta Ottawa Hotel and Suites** has unofficially earned the local title of tops for children, due not least to the popularity of its two-story indoor waterslide. But I equally recommend the **Minto Place Suite Hotel** and the **Cartier Place Suite Hotel.** In addition to the properties named above, the **Ottawa Marriott Hotel** received a local seal of approval as a child- and youth-friendly hotel in 2004.

• **Best Luxury Hotel:** The breathtaking splendor of the **Hilton Lac Leamy,** adjacent to Casino du Lac-Leamy (3 boulevard du Casino, Gatineau © **866/488-7888** or 819/790-6444), set a new standard of luxury in Canada's capital region when it opened in 2001. The main lobby features a spectacular blown-glass sculpture. Public areas are adorned with ceramic and marble. Views of Lac Leamy, Lac de la Carrière with its trademark fountain, and the Ottawa skyline are stunning. Guest facilities include spa, indoor/outdoor pool, tennis courts, fitness center, adjacent performance hall, and adjacent award-winning fine-dining restaurant.

• **Best Budget Accommodation:** Between May and August, head to the **University of Ottawa.** Their downtown, apartment-style residences are 2-bedroom units with double beds, TV, kitchenette, and private bathroom. Up to four people can stay for a flat fee of C$99 (US$81) per night. And they are clean, clean, clean.

• **Most Unusual Accommodation:** The **Ottawa International Hostel** (75 Nicholas St. © **613/235-2595**) is housed in the former Carleton County Gaol (1862–1972).

Your bed for the night is a jail cell bunk. If you'd rather not sleep behind bars, you can overnight in one of the dorms. Guided tours of the former prison are available through Haunted Walks Inc. (see chapter 6).

- **Best Suite Hotel:** There's an abundance of good suite hotels in the city, as you'll see if you browse through chapter 4, "Accommodations." Sharing the top spot by a whisker are the **Marriott Residence Inn** (161 Laurier Ave. W. ✆ **800/ 331-3131** or 613/231-2020) and **Minto Place Suite Hotel** (433 Laurier Ave. W. ✆ **800/267-3377** or 613/782-2350). Both have beautifully appointed, spacious suites with well-equipped kitchens. Their convenient downtown locations, clean indoor pools, and courteous, friendly staff earn them top marks.

- **Best Location: The Lord Elgin** (100 Elgin St. ✆ **800/267-4298** or 613/235-3333) could not be better located as a base for visitors to Ottawa. Directly across the street is Confederation Park, a small but pretty city park that's a leafy respite in summer and a glittering ice palace in winter (during the Winterlude festival). The National Arts Centre is across the street; Parliament Hill, the Rideau Canal, ByWard Market, and Rideau Shopping Centre are literally a five-minute stroll away. If you venture south along Elgin Street, you'll find plenty of pleasant eateries, lively pubs, and shops. **The Westin Ottawa** (11 Colonel By Dr. ✆ **888/625-5144** or 613/ 560-7000), on the opposite side of the Rideau Canal from The Lord Elgin, is also just steps from Parliament Hill and the ByWard Market. The third floor of the hotel provides direct access to the Rideau Shopping Centre.

- **Best Resort:** Leisure and recreational activities are outstanding at the new Brookstreet Resort in Ottawa's west end, the heart of Silicon Valley North (525 Legget Dr., ✆ **888/826-2220** or 613/ 271-1800). Their 18-hole golf course, The Marshes, was the final father-and-son Robert Trent Jones design collaboration. There's a state-of-the-art health club and spa onsite. Guest rooms have a boutique-hotel feel. "Perspectives" restaurant features contemporary Canadian fine dining with an Asian influence. **Chateau Cartier Resort** (1170 chemin Aylmer, Aylmer, Quebec ✆ **800/807-1088** or 819/777-1088), just a short drive from Ottawa, features an 18-hole golf course. Activities abound here — guests can also enjoy racquetball, squash, tennis, ice-skating, cross-country skiing, and more. Relax in the luxurious spa. Most rooms here are junior suites, above average in amenities and decor.

- **Best Retreat: The Carmichael Inn & Spa** (46 Cartier St. ✆ **613/ 236-4667**) is a quiet oasis in the heart of the busy city. Enjoy the calm, restful atmosphere. Relax on the sheltered veranda in spring and summer or curl up in an armchair by the fireplace in colder weather. A luxurious spa is located on the lower level. Day or overnight packages and special getaways for couples are popular features.

- **Friendliest B&B:** You'll feel completely at ease at **A Rose On Colonel By** (9 Rosedale Ave. ✆ **613/291-7831**). Owner Ann Sharp cheerfully welcomes guests, and her friendly nature ensures a relaxing stay in this charming home.

- **Best Period Décor:** You'll find many period details throughout the distinguished **Auberge "The**

King Edward" B&B (525 King Edward Ave. ℂ 800/841-8786 or 613/565-6700). The front parlor is a peaceful oasis of tropical plants, accented by a trickling fountain. Antiques are featured throughout the principal rooms. Original fireplaces, plaster moldings, pillars, and stained glass windows complete the picture. During the Christmas season, a 3.6 m (12 ft.) tall Christmas tree trimmed with Victorian decorations is a sight to behold.

- **Best All-Around B&B:** There's lots to like about **Alanbury House** (119 Strathcona Ave. ℂ 613/

234-8378). The owners are pleasant and welcoming. The interior has been meticulously decorated with chic Montreal style and taste. Fabrics and furnishings, including several antique pieces, have been carefully selected to complement this beautiful three-story Victorian home. The Willow Room features a fireplace, wrought-iron bed, and double Jacuzzi tub — perfect for a romantic getaway. The location is close to downtown, the Canal, the shops of the Glebe, and pretty little Central Park.

3 Best Dining Bets

- **Best Afternoon Tea:** There is nothing more civilized than afternoon tea, and **Zoe's Lounge** at the **Fairmont Château Laurier** (1 Rideau St. ℂ 613/241-1414) does it very well. Guests will appreciate the white linen, silver tea service, Victorian scones with Devonshire cream and strawberry jam, and attentive service from gracious waiters in waistcoats and bow ties.
- **Best Vegetarian: The Table** (1230 Wellington St. W. ℂ 613/ 729-5973) is a casual eatery with buffet-style service. Many dishes are certified organic. Choose from vegetable stir-fries, tofu, pasta, salads, breads, fresh fruit, cakes, and pies.
- **Best Desserts:** The beautifully sculpted Italian pastries are a feast for the eyes as well as the stomach at **Pasticceria Gelateria Italiana Ltd.** (200 Preston St. ℂ 613/233-6199). They also serve superb homemade gelato. Mandarin orange is my favorite here.
- **Best Crepes:** On a little side street in the Hull sector of Gatineau, **L'Argoät** (39A rue Laval ℂ 819/ 771-6170) is the perfect *crêperie*.

The menu has a satisfyingly long list of galettes (savory Breton crepes made with buckwheat flour) and sweet dessert crepes. Authentic Breton cider is served in small bowls. The decor is French country and the service is all Gallic charm.

- **Best Coffeehouse:** The atmosphere at **Bridgehead** (1277 Wellington St. W. ℂ 613/725-5500) is very urban neighborhood, and epitomizes the concept of the coffeehouses of today rather than the cafes of yesterday. Serving only fairly traded, organic, shade-grown coffees and offering itself as a wireless Internet hotspot, Bridgehead delivers what city folk want.
- **Best Gourmet Takeout:** For an ever-changing selection of take-home food, visit **Thyme & Again** (1255 Wellington St. W. ℂ 613/ 722-6277). The list of soups, salads, side dishes, main dishes, dips, vinaigrettes, and desserts reads like a fine-dining menu. Honorable mention must go to two other gourmet-to-go destinations: **A Culinary Conspiracy** (541 Rideau St. ℂ 613/241-3126) and

Epicuria (419 Mackay St. ℂ **613/ 745-7356**). You may never cook again!

- **Best Canadian:** The freshest available regional, seasonal, and often organic products are employed to create uniquely Canadian dishes on the constantly changing menu at **Domus** (87 Murray St. ℂ **613/241-6007**).

- **Best Classic French Cuisine:** If you seek an exemplary classic French cuisine dining experience, look no further than **Signatures** (453 Laurier Ave. E. ℂ **613/236-2499**). The only Cordon Bleu restaurant in North America, Signatures is located in an elegant Victorian mansion. The kitchen and the service excel, and a truly memorable evening awaits those who choose to dine here.

- **Best Italian:** Housed in a heritage stone building, **Mamma Grazzi's Kitchen** (25 George St. ℂ **613/ 241-8656**) is especially pleasant in the summer, when you can dine alfresco in the cobblestone courtyard at the rear. I've been coming here for years and have never been disappointed with the food or the service.

- **Best Young Chefs:** The co-chefs/ owners of **The Urban Pear** (151 Second Ave. ℂ **613/569-9305**) are so clearly passionate about their food and their restaurant they deserve a mention. Summer Lichty and Ben Baird, who both trained at Stratford Chef School, opened The Urban Pear in 2002. The menu focuses on fresh, local produce and therefore changes daily. Dishes are carefully prepared and delightfully plated.

- **Best Fusion:** Intense Caribbean colors surround diners at **Savana Café** (431 Gilmour St. ℂ **613/ 233-9159**). West African–style vegetable stir-fry, sweet basil shrimp,

coconut rice, and pad Thai are just a few of the divine dishes.

- **Best American:** Ottawa's **Hard Rock Cafe** (73 York St. ℂ **613/ 241-2442**) caters to rock music fans and lovers of burgers, steaks, fajitas, ribs, barbecued chicken, milkshakes, and ice cream sundaes. The collection of memorabilia from rock's most legendary performers is jaw-dropping.

- **Best Croissants:** Reputed to have the flakiest, richest, most buttery croissants in the city, the **French Baker/Le Boulanger Français,** 119 Murray St. (ℂ **613/789-7941**) also has authentic baguettes and other breads and pastries.

- **Best Ice Cream:** I always say you can never have too much ice cream, and it's impossible for me to walk or drive past **Pure Gelato** (350 Elgin St. ℂ **613/237-3799**) without stopping in for a dish of their delicious gelato.

- **Best Pasta: Luciano's,** a take-home-only pasta shop (106 Preston St. ℂ **613/236-7545**), is the place to go to stock your freezer with ravioli, agnolotti, and tortellini stuffed with yummy fillings like sun-dried tomato, spinach and ricotta, and butternut squash. Choose spaghetti, fettuccine, linguine, or rigatoni and top it with one of their homemade sauces.

- **Best Pizza:** Pizzas almost fly from the oven onto tables and out the door at **Café Colonnade** (280 Metcalfe St. ℂ **613/237-3179**). Their famous pizza has a thick crust with a sprinkling of cheese around the edge, a generous smear of tangy tomato sauce, and gooey mozzarella to hold the toppings in place. On warm summer days and evenings you can hang out on the outdoor terrace that stretches along one side of the building. Takeout is also available.

- **Best Seafood:** You know how fresh the fish is at the **Pelican Fishery & Grill** (1500 Bank St. ✆ **613/526-0995**) because you walk right past the eye-catching display of fresh fish and seafood on the way to your table. The menu changes daily, depending on what's available.
- **Best Bistro:** One of the best places to eat in the ByWard Market area, the **Black Tomato** (11 George St. ✆ **613/789-8123**) gets top marks for the food and the surroundings. The kitchen has heaps of culinary talent, so prepare yourself for a hedonistic culinary experience.
- **Best Alfresco Dining:** Having the distinct advantage of a converted boathouse setting, the **Canal Ritz** (375 Queen Elizabeth Dr. ✆ **613/238-8998**) boasts an outstanding terrace alongside the Rideau Canal, giving diners a constantly changing panorama. In summer, boats glide right past the terrace. In the winter, the Canal Ritz wins for best view: when the canal freezes and transforms itself

into the world's longest skating rink, you can watch the myriad skaters slipping and sliding along the ice as you gaze through the picture windows.
- **Best Hotel Dining: The ARC Lounge & Restaurant** (140 Slater St. ✆ **613/238-2888**) evokes the same feeling of simple good taste that prevails throughout the hotel. Subdued lighting, rich dark wood, and contemporary decor combine to create a sophisticated yet relaxing atmosphere. Dishes get top marks for presentation, with taste to match.
- **Best Wine List:** The wine list at **Luxe Bistro** (47 York St. ✆ **613/241-8805**) has been enjoying the limelight, winning acclaim for its length as much as its breadth. With so many good wines to choose from, and a generous proportion of them available by the glass, the best way to go is to create your own wine tasting by selecting any four wines-by-the-glass at 3 oz. each for a total of C$22 (US$18).

4 The Best of Ottawa for Families

There are as many different kinds of children as there are parents. Some families like to be active outdoors, others like to explore museums, and many like to join in local festivals and special events. Whatever your family's favorite kind of vacation, Ottawa and the surrounding region delivers. There's so much to see and do, you'll find yourself planning a return visit even before the first is over.

- **Best Attractions:** Ottawa has so many top attractions appealing to all age groups that it's difficult and perhaps a little unfair to single out a few. Visit the exceptional **Canadian Museum of Civilization,** with its world-class exhibits, IMAX films, and **Children's**

Museum, and the new **Canadian War Museum,** with its stunning architecture and state-of-the-art exhibits. At the **RCMP Musical Ride Centre,** tour the stables and watch the Mounties rehearse their routines free of charge. Browse the animal barns, demonstrations, and special events at the **Canada Agriculture Museum,** and take in the dinosaurs, rocks and minerals, and creepy critters at the **Museum of Nature.** Visit the **Canada Aviation Museum,** with its large collection of authentic aircraft, and get involved in the hands-on **Canada Science and Technology Museum.** See chapter 6.

- **Best Accommodations:** Although you may think a one- or two-bedroom hotel suite is out of the reach of a family budget, many suite hotels are competitively priced and offer packages during peak holiday periods. You may well find the cost is similar to other types of accommodation, and when you're traveling with children a suite is the only way to go. The flexibility of having at least one separate bedroom and the convenience of a kitchen in which to prepare snacks and meals makes the entire vacation less stressful for everyone. See chapter 4.
- **Best Outdoors:** Head for Gatineau Park across the river in Quebec in any season and enjoy the trails. Drop in to the visitor center before you hike, bike, or ski and buy a trail map showing the topography in detail so you can select trails to suit your fitness level and ability. See chapter 10, page 208.
- **Best Events:** Join the fun at **Winterlude,** celebrating Canada's chilliest season. The first three weekends of February are filled with snow, ice, and loads of family fun. In mid-May, the **Canadian Tulip Festival** will dazzle young and old with the blooming of more than three million tulips in a rainbow of colors. Between May and October, the **RCMP Musical Ride** performs a musical show with their majestic horses. They tour throughout Canada, with some Ottawa dates. Not to be missed is the **Changing of the Guard,** a half-hour ceremony performed daily (weather permitting) on Parliament Hill between late June and late August. Finally, it's worth braving the crowds to experience **Canada Day (July 1)** in the nation's capital.
- **Most Fun Dining:** Experience the unique atmosphere of Marchélino (Rideau Shopping Centre, 50 Rideau St. ✆ **613/569-4934**). Wander among the colorful displays of fruits, salads, breads, and pastries and watch the staff at work rolling out dough, baking bread, roasting chickens, sliding pizzas in and out of the stone hearth oven, assembling sushi, and flipping crepes. See chapter 5, page 96.
- **Best Casual Dining:** The Elgin Street Diner (374 Elgin St. ✆ **613/ 237-9700**) is a comfy, neighborhood kind of place where you can saunter in, flop into a chair, and hang out with a coffee while the kids slurp milkshakes and chomp peanut butter and jam sandwiches. There are plenty of old-fashioned dinners on the menu, including meat loaf, shepherd's pie, and liver and onions. See chapter 5, page 91.

2

Planning Your Trip to Ottawa

Whether your trip planning style leans toward thorough research and meticulous attention to detail or last-minute and anything goes in terms of when, where, and how, taking time to plan will help you make the most of Ottawa's extensive choice of visitor attractions, activities, and unique experiences. Moreover, in today's climate of heightened travel security it's in your best interests to ensure you understand the rules and requirements for transportation and, for those who are arriving from abroad, the entry requirements for Canada.

1 Visitor Information

FROM NORTH AMERICA

Within Canada, your starting point is the **Capital Infocentre,** 90 Wellington St., Ottawa (*C* **800/465-1867** or 613/ 239-5000; **www.canadascapital.gc.ca**), located directly across the street from the Parliament Buildings. The **Capital Infocentre** provides information on Ottawa and the surrounding region and is administered by the National Capital Commission (NCC). During the main tourist season, from mid-May to Labour Day (first Monday in September), the **Capital Infocentre** is open daily 8:30am to 9pm. The rest of the year it's open daily 9am to 5pm. To receive printed material on Ottawa and the entire National Capital Region, write to the Capital Infocentre's mailing address at 40 Elgin St., Room 202, Ottawa, ON K1P 1C7.

The **Ottawa Tourism and Convention Authority Inc. (OTCA),** 130 Albert St., Suite 1800, Ottawa, ON K1P 5G4, maintains a comprehensive website with visitor information at **www.ottawatourism.ca.** The **OTCA** publishes a comprehensive annual visitor guide, which includes maps and listings of cultural sites, things to see and do, accommodations, places to dine and shop, and services. You can obtain a free printed copy of the guide by phoning the **Capital Infocentre** (*C* **800/465-1867**). Allow ten business days for delivery. You can also pick up a copy at the **Capital Infocentre** when you arrive in the city.

The **Ontario East Tourism Association,** *C* **800/567-3278; www. ontarioeast.com,** can provide details of Eastern Ontario attractions, including the Thousand Islands and St. Lawrence Valley Corridor, the Rideau Heritage Corridor, and the Ottawa Valley.

Visitors to Canada from the U.S. can visit the Canadian federal government's Department of Foreign Affairs and International Trade website, **www. dfait-maeci.gc.ca/can-am,** which specifically deals with issues pertaining to Canada–U.S. relations. Contact information for Canadian government offices in the U.S. is listed, as well as links for tourism information. In addition to the Canadian Embassy, located in Washington, D.C., there are about a dozen Canadian consulate general offices and several consulates located throughout the U.S.

From Abroad

Visit the official travel site of the **Canadian Tourism Commission, www.travelcanada.ca,** and click on your country of residence to access customized visitor information, including advice on traveling to Canada and contact information for tour operators and travel agents in your country who specialize in Canada as a destination.

There are more than 300 Government of Canada diplomatic and consular missions overseas, which can provide information on traveling to Canada and direct you to the appropriate sources for tourist information. If your country of residence is other than those listed below, you can access the full directory online at **www.dfait-maeci.gc.ca/world/ embassies/menu-en.asp.**

U.K.: The **Canadian High Commission,** 1 Grosvenor Sq., London W1K 4AB (© **0207/258-6600**).

Ireland: The **Canadian Embassy,** 65 St. Stephen's Green, Dublin 2 (© **01/417-4100**).

Australia: The **Canadian High Commission,** Commonwealth Avenue, Canberra, ACT, 2600 (© **02/6270-4000**), or the Consulate General of Canada, Level 5, Quay West Building, 111 Harrington St., Sydney, NSW, 2000 (© **02/9364-3000**). There are also Consulates in Perth and Melbourne.

New Zealand: The **Canadian High Commission,** 61 Molesworth St., 3rd Floor, Thorndon, Wellington (© **04/473-9577**).

South Africa: The **Canadian High Commission,** 1103 Arcadia St., Hatfield, Pretoria (© **012/422-3000**). There is also a Canadian High Commission in Capetown and a Consulate in Durban.

2 Entry Requirements & Customs

ENTRY REQUIREMENTS

The following guidelines regarding entry documents should be followed carefully. Security has been heightened at border crossings and other points of entry since the September 11, 2001 terrorist attacks. Laws, restrictions, and entitlements that affect visitors are subject to change at any time. It's best to check before you travel.

All visitors to Canada must show proof of citizenship. A valid passport is the preferred entry document, and is a requirement for most visitors. U.S. citizens and permanent U.S. residents do not need a passport to enter Canada, though it is the easiest and most convenient method of proving citizenship. U.S. citizens may present one of the following documents, provided it is accompanied by official photo ID: certificate of citizenship, birth certificate, or certificate of naturalization. U.S. permanent residents must also carry their Alien Registration Card (Green Card). If you plan to drive into Canada, be sure to bring

your car's registration papers and insurance documents. If you are traveling with children, make sure they have identification documents. Parents who share custody of their children should carry copies of the legal custody documents. If you are not the parent or legal guardian of the children traveling with you, you should carry a written statement from the children's parent or guardian, granting permission for the children to travel to Canada under your supervision.

Citizens of most European countries, Commonwealth countries, and former British colonies, as well as certain other countries, do not need visas but must carry passports. Entry visas are required for citizens of more than 140 countries. You must apply for and receive your visa from the Canadian embassy, high commission, or consulate in your home country. For a complete list of countries and territories whose citizens require visas in order to enter Canada as visitors, visit **www.cic.gc.ca.**

CUSTOMS
WHAT YOU CAN BRING INTO CANADA

Generally, you are allowed to bring in goods for personal use during your trip to Canada, although there are restrictions and controls on the importation of certain goods, such as firearms, ammunition, fireworks, meat and dairy products, animals, plants and plant products, firewood, fresh fruits and vegetables, and certain food and drug products. Outdoor sportsmen and women should note that fishing tackle can be brought into Canada, but the bearer must posses a non-resident license for the province where he or she plans to use it. However, there are severe restrictions on firearms and weapons, and visitors are strongly advised to contact the Canadian Firearms Centre (© 800/731-4000 in Canada and the U.S., © 506/624-5380 from other countries) prior to travel.

If you meet the minimum age requirement of the province or territory through which you enter Canada (the age is 19 in Ontario), you can bring in, free of duty or taxes, no more than 1.14 liters (40 fl. oz.) of liquor, or 1.5 liters (52 fl. oz.) of wine, or 24 containers of beer (355 mL, or 12 fl. oz. each). Visitors entering Ontario who are aged 19 or older can also bring up to 200 cigarettes, 50 cigars or cigarillos, 200 grams (7 oz.) of manufactured tobacco, and 200 tobacco sticks duty-free. Dogs and cats in good health can enter Canada from the U.S. with their owners, but you should bring a valid rabies vaccination certificate with you. Check with the Canadian Food Inspection Agency's Import Service Centre © 800/835-4486 if you wish to bring other kinds of animals from the U.S., or any animal from another country.

For more information on customs matters, contact your nearest Canadian embassy or consulate, or call the **Automated Customs Information Service** (© 204/983-3500 or 506/636-5064). Information is available online at **www.cbsa-asfc.gc.ca.** Print publications can be ordered by calling © 800/959- 2221.

What You Can Take Home from canada

Returning **U.S. citizens** who have been away for at least 48 hours are allowed to take back, once every 30 days, $800 worth of merchandise duty-free. You'll be charged a flat rate of duty on the next $1,000 worth of purchases. Any dollar amount beyond that is dutiable at whatever rates apply. On mailed gifts, the duty-free limit is $200. Be sure to have your receipts or purchases handy to expedite the declaration process. *Note:* If you owe duty, you are required to pay on your arrival in the United States, either by cash, personal check, government or traveler's check, or money order, or in some locations, a Visa or MasterCard.

To avoid having to pay duty on foreign-made personal items you owned before you left on your trip, bring along a bill of sale, insurance policy, jeweler's appraisal, or receipt of purchase. Or you can register items

---

(*Tips* **Passport Savvy**

Allow plenty of time before your trip to apply for a passport; processing can take several weeks. Keep in mind that if you need a passport in a hurry, you'll pay a higher processing fee. When traveling, safeguard your passport in an inconspicuous, inaccessible place like a money belt and keep a copy of the critical pages with your passport number in a separate place. If you lose your passport, visit the nearest consulate or embassy of your native country as soon as possible for a replacement.

that can be readily identified by a permanently affixed serial number or marking — think laptop computers, cameras, and CD players — with Customs before you leave. Take the items to the nearest Customs office or register them with Customs at the airport from which you're departing. You'll receive, at no cost, a certificate of registration, which allows duty-free entry for the life of the item.

With some exceptions, you cannot take fresh fruits and vegetables into the United States. Also, Cuban tobacco products purchased in Canada cannot be taken back into the U.S. For specifics on what you can take back, download the invaluable free pamphlet *Know Before You Go* online at **www.cbp.gov.** (Click on "Travel," and then click on "Know Before You Go! Online Brochure.") Or contact the **U.S. Customs & Border Protection (CBP),** 1300 Pennsylvania Ave. NW, Washington, DC 20229 (© **877/287-8667**) and request the pamphlet.

Citizens of the U.K. who are returning from a non–EU country have a customs allowance of 200 cigarettes; 50 cigars; 250 grams of smoking tobacco; 2 liters of still table wine; 1 liter of spirits or strong liqueurs (over 22% volume); 2 liters of fortified wine, sparkling wine, or other liqueurs; 60cc perfume; 250cc toilet water; and £145 worth of all other goods, including gifts and souvenirs. People under age 17 cannot have the tobacco or alcohol allowance. For more information, contact **HM Customs & Excise** at

© **0845/010-9000** (from outside the U.K., 020/8929-0152), or consult their website at **www.hmce.gov.uk.**

The duty-free allowance in **Australia** is A$400, or for those under age 18, A$200. Citizens can take in 250 cigarettes or 250 grams of loose tobacco, and 1,125 milliliters of alcohol. If you're returning with valuables you already own, such as foreign-made cameras, you should file form B263. A helpful brochure available from Australian consulates or customs offices is *Know Before You Go.* For more information, call the **Australian Customs Service** at © **1300/363-263** or log on to **www.customs.gov.au.**

The duty-free allowance for **New Zealand** is NZ$700. Citizens over age 17 can take in 200 cigarettes, 50 cigars, or 250 grams of tobacco (or a mixture of all three if their combined weight doesn't exceed 250g), plus 4.5 liters of wine and beer, or 1.125 liters of liquor. New Zealand currency does not carry import or export restrictions. Before you leave, fill out a certificate of export listing the valuables you are bringing out of the country; that way, you can take them back without paying duty. Most questions are answered in a free pamphlet available at New Zealand consulates and customs offices: *New Zealand Customs Guide for Travellers, Notice No. 4.* For more information, contact **New Zealand Customs,** The Customhouse, 17–21 Whitmore St., Box 2218, Wellington (© **04/473-6099** or 0800/428-786; **www.customs.govt.nz**).

3 Money

CURRENCY

The currency of Canada is the Canadian **dollar,** made up of 100 **cents.** U.S. visitors will still find their dollar buys more in Canada than at home, but the heady days of highly favorable exchange rates have passed and the

Canadian dollar is hovering around 82 cents in U.S. money, give or take a couple of points' variation. What this means is that your American money gets you about 20% more the moment you exchange it for local currency. The British pound has been sitting at around $2.30, a little lower than in recent years, but still translating into excellent value for visitors from the U.K. (You might want to visit a website such as **www.xe.com/ucc** for up-to-the-minute exchange rate information.)

Be aware that although sales taxes are high in Canada (15% tax is added to retail goods purchased in Ontario, with taxes for restaurant meals even higher), as a visitor you may be eligible to claim a partial tax refund for some purchases (see "Taxes" under "Fast Facts" in chapter 3, "Getting to Know Ottawa"). Paper currency comes in $5, $10, $20, $50, and $100 denominations. Coins come in 1¢, 5¢, 10¢, and 25¢ (penny, nickel, dime, and quarter) and $1 and $2 denominations.

Most tourist establishments in Canada will accept U.S. cash, but to get the best rate change your funds into Canadian currency upon arrival. If you do spend American money at Canadian establishments, you should understand how the conversion is calculated. Often there is a sign at the cash register stating U.S. CURRENCY XX%. The stated percentage, for example

20%, is the "premium," which means that for every U.S. greenback you hand over, the cashier will consider it equivalent to $1.20 Canadian. For example, to pay a $24 tab you'll need only $20 in U.S. currency. Be aware that the exchange rate may not be as favorable as you would get at a bank or currency-exchange booth — you pay a price for convenience.

It's a good idea to bring some Canadian funds to take you through your first day or so, when you'll likely need cash for cab or bus fare and a snack. That way, you can avoid lines at airport ATMs (automated teller machines). In the U.S., you can exchange money at your local American Express or Thomas Cook office before you leave on your trip. Banks in Ottawa generally offer currency-exchange services. If you're far away from a bank with currency-exchange services, American Express offers traveler's checks and foreign currency, though with a US$15 order fee and additional shipping costs, at www.americanexpress.com or ✆ **800/807-6233.**

The Canadian Dollar, the U.S. Dollar & the British Pound

The prices in this guide are given first in Canadian dollars, then in U.S. dollars. Amounts over $5 have been rounded to the nearest dollar. Note that the Canadian dollar is worth about 20% less than the U.S. dollar. At the time of writing, C$1 was worth about US$0.82 and that was the equivalency used to figure the prices in this guide. The U.K. pound is included here for your reference, with C$1 worth about £0.44. Note that exchange rates are subject to fluctuation, and you should always check the most recent currency rates when preparing for your trip. Here's a quick table of equivalents:

C$	US$	UK£	US$	C$	UK£
1	0.82	0.44	1	1.22	0.53
5	4.10	2.20	5	6.10	2.65
10	8.20	4.40	10	12.20	5.30
50	41.00	22.00	50	61.00	26.50
80	65.60	35.20	80	97.60	42.40
100	82.00	44.00	100	122.00	53.00

⌜ *Fun Fact*

The common name for the $1 coin is the "loonie" because of the loon on the reverse side. When the bi-metallic $2 coin was subsequently introduced into circulation, it was instantly dubbed the "toonie."

ATMS

The easiest and best way to get cash away from home is from an **ATM** (automated teller machine). The **Cirrus** (✆ **800/424-7787; www.mastercard. com**) and **PLUS** (✆ **800/843-7587; www.visa.com**) networks span the globe; look at the back of your bank card to see which network you're on, then call or check online for ATM locations at your destination. Be sure you know your personal identification number (PIN) and your daily withdrawal limit before you leave home. Also keep in mind that many banks impose a fee every time a card is used at a different bank's ATM, and that fee can be higher for international transactions than for domestic ones. On top of this, the bank from which you withdraw cash may charge its own fee.

You can also get cash advances on your credit card at an ATM. Keep in mind that credit card companies try to protect themselves from theft by limiting the funds someone can withdraw outside their home country, so call your credit card company before you leave home. And keep in mind that you'll pay interest from the moment of your withdrawal, even if you pay your monthly bills on time.

TRAVELER'S CHECKS

Traveler's checks are something of an anachronism from the days before the ATM made cash accessible at any time. Traveler's checks used to be the only sound alternative to traveling with dangerously large amounts of cash. They were as reliable as currency, but, unlike cash, could be replaced if lost or stolen.

These days, traveler's checks are less necessary because most cities have 24-hour ATMs that allow you to withdraw small amounts of cash as needed. However, keep in mind that you will likely be charged an ATM withdrawal fee if the bank is not your own, so if you're withdrawing money every day you might be better off with traveler's checks — provided that you don't mind showing identification every time you want to cash one.

Visitors from the U.S.: You can get traveler's checks at almost any American bank. **American Express** offers denominations of $20, $50, $100, $500, and (for cardholders only) $1,000. You'll pay a service charge ranging from 1% to 4%. You can also get American Express traveler's checks over the phone by calling ✆ **800/221-7282;** Amex gold and platinum cardholders who use this number are exempt from the 1% fee.

Visa offers traveler's checks at Citibank locations nationwide, as well as at several other banks. The service charge ranges between 1.5% and 2%; checks come in denominations of

⌜ *Tips* **Small Change**

When you change money, ask for some small bills. Petty cash will come in handy for tipping and public transportation. Consider keeping the change and a few small bills separate from your larger bills, so that it's readily accessible and you'll be less of a target for theft.

$20, $50, $100, $500, and $1,000. Call ℂ **800/732-1322** for information. AAA members can obtain Visa checks without a fee at most AAA offices or by calling ℂ **866/339-3378. MasterCard** also offers traveler's checks. Call ℂ **800/ 223-9920** for a location near you.

American Express, Thomas Cook, Visa, and **MasterCard** offer foreign-currency traveler's checks. You'll pay the rate of exchange at the time of your purchase (so it's a good idea to monitor the rate before you take the plunge), and most companies charge a transaction fee per order (and a shipping fee if you order online). However, almost all hotels, restaurants, shops, and attractions accept U.S.–dollar traveler's checks, and you can exchange them for cash at local banks if you show ID, although there may be a charge for this service.

If you choose to carry traveler's checks, be sure to keep a record of their serial numbers (separately from your checks, of course), so you're ensured a refund if they are lost or stolen.

CREDIT CARDS

Credit cards are invaluable when traveling — they provide a safe way to carry money, a convenient record of all your expenses, and they generally offer relatively good exchange rates.

You can also withdraw cash advances from your credit cards at banks or ATMs, provided you know your PIN. If you've forgotten yours, or didn't even know you had one, call the number on the back of your credit card and ask the bank to send it to you. It usually takes 5 to 7 business days, though some banks will provide the number over the phone if you can provide certain personal information to prove your identity. Keep in mind that when you use your credit card abroad, most banks assess a 2% fee above the 1% fee charged by Visa or MasterCard or American Express for currency conversion on credit charges. But credit cards still may be the smart way to go when you factor in things like exorbitant ATM fees and higher traveler's check exchange rates (and service fees).

Almost every credit card company has an emergency toll-free number to call if your card is lost or stolen (this number is often printed on the card, so it is wise to print the number on a piece of paper stored separately from the card location). The credit card company may be able to wire you a cash advance from your card immediately, and in many places they can deliver an emergency card in a day or two. In Canada, **MasterCard** holders

---

⸢*Tips* **Dear Visa: I'm Off to Ottawa!**

Some credit card companies recommend that you notify them of any impending trip abroad so that they don't become suspicious when the card is used numerous times in a foreign destination and block your access. Even if you don't call your credit card company in advance, you can always call the card's toll-free emergency number (see "Credit Cards" above, or "Fast Facts" later in this chapter) if a charge is refused — a good reason to carry the phone number with you. But perhaps the most important lesson here is to carry more than one card on your trip; a card might not work for any number of reasons, so having a backup is the smart way to go.

What Things Cost in Ottawa	C$	U.S.$	U.K.£
Shuttle from airport to downtown hotel	12.00	9.84	5.28
Newspaper	1.00	.82	.44
Local telephone call	.25	.20	.11
Movie ticket	10.00	8.20	4.40
Theater ticket for the National	25.00–	20.50–	11.00–
Arts Centre	150.00	123.00	66.00
Taxi fare, typical ride between	6.00–	4.90–	2.64–
downtown attractions	10.00	8.20	4.40
Bus ticket (adult single cash fare)	2.60	2.15	1.15
Bus day pass (unlimited travel)	6.25	5.13	2.75
Two course lunch for one (moderate)*	25.00	20.50	11.00
Three course dinner for one (moderate)*	40.00	32.80	17.60
Parking meter, downtown per hour	2.50	2.05	1.10
Museum entrance fee, typical adult	7.00	5.75	3.08
Disposable camera	12.00	9.84	5.28
Regular latte	3.50	2.87	1.54
Bottle of water	2.00	1.64	.88
Hot dog from corner umbrella cart	2.00	1.64	.88
Large takeout pizza	20.00	16.40	8.80

*Includes tax, tip, and nonalcoholic beverage

should call ① **800/MC-ASSIST (622-77578); Visa** customers should call ① **800/847-2911; and American Express** cardholders should call collect ① **363/393-1111.** Information is available online at **www.mastercard.com, www.visa.com,** and **www.american** express.com. You can call a toll-free information directory at ① **800/555-1212** to get Canadian toll-free numbers. The best and quickest way to get assistance when you are in your home country is to call your card issuer.

4 When to Go

THE CLIMATE

Spring in Ottawa runs from late March to mid-May (although some years there is a late snowfall in April); **summer,** mid-May to mid-September; **fall,** mid-September to mid-November; and **winter,** mid-November to late March. The average annual high is 10°C (50°F), and the average annual low is 0°C (32°F). In winter, fluctuations in temperature sometimes cause freezing rain, a serious hazard for drivers (and pedestrians).

Ottawa's Average Temperatures (°C/°F)

	Jan	Feb	Mar	Apr	May	June	July	Aug	Sept	Oct	Nov	Dec
High	–4/25	–6/22	3/37	9/48	17/63	20/69	23/74	22/72	18/64	12/54	5/42	–3/27
Low	–18/0	–18/0	–13/9	–1/31	8/47	14/58	17/62	15/59	11/52	2/36	–6/21	–15/5

Tips Full House

Hotel rooms fill up quickly during the most popular events in Ottawa: Winterlude, a winter festival held during the first three weekends in February, the Canadian Tulip Festival, a 10-day event in mid-May, and Canada Day weekend, incorporating Canada Day on July 1. If you plan to visit during these times, reserve accommodation several weeks or even months ahead, and when comparing accommodations ask whether special packages are available, which may include tickets or entrance fees to attractions.

HOLIDAYS

On most public holidays, banks, government offices, schools, and post offices are closed. Museums, retail stores, and restaurants vary widely in their policies for holiday openings and closings, so call before you go to avoid disappointment.

Note that most museums in Ottawa are closed on Mondays between mid-October and late April. Ottawa celebrates the following holidays: New Year's Day (January 1), Good Friday and/or Easter Monday (March or April, varies each year), Victoria Day (Monday following the third weekend in May), Canada Day (July 1), Civic Holiday (first Monday in August), Labour Day (first Monday in September), Thanksgiving (second Monday in October), Remembrance Day (November 11), Christmas Day (December 25), and Boxing Day (December 26).

OTTAWA CALENDAR OF EVENTS

The following list of events will help you plan your visit to Ottawa. Contact the **Capital Infocentre** (© 800/465-1867) to confirm details if a particular event is a major reason for your vacation. Even the largest, most successful events sometimes retire, a few events are biennial, and dates may change from those listed here. In addition to the following events, numerous smaller community and cultural events take place throughout the year. **Lansdowne Park,** a multi-purpose sports and entertainment facility, hosts many trade and consumer shows catering to special interests — call them at © **613/580-2429** for information on upcoming events. There are numerous websites listing annual events and festivals for Ottawa. Check out **www. canadascapital.gc.ca**, **www.ottawatourism.ca**, **www.ottawakiosk.ca,** and **www.ottawastart.com**.

January

The Governor General's New Year's Day Levee is held at Rideau Hall, the official residence of the governor general. Members of the public are invited to meet the governor general, visit the historic residence's public rooms, and enjoy entertainment and light refreshments. Note that in some years the date may be brought forward to December, depending upon the governor general's official duties. © **866/842-4422.** www.gg.ca

February

Winterlude. Every year, the first three weekends of February are filled with family winter fun in the snow and ice, as the city celebrates its chilliest season. Downtown Ottawa and Hull are transformed into winter wonderlands filled with gigantic snow sculptures, glittering ice sculptures, and a Snowflake Kingdom especially for kids. Children's entertainment, craft workshops, horse-drawn sleigh rides, snowboarding demonstrations, dogsled rides, and more are on offer for little ones. Activities are based at Parliament Hill, New Ottawa City Hall and Festival Plaza, Confederation Park, the Rideau Canal Skateway at Fifth Avenue, Dow's Lake, and Jacques-Cartier Park in Hull. A free shuttle bus operates between sites. ✆ **800/ 465-1867.** www.canadascapital.gc.ca

Canadian Ski Marathon. The world's longest cross-country ski tour is a skier's paradise and offers some of the best wilderness trails anywhere. You can ski as little as 15km (9 miles) or as much as 160km (99 miles) — you set the pace. The marathon attracts 2,000 novice and veteran skiers from ages 4 to 86. ✆ **819/ 770-6556.** www.csm-mcs.com

Keskinada Loppet. Close to 3,000 skiers from more than a dozen countries gather to participate in Canada's biggest cross-country ski event, held annually in Gatineau Park. Events include 50-km (31-mile) and 25-km (16-mile) classic and freestyle races. Kids under age 13 can ski, snowshoe, or walk the 2-km (1.25-mile) Mini-Keski. ✆ **800/ 465-1867** or 819/595-0114. www.keskinada.com

Ottawa Boat, Sportsmen's & Cottage Show. Revel in the outdoors at this show for fishers, hunters, and weekend cottagers, held at Lansdowne Park. Dozens of demos feature everything from tying a fly to paddling a canoe. ✆ **613/580-2429.**

March

The Ottawa-Gatineau International Auto Show at the Ottawa Congress Centre (adjoining the Rideau Centre) brings you up to date on what's happening in the world of cars, minivans, pickups, and SUVs. ✆ **613/ 563-1984.** www.ottawa gatineauautoshow.com

April

The Ottawa Lynx. Ottawa's premier baseball team, the Triple-A affiliate of the Montreal Expos, provides fun and affordable family entertainment at JetForm Park. The Lynx play 72 home games between April and September. The 10,332-seat stadium boasts a full-service restaurant, luxury suites, and a picnic area. ✆ **613/747-LYNX (5969).** www.ottawalynx.com

May

Canadian Tulip Festival. A visit to this spring festival in mid-May will dazzle you with the blooming of more than three million tulips in a rainbow of colors. The tulip festival, expanded to more than 2 weeks of activities, includes concerts, an arts and crafts market, fireworks displays, and the colorful Tulip Flotilla, a floating parade on the Rideau Canal. Stroll along the banks of the canal and through the gardens at Dow's Lake to catch the full effect of the carpet of flowers. ✆ **800/66-TULIP (668-8547)** or 613/567-4447. www.tulipfestival.ca

National Capital Race Weekend. Thousands of runners, volunteers, spectators, and visitors gather for this world-class 42-km (26-mile) marathon. Several other events, ranging from 2km (1 mile) to 21km (13 miles) are held. Families, in-line skaters, and beginner runners are welcome. ✆ **613/234-2221.** www.ncm.ca

Classic Cars. Owners and enthusiasts are invited to "Cruisin' Night" at Place d'Orléans Shopping Centre on Wednesday evenings from 6pm to 9pm, May to September, to view 350 classic cars during this outdoor, family event. ✆ **613/824-9050.**

Odawa Annual Pow Wow. Held at Ottawa Municipal Campground, this energetic and colorful event is designed to bring First Nations culture to Native and non-Native audiences through the sharing of music, dance, art, and food. ✆ **613/722-3811.** www.odawa.on.ca

RCMP Musical Ride. From May to October, the world-famous Royal Canadian Mounted Police and their majestic horses perform a musical show for appreciative audiences throughout Canada. The Musical Ride performs its sunset ceremonies for several evenings in Ottawa in late June, and gives a special performance on Parliament Hill on Canada Day. Tours of the stables are offered year-round. ✆ **613/998-8199.** www.rcmp-grc.gc.ca

June

Ottawa International Children's Festival. This event brings the best of live theatrical arts to children at sites in and around the Canada Science and Technology Museum. Families will enjoy music, theater, crafts, and other kids' entertainment. Other performing arts events for children are staged throughout the year at various local venues. ✆ **613/241-0999.** www.ottawachildrens festival.ca

Ottawa Renegades CFL Football. Ottawa's CFL team battles through the football season from June to October. ✆ 613/231-5608. www.ottawarenegades.net

Magnetic North Theatre Festival. Contemporary English-language theater is featured at this Ottawa-based organization, which goes on the road across Canada in alternate years. ✆ **613/947-7000.** www.magneticnorthfestival.ca

Gloucester Fair. This old-fashioned fair offers agricultural displays, gymkhana and western horse shows, a demolition derby, a lumberjack show, midway rides, bubblegum-blowing contests, pony rides, face

painting, and more. ✆ **613/744-2671.** www.gloucester-fair.on.ca

Festival Franco-Ontarien. One of the most important French celebrations in North America is held in the ByWard Market area, with a variety of musical and theatrical performances to entertain all ages. ✆ **613/755-2553.** www.ffo.ca

Ottawa Dragon Boat Race Festival. Held at the Rideau Canoe Club at Mooney's Bay Park, this festival features dragon boat races, multicultural stage performers, exhibits, and activities for children. Admission is free. ✆ **613/238-7711.** www.dragonboat.net

Changing of the Guard. This half-hour ceremony is one of Ottawa's most outstanding attractions. From late June to late August, the Ceremonial Guard parades from the Cartier Square Drill Hall to Parliament Hill daily between 9:30 and 10am. The ceremony begins at 10am, weather permitting. ✆ **800/465-1867.** www.parl.gc.ca

ByWard Market Auto Classic. On the first Sunday in June, the ByWard Market hosts the Auto Classic, a showcase of automotive history with more than 150 vintage, classic, and high-performance cars on display for fun and prizes. The event is free to the public. ✆ 613/562-3325. www.byward-market.com

Italian Week. Corso Italia (Preston Street), the commercial heart of Ottawa's Little Italy, is the place to be in mid-June to celebrate the food, music, pageantry, and art that is Italy. ✆ 613/726-0920. www.prestonstreet.com

Carnival of Cultures. The picturesque outdoor Astrolabe Theatre is the setting for a summer kaleidoscope of cultures, with music, food, and dance from around the world. The dynamic entertainment includes international artists and Ottawa's top folk dancers, singers, and musicians. ℭ **613/742-6952.** www.carnival ofcultures.ca

UniSong. More than 400 members of youth and children's choirs from across Canada perform four days of concerts at the National Arts Centre and other locations. Enjoy a full program of Canadian music and celebrations, including a massed performance on Canada Day. ℭ **613/ 234-3360.** www.abc.ca

Garden Party at Rideau Hall. The governor general hosts the annual garden party at Rideau Hall in June (the date varies according to the governor general's official duties). Her Excellency greets visitors on the upper terrace of the gardens. The first Changing of the Guard ceremony of the summer is held before the party. Guests can explore the residence's public rooms, gardens, and greenhouses, and children can enjoy many special activities on the grounds, including entertainment and crafts. Light refreshments are served. ℭ **866/842-4422** or 613/ 991-4422. www.gg.ca

Canada Dance Festival. This biennial festival, next scheduled for early June 2006, showcases the finest in new Canadian contemporary choreography. Performances fill the stages, streets, and parks of Ottawa and feature emerging independent artists as well as established companies. ℭ **613/996-5051.** www.canadadance.ca

Ottawa Fringe Festival. A wide range of exciting and vibrant theatre, dance, music, visual arts, video, and film can be enjoyed on six stages in the heart of Ottawa's arts and theatre district. More than 70 companies stage more than 300 shows. ℭ **613/ 232-6162.** www.ottawafringe.com

July

Canada Day. Each July 1, hundreds of thousands of Canadians gather in Ottawa to celebrate Canada's birthday. Activities center around Parliament Hill, Major's Hill Park, and Jacques-Cartier Park in Hull. Shows, street performers, and concerts mark the event. Don't miss the spectacular fireworks display over the Ottawa River. ℭ **800/465-1867.** www.canadascapital.gc.ca

Wind Odyssey Sound and Light Show on Parliament Hill. This free, dynamic show illuminates Parliament Hill on summer evenings, running from July to September. The accomplishments and experiences of Canadians are featured, revealing the essence of Canada through stirring music and visual projections on the Parliament Buildings. ℭ **800/465-1867.** www.canadascapital.gc.ca

Helping Other People Everywhere (HOPE). HOPE, a nonprofit charitable organization, holds the largest beach volleyball tournament in the world, with 1,000 teams playing on 79 courts. The tournament attracts more than 30,000 participants and spectators, who flock to Mooney's Bay in support of HOPE. ℭ **613/237-1433.** www.hopehelps.com

International Youth Orchestra Festival. The festival offers joint shared concerts, broadcasts, demonstrations, and a gala mass concert. Call the Capital Infocentre ℭ **800/465-1867.**

The Ottawa Chamber Music Festival. North America's largest chamber music festival and one of Canada's most respected cultural events features the finest musicians from across Canada, the United States, and Europe. Some of the most beautiful churches in downtown

Ottawa host 78 concerts over 2 weeks in late July and early August. ☎ **613/234-8008.** www.chamber fest.com

Ottawa International Jazz Festival. For 10 days in July, the finest jazz musicians in the world perform in intimate studio spaces and open-air venues for thousands of fans. Dates vary slightly; sometimes the festival begins in late June. ☎ **613/241-2633.** www.ottawajazzfestival.com

Cisco Systems Bluesfest. Canada's biggest blues festival presents an outstanding array of blues musicians, plus Gospel, roots, world, and popular music. Headliners are usually announced by the end of April each year. ☎ **613/247-1188.** ottawa-bluesfest.ca

Pride Week Festival. The Ottawa area highlights its gay, lesbian, bisexual, and transgender community with a week of events including the annual Pride Parade. ☎ **613/238-2424.** www.prideottawa.com

Capital Classic Show Jumping Tournament. Canada's top equestrians compete at this annual event. Held at the National Capital Equestrian Park, the tournament draws lots of family spectators. Call the Capital Infocentre ☎ **800/465-1867.** www.capitalclassic.ca

Children's Hospital of Eastern Ontario Teddy Bear Picnic. Bring your kids and their bears to this annual picnic, held on the beautiful grounds of Rideau Hall on the second Saturday of July. Meet a Mountie, enjoy a pancake breakfast, visit the petting zoo, and watch live entertainment. ☎ **613/737-7600.**

August

Ottawa Folk Festival. This gathering celebrates Canada's rich folk traditions with music, dance, storytelling, and crafts. Some of Canada's finest acoustic musicians perform evening concerts on the main stage, and afternoon musical stages feature such themes as song writing, Ottawa Valley fiddling and step dancing, Celtic music, and vocal harmonics. A fun-filled area offers crafts, activities, costumes, and children's performers. ☎ **613/230-8234.** www.ottawafolk.org

Caribe-Expo: The Ottawa Caribbean Carnival is a 4-day extravaganza featuring the much-anticipated street parade. ☎ **613/729-1408.** www.caribe-expo.com

Central Canada Exhibition. This is wholesome family entertainment at a great price. "The Ex" combines interactive theme exhibits, agricultural programs, entertainment, and a large midway with more than 60 rides, including a roller coaster. ☎ **613/237-7222.** www.ottawa superex.com

The Sparks Street Mall International Busker Festival. Jugglers, comedians, storytellers, fire-eaters, mimes, musicians, and magicians entertain audiences of all ages. ☎ **613/230-0984.**

September

Gatineau Hot Air Balloon Festival. Some 150 balloons take to the skies at Canada's largest balloon festival, held on Labour Day weekend. There are plenty of shows and activities, fairground rides, and a dazzling fireworks display. ☎ **800/668-8383** or **819/243-2330.** www.balloongatineau.com

Ottawa Senators. The Sens take on the National Hockey League's best at the Corel Centre. The regular season runs from September to April. ☎ **613/599-0300.** www.ottawa senators.com

Fall Rhapsody. Workshops, guided tours, nature interpretation programs, and other outdoor activities take place in Gatineau Park against a spectacular backdrop of fall leaves.

Kids can watch and participate in games and crafts. The towns and villages surrounding Gatineau Park celebrate autumn with exhibits of arts and crafts and activities for the whole family. ✆ **819/827-2020.** www.canadascapital.gc.ca

Ottawa International Writers Festival. A celebration of the finest new and established writing from Canadian and international creators. ✆ **613/562-1243.** www.writers fest.com

October

International Student Animation Festival of Ottawa. This biennial animation event, which alternates with the Ottawa International Animation Festival (see below), is devoted to students and first-time animators. Competitions, workshops, recruiting, and a trade fair are part of the event. ✆ **613/232-8769.**

Great Pumpkin Weigh-off. At the ByWard Market on the first Saturday in October, growers from Ontario, Quebec, and the northeastern United States bring their entries to compete for the title of the Great Pumpkin. Some of the monsters weigh in at 450kg (1,000 lb.). Expert carvers are on hand to produce jack o' lanterns. ✆ **613/562-3325.** www.byward-market.com

Ottawa International Animation Festival. Film industry people from around the world gather in Ottawa for this biennial event (alternating with the Student Animation Festival, see above). Programs include competitions, retrospectives, workshops, children's days, and more. ✆ 613/ 232-8769. www.awn.com/ottawa

November

Ottawa Wine and Food Show. Thousands flock to this annual event at the Ottawa Congress Centre. Sample fine wines, beers, and spirits from around the world. Taste the delicious food, be entertained by celebrity chefs, or attend a wine seminar. Limited to ages 19 and over. ✆ **613/563-1984.** www.playerexpo.com

Help Santa Toy Parade. On the third or fourth weekend in November, the annual Santa Claus Parade winds its way through downtown Ottawa. Floats, bands, and clowns entertain the crowds lining the streets. The Professional Firefighters' Association collects toys along the parade route and distributes them to less fortunate children in the Ottawa area. ✆ **613/526-2706.** www.toyparade.org

December

Christmas Lights Across Canada. Originating in the heart of the capital, more than 300,000 colorful lights now glow throughout the National Capital Region to celebrate the beginning of the Canadian winter and to welcome the New Year. ✆ **800/465-1867.** www.canadascapital.gc.ca

Christmas Carollers. Leading up to Christmas, local choirs sing Christmas carols in the historic ByWard Market district. Visitors can enjoy free horse-drawn carriage rides and listen to the seasonal music. ✆ **613/562-3325.** www.byward-market.com

5 Travel Insurance

Before you buy travel insurance, check your existing insurance policies and credit card coverage. You may already be covered for lost luggage, cancelled tickets, or medical expenses. The cost of travel insurance varies widely depending on the cost and length of your trip, your age and health, and the type of trip you're taking, but expect to pay between 5% and 8% of the vacation itself.

TRIP-CANCELLATION INSUR-ANCE—Trip-cancellation insurance helps you get your money back if you have to back out of a trip, if you have to go home early, or if your travel supplier goes bankrupt. Allowed reasons for cancellation can range from sickness to natural disasters to government travel advisories that declare your destination unsafe for travel. Insurance policy details vary, so read the fine print — and make sure that your airline is on the list of carriers covered in case of bankruptcy. Protect yourself further by paying for the insurance with a credit card — you may, depending on the laws of your country, get your money back on goods and services not received if you report the loss within 60 days after the charge is listed on your credit card statement.

Note: Many tour operators, particularly those offering trips to remote or high-risk areas, include insurance in the cost of the trip or can arrange insurance policies through a partnering provider, a convenient and often cost-effective way for the traveler to obtain insurance. Make sure the tour company is a reputable one, however: Some experts suggest you avoid buying insurance from the tour or cruise company you're traveling with, saying it's better to buy from a third-party insurer than to put all your money in one place.

U.S. Citizens: For more information, contact one of the following recommended insurers: Access America (℡ 866/807-3982; www.accessamerica.com); Travel Guard International (℡ 800/826-4919; www.travelguard.com); Travel Insured International (℡ 800/243-3174; www.travelinsured.com); and Travelex Insurance Services (℡ 888/457-4602; www.travelex-insurance.com).

MEDICAL INSURANCE—Medical care in Ontario is provided to all residents through the Ontario Health Insurance Plan (OHIP), administered by the provincial government. Visitors from abroad are ineligible for OHIP coverage and should arrange for **health insurance** coverage before entering Canada. For more information, contact a private insurance company directly, or call the **Canadian Life and Health Insurance Association** ℡ 800/268-8099; www.clhia.ca. Canadian travelers are protected by their home province's health insurance plan for a limited time period. Check with your province's health insurance agency before traveling.

U.S. Citizens: Most health plans (including Medicare and Medicaid) do not provide coverage if you get sick away from home. Even if your plan does cover treatment, most out-of-country hospitals make you pay your bills up front, and send you a refund only after you've returned home and filed the necessary paperwork with your insurance company. If you require additional medical insurance, try **MEDEX Assistance** (℡ 410/453-6300; www.medexassist.com) or **Travel Assistance International** (℡ 800/821-2828; www.travelassistance.com; for general information on services, call the company's Worldwide Assistance Services, Inc., at ℡ **800/777-8710.**

LOST-LUGGAGE INSURANCE—If you are a homeowner or have contents insurance for a rental property, see if your policy covers off-premises **theft and loss** wherever it occurs. Ask your insurance agent what procedures you need to follow to make a claim. Be sure to keep any valuables or irreplaceable items with you in your carry-on luggage, as many valuables (including books, money, and electronics) aren't covered by insurance policies. Otherwise, you should take out a separate policy to cover lost luggage.

If your luggage is lost, immediately file a lost-luggage claim at the airport, detailing the luggage contents. For most airlines, you must report delayed, damaged, or lost baggage within four hours of arrival. The airlines are required to deliver luggage, once found, directly to your house or destination free of charge.

RENTAL CAR INSURANCE—If you plan to rent a car, check with your credit card issuer to see if they pick up the **collision damage waiver fee (CDW)** in Canada. Many credit card companies cover the CDW, as long as you pay for the entire rental cost with the credit card. If you pre-book the rental, remember to bring the same credit card with you when you pick up the vehicle. The CDW can run as high as C$20 (US$16) per day, adding a considerable amount to the cost of car rental. Check your car insurance policy, too — it might cover the CDW.

6 Health & Safety

GENERAL AVAILABILITY OF HEALTH CARE

Contact the International Association for Medical Assistance to Travelers (IAMAT) (✆ **416/652-0137** in Canada; 716/754-4883 in the U.S., or visit **www.iamat.org**) for tips on travel and health concerns in Canada, and lists of local doctors. The United States Centers for Disease Control and Prevention (✆ **800/311-3435; www.cdc.gov**) provides up-to-date information on health hazards by region or country and offers tips on food safety.

WHAT TO DO IF YOU GET SICK AWAY FROM HOME

For non–life threatening emergencies that require a physician consultation, go to a **walk-in clinic.** These clinics operate just as the name implies — you walk in and wait your turn to see a doctor. Look in the Yellow Pages or ask your hotel to recommend one. Payment procedures and opening hours vary among clinics, so call ahead and ask about their billing policy for non-residents of Ontario or Canada. Most clinics will accept health cards from other provinces, although Quebec residents may be required to pay cash and obtain reimbursement from their provincial government. Out-of-country patients may be required to pay cash — checks or credit cards may not be accepted. Some doctors will make house calls to your hotel.

If you are suffering from a serious medical problem and are unable to wait to be seen at a walk-in clinic, visit the nearest hospital emergency room. Emergency rooms operate on a triage system, where patients are assessed upon arrival and those who need care the most urgently are seen first. There are emergency services available at several hospitals in the Ottawa area. For adults, **Ottawa Hospital** offers emergency care at two sites: the **General Campus** at 501 Smyth Rd., ✆ **613/737-8000,** and the **Civic Campus** at 1053 Carling Ave., ✆ **613/761-4621.** In addition, the **Children's Hospital of Eastern Ontario (CHEO)** is a large pediatric teaching hospital with emergency care services, located at 401 Smyth Rd., ✆ **613/737-7600.** Ontario emergency rooms are extremely busy and wait times for non-urgent cases are typically several hours. If at all possible, use the walk-in clinics. For minor health problems, consult a **pharmacist.** These professionals are trained in health consultation and will recommend whether you should see a doctor about your particular condition. Many pharmacies are open evenings and weekends and advertise their hours in the Yellow Pages. **Shopper's Drug Mart** has three **24-hour drugstores** in the Ottawa area; the closest location to downtown Ottawa is 1460 Merivale Rd. (at Baseline Road), ✆ **613/224-7270.**

If you suffer from a chronic illness, consult your doctor before your departure. For conditions like epilepsy, diabetes, or heart problems, wear a MedicAlert identification tag (© 800/668-1507 in Canada; **888/633-4298** in the U.S.; www.medicalert.ca or www.medicalert.org), which will immediately alert doctors to your condition and give them access to your records through MedicAlert's 24-hour hotline.

Pack prescription medications in your carry-on luggage, in their original containers with pharmacy labels — otherwise, they may not make it through airport security. Also bring along copies of your prescriptions in case you lose your pills or run out, and carry the generic name of your prescription medicines in case a local pharmacist is unfamiliar with the brand name. Don't forget an extra pair of contact lenses or prescription glasses.

For Canadian citizens, most reliable health-care plans provide coverage if you get sick away from home. If you are visiting Canada from the U.S. or overseas, you may have to pay all medical costs up front and be reimbursed later. See "Medical Insurance," under "Travel Insurance," above.

STAYING SAFE

As large cities go Ottawa is generally safe, but be alert and use common sense, particularly at night. Sadly, in recent years the number of homeless people and panhandlers has increased, but they are not generally aggressive in nature. The liveliest and rowdiest areas tend to be around the bars in the ByWard Market and Elgin St. neighborhoods, especially late at night.

7 Specialized Travel Resources

FOR TRAVELERS WITH DISABILITIES

Most disabilities shouldn't stop anyone from traveling. There are more options and resources out there than ever before. To find out which attractions, accommodations, and restaurants in Ottawa are accessible to people with disabilities, refer to the Ottawa Visitor Guide, available from the **Capital Infocentre,** © **800/465-1867.** The guide includes symbols next to each listing to indicate whether the entry and washrooms are accessible. **Full accessibility** is defined as independently accessible to people using wheelchairs or with limited upper-body strength. Services should include automatic front doors, ramps, sufficient turning space for a wheelchair in the rooms or bathrooms, and wider doorways (84 cm, or 33 in.). **Basic accessibility** indicates that people using wheelchairs may require assistance to use the services within the establishment. The owners and managers of each establishment determine whether their property is accessible. For more information, contact **Disabled Persons Community Resources (DPCR),** 1150 Morrison Dr., Suite 100, Ottawa © **613/724-5889,** or **www.dpcr.ca.** This non-profit organization publishes an *Accessibility Guide,* which covers cinemas and theaters, financial institutions, hotels and motels, medical facilities, museums and tourist attractions, parks, religious facilities, restaurants, shopping malls, retail stores, and transportation. The guide can be ordered online.

OC Transpo, which provides **public transit** in Ottawa, is committed to accessible public transit. Call their hotline at © **613/842-3625** Mon–Fri 9am–5pm to find out more about accessible services on conventional transit. Note that if you use a wheelchair, scooter, or walker, you can ride conventional transit service and the **O-Train** at no charge. The low-floor trains and stations are fully accessible, but you must be able to get to and from the station. Additionally, there are 45 designated accessible bus routes that use fully accessible buses. These buses have low floors and no stairs to climb, providing easier access for seniors, passengers with limited mobility, people using wheelchairs, and parents with small children or strollers. The buses lower themselves to the curb and have an extendable ramp for wheelchair users. You can spot low-floor buses by the blue and white wheelchair symbol on the upper corner of the front of the bus. Call ☎ 613/741-4390 for more information on these routes. Blind and visually impaired travelers can obtain information on how to make the most of their trip to Ottawa by calling the **Canadian National Institute for the Blind (CNIB)** Information Centre at ☎ 613/563-4021.

For persons with permanent or short-term disabilities who are unable to walk to, or board, conventional transit, **Para Transpo** is available. Both visitors and residents can use this service, but you must register and book a reservation a day in advance. You must also have the application form signed by an appropriate health professional. Para Transpo uses a large fleet of modern, air-conditioned cars and lift-equipped vans. Call ☎ 613/244-1289 Mon–Fri 9am–5pm for information and registration; ☎ 613/244-7272 for reservations.

FOR GAY & LESBIAN TRAVELERS

Canada is one of the world's most progressive countries, and the December 2004 Supreme Court of Canada equal-marriage decision demonstrated the country's commitment to human rights and strengthened its position as a gay-friendly travel destination. In Ottawa, the social life and entertainment for the gay and lesbian community is clustered around Bank Street in the vicinity of Frank

Street, Somerset Street W., and Lisgar Street. There are also several bars and clubs in the ByWard Market district (see chapter 9, "Ottawa After Dark"). To find out what's happening in Ottawa that's of interest to gays and lesbians, pick up a copy of **Capital Xtra!,** a monthly newspaper distributed widely throughout the Ottawa area, Eastern Ontario, and Montreal. News, arts, culture, entertainment, and local events are covered. To receive a copy in advance of your visit, write to Capital Xtra!, 251 Bank St., Suite 503, Ottawa, ON K2P 1X3. Alternatively, you can call ☎ 613/237-7133 or visit **www.xtra.ca.**

FOR SENIORS

Many city attractions grant senior discounts, and some hotels offer special rates. Carry a form of photo ID that includes your birth date. Becoming a member of a seniors' organization may earn you a discount on travel arrangements. Consider joining the **Canadian Association of Retired Persons (CARP),** 27 Queen St. E., Suite 1304, Toronto, ON M5C 2M6 (☎ 416/363-8748). The website has a comprehensive travel section for members that features hotels, packages, transportation, and travel insurance. The U.S. equivalent is **AARP** (formerly known as the American Association of Retired Persons), 601 E. St. NW, Washington, DC 20049 (☎ 888/687- 2277; **www.aarp.org**). Members get discounts on hotels, airfares, and car rentals. AARP offers members a wide range of benefits, including *AARP: The Magazine* and a monthly newsletter. Anyone over age 50 can join.

Recommended publications offering travel resources and discounts for seniors include the quarterly magazine *Travel 50 & Beyond* (www.travel50 andbeyond.com); *Travel Unlimited: Uncommon Adventures for the Mature Traveler* (Avalon); *101 Tips for Mature Travelers,* available from Grand Circle

Travel (© 800/221-2610 or 617/ 350-7500; www.gct.com); and *Unbelievably Good Deals and Great Adventures That You Absolutely Can't Get Unless You're Over 50,* by Joan Rattner Heilman (McGraw-Hill).

FOR FAMILIES

Luckily for visitors with kids in tow, Ottawa has a good selection of suite hotels that are equipped with kitchenettes or full kitchens and one or two bedrooms; some have two bathrooms. Prices are usually comparable to the cost of two hotel rooms (sometimes cheaper), but you get the advantage of food preparation facilities and accommodation for the entire family in one unit, which are important considerations when you have young children with you. Suite hotels often encourage families, offering children's programs, play centers, or indoor pools. When booking your accommodation, always ask if family packages are available.

When you're deciding which time of year to visit, try to schedule your trip during school vacation periods, which in Ontario run for two weeks during Christmas/New Year, one week in mid-March, and the months of July and August. Special events and festivals aimed particularly at families are held at various museums and other locations during school holidays. Many of Ottawa's attractions are clustered downtown within walking distance of one another, so it's possible to enjoy a break in Ottawa without the need for a vehicle.

To locate those accommodations, restaurants, and attractions that are particularly kid-friendly, refer to the "Kids" icon throughout this guide. Recommended family travel Internet sites include Family Travel Forum (www.familytravelforum.com), a comprehensive site that offers customized trip planning; Family Travel Network (www.familytravelnetwork.com), an award-winning site that offers travel features, deals, and tips; **Traveling Internationally with Your Kids** (www.travelwithyourkids.com), a comprehensive site offering sound advice for long-distance and international travel with children; and **Family Travel Files** (www.thefamilytravel files.com), which offers an online magazine and a directory of off-the-beaten-path tours and tour operators for families.

FOR STUDENTS

Students seem to always be on a shoestring budget. If you're between the ages of 12 and 25 and a full-time student, obtaining an **International Student Identity Card (ISIC)** will get you substantial savings on rail passes, plane tickets, and entrance fees, and often you'll get discounts on accommodation, food, and retail purchases. It also provides you with basic health and life insurance and a 24-hour help line. The card is available for C$16 (US$13). If you're no longer a student but are still under 26, you can get an **International Youth Travel Card (IYTC)** for the same price from the same people that entitles you to some discounts. You can get your ISIC or IYTC card from **Travel CUTS** (© **800/FLY-CUTS** or **359-2887; www.travelcuts.com**) or **STA Travel** (© **800/781-4040; www.statravel. com**) for both Canadian and U.S. residents. Irish students may prefer to turn to **USIT** (© **01/602-1600;** www.usitnow.ie), an Ireland-based specialist in student, youth, and independent travel.

Students who would like to attend lectures, seminars, concerts, and other events can contact **Carleton University,** 1125 Colonel By Dr. (© **613/ 520-7400; www.carleton.ca**) or the **University of Ottawa,** 550 Cumberland (© **613/562-5700; www.uottawa.ca**).

FOR WOMEN

Journeywoman (www.journeywoman. com) is a great travel resource for female travelers. The website offers a free monthly e-mail newsletter, message boards, and an extensive library of articles. **Women Welcome Women Worldwide (5W) (℃ 203/259-7832; www.womenwelcomewomen.org.uk)** encourages international friendships by facilitating women from different countries to visit one another. Men may accompany women on their travels, but they cannot join the club. The organization has more than 3,000 members in around 70 countries. *Safety and Security for Women Who Travel,* by Sheila Swan Laufer and Peter Laufer (Traveler's Tales, Inc.) contains travel tips and common-sense advice.

8 Planning Your Trip Online

SURFING FOR AIRFARES

The "big three" online travel sites, **Expedia.com, Travelocity.com,** and **Orbitz.com,** sell most of the air tickets bought on the Internet. (Canadian travelers should try **Expedia.ca** and **Travelocity.ca;** U.K. residents can go for expedia.co.uk and opodo.co.uk). Each has different business deals with the airlines and may offer different fares on the same flights, so it's wise to shop around. Expedia and Travelocity will also send you **e-mail notification** when a cheap fare becomes available to your favorite destination. Of the smaller travel agency websites, **SideStep** (www.sidestep.com) has received the best reviews from Frommer's authors. It's a browser add-on that purports to "search 140 sites at once," but in reality beats competitors' fares only as often as other sites do.

Also remember to check **airline websites,** especially those for low-fare carriers, whose fares are often misreported on or simply missing from travel agency websites. Even with major airlines, you can often shave a few bucks from a fare by booking directly through the airline and avoiding a travel agency's transaction fee. But you'll get these discounts only by **booking online:** most airlines now offer online-only fares that even their phone agents know nothing about. For the websites of airlines that fly to and from your destination, see "Getting There," later in this chapter.

Great **last-minute deals** are available through free weekly e-mail services provided directly by the airlines. Most of these are announced on Tuesday or Wednesday and must be purchased online. Most are only valid for travel that weekend, but some (such as Southwest's) can be booked weeks or months in advance. Sign up for weekly e-mail alerts at airline websites or check megasites that compile comprehensive lists of last-minute specials, such as **SmarterTravel.com.** For last-minute trips, **Site59.com** and **Lastminutetravel.com** in the U.S. and **Lastminute.com** in Europe often have better air-and-hotel package deals than the major-label sites.

If you're willing to give up some control over your flight details, use what is called an **"opaque" fare service** like **Priceline.com** (www.priceline.co.uk for Europeans) or its smaller competitor **Hotwire.com.** Both offer rock-bottom prices in exchange for travel on a "mystery airline" at a mysterious time of day, often with a mysterious change of planes en route. The mystery airlines are all major, well-known carriers — and the possibility of being sent from Philadelphia to Chicago via Tampa is remote; the airlines' routing computers perform a lot better than they used to. But your chances of getting a 6am or 11pm flight are pretty high. Hotwire tells you flight prices before you buy; Priceline usually has better deals than Hotwire, but you have to play their "name your price" game. If you're new at this, the helpful folks at **BiddingForTravel.com** do a good job of demystifying Priceline's prices and strategies. Priceline and Hotwire are great for flights within North America and between the U.S. and Europe. But for flights to other parts of the world, consolidators will almost always beat their fares. *Note:* In 2004 Priceline added non-opaque service to its roster. You now have the option to pick exact flights, times, and airlines from a list of offers — or to bid on opaque fares as before.

For much more about airfares and savvy air-travel tips and advice, pick up a copy of *Frommer's Fly Safe, Fly Smart* (Wiley Publishing, Inc.).

SURFING FOR HOTELS

Shopping online for hotels, which is much easier in the U.S., Canada, and certain parts of Europe than it is in the rest of the world, is generally done in one of two ways: by booking through the hotel's own website or through an independent booking agency (or a fare-service agency like Priceline; see below). These Internet hotel agencies have multiplied in mind-boggling numbers of late, competing for the business of millions of consumers surfing for accommodations around the world. This competitiveness can be a boon to consumers who have the patience and time to shop and compare the online sites for good deals — but shop they must, for prices can vary considerably from site to site. And keep in mind that hotels at the top of a site's listing may be there for no other reason than that they paid money to get the placement.

Of the "big three" sites, **Expedia** offers a long list of special deals and "virtual tours" or photos of available rooms so you can see what you're paying for (a feature that helps counter the claims that the best rooms are often held back from bargain

booking websites). **Travelocity** posts unvarnished customer reviews and ranks its properties according to the AAA rating system. Also reliable are **Hotels.com** and **Quikbook.com. TravelAxe** (www.travelaxe.net) is an excellent free program that can help you search multiple hotel sites at once, even ones you may never have heard of — and conveniently lists the total price of the room, including the taxes and service charges. Another booking site, **Travelweb** (www.travelweb.com), is partly owned by the hotels it represents (including the Hilton, Hyatt, and Starwood chains), and is therefore plugged directly into the hotels' reservations systems — unlike independent online agencies, which have to fax or e-mail reservation requests to the hotel, a good portion of which get misplaced in the shuffle. More than once, travelers have arrived at their hotel only to be told that they have no reservation. To be fair, many of the major sites are undergoing improvements in service and ease of use, and Expedia will soon be able to plug directly into the reservations systems of many hotel chains — none of which can be bad news for consumers. In the meantime, it's a good idea to **get a confirmation number and make a printout** of any online booking transaction.

In the opaque website category, **Priceline** and **Hotwire** are even better for hotels than for airfares; with both, you're allowed to pick the neighborhood and quality level of your hotel before offering up your money. Priceline's hotel product even covers Europe and Asia, though it's much better at getting five-star lodging for three-star prices than at finding anything at the bottom of the scale. On the downside, many hotels stick Priceline guests in their least desirable rooms. Be sure to go to **BiddingforTravel.com** before bidding on a hotel room on Priceline; it features a fairly up-to-date list of hotels that Priceline uses in major cities. For both

Frommers.com: The Complete Travel Resource

For an excellent travel-planning resource, we highly recommend **Frommers.com,** voted Best Travel Site by *PC Magazine*. We're a little biased, of course, but we guarantee that you'll find the travel tips, reviews, monthly vacation giveaways, bookstore, and online-booking capabilities thoroughly indispensable. Among the special features are our popular **Destinations** section, where you'll get expert travel tips, hotel and dining recommendations, and advice on the sights to see for more than 3,500 destinations around the globe; the **Frommers.com Newsletter,** with the latest deals, travel trends, and money-saving secrets; our **Community** area featuring **Message Boards,** where Frommer's readers post queries and share advice (sometimes our authors even show up to answer questions); and our **Photo Center,** where you can post and share vacation tips. When your research is done, the **Online Reservations System** (www.frommers.com/ book_a_trip) takes you to Frommer's preferred online partners for booking your vacation at affordable prices.

Priceline and Hotwire, you pay up front and the fee is nonrefundable. *Note:* Some hotels do not provide loyalty program credits or points or other frequent-stay amenities when you book a room through opaque online services.

In the Ottawa area, accommodation packages and hotel reservations can be made online by visiting **www.ottawatourism.ca.** Detailed contact information for accommodations can be found on this site, and also at **www.canadascapital.gc.ca.** If you like the homey atmosphere and comfort of a bed-and-breakfast (B&B), try surfing **www.bbcanada.com.**

SURFING FOR RENTAL CARS

For booking rental cars online, the best deals are usually found at rental car company websites, although all the major online travel agencies also offer rental car reservations services. Priceline and Hotwire work well for rental cars, too; the only "mystery" is which major rental company you get, and for most travelers the difference between Hertz, Avis, and Budget is negligible.

9 The 21st-Century Traveler

INTERNET ACCESS AWAY FROM HOME

Travelers have any number of ways to check their e-mail and access the Internet on the road. Of course, using your own laptop — or even a **PDA (personal digital assistant)** or electronic organizer with a modem — gives you the most flexibility. But even if you don't have a computer, you can still access your e-mail and even your office computer from cybercafes.

WITHOUT YOUR OWN COMPUTER

It's hard nowadays to find a city that *doesn't* have a few cybercafes. Although there's no definitive directory for cybercafes — these are independent businesses, after all — two places to start looking are at **www.cybercaptive.com** and **www.cybercafe.com.** Some hotels now offer in-room wireless Internet access. If it's important to you to have access to your e-mail, make your accommodation reservation by phone and confirm you will have Internet access available. Avoid **hotel business centers,** however, unless you're willing to pay exorbitant rates. Public libraries offer Internet access, although you may have to reserve a computer terminal a day or so in advance.

To retrieve your e-mail, ask your **Internet Service Provider (ISP)** if it has a Web-based interface tied to your existing e-mail account. If your ISP doesn't have such an interface, you can use the free **mail2web** service (www.mail2web.com) to view and reply to your home e-mail. For more flexibility, you may want to open a free, Web-based e-mail account with **Yahoo! Mail** (http://mail.yahoo.com). Your home ISP may be able to forward your e-mail to the Web-based account automatically.

If you need to access files on your office computer, look into a service called **GoToMyPC** (www.gotomypc.com). The service provides a Web-based interface for you to access and manipulate a distant PC from anywhere — even a cybercafe — provided your "target" PC is switched on and has an always-on connection to the Internet. The service offers top-quality security, but if you're worried about hackers, use your own laptop rather than a cybercafe computer to access the GoToMyPC system.

WITH YOUR OWN COMPUTER

Wi-Fi (wireless fidelity) is the buzzword in computer access, and more and more hotels, cafes, and retailers are signing on as wireless "hotspots" from where you can get high-speed connection without cable wires, networking hardware, or a phone line (see below). You can get Wi-Fi connection one of several ways. Many laptops sold in the last year have built-in Wi-Fi capability (an 802.11b wireless Ethernet connection). Mac owners have their own networking technology, Apple AirPort. For those with older computers, an 802.11b/ **Wi-Fi card** can be plugged into your laptop. You sign up for wireless access service much as you do cellphone service, through a plan offered by one of several commercial companies that have made wireless service available in airports, hotel lobbies, and coffee shops, primarily in the U.S. (followed by the U.K. and Japan). Canada is increasingly wireless, and many Ottawa hotels now offer wireless Internet access, although a fee is charged in some instances.

T-Mobile Hotspot (www.t-mobile. com/hotspot) serves up wireless connections at more than 1,000 Starbucks coffee shops nationwide. **Boingo (www.boingo.com)** and **Wayport (www.wayport.com)** have set up networks in airports and high-class hotel lobbies.

There are also places that provide free wireless networks in cities around the world. To locate these free hotspots, go to **www.personaltelco. net/index.cgi/WirelessCommunities.** In Ottawa, **Bridgehead Coffee House (www.bridgehead.ca)** has several locations, all of which offer free wireless Internet access.

Most hotels in Ottawa offer dataports for laptop modems, and/or free high-speed Internet access using an Ethernet network cable. You can bring your own cables, or rent from the hotel. Call your hotel in advance to see what your options are.

In addition, major ISPs have local access numbers around the world, allowing you to go online by simply placing a local call. Check your ISP's website or call its toll-free number and ask how you can use your current account away from home, and how much it will cost.

If you're traveling outside the reach of your ISP, the iPass network has dial-up numbers in most of the world's countries. You'll have to sign up with an iPass provider, who will then tell you how to set up your computer for your destination(s). For a list of iPass providers, go to www.ipass.com and click on "Individual Purchase." One solid provider is i2roam (www.i2roam.com; ☎ 866/811-6209 or 920/235-0475).

Wherever you go, bring a **connection kit** of the right power and phone adapters, a spare phone cord, and a spare Ethernet network cable — or find out whether your hotel supplies them to guests. The electrical current in Canada is the same as in the U.S. (110–115V AC).

USING A CELLPHONE

The three letters that define much of the world's **wireless capabilities** are GSM (Global System for Mobiles), a big, seamless network that makes for easy cross-border cellphone use throughout Europe and dozens of other countries worldwide. In the U.S., T-Mobile, AT&T Wireless, and Cingular use this quasi-universal system; in Canada, Microcell and some Rogers customers are GSM, and all Europeans and most Australians use GSM.

If your cellphone is on a GSM system and you have a world-capable multiband phone, such as many Sony Ericsson, Motorola, or Samsung models, you can make and receive calls across civilized areas on much of the globe, from Andorra to Uganda. Just call your wireless operator and ask for "international roaming" to be activated on your account. Unfortunately, per-minute charges can be high — usually US$1–US$1.50 (C$1.22–C$1.83) in Western Europe and up to US$5 (C$6) in places like Russia and Indonesia.

That's why it's important to buy an "unlocked" world phone from the get-go. Many cellphone operators sell "locked" phones that restrict you from using any other removable computer memory phone chip (called a SIM card) other than the ones they supply. Having an unlocked phone allows you to install a cheap, prepaid SIM card (found at a local retailer) in your destination country. (Show your phone to the salesperson; not all phones work on all networks.) You'll get a local phone number — and much, much lower calling rates. Getting an already locked phone unlocked can be a complicated process, but it can be done; just call your cellular operator and say you'll be going abroad for several months and want to use the phone with a local provider.

For many, **renting** a phone is a good idea. (Even worldphone owners will have to rent new phones if they're traveling to non-GSM regions, such as Japan or Korea.) While you can rent a phone from any number of overseas sites, including kiosks at airports and at car-rental agencies, we suggest renting the phone before you leave home. That way you can give loved ones and business associates your new number, make sure the phone works, and take the phone wherever you go — especially helpful for overseas trips through several countries, where local phone-rental agencies often bill in local currency and may not let you take the phone to another country. Two good wireless rental companies are **InTouch USA** (☎ 800/872-7626; www.intouchglobal.com) and **RoadPost** (☎ 888/290-1606 or 905/272-5665; www.roadpost.com). Give them your itinerary, and they'll tell you what wireless products you need. InTouch will also, for free, advise you on whether your existing phone will work overseas; simply call ☎ **703/222-7161** between 9am and 4pm EST, or go to http:// intouchglobal.com/travel.htm.

Online Traveler's Toolbox

Veteran travelers usually carry some essential items to make their trip easier. Following is a selection of handy online tools to bookmark and use.

- **Airplane Seating** and Food. Find out which seats to reserve and which to avoid (and more) on all major domestic airlines at Seatguru.com. And check out the type of meal (with photos) you'll likely be served on airlines around the world at Airlinemeals.com.
- **Foreign Languages for Travelers** (www.travlang.com). Learn basic terms in more than 70 languages and click on any underlined phrase to hear what it sounds like.
- **Intellicast.com** and **Weather.com** give weather forecasts for all 50 states and for cities around the world.
- **Mapquest** (www.mapquest.com). This best of the mapping sites lets you choose a specific address or destination, and in seconds will return a map and detailed directions.
- **Subway Navigator** (www.subwaynavigator.com). Download subway maps and get savvy advice on using subway systems in dozens of major cities around the world.
- **TimeAndDate.com.** See what time (and day) it is anywhere in the world.
- **Universal Currency Converter** (www.xe.com/ucc). See what your dollar or pound is worth in more than 100 other countries.
- **Travel Warnings** (www.travel.state.gov, www.fco.gov.uk/travel, www.voyage.gc.ca, www.dfat.gov.au/consular/advice). These sites report on places where health concerns or unrest might threaten American, British, Canadian, and Australian travelers. Generally, U.S. warnings are the most paranoid; Australian warnings are the most relaxed.
- **Visa ATM Locator** (www.visa.com), for locations of PLUS ATMs worldwide, or **MasterCard ATM Locator** (www.mastercard.com), for locations of Cirrus ATMs worldwide.

10 Getting There

BY PLANE

Wherever you're traveling from, shop around among the airlines that service your destination and hunt determinedly for the lowest fare possible, while meeting your other requirements. If your arrival and departure dates can be flexible, you'll have a better chance of landing a deal.

The weekend Travel section of major city newspapers often carries advertisements for ticket brokers and consolidators. These companies buy airline tickets in bulk and sell them at a discount. By purchasing your tickets through these companies, you may be able to fly for less than the standard advance (APEX) fare. You may not be able to get the lowest price quoted in the ad, but you're likely to pay less than the price quoted by the major airlines. Be aware that tickets purchased in this way are often nonrefundable. If you change your itinerary after purchase, you will probably be charged a stiff penalty.

Since the September 11, 2001 terrorist attacks, airport security has been enhanced (see "Getting Through the Airport," below). Changes in procedures may cause increased processing times for passengers, both at the check-in counters and the security checkpoints. Ask your airline for recommended check-in times.

If you're traveling with children, ask your air carrier in advance about child safety restraints, transport of strollers, times of meal service, availability of children's meals, and bulkhead seating (which has extra room to stretch out). Mention any food allergies or medical concerns.

Note that the term "direct flight" may include an enroute stop but not an aircraft change.

WITHIN CANADA—Air Canada, which also operates under the "Jazz" logo, offers direct flights to Ottawa from the following Canadian cities: Calgary, Edmonton, Fredericton, Halifax, London, Montreal (Dorval), Quebec City, Toronto (Pearson and City Centre), Vancouver, and Winnipeg. The central reservation number for Air Canada is © **888/247-2262; www.aircanada.ca.** Bearskin Airlines © **800/465-5039; www.bearskinair lines.com** serves Buttonville Airport northeast of Toronto and several cities in Northern Ontario, including North Bay, Sudbury, and Thunder Bay. For direct flights from Iqualuit, contact Canadian North © **800/661-1505; www.canadiannorth.com** or First Air © **800/267-1247; www.firstair.ca.** CanJet Airlines serves Halifax, Montreal, and Deer Lake © **800/ 809-7777; www.canjet.com.** Primarily serving the high-tech business sector, QuikAir (© **800/551-7845; www. quikair.ca**) flies between Silicon Valley North (aka Ottawa) and Kitchener-Waterloo. For a direct flight from Regina, Saskatoon, or Calgary, contact WestJet (© **800/538-5696; www.westjet.com.**

FROM THE U.S.—Direct flights from Boston, Chicago, New York (LaGuardia and Newark), and Washington (Dulles) are operated by Air Canada (© **888/247-2262; www.aircanada.ca**). American Airlines (© **800/433-7300; www.aa.com**) and United Express (Air Wisconsin) (© **800/864-8331; www.airwis.com**) fly direct to Ottawa from Chicago. ASA-Delta Connection (© **800/221-1212; www.delta.com**) operates direct flights from Atlanta. From Albany, Continental Connection © **800/231-0856; www.continental.com**) flies direct to Ottawa. Travelers in the Newark area can fly with Continental Express (© **800/784-4444; www. continental.com**). Northwest Airlink (© **800/225-2525; www.nwa.com**) flies direct to Ottawa from Detroit. US Airways (© **800/428-4322; www. usairways.com**) operates direct flights from Philadelphia and Pittsburgh.

FROM ABROAD—Air Canada flies direct to Ottawa from London (Heathrow). Zoom Airlines Inc. (© **866/359-9666; www.flyzoom.ca**) is a recently established discount carrier that flies direct to Ottawa from Glasgow and London (Gatwick).

GETTING THROUGH THE AIRPORT

With the federalization of airport security, security procedures at Canadian and U.S. airports are more stable and consistent than ever. Generally, you'll be fine if you check in **1 hour** before a domestic flight and **2 hours** before an international flight; if you show up late, tell an airline employee and you may get whisked to the front of the line. To board flights within Canada, a current, government-issued photo ID is required. Most Canadians use a driver's license as ID for domestic flights. Proof of citizenship is required for entry at all Canadian border crossings, including airports, and a passport is the most recommended document to carry. For requirements for U.S. citizens arriving in Canada, see "Entry Requirements" earlier in this chapter. Citizens of most European countries, Commonwealth countries, and former British colonies, as well as certain other countries, do not need visas but must carry passports. Entry visas are required for citizens of more than 140 countries. Keep your ID at the ready to show at check-in, the security checkpoint, and sometimes even the gate.

E-tickets have made paper tickets nearly obsolete. Passengers with e-tickets can beat the ticket-counter lines by using airport **electronic kiosks** or even **online check-in** from your home computer. Online check-in involves logging on to your airline's website, accessing your reservation, and printing out your boarding pass — and the airline may even offer you bonus miles to do so! If you're using a kiosk at the airport, bring the credit card you used to book the ticket or your frequent-flier card. Print out your boarding pass from the kiosk and simply proceed to the security checkpoint with your pass and a photo ID. If you're checking bags or looking to snag an exit-row seat, you will be able to do so using most airline kiosks. Even the smaller airlines are employing the kiosk system, but always call your airline to make sure these alternatives are available. **Curbside check-in** is also a good way to avoid lines, although a few airlines still ban curbside check-in; call before you go.

Security checkpoint lines are shorter than they were in the months following the September 11, 2001 terrorist attacks, but at times they can be slow going. If you have trouble standing for long periods of time, tell an airline employee; the airline will provide a wheelchair. Speed up security by **not wearing metal objects** such as big belt buckles. If you've got metallic body parts, a note from your doctor can prevent a long chat with the security

screeners. Keep cellphones, laptops, personal CD players, and other electronics easily accessible and be prepared to have these items hand checked by security staff — this may include a request to switch on the item in question. Keep in mind that only **ticketed passengers** are allowed past security.

Federalization has stabilized **what you can carry on and what you can't.** The general rule is that sharp things are out, nail clippers are okay, and food and beverages must be passed through the X-ray machine. Bring food in your carry-on rather than checking it, as explosive-detection machines used on checked luggage have been known to mistake food (especially chocolate, for some reason) for bombs. Travelers in Canada and the U.S. are allowed one carry-on bag, plus a "personal item" such as a purse, briefcase, or laptop bag, although if flights are fully booked the airline may ask you to check your carry-on luggage. The U.S. Transportation Security Administration (TSA) has issued a list of restricted items; check its website (www.tsa.gov/public/index.jsp) for details.

Airport screeners may decide that your checked luggage needs to be searched by hand. You can now purchase luggage locks that allow screeners to open and relock a checked bag if hand searching is necessary. Look for Travel Sentry certified locks at luggage or travel shops and Brookstone stores (you can buy them online at www.brookstone.com). These locks, approved by the TSA, can be opened by luggage inspectors with a special code or key. For more information on the locks, visit www.travelsentry.org. If you use something other than TSA-approved locks, your lock will be cut off your suitcase if a TSA agent needs to hand-search your checked luggage and you are not available to provide the key or combination.

GETTING INTO TOWN FROM THE AIRPORT

From the Ottawa International Airport, which is located in the south end of the city, you have several options for traveling downtown. The Ottawa Airport Shuttle (© 613/260-2359) runs between the airport and several downtown locations and departs from the airport at the Level 1 curb outside the terminal in the arrivals area. The cost is C$12 (US$10) per adult one way, and C$20 (US$16) round trip. The shuttle operates daily with departures every 30 minutes, starting at 5am downtown; 5:35am at the airport. The major hotels have scheduled stops; other hotels are serviced upon request. An airport limo can be summoned by calling (© 613/523-1560). You can also hop into a regular cab; the fare will be around C$25 (US$20) to downtown. If you wish to use the public transit system, OC Transpo provides high-frequency rapid service along the scenic Transitway, a roadway built specifically for buses. Route 97 departs the terminal at the curb outside the Arrivals area. Adult cash fare (exact change only) is C$2.60 (US$2.15). Tickets are available at the Ground Transportation Desk located on Level 1 of the terminal building. Two tickets, at a cost of C90¢ (US75¢) each, are needed for one adult to travel downtown. Several major car-rental companies are located in the arrivals area of the terminal building. A 20-minute drive north along the Airport Parkway will take you to the heart of downtown.

FLYING FOR LESS: TIPS FOR GETTING THE BEST AIRFARE

Passengers sharing the same airplane cabin rarely have paid the same fare. Travelers who need to purchase tickets at the last minute, change their itinerary at a moment's notice, or fly one-way often get stuck paying the premium rate. Here are some ways to keep your airfare costs down.

- Passengers who can book their ticket **long in advance,** who can **stay over Saturday night,** or who **fly midweek** or **at less-trafficked hours** may pay a fraction of the full fare. If your schedule is flexible, say so, and ask if you can secure a cheaper fare by changing your flight plans.

- You can also save on airfares by keeping an eye out in local newspapers for **promotional specials** or **fare wars,** when airlines lower prices on their most popular routes. You rarely see fare wars offered for peak travel times, but if you can travel in the off-months you may snag a bargain.

- Search **the Internet** for cheap fares (see "Planning Your Trip Online").

- Try to book a ticket **in its country of origin.** For instance, if you're planning a one-way flight from Johannesburg to Bombay, a South Africa–based travel agent will probably have the lowest fares. For multi-leg trips, book in the country of the first leg; for example, book New York–London–Amsterdam–Rome–New York in the U.S.

- **Consolidators,** also known as bucket shops, are great sources for international tickets, although they usually can't beat the Internet on fares within North America. Start by looking in weekend newspaper travel sections; U.S. travelers should focus on the *New York Times, Los Angeles Times,* and *Miami Herald. **Warning:*** Bucket-shop tickets are usually non-refundable or rigged with stiff cancellation penalties, often as high as 50% to 75% of the ticket price, and some put you on charter airlines, which may leave at inconvenient times and experience delays. Several reliable consolidators are worldwide and available on the Net. **STA Travel** is now the world's leader in student travel, thanks to its purchase of Council Travel. It also offers good fares for travelers of all ages. ELTExpress **eltexpress.com; Flights.com** (*©* **312/332-0090** Mon-Fri 10am–6pm; *©***206/860-7325** Sat-Sun 12noon–8pm) started in Europe and has excellent fares worldwide, but particularly to that continent. It also has "local" websites in 12 countries. **Lowestfare.com** (*©* **800/FLY-CHEAP**) is owned by package-holiday megalith MyTravel and so has especially good access to fares for sunny destinations. **AirTicketsDirect.com** (*©* **800/778-3447**) is based in Montreal and leverages the Canadian dollar for low fares; it'll also book trips to places that U.S. travel agents won't touch, such as Cuba.

• Join **frequent-flier clubs.** Accrue enough miles, and you'll be rewarded with free flights and elite status. It's free, and you'll get the best choice of seats, faster response to phone inquiries, and prompter service if your luggage is stolen, your flight is canceled or delayed, or you want to change your seat. You don't need to fly to build frequent-flier miles — **frequent-flier credit cards** can provide thousands of miles for doing your everyday shopping.

• For many more tips about air travel, including a rundown of the major frequent-flier credit cards, pick up a copy of *Frommer's Fly Safe, Fly Smart* (Wiley Publishing, Inc.).

BY CAR

With the completion of Highway 416 several years ago, which serves as a direct link between Highway 401 and Ottawa, the approach from the south and west of Canada's capital is a smooth and easy drive. Unless you're headed for the west end of the city, take exit 57 from Highway 416 — look for the sign that reads BANK-FIELD ROAD (COUNTY ROAD 8)/AIRPORT/SCENIC ROUTE. Follow County Road 8 east to Highway 73 north through the countryside until you reach Hunt Club Road on the southern edge of the city. From here, you can take one of several routes downtown — Prince of Wales Drive and Riverside Drive are the most pleasant. The Airport Parkway/Bronson Avenue is the most direct route downtown, and Bank Street will take you past the most shops. From Montreal and Eastern Canada, travel west along Highway 417 and enter the city via Montreal Road. Keep an eye out for the handy, easy-to-read MapArt plasticized folding road map in local stores, which has a map of the region, a city map, and a large print map of downtown that includes one-way streets, churches, major attractions, and some hotels. *Warning:* Be alert to the possibility of deer suddenly appearing in the roadway in rural forested areas, particularly on Highway 416, most often at night.

If you're arriving from south of the border, there are several convenient crossing points. From Vermont, enter Canada via Interstate 89 or 91, travel toward Montreal, and pick up the westerly route (Highway 417). In New York State, Interstate 81 crosses at Hill Island to Highway 401; you can also take Route 37 and enter at Ogdensburg–Johnstown or Roosevel-town–Cornwall. On Interstate 87 in New York State, cross into Quebec, travel toward Montreal, and keep to the west of the city, heading onto Highway 417. If you're driving from Michigan, you'll enter Ontario at Detroit–Windsor (via I-75 and the Ambassador Bridge or tunnel) or Port Huron–Sarnia (via I-94 and the Blue-water Bridge).

Here are some approximate driving distances in kilometers to Ottawa: from Montreal, 200km; from Toronto, 450km; from Quebec City, 475km. And in miles from these U.S. cities: from Boston, 465 miles; Buffalo, 335 miles; Chicago, 800 miles; Detroit, 525 miles; New York City, 465 miles; Washington, D.C., 580 miles.

Be sure to carry your driver's license and car registration and insurance documents if you plan to drive your own vehicle. If you are a member of the American Automobile Association (AAA), the **Canadian Automobile Association (CAA)** North and East Ontario branch provides emergency roadside assistance (✆ **800/222-4357,** or 613/820-1400 within the City of Ottawa area).

If you decide to rent a car, try to make arrangements in advance to be sure the vehicle you want will be available. If you are traveling from outside Canada, you may obtain a reasonable discount by booking before you leave home. The rental fee depends on the type of car, but a typical fee for a midsize car with automatic transmission is around C$50 (US$41) a day, plus taxes. This price will vary according to season, availability, and length of rental (a full week's rental will often give you a lower price than the daily rate multiplied by 7). The price quoted usually does not include insurance, but some credit card companies offer automatic insurance coverage if you charge the full amount of the car rental to the card (check with your credit card issuer before you travel). Be sure to read the fine print of the agreement and undertake a thorough visual check for damage before accepting the vehicle. Some companies add conditions that will boost your bill if you don't fulfill certain obligations, such as filling the gas tank before returning the car. Major rental companies with offices at Ottawa

International Airport and downtown locations include **Avis** ✆ **800/879-2847, Budget** ✆ **800/268-8900, Enterprise** ✆ **800/325-8007, Hertz** ✆ **800/263-0600,** and **National** ✆ **800/227-7368.** Note that rental car companies customarily impose a minimum age of 25 for drivers, and some companies have a maximum age of 70 or 75.

BY TRAIN

VIA Rail trains to Ottawa operate as part of the Windsor–Quebec City corridor. The **Ottawa VIA Rail Station** is located at 200 Tremblay Rd., near the Riverside Drive exit from Highway 417, just east of downtown. VIA Rail often has special fares, and booking in advance may also get you a substantial discount. For rail information, contact **VIA Rail Canada** at ✆ **888/VIA-RAIL** (888/842-7245); www.viarail.ca. If you're traveling from the United States, call **Amtrak** at ✆ **800/USA-RAIL** (800/872-7245); www.amtrak.com. Several major car rental companies have offices near the rail station and offer free pickup and dropoff service at the station for their customers. Taxi cabs and city buses will take you downtown in around a quarter of an hour, depending on traffic conditions.

BY BUS

The **Ottawa Bus Terminal** (✆ **613/238-5900**) is located at 265 Catherine St., near the Kent Street exit from Highway 417, on the edge of the downtown core. **Greyhound Canada** (✆ **800/661-8747**) provides coast-to-coast service with connections to Ottawa. Book online or obtain schedule and fare information at www.greyhound.ca. **Greyhound Lines, Inc.** (✆ **800/229-9424;** www.greyhound.com) provides bus service between the U.S. and Canada.

Traveling by bus may be faster and cheaper than the train, and if you want to stop to visit towns along the way its routes may offer more flexibility. But there's also less space to stretch out, toilet facilities are meager, and meals are taken at roadside rest stops, so consider carefully, particularly if you're planning to bring children with you.

Investigate offers such as unlimited-travel passes and discount fares. It's tough to quote typical fares because bus companies, like airlines, are adopting yield-management strategies, resulting in frequent price changes depending on demand.

11 Packages for the Independent Traveler

Before you start your search for the lowest airfare, you may want to consider booking your flight as part of a travel package. Package tours are not the same thing as escorted tours. Package tours are simply a way to buy the airfare, accommodations, and other elements of your trip (such as car rentals, airport transfers, and sometimes even activities) at the same time and often at discounted prices — kind of like one-stop shopping. Packages are sold in bulk to tour operators — who resell them to the public at a cost that usually undercuts standard rates.

One good source of package deals is the airlines themselves. Most major airlines offer air/land packages, including **American Airlines Vacations** (✆ 800/321-2121; www.aavacations.com), **Delta Vacations** (✆ 800/221-6666; www.deltavacations.com), **Continental Airlines Vacations** (✆ 800/301-3800; www.covacations.com), and **United Vacations** (✆ 888/854-3899; www.unitedvacations.com). Several big **online travel agencies** — Expedia, Travelocity, Orbitz, Site59, and Lastminute.com — also do a brisk business in packages. If you're unsure about the pedigree of a smaller packager, check with the **Better Business Bureau** in the city where the company is based, or go online at www.bbb.org. If a packager won't tell you where they're based, don't fly with them.

Travel packages are also listed in the travel section of your local weekend newspaper. Or check ads in the national travel magazines, such as *Arthur Frommer's Budget Travel Magazine*, *Travel & Leisure*, *National Geographic Traveler*, and *Condé Nast Traveler*.

Package tours can vary by leaps and bounds. Some offer a better class of hotels than others. Some offer the same hotels for lower prices. Some offer flights on scheduled airlines, while others book charters. Some limit your choice of accommodations and travel days. You are often required to make a large payment up front. On the plus side, packages can save you money, offering group prices but allowing for independent travel. Some even let you add on a few guided excursions or escorted day trips (also at prices lower than if you booked them yourself) without booking an entirely escorted tour.

Before you invest in a package tour, get some answers. Ask about the **accommodations choices** and prices for each. Then look up the hotel reviews in a *Frommer's* guide and check their rates online for your specific dates of travel. You'll also want to find out what **type of room** you get. If you need a certain type of room, ask for it; don't take whatever is thrown your way. Request a nonsmoking room, a quiet room, a room with a view, or whatever you fancy.

Finally, look for **hidden expenses.** Ask whether airport departure fees and taxes, for example, are included in the total cost.

12 Tips on Accommodations

SAVING ON YOUR HOTEL ROOM

The **rack rate** is the maximum rate that a hotel charges for a room. Hardly anybody pays this price, however, except in high season or on holidays. To lower the cost of your room:

- **Ask about special rates or other discounts.** Always ask whether a room less expensive than the first one quoted is available, or whether any special rates apply to you. You may qualify for corporate, student, military, senior, or other discounts. Mention membership in AAA, AARP, frequent-flier programs, or trade unions, which may entitle you to special deals as well. Find out the hotel policy on children — do kids stay free in the room, or is there a special rate?

- **Dial direct.** When booking a room in a chain hotel, you'll often get a better deal by calling the individual hotel's reservation desk rather than the chain's main number.

- **Book online.** Many hotels offer Internet-only discounts, or supply rooms to Priceline, Hotwire, or Expedia at rates much lower than the ones you can get through the hotel itself. Shop around. And if you have special needs — a quiet room, a room with a view — call the hotel directly and make your needs known after you've booked online.

- **Remember the law of supply and demand.** Resort hotels are most crowded and therefore most expensive on weekends, so discounts are usually available for midweek stays. Business hotels in downtown locations are busiest during the week, so you can expect big discounts over the weekend. Many hotels have high-season and low-season prices, and booking the day after "high season" ends can mean big discounts.

- **Look into group or long-stay discounts.** If you come as part of a large group, you should be able to negotiate a bargain rate, since the hotel can then guarantee occupancy in a number of rooms. Likewise, if you're planning a long stay (at least five days), you might qualify for a discount. As a general rule, expect one night free after a seven-night stay.

- **Avoid excess charges and hidden costs.** When you book a room, ask whether the hotel charges for parking. Use your own cellphone, pay phones, or prepaid phone cards instead of dialing direct from hotel phones, which usually have exorbitant rates. And don't be tempted by the room's minibar offerings: Most hotels charge through the nose for water, soda, and snacks. Finally, ask about local taxes and service charges, which can increase the cost of a room by 15% or more. If a hotel insists upon tacking on a surprise "energy surcharge" that wasn't mentioned at check-in, or a "resort fee" for amenities you didn't use, you can often make a case for getting it removed.

- **Book a suite.** A room with a kitchenette allows you to shop for groceries and cook your own meals. This is a big money saver, especially for families on long stays.

- **Consider enrolling in hotel "frequent-stay" programs,** which reward repeat customers who accumulate enough points or credits to earn free hotel nights, airline miles, complimentary in-room amenities, or even merchandise. These are offered not only by many chain hotels and motels (Hilton HHonors, Marriott Rewards, Wyndham ByRequest, to name a few), but also by individual inns and B&Bs. Many chain hotels partner with other hotel chains, car-rental firms, airlines, and credit card companies to give consumers additional ways to accumulate points in the program.

3

Getting to Know Ottawa

Ottawa enjoys a reputation as one of the world's most beautiful capital cities, proudly standing at the confluence of three picturesque rivers: the Rideau, the Gatineau, and the mighty Ottawa.

Ottawa presents itself as a city of contrasts, with a personality that is both refreshing and eclectic. Parliament Hill — the seat of Canada's federal government, crowned by the magnificent copper roofs and sandstone-block construction of the Parliament Buildings — is Ottawa's most famous landmark. Farther along the banks of the Ottawa River, within sight of the Parliament Buildings, the stark grace of the steel and glass of the National Gallery of Canada glitters and gleams. Downtown, white-collar civil servants from the many federal government buildings share sidewalk space with university students and tourists.

With its proximity to Quebec and its high concentration of government employees, Ottawa is a truly bilingual city, offering a stimulating blend of English and French culture. As you stroll around the city, you are as likely to hear French spoken as English (and often in the same conversation, as bilingual Canadians switch back and forth between languages with ease).

But don't despair if you don't speak French. The people you will meet as a visitor to Canada's capital — hotel staff, restaurant servers, museum and attractions employees — are usually fluent in both official languages.

Ottawa is an easy city to navigate as a visitor, since the downtown core is compact and a good majority of the most popular tourist destinations are centrally located and accessible on foot. The extensive network of bike paths and recreational trails also provides an ideal way to explore the city for those who enjoy cycling.

Home to a host of national museums and attractions, Ottawa is considered Canada's cultural capital. Visual and performing arts are celebrated in style in Ottawa, and the city is home to many annual festivals and events.

Ottawa is a wonderful city to explore. Its people are friendly, the streets and parks are clean and safe, and there's plenty to keep visitors entertained, no matter what the season. Experience one of the many lively festivals, visit two or three of the national museums, and leave plenty of time to play or relax in the region's ample greenspace, numerous parks, and scenic waterways. Enjoy!

1 Orientation

VISITOR INFORMATION

Across the street from the Parliament Buildings and within easy walking distance of many major tourist attractions is the **Capital Infocentre,** at 90 Wellington St. The building has a windowed gallery facing Parliament Hill, offering a dramatic photo opportunity. The Terry Fox Memorial is situated in the square out front.

The Capital Infocentre is packed with brochures and dynamic exhibits. As you enter the building, you'll see a great orientation tool — a huge three-dimensional map of the central region. For a dazzling overview of Canada's capital and what's on offer for visitors, attend a presentation at the multimedia theater. Also check out the souvenir shop, which offers maps, guide books, clothing, and a few items for children.

To customize your itinerary in the capital, visit one of the "passport kiosks" in the Infocentre. Using the touch-sensitive screens, you can ask the computer for information on sites and attractions that suit your tastes and interests. The system then prints out a personalized passport with your chosen itinerary. If you prefer more personal interaction, orientation counselors are available to answer questions on Ottawa and the surrounding region and to help you plan your visit. For phone inquiries, contact the **Capital Call Centre** at ℂ **800/465-1867** or 613/239-5000, open Monday to Friday 8:30am to 8pm and weekends 8:30am to 5pm from mid-May to Labour Day. The rest of the year it's open Monday to Friday 8:30am to 5pm and Saturday to Sunday 9am to 5pm. Online, visit the Capital Infocentre website at **www.canadascapital.gc.ca.** Other websites with visitor information include **www.canada.com, www.ottawakiosk.com,** and **www.festivalseeker.com.**

The **Ottawa Tourism and Convention Authority (OTCA)** publishes an annual visitor guide, with maps and descriptions of cultural sites, things to see and do, accommodations, places to dine and shop, and services. The guide is available at the Capital Infocentre and at other locations around the city. The OTCA can be reached at ℂ **800/363-4465** for general visitor information or via the toll-free number for the Capital Call Centre listed above. The OTCA also operates a comprehensive tourism information portal at **www.ottawatourism.ca.** Leisure packages can be viewed at **www.ottawagetaways.ca.**

For listings of upcoming events, pick up a copy of *Where,* a free monthly guide to entertainment, shopping, and dining, available at hotels and stores throughout the city. The daily newspapers are the *Ottawa Citizen,* the *Ottawa Sun,* and *Le Droit,* Ottawa's French-language newspaper. The *Ottawa Citizen* includes a comprehensive Arts section on Fridays, with film listings and reviews, and a special Going Out section on Saturdays, with listings of upcoming live entertainment events. *Capital Parent,* a free monthly newspaper, contains articles of interest to parents and often advertises family-friendly events. For news and information about regional arts events and activities, drop in to **Arts Court,** 2 Daly Ave. (ℂ 613/564-7240), or call the **Council for the Arts in Ottawa (CAO)** (ℂ 613/569-1387). Canada's capital region is well served by weekly arts and entertainment newspapers. *Xpress* serves the English-speaking community and

---

⌐Tips **Smoke-Free City**

All public places and workplaces, including restaurants, bars, bingo halls, billiards halls, and all places of employment, were declared smoke-free as of August 1, 2001. The bylaws are designed to protect Ottawa's citizens from the health risks associated with secondhand smoke.

Voir highlights francophone events and news. Ottawa's gay and lesbian community has several publications including ***Capital Xtra!,*** a monthly newspaper.

CITY LAYOUT

The Ottawa River — Canada's second longest, at more than 1,100km (700 miles) — sweeps around the northern edge of the city. Most of the major attractions are clustered in the downtown area on the south bank of the Ottawa River. The **Rideau Canal** takes center stage, curving through the city and dividing the downtown area in two: **west of the canal** (often called **Centretown**), and **east of the canal** (often called **Lower Town**).

In the downtown area west of the canal you'll find **Parliament Hill,** the **Supreme Court,** the new **Canadian War Museum,** and the **Canadian Museum** of Nature (a few blocks south). Situated on the east side of the **Ottawa Locks** where the Rideau Canal meets the Ottawa River is the majestic **Château Laurier,** Ottawa's most elegant hotel, with the **Canadian Museum of Contemporary Photography** nestled along its west wall. Continuing east, the **ByWard Market** district hosts dozens of restaurants, boutiques, bars, and clubs. Along **Sussex Drive** (which follows the south bank of the Ottawa River), you'll find the **National Gallery,** the **Royal Canadian Mint,** and the **prime minister's residence.** Crossing the Rideau River, as Sussex Drive changes name to Rockcliffe Parkway, you can pass by the gates of many embassies and their official residences. **Rideau Hall, Rockcliffe Park, the Canada Aviation Museum,** and the **RCMP Musical Ride Centre (Rockcliffe Stables)** are all east of the Rideau River. The area south of the Queensway (Hwy 417), west to Bronson Avenue, and east to the canal is known as **the Glebe** and offers boutique shopping and trendy cafes along **Bank Street.** North across the river, in the **province of Quebec,** lies the city of **Gatineau,** connected to the east end of Ottawa by the Macdonald-Cartier and Alexandra bridges and to the west by the Portage and Chaudière bridges. At the north end of the Alexandra Bridge stands the architecturally stunning **Canadian Museum of Civilization.** The **Casino du Lac-Leamy,** with its theater, convention center, and luxury hotel, is situated on Lake Leamy in Gatineau. North and west of Gatineau stretches breathtaking **Gatineau Park,** 361 sq. km (141 sq. miles) of wilderness managed by the National Capital Commission.

Finding your way around town in Ottawa can be a challenge, since some streets halt abruptly and then reappear a few blocks farther on, one-way streets are common in the downtown core, and some streets change names several times. Ottawa's main east–west street, for example, starts as Scott Street, changes to Wellington Street as it passes through downtown in front of the Parliament Buildings, switches to Rideau Street in downtown east, and finally becomes Montreal Road on the eastern fringes of town. Take my advice: Carry a map.

Tips The Main Streets Downtown

The main streets running east–west through downtown are **Wellington, Laurier,** and **Somerset;** the **Rideau Canal** separates east from west (Lower Town and Centretown); and the main north–south streets are **Bronson, Bank,** and **Elgin.**

Ottawa–Gatineau

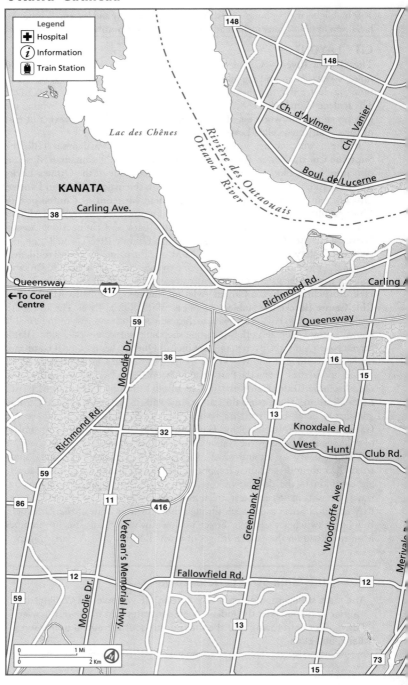

Legend
- Hospital
- Information
- Train Station

148

148

Ch. d'Aylmer

Ch. Vanier

Boul. de Lucerne

Lac des Chênes

Rivière des Outaouais
Ottawa River

KANATA

38 Carling Ave.

Queensway

417

←To Corel Centre

Richmond Rd.

Carling A

Queensway

59

36

16

15

Moodie Dr.

13

Knoxdale Rd.

Richmond Rd.

32

West Hunt Club Rd.

59

Greenbank Rd.

Woodroffe Ave.

86

11

416

Merivale

12

Veteran's Memorial Hwy.

Fallowfield Rd.

12

59

Moodie Dr.

13

0   1 Mi
0   2 Km

15

73

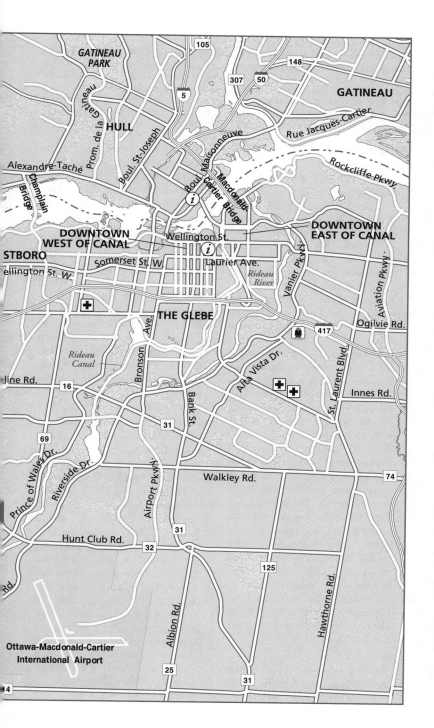

GATINEAU PARK

105

148

307

50

5

GATINEAU

HULL

Prom. de la Gatineau

Rue Jacques-Cartier

Rockcliffe Pkwy.

Alexandre-Taché

Boul. St-Joseph

Boul. Maisonneuve

Macdonald-Cartier Bridge

Champlain Bridge

DOWNTOWN WEST OF CANAL

Wellington St.

DOWNTOWN EAST OF CANAL

STBORO

Somerset St. W.

Laurier Ave.

Vanier Pkwy.

Aviation Pkwy.

ellington St. W.

Rideau River

THE GLEBE

Bronson Ave.

Rideau Canal

417

Ogilvie Rd.

ine Rd.

16

Bank St.

Alta Vista Dr.

St. Laurent Blvd.

Innes Rd.

31

69

Prince of Wales Dr.

Riverside Dr.

Airport Pkwy.

Walkley Rd.

74

Hunt Club Rd.

32

31

125

Albion Rd.

Hawthorne Rd.

Ottawa-Macdonald-Cartier International Airport

Rd.

25

31

4

NEIGHBORHOODS IN BRIEF

The architecture and layout of the city of Ottawa has been said to reflect Canada's bilingual heritage. Many residents speak or understand both French and English, and a number of ethnic groups have also brought their cultures to the city. Nowhere is this diversity more apparent than in Ottawa's distinct neighborhoods. The various business and residential areas each have their own mix of shops, cuisine, architecture, and sights and sounds, representing different cultures and traditions from around the globe. Strolling through the various neighborhoods will give you an appreciation of the city's heart and soul — its people.

ByWard Market and Downtown East of the Canal

Situated northeast of the Parliament Buildings, on the east side of the Rideau Canal and bordered to the east by the Rideau River, this historic neighborhood is the oldest section of Ottawa. Originally, downtown east of the canal (also known as Lowertown) was an uninhabitable cedar swamp. During the construction of the Rideau Canal, the land was drained and a mix of settlers soon moved in, including canal workers, shantymen, rivermen, and their families. The area was populated by poor Irish immigrants and French Canadians, and a reputation for general rowdiness and unlawfulness soon took hold. The building of the farmers' market in the mid-19th century helped to boost the local economy. The ByWard Market district, with its eclectic mix of boutiques, cafes, and bars, is now a prosperous, attractive city neighborhood with a vibrant personality. This is where to hang out to shop in one-of-a-kind boutiques, enjoy a drink or two in a pub or bar, or stroll around checking out restaurant menus to decide where to dine. Several major hotels are right on the doorstep, including the Fairmont Château Laurier, Les Suites Ottawa, the Lord Elgin, Novotel, and the Westin.

Sussex Drive

Winding along the south shore of the Ottawa River, historic Sussex Drive is a grand boulevard featuring many well-known landmarks. The National Gallery of Canada, the Royal Canadian Mint, the Notre Dame Basilica, the U.S. Embassy, the French Embassy, the residence of the prime minister of Canada (24 Sussex Dr.), and Rideau Hall (home of the governor general) are all found on this route. Also on Sussex Drive are the scenic Rideau Falls and the imposing Lester B. Pearson Building, home of the federal Department of Foreign Affairs. Earnscliffe, the residence of the British high commissioner, was originally the home of Canada's first prime minister, Sir John A. Macdonald. It sits high on a cliff overlooking the Ottawa River. This area can be explored on foot, by bicycle, or as part of a scenic drive.

Downtown West of the Canal

Ottawa's downtown business district (also referred to as Centretown) is a maze of office towers in an area stretching several blocks to the south of Parliament Hill. ARC the.hotel, an upscale boutique hotel, and a number of worldwide chains including Delta, Marriott, and Sheraton are located here. There are many excellent restaurants and shops in the area, tucked in and around the office buildings. The Sparks Street Mall, Canada's first pedestrian shopping street, runs between Elgin Street in the east and Lyon Street in the west, one block south of Parliament Hill. The streets tend to be quiet in the evenings, particularly when compared to the ByWard Market area, whose activity escalates as the evening wears on.

Somerset Village

This small downtown neighborhood, centered on a one-block stretch of Somerset Street between Bank and O'Connor streets, is considered a heritage district, characterized by a cluster of attractive Victorian redbrick dwellings. One of Ottawa's first commercial districts, Somerset Village was revitalized in the mid-1980s. Trees and shrubs, five-globe streetlamps, redbrick sidewalks, and benches now line the 19th-century streets. The village encompasses 14 buildings, 12 of which were built around 1900 or earlier, with a lively mix of shops, offices, bars, restaurants, and residential structures. In addition, several embassies are located here. Worth a stroll to find somewhere for lunch or dinner.

Somerset Heights

Step into the Far East as you travel farther west along Somerset Street to the neighborhood stretching from Bay to Rochester streets. Intriguing markets sell a variety of Asian produce, crafts, traditional Chinese medicinal ingredients, hand-painted silk garments, and many more fascinating treasures. Thai, Vietnamese, and Chinese restaurants appear on every corner, tempting visitors with their distinctive cuisine. The stores and restaurants are owned and frequented by local residents and therefore offer an authentic ethnic neighborhood experience.

Wellington Street West & Westboro Village

Farther west along Somerset Street West, the road changes name to Wellington Street West as it enters an eclectic neighborhood with down-to-earth cafes and shops. The area doesn't fit under a neat moniker, but a visit will prove to be one of those journeys of discovery sometimes experienced when exploring a city.

Continuing west, the next commercial district is Westboro. Originally a small village on the outskirts of the city, Westboro has retained its friendly small-town atmosphere. This traditional city neighborhood west of downtown has enjoyed a revitalization that began in the late 1990s. The addition of Richmond Road Mountain Equipment Co-op spurred retail growth in the west end of Westboro's commercial ribbon, and there is hope that the area will eventually link with Wellington Street West to form a shopping district much like the ByWard Market and the Glebe.

Little Italy

The heart of Ottawa's Italian immigrant population is Preston Street, also fondly known as Corso Italia (both names appear on the official street signs). The area serves as the commercial and cultural center of Little Italy. An abundance of cafes, *trattorie,* and pizzerias celebrate the essence of Italy — its delicious cuisine. Irish, French, and Asian Canadians also call the neighborhood home. Every June, the street comes alive with the festivities of Italian Week, culminating in a street party stretching over three evenings. Grab a cab out here one evening for a memorable Italian meal.

The Glebe

Just south of downtown, between the Queensway and Lansdowne Park, lies Ottawa's first suburb. In the 1870s, residential development began to encroach on farmland south of the city. The construction of exhibition grounds at Lansdowne Park and of a streetcar link between the Glebe and the city fueled the growth of this neighborhood. The middle classes settled here in large numbers. Today, the Glebe is an upscale middle-class neighborhood served by a stretch of trendy, high-end stores, services, and eateries on Bank Street. It's well worth spending a morning or afternoon strolling up one side of the street and down the other. If you begin at the north end, take a break near the canal before making your return journey. Brown's Inlet and Park are tucked a block or two west of Bank Street, north of Queen Elizabeth Drive. If you start at the canal end, rest in Central Park, which straddles Bank Street in the vicinity of Powell and Clemow avenues. For winter strolling, take refuge in the atrium at Fifth Avenue Court, about midway down this section of Bank Street, or in one of the many cafes along the way.

Hey, I Didn't Know That about Ottawa!

- The name Ottawa is adapted from *Outaouak,* the name of the Algonquin people who settled and traded furs in the area.
- The world's largest gold depository is found in the Bank of Canada gold vaults, which lie under one of Ottawa's main streets, Wellington Street.
- Ottawa's official relationship with tulips began in 1945, when Queen Juliana of the Netherlands presented 100,000 bulbs to the city as a gift. They were given in appreciation of Canada's granting of a safe haven to the Dutch Royal Family during World War II and in recognition of the role that Canadian troops played in liberating the Netherlands. Half a century later, three million tulips bloom in the city's parklands in May.
- The sport of basketball was invented by Dr. James Naismith, who hailed from Almonte, a small town just west of Ottawa.
- Canada's last public hanging took place at Ottawa's first jail. The building is now operated by Hostelling International, and guests can actually sleep behind bars in the cells.
- The Governor General's New Year's Day Levee at Rideau Hall originated from the French governor's practice of shaking hands and wishing a happy New Year to the citizens of Quebec City, a tradition begun in 1646.
- The grounds of Parliament Hill were laid out in 1873 by Calvert Vaux, the same landscape architect who designed New York's Central Park.
- The 7.8-km (4.5-mile) Rideau Canal Skateway, the world's longest skating rink, is used by approximately 750,000 skaters each winter and has an average skating season of 64 days.
- The world's first international telephone call was made from Ottawa in 1927, when Canadian prime minister Mackenzie King called the British prime minister.
- North American entertainment stars Paul Anka and Rich Little were born in Ottawa and have streets named after them in the city's south end.
- Actor Dan Ackroyd was born in the region and attended Carleton University. Singer Alanis Morrisette was also born here, and rock star Bryan Adams went to school in Ottawa.
- The Ottawa Senators was originally the name of a local football club in the 1920s. In 1992, the name was reclaimed for Ottawa's first National Hockey League team.
- The Stanley Cup was born in Ottawa. In 1892, Governor General Lord Stanley Preston commissioned a silversmith in England to make a gold-lined silver bowl on an ebony base, which became the premier trophy of professional hockey in North America.

2 Getting Around

BY PUBLIC TRANSPORTATION

CITY BUSES   Public transit in Ottawa is provided by **OC Transpo.** This is an economical and efficient way to get around, since buses can bypass rush-hour traffic through the Transitway, a rapid-transit system of roadways reserved exclusively for buses. Routes 95, 96, and 97 are the three main Transitway routes, operating 22 hours a day. All OC Transpo bus routes travel along parts of the Transitway or connect at one of the stations. OC Transpo stations, many of which are located next to major shopping or employment centers, offer convenient transfer points with heated waiting areas, information displays, and pay phones. Many have bike racks and vendor kiosks. For transit information call © **613/741-4390;** www.octranspo.com. There are four sales and information centers in the city — one in the Rideau Centre shopping mall in downtown Ottawa, and three more at transit stations: Lincoln Fields Station in west Ottawa, and St. Laurent Station and Place d'Orléans station in the east.

The regular exact-cash fare is C$2.60 (US$2.15) adult single or C$1.35 (US$1.10) child. It's cheaper to use tickets, at C90¢ (US75¢) each, since the adult fare is two tickets and the child fare is one ticket. The exception is during weekday rush hours, when some express routes charge a three-ticket fare. Day passes are a good buy at C$6 (US$5) in advance at a vendor or C$6.50 (US$5.35) on the bus for unlimited rides. The Family Day Pass is a real bargain. Just one day pass will entitle a family of up to 2 adults and 4 children aged 11 and under to unlimited same-day travel on Sundays and statutory holidays. You can buy bus passes and tickets at more than 300 vendor locations across the city. Day passes can also be purchased at the National Capital Infocentre at 90 Wellington St. in front of the Parliament Buildings and at many downtown hotels.

The number of buses that are fully accessible to **people with disabilities** has increased dramatically in recent years. Forty-five bus routes currently support fully accessible low-floor buses, although some trips each day may use nonaccessible buses so it's best to check before starting out on a trip. A telephone hotline has been set up to help customers find out more about accessible services on conventional transit © **613/842-3625.** For information on designated accessible bus routes, call the main OC Transpo phone line at © **613/741-4390.** Fully accessible buses, marked by a blue and white wheelchair symbol on the front of the bus, have low floors to provide access for seniors, people with limited mobility, people using wheelchairs, and parents with small children or strollers. The buses lower to the curb so there are no stairs to climb, and drivers can extend a ramp to accommodate wheelchairs. In addition, these buses are equipped with air-conditioning, cloth seats, yellow grab rails and pull cords, and easy-to-reach stop-request buttons.

For persons with permanent or short-term disabilities who are unable to walk to or board regular transit, **Para Transpo** is available. Both visitors and residents can use this service but you must register, and the application form must be signed by an appropriate health professional. Reservations must be made one day before your trip. Call © **613/244-1289** for information and registration, or © **613/244-7272** for reservations (the reservations office is open daily 9am to 5pm).

Public transit throughout the city of **Gatineau** and the **Outaouais region** on the Quebec side of the Ottawa River is provided by **Société de transport de** l'Outaouais (STO) (𝓒 819/770-3242 for information; an information office is located at 111 Jean-Proulx St. in Gatineau (Hull Sector), open Monday to Saturday 7am to 9pm and Sunday 9:30am to 8:30pm; www.sto.ca).

LIGHT RAIL TRAIN (O-Train)   The Light Rail pilot project was launched in October 2001. Designed to go where the Transitway doesn't, the O-Train uses an 8-km (5-mile) stretch of existing Canadian Pacific rail line running between Greenboro Transitway Station in the south end and Bayview Station in the north end of the city, close to downtown. Greenboro Station has parking available for more than 600 vehicles and connects to Ottawa International Airport via bus route 97. Confederation Station is close to Vincent Massey Park. Carleton Station serves students and staff of Carleton University. Carling Station is conveniently close to Dow's Lake and Little Italy. Bayview Station is minutes from downtown, with a high-frequency bus service. Each state-of-the-art train, built by the Canadian company Bombardier, consists of three air-conditioned cars, accommodating 135 seated and 150 standing passengers. The front and rear diesel-powered units allow the train to travel in either direction on the track without having to turn around. A low-floor design ensures easy access for passengers and a quiet, comfortable ride.

Operating hours are Monday to Saturday 6:30am to midnight, and Sunday and holidays 7:30am to 11pm. The fare is C$2 (US$1.65). Children 11 and under ride free on the O-Train. Tickets can be purchased from the vending machines on the station platform. You may transfer to an OC Transpo bus at no extra charge, except on rush-hour routes, which require a top-up of a single bus ticket or C$1.15 (US95¢). Children ages 6 to 11 who transfer to a bus must pay the child's bus fare.

The current rail line is the first step toward citywide light rail transit. Several extensions are being considered, including links to Ottawa's downtown core, Gatineau, and Ottawa International Airport.

BY TAXI

You can hail a taxi on the street, but you'll find one more readily at taxi stands in front of most hotels, many government buildings, and some museums. You can also summon a taxi by phone. In the Ottawa area, 24-hour cab companies include **Blue Line** (𝓒 613/238-1111), with a fleet of more than 600 cabs, and **Capital Taxi** (𝓒 613/744-3333). West-Way Taxi (𝓒 613/727-0101) has drivers who have been trained to transport people with disabilities.

BY TOUR BUS

There are so many interesting buildings, monuments, attractions, and views in Ottawa that hopping on a tour bus is a great idea, especially if it's your first visit to Canada's capital. Tours are fully narrated so you don't miss anything while you're cruising around town. On-and-off privileges allow you to take a break to stretch your legs, or if you see somewhere you'd like to visit you can just hop off the bus and join it again later.

Choose an open-top double-decker bus or a vintage trolley bus operated by **Gray Line Sightseeing Tours** for a 90-minute tour. Step on or off the bus at any of the 15 designated stops as many times as you wish as you pass the following major tourist attractions: Parliament Hill, Canadian Museum of Civilization, Notre Dame Basilica, Rideau Hall, RCMP Musical Ride Centre and Stables, Canada Aviation Museum, and the ByWard Market. The tours officially start at the corner of Sparks and Metcalfe streets. Tickets are valid for two days,

The View from Here

- For views of Parliament Hill and the Ottawa River, visit Major's Hill Park or Nepean Point.
- To take in the Ottawa skyline facing south, as well as Parliament Hill, look across from Victoria Island or the Canadian Museum of Civilization.
- For a photo of the stunning architecture of the Museum of Civilization, look across the Ottawa River from Parliament Hill.
- To capture tulips on film, visit the numerous public parks and gardens throughout the city during the month of May. Visit the Dutch tulip gardens at the northern tip of Dow's Lake in Commissioner's Park, where 300,000 bulbs create a breathtaking display of color.
- To see beautiful waterfalls, visit Rideau Falls and Hog's Back Falls.
- View the Ottawa skyline facing north from the Arboretum and the Central Experimental Farm.
- Enjoy a vista of the Ottawa Valley from Champlain Lookout in Gatineau Park.
- To see the wide sweep of the Ottawa River and the Quebec shoreline, pay a visit to Rockcliffe Lookout.

and the tour buses run in a continuous circle between 10am and 4pm. Tours operate from May to October. A family of four can get a two-day, on/off-privilege ticket for C$80 (US$66); an adult single is C$30 (US$25). For departure times and other information, call Gray Line at © **800/297-6422** or © 613/ 565-5463; www.grayline.ca.

BY CAR

So many of Ottawa's attractions are downtown and within walking distance of each other that you can have an action-packed vacation without ever getting behind the wheel. If you traveled to Ottawa by car, leave it in the hotel parking garage unless you're planning to venture out on a day trip. If you arrived in the city by plane, train, or bus, you could rent a car for a day or two to explore Ottawa's surrounding regions, and spend the rest of the time traveling by city bus, by tour bus, by bicycle, or on foot.

If you do decide to drive, be prepared for one-way streets that don't follow any predictable pattern. Keep an eye out, as well, for traffic blocks designed to prevent vehicles from using residential streets as thoroughfares. Some streets change names several times along their length, and others stop abruptly only to continue a few blocks over. Needless to say, a map is essential if you're driving in city areas. You'll have the added convenience of being able to locate major tourist attractions, parking lots, and other useful destinations.

RENTAL CARS   If you decide to rent a car during the high season, try to make arrangements well in advance to ensure the vehicle you want will be available. If you are traveling from outside Canada, you may obtain a reasonable discount by booking before you leave home. The rental fee depends on the type of car, but the starting point is around C$30 to C$50 (US$25–US$41) a day for a compact or midsize vehicle, plus taxes. This price does not include insurance, but some credit cards offer automatic coverage if you charge the full amount of the car rental to the card (check with your credit card issuer before you travel). Be sure to read the fine print of the agreement and complete a thorough visual

> ⌒ **Tips** **Overnight Winter Parking Ban**
>
> From November 15 to April 1 there are parking restrictions on city streets between 1 and 7am when an accumulation of 7cm (3 in.) of snow or more is forecast. Call the City of Ottawa Snowline at ℂ **613/580-2460.** Motorists should be aware that snow-removal crews may be working to remove snow from recent storms at any time; signs informing the public are placed in snowbanks several hours before beginning work.

check for damage before accepting the vehicle. Some companies add conditions that will boost your bill if you don't fulfill certain obligations, such as filling the gas tank before returning the car. Major rental companies with offices at Ottawa International Airport (either at the terminal or close by) and locations throughout the city include **Avis** (ℂ **800/879-2847**), **Budget** (ℂ **800/268-8900**), **Enterprise** (ℂ **800/325-8007**), **Hertz** (ℂ **800/263-0600**), **National** (ℂ **800/227-7368**), and **Thrifty** (ℂ **800/847-4389**).

Note: If you're under age 25 or over 70, tell the rental company when you book — most companies have a minimum age policy, and some have implemented a maximum age as well.

PARKING   When parking downtown, you have a choice of meters or lots. Parking meters are color-coded: meters with a 1-hour time limit have gray domes, those with a 2-hour limit have green domes, and those for tour-bus parking only have yellow domes. Meters accept quarters, loonies, and toonies.

Always read the signs posted near parking meters to find out if there are any parking restrictions. One of the most common restrictions is a ban on parking weekdays between 3:30 and 5:30pm on certain streets, to improve traffic flow during the evening rush hour. Generally, short-term parking rates downtown are C50¢ (US41¢) for 12 minutes. Your best bet is to use a municipal parking lot, marked with a large white "P" in a green circle. On weekends, parking is free at city lots and meters in the area west of the canal, east of Bronson Avenue, and north of the Queensway. If you must leave your vehicle on a city street overnight, ask hotel staff or your B&B host whether there are parking restrictions.

DRIVING RULES   In Ontario, a right turn on a red light is permitted after coming to a complete stop unless posted otherwise, provided you yield to oncoming traffic and pedestrians. Be aware that once you cross the Ottawa River you enter the province of Quebec, where you cannot turn right on a red light. There have been experiments in some communities to introduce right turns on reds, but the idea strikes fear in the hearts of most Quebec pedestrians so the jury is still out on whether the law will change. Better to err on the side of caution. Wearing your seat belt is compulsory; fines for riding without a seat belt are substantial. Speed limits are posted and must be obeyed at all times. Always stop when pedestrians are using the crosswalks, but also be careful of pedestrians crossing against the lights — Ottawans seem to have a mild disregard for pedestrian-crossing signals in the downtown core. Beware, as well, of drivers running red lights. Always check that an intersection is clear before advancing when the light turns green, especially if your vehicle is going to be the first one through. In 2000, Ottawa began a pilot intersection safety program, using two cameras rotated among eight city intersections, with the aim of reducing the number of drivers who run red lights. According to a report by the City of Ottawa the pilot

---

Tips **Watch for Cyclists!**

With the excellent network of bike pathways in the city, Ottawa has a large population of cyclists. Keep your eyes open for cyclists, especially when opening your car door on the street. Opening your door into a cyclist's path is a traffic violation — and even worse, could cause serious injury to the cyclist.

---

program has been hugely successful, reducing the number of right-angle collisions at these intersections by 32% and issuing almost 10,000 tickets to errant drivers in the first three years. Plans are underway to increase the number of intersections fitted with red-light cameras.

BY BICYCLE

A great way to get around in Ottawa is by bicycle. Ottawa and the surrounding regions offer a comprehensive network of pathways and parkways where people can bike and in-line skate through beautiful natural scenery. A number of city streets also have designated bike lanes. For maps of the pathways and more information, drop in to the **Capital Infocentre,** opposite Parliament Hill at 90 Wellington St. (© **800/465-1867;** www.canadascapital.gc.ca). If you find your planned bike route overly ambitious, hop on the bus: **OC Transpo** has installed **bike racks** on 170 buses, including most buses on routes 2, 95, and 97. Each rack holds two bikes, and loading and unloading is quick and easy. There's no additional cost to use the rack. The program runs from spring through fall.

If you didn't bring your own equipment, numerous places in Ottawa rent out bicycles and in-line skates. See chapter 7, "Active Ottawa," for a list of rental outfits.

Some specific rules apply to cyclists. All cyclists under age 18 must wear a bicycle **helmet.** Cyclists cannot ride on the sidewalk and must not exceed speeds of 20km per hour (12.5mph) on multi-use pathways. Be considerate of other road or pathway users, and keep to the right. Pass only when it is safe to do so, and if you're on a bicycle use your bell or voice to let others know you're about to pass.

If you're in the vicinity of the Rideau Centre and the ByWard Market, you can **park** your bike at a supervised facility. Located at Rideau and William streets, the facility operates daily 8:30am to 5:30pm, from Victoria Day until Labour Day weekend (third Saturday in May to first Monday in September).

FAST FACTS: **Ottawa**

Airport For general inquiries and for information on flights, baggage, and air freight, call the appropriate airline company — see "Getting There" in chapter 2. You can also obtain general information from the Airport switchboard (© **613/248-2000**) and on the Web at **www.ottawa-airport.ca**. The airport is located in the south end of the city at the southern end of Airport Parkway. For information on transportation from the airport to downtown, see "Getting There" in chapter 2.

Air Travel Complaints The Canadian Transportation Agency's Air Travel Complaints Commissioner handles unresolved passenger complaints against air carriers. Information and complaint forms are available at **www.cta.gc.ca**. For more information call the Canadian Transportation Agency ℂ **888/222-2592**.

American Express For card member services, including traveler's checks and lost or stolen cards, call ℂ **800/869-3016** or ℂ 363/393-1111 collect (only if your card is lost or stolen). There is an American Express Travel Agency, which provides travel and financial services, at 220 Laurier Ave. W. ℂ **613/563-0231**.

Area Codes The telephone area code for Ottawa is 613; for Gatineau and surrounding areas it's 819. When calling from Ottawa to Gatineau, you don't need to use the area code.

ATMs Walk-up cash machines that link to the Cirrus or PLUS networks can be found every few blocks at various bank branches. You can also get cash advances against your MasterCard or Visa at an ATM, but you'll need a separate personal identification number (PIN) and will likely be charged interest from the time of withdrawal. ATMs generally charge a fee for each withdrawal unless the machine is operated by your own banking institution.

Babysitting Hotel concierge or front desk staff can usually supply names and phone numbers of reliable sitters.

Business Hours Most **stores** are open Monday to Saturday from 9:30 or 10am to 6pm, and many have extended hours one or more evenings. Sunday opening hours are generally from noon to 5pm, although some stores open at 11am and others are closed all day. **Banks** generally open at 9:30am and close by 4pm, with extended hours one or more evenings; some are open Saturdays. **Restaurants** open at 11 or 11:30am for lunch and at 5pm for dinner, although many in the ByWard Market district stay open all day. Some **museums** are closed on Mondays from October to April; some also close Tuesdays in the winter months. Many stay open on Thursdays until 8 or 9pm.

Camera Repair See "Cameras and Electronics" in chapter 8.

Car Rentals See "Getting Around," earlier in this chapter.

Climate See "When to Go" in chapter 2.

Currency Exchange Generally, the best place to exchange your currency is at a bank or by obtaining local currency through an ATM. There are a number of foreign exchange services in Ottawa. **Calforex** in the Rideau Centre, 50 Rideau St. (ℂ **800/769-2025** or 613/569-4075), is open daily and provides no-fee American Express traveler's checks and other foreign currency services. **Custom House Currency Exchange** is located at 153 Sparks St. (ℂ **613/234-6005**).

Dentists For emergency dental care, ask the front desk staff or concierge at your hotel for the name of the nearest dentist, or call Ottawa Dental Society Emergency Service ℂ **613/523-4185**.

Directory Assistance For numbers within the same area code, call ℂ **411**. For other numbers, call ℂ **555-1212**, prefixed by the area code of the number you're searching for. There is a charge for these services.

Disability Services Most of Ottawa's museums and public buildings, as well as many theaters and restaurants, are accessible to travelers with disabilities. For details, refer to the Ottawa visitor guide available from the Capital Infocentre, 90 Wellington St. (across from Parliament Hill) (© **800/465-1867** or 613/239-5000). Public transit (OC Transpo) is increasingly accessible for passengers with disabilities. For those who are unable to board regular transit, Para Transpo provides alternative transportation. See "Tips for Travelers with Disabilities" in chapter 2.

Doctors Ask hotel staff or the concierge to help you locate a doctor. Some physicians will visit hotels. Walk-in clinics are available to out-of-province and foreign visitors, but be prepared to pay for services on the spot with cash. For more information, see "Health & Safety" in chapter 2.

Documents See "Entry Requirements" in chapter 2.

Driving Rules See "Getting Around," earlier in this chapter.

Drugstores **Shopper's Drug Mart** has one **24-hour** location: 1460 Merivale Rd. (at Baseline Rd.) (© 613/224-7270).

Electricity It's the same as in the United States: 110–115 volts AC.

Embassies/Consulates All embassies in Canada (more than 100 in total) are located in Ottawa; consulates are primarily located in Toronto, Montreal, and Vancouver. Embassies include the Australian High Commission, 50 O'Connor St., Suite 710, Ottawa, ON K1P 6L2 (© 613/236-0841); the British High Commission, 80 Elgin St., Ottawa, ON K1P 5K7 (© **613/237-1530**); the Embassy of Ireland, 130 Albert St., Ottawa, ON K1P 5G4 (© **613/233-6281**); the New Zealand High Commission, 727–99 Bank St., Ottawa, ON K1P 6G3 (© **613/238-5991**); the South African High Commission, 15 Sussex Dr., Ottawa, ON K1M 1M8 (© **613/744-0330**); and the Embassy of the United States of America, 490 Sussex Dr., Ottawa, ON K1N 1G8 © 613/**238-5335;** www.usembassycanada.gov for general inquiries.

Emergencies Call © **911** emergency services for fire, police, or ambulance. For Poison Control, call © **613/737-1100.**

Eyeglasses For same-day service (it may be as quick as 1 hour) on most prescriptions, call **Hakim Optical,** which has seven Ottawa locations including the downtown store at 229 Rideau St. (© **613/562-1234**). **Lenscrafters,** open 7 days a week, is conveniently located in major malls, including Bayshore, Place d'Orléans, the Rideau Centre, and St. Laurent Shopping Centre.

Homeopathic and Naturopathic Pharmacy The **Ottawa Natural Clinic Pharmacy** has a comprehensive selection of homeopathic and naturopathic remedies, health foods, and related books and literature. Consultations can be arranged by appointment. Located at 151 Slater St. © 613/235-3993.

Hospitals The **Children's Hospital of Eastern Ontario (CHEO),** 401 Smyth Rd. (© **613/737-7600**), is a pediatric teaching hospital affiliated with the University of Ottawa that services a broad geographical area, including Eastern Ontario and Western Quebec. The hospital has an emergency department. For adult care, the **Ottawa Hospital** is a large multi-campus academic health sciences center with emergency departments at two sites: the **Civic** campus at 1053 Carling Ave. (© **613/761-4621**), and the **General** campus at 501 Smyth Rd. (© **613/737-8000**). Ontario emergency rooms are extremely busy and wait times for non-urgent cases are typically several hours. If at all possible, use a walk-in clinic; for more information see "Health & Safety," chapter 2.

Internet Access   You can check your e-mail and send messages at the **Internet Café,** 288 Bank St., at Somerset (© **613/230-9000**) or **Agora Bookstore Student Federation** at 145 Besserer St. (© **613/562-4672**). New wireless "hot spots" are popping up all over the place, so if you're equipped with the technology you should find it fairly easy to go online. Otherwise, try the Public Library. See "Libraries," below.

Kids Help Phone   Kids or teens in distress can call © **800/668-6868** for help.

Laundry/Dry-Cleaning   Most hotels provide same-day laundry and dry-cleaning services or have coin-operated laundry facilities.

Libraries   The city of Ottawa now has 34 branches of the Ottawa Public Library. Drop in to any branch to pick up a current brochure of special events, or visit the website at www.library.ottawa.on.ca. The main branch is located at 120 Metcalfe St. (© **613/236-0301**).

Liquor   You must be **19 years of age or older** to consume or purchase alcohol in Ontario. Bars and retail stores are strict about enforcing the law and will ask for proof of age if they consider it necessary. The **Liquor Control Board of Ontario (LCBO)** sells wine, spirits, and beer. Their flagship retail store, at 275 Rideau St. (© **613/789-5226**), has two floors of fine products from around the world, as well as a Vintages section with a wide selection of high-quality products. Wine accessories are also available, and seminars and tastings are regularly scheduled. This store is well worth a visit. Ontario wines are available at individual winery outlets. Beer is also available at the Beer Store, with about 20 locations in Ottawa.

Mail   Mailing letters and postcards within Canada costs C50¢ (US41¢). Postage for letters and postcards to the United States costs C85¢ (US70¢), and overseas C$1.45 (US$1.19).

Maps   Maps of Ottawa are readily available in convenience stores and bookstores, as well as at the **Capital Infocentre,** 90 Wellington St. (© **800/465-1867** or 613/239-5000). For a good selection of maps and travel guides, visit **Place Bell Books,** 175 Metcalfe St. (© **613/233-3821**). Specializing in city and country travel books and maps, this bookstore has a hefty selection of vacation guides. Local guide books and scenic photography books of the Ottawa region are also on hand. Another good source is **A World of Maps,** 1235 Wellington St. W. (© **800/214-8524** or 613/724-6776).

Members of Parliament   Call the **Government of Canada** information line at © **800/O-CANADA** (622-6232) Monday to Friday 8am to 8pm. Service is provided in English and French.

Newspapers/Magazines   The daily newspapers are the **Ottawa Citizen,** the **Ottawa Sun,** and **Le Droit,** Ottawa's French-language newspaper. Keep an eye out for **Capital Parent,** a local free publication that advertises family-friendly events. **Where Ottawa** is a free monthly guide to shopping, dining, entertainment, and other tourist information. You can find it at most hotels and at some restaurants and retail stores. **Ottawa City**

Magazine and *Ottawa Life* are city monthlies. Arts and entertainment newspapers include the English-language *Xpress* and the French-language *Voir.* Gays and lesbians should check out *Capital Xtra!*. For a great variety of international publications, visit **Mags and Fags,** at 254 Elgin St. (✆ **613/233-9651**), or **Planet News,** at 143 Sparks St. (✆ **613/232-5500**).

Police In a life-threatening emergency or to report a crime in progress or a traffic accident that involves injuries or a vehicle that cannot be driven, call ✆ **911**. For other emergencies (a serious crime or a break-and-enter) call ✆ **613/230-6211**. For all other inquiries, call ✆ **613/236-1222**.

Post Offices Many convenience stores and drugstores offer postal services, and some have a separate counter for shipping packages during regular business hours. Look for the sign in the store window advertising such services. Downtown, postal services are available at **Minto Place Postal Outlet,** 440 Laurier Ave. W. (✆ **613/782-2260**), and **ByWard Market Postal Outlet,** 298 Dalhousie St. (✆ **613/241-3264**).

Radio The **Canadian Broadcasting Corporation (CBC)** broadcasts on **91.5FM** and **103.3FM**. Pop music hits from the past 20 years are played on **BOB FM93.9**. For news and talk radio, tune in to **CFRA 580AM**. Ottawa's classic rock station is **CHEZ 106FM**. The local easy-listening music station is **Majic 100FM. The BEAR,** on **106.9FM,** broadcasts a mix of current and classic rock. To keep up with the latest on the sports scene, including broadcasts of the Ottawa Senators and Ottawa 67's, listen to **The Team, Sports Radio 1200. KOOL 93.9FM** broadcasts a mix of hits and fun. For country music fans, there's **Young Country Y101.1FM**.

Safety Ottawa is generally safe, but be alert and use common sense, particularly at night. The ByWard Market area and Elgin Street are busy at night with the bar crowd.

Taxes The national Goods and Services Tax (GST) is 7%. The provincial retail sales tax (PST) is 8% on most goods; certain purchases, such as groceries and children's clothing, are exempt from provincial sales tax. The accommodations tax is 5%.

In general, nonresidents may apply for a tax refund. They can recover the accommodations tax, the sales tax, and the GST for nondisposable merchandise that will be exported for use, provided it is removed from Canada within 60 days of purchase. The following do not qualify for rebate: meals and restaurant charges, alcohol, tobacco, gas, car rentals, and such services as dry-cleaning and shoe repair.

The quickest and easiest way to secure the refund is to stop at a duty-free shop at the border. You must have original receipts with GST registration numbers. You can also apply through the mail, but it will take several weeks to receive your refund. For an application form and information, write or call the **Visitor Rebate Program** Enquiries Line, ✆ **800/668-4748** within Canada. You can also get information and an application form online at www.cra-arc.gc.ca/visitors. The forms are also available at tourism kiosks around town and in some shops.

Taxis See "Getting Around," earlier in this chapter.

Telephone A local call from a telephone booth costs C25¢ (US21¢, but note that Canadian and U.S. coins are accepted at face value. Watch out for hotel surcharges on local and long-distance phone calls; often a local call will cost at least C$1 (US82¢) from a hotel room. The United States and Canada are on the same long-distance system. To make a long-distance call between the United States and Canada, use the area codes as you would at home. Canada's international prefix is **1.** Phone cards can be purchased at convenience stores and drugstores.

Time Ottawa is on **Eastern Standard Time. Daylight saving time** is in effect from the first Sunday in April (clocks are moved ahead 1 hour) to the last Sunday in October (clocks are moved back 1 hour).

Tipping Basically, it's the same as in major U.S. cities — 15% in restaurants (up to 20% in higher-end restaurants or for exceptional service and food), 10 to 15% for taxis, C$1 (US82¢) per bag for porters, C$2 (US$1.64) per day for hotel housekeepers.

Transit Information The public transit system is a bus service provided by Ottawa-Carleton (OC) Transpo (© **613/741-4390**). Besides using public roads, OC Transpo has a convenient system of roadways used exclusively by buses — the Transitway. Two main lines operate on the Transitway, with transfers possible at many stations along the routes. Route 95 connects the southwest end of the city with the east via downtown. Route 97 runs between Kanata in the west to the airport in the south via downtown. In addition, there is a light rail train providing all-day service at a limited number of stations. For more information, see "Getting Around" earlier in this chapter.

Weather For the weather forecast, check the daily newspaper, catch a radio broadcast, or tune in to the weather channel on TV. Some hotels post weather information at the front desk.

Where to Stay

Visitors looking for a place to stay in the National Capital Region will find accommodations to fit every style and budget. Whether your idea of the perfect place to call home during your vacation is a grandly proportioned Loire Valley Renaissance château, an ultra-modern self-catering suite, a romantic B&B, or a chic boutique hotel, you'll find a listing in this chapter to meet your needs. If all you're looking for is a clean place to rest your head, you'll find that, too — university digs, airport inns, and even a converted jail.

If you're traveling with children, I strongly recommend staying in a one- or two-bedroom suite if your budget will allow. In return for your investment, you'll get a comfortable base with space for everyone to spread out, a place to make meals on your own schedule (you'll also save money by not having to eat out all the time), and usually more than one TV. You may even get a private balcony to sneak onto once the kids are asleep, where you can enjoy a glass of wine with your spouse as you watch the city lights twinkle.

Many of the properties listed in this chapter are within walking distance of the capital's major attractions. Others are only a short drive from downtown but may be more convenient for you if you want to be near the train station, Corel Centre, Carleton University, Lansdowne Park, the airport, or Gatineau Park.

PARKING If you have a vehicle with you, remember to factor in parking charges when estimating the cost of your chosen accommodation. Hotel parking rates vary from C$4 (US$3.25) to C$29 (US$24) per night in the downtown area. Most lots are underground and a few do not allow in-and-out privileges, which restricts your flexibility. Overnight street parking is allowed where signs are posted. From November 15 to April 1, a city bylaw prohibits overnight on-street parking from 1 to 7am if a snowfall of 7cm (3 in.) or more is forecast (including ranges such as 5–10cm, or 2–4 in.). When the parking ban is in effect, the information will be broadcast through the local media. These bans are actively enforced, and those who fail to comply could find their vehicle ticketed and towed to a nearby street. Call the Snowline at © **613/580-2460** to find out if the parking restrictions are currently being enforced.

AN IMPORTANT NOTE ON PRICES The prices quoted in this chapter are generally a range from the cheapest low-season rate up to corporate or rack rates (rack rates are the highest posted rates, although rooms are rarely sold at the full rack rate). In each listing, the prices include accommodation for two adults sharing. Discounts can result in a dramatic drop from the rack rate, typically anywhere from 10% to 50%. Almost every hotelier I spoke with mentioned that weekend specials or family packages are available at various times throughout the year. See section 12, "Tips on Accommodations," in Chapter 2, for more on getting the best rates. Note also that 5% accommodations tax and 7% GST (Goods and Services Tax) are required by law to be added to your bill, but the taxes are refundable to nonresidents upon application (see "Taxes" under "Fast Facts: Ottawa" in chapter 3).

A NOTE TO NONSMOKERS Most hotels in Ottawa are almost exclusively nonsmoking, partly due to a reduced demand for smoking rooms and partly due to the city smoking bylaw that prohibits smoking in public places. Typically, 10% of the rooms in any given hotel are reserved for smokers. However, people who want a smoke-free environment should make that clear when reserving a room. Rooms for smokers are often clustered together at one end of the hallway, and the rooms and even the hallways adjacent to those areas tend to smell strongly of smoke even in the cleanest hotels. Never assume that you'll get a smoke-free room if you don't specifically request one. The smoking bylaws in the city of Ottawa and the new city of Gatineau (which includes Hull) differ enormously. You'll find smoking bans in all public areas in Ottawa, whereas in Quebec smokers can light up in most places. You can't really get away from secondhand smoke in Quebec, which will irritate some people and not bother others. I'm just letting you know in advance what to expect.

A NOTE ABOUT POOLS Please be aware that hotel pools are almost always not supervised by hotel staff. If you have children with you, please make sure they are under your direct supervision in pool areas at all times.

BED-AND-BREAKFASTS Ottawa has an abundance of gracious older homes, some of which have been transformed into charming B&Bs. For the most part, B&Bs in Ottawa are located in quiet residential neighborhoods with tree-lined streets. If you're traveling solo or as a couple, then a B&B presents an economical and delightful alternative to a hotel room; families will usually need to rent two rooms in order to secure enough sleeping area, and that must be taken into account when estimating costs. Also, be aware that B&Bs and inns are usually geared to adult visitors. Many homes have expensive antiques on display and guests are expecting a quiet, restful stay. If you have children with you and they're young, boisterous, or both, then you're better off in a downtown suite hotel with a pool.

Two organizations in the city can help you choose a B&B. The Ottawa Tourism and Convention Authority (OTCA; 130 Albert St., Suite 1800, Ottawa, ON K1P 5G4 (**℡ 800/465-1867** or 613/239-5000; www.ottawatourism.ca) has around 18 B&Bs and inns listed as members. OTCA also operates a walk-in accommodations reservation desk at the Capital Infocentre, 90 Wellington St. (across from Parliament Hill), Ottawa, ON (**℡ 800/465-1867** or 613/239-5000). Online, visit **BBCanada.com** and have a look at more than 75 properties in the city and around the region that offer bed-and-breakfast accommodation. The **Association of Ottawa Bed and Breakfasts** represents a group of about a dozen BBCanada members who operate B&Bs in distinctive historical properties.

CAMPING Across the Ottawa River in Quebec, Gatineau Park's 36,000 hectares (88,000 acres) of woodlands and lakes has two campgrounds. Philippe Lake Family Campground has around 300 sites, and La Pêche Lake has a limited number of canoe camping sites. For details on these and other camping facilities, contact the Gatineau Park Visitor Centre, 318 Meech Lake Rd., Old Chelsea, QC J0X 1N0 (**℡ 819/ 827-2020**), or call the National Capital Commission at **℡ 800/465-1867**.

REDUCING YOUR ROOM RATE *Always* ask for a deal. Corporate discounts, club memberships (CAA, AAA, and others), and discounts linked to credit cards are just a few of the ways you can get a lower price. In Ottawa, hotels are especially eager to boost their occupancy rates with families on weekends, when their corporate and government clients desert them. Weekend rates and family packages are often available. Even though Winterlude, March break, the Canadian Tulip Festival, and the summer months are all peak tourist times, many hotels offer packages that may include complimentary museum passes, restaurant vouchers, or other money-saving deals.

1 Downtown (West of the Canal)

This area has the highest concentration of high-rises and the most traffic congestion, complicated by one-way streets, occasional traffic blocks, and time-limited meter parking, but it's close to most of the major attractions. Parliament Hill spreads majestically along the banks of the Ottawa River at the north end of this district. In addition to the Parliament Buildings, where you can catch the Changing of the Guard and the RCMP Musical Ride during the summer, you'll find the spectacular new Canadian War Museum, the National Arts Centre, the Ottawa Locks, the Museum of Nature, and extensive greenspace and pathways along the banks of the Ottawa River and Rideau Canal. Bank, Elgin, and Sparks streets are lined with restaurants and shops. Many other attractions, including the National Gallery, the Royal Canadian Mint, ByWard Market, and the Rideau Centre indoor shopping mall, are just across the canal to the east.

VERY EXPENSIVE

ARC the.hotel ★★★   Aiming to blend efficiency with luxury, ARC the.hotel focuses on meeting the needs of sophisticated travelers. The ARC boutique-hotel experience will leave you feeling relaxed, pampered, and refreshed. Even the hallways are delicately scented with aromatherapy fragrances. Down-filled duvets, oversize pillows, Egyptian cotton sheets, Frette bathrobes, Aveda toiletries — the list goes on. (Guests with allergies can request non-allergenic bedding and toiletries.) The nightly turndown service thoughtfully includes cold spring water, Godiva chocolates, and a fresh Granny Smith apple. You can put a little background music on the CD player, enjoy a complimentary glass of sparkling wine (served after 5pm daily), or catch up on your reading in the library. If you wish to customize your return visit, make your preferences known to the front desk staff and on your next trip you'll feel even more at home. The ARC lounge serves signature martinis at the cocktail hour, and the fine-dining restaurant features the best hotel dining in the city.

140 Slater St., Ottawa, ON K1P 5H6. © 800/699-2516 or 613/238-2888. Fax 613/235-8421. www.arcthe hotel.com. 112 units. C$190–C$250 (US$156–US$205) std. double; C$310 (US$254) junior suite; C$425 (US$349) executive 1-bedroom suite. Children under 16 stay free in parent's room. AE, DC, DISC, MC, V. Valet parking C$20 (US$16). **Amenities:** Lounge/restaurant; exercise room; concierge; business center; limited room service; massage; babysitting; same-day dry-cleaning/laundry; executive suites. *In room:* A/C, TV w/pay movies, dataport, minibar, coffeemaker, hair dryer, safe.

Crowne Plaza Ottawa ★★   If you're looking for contemporary luxury in a traditional hotel, this is a fine place to stay. The public areas reflect a sophisticated Art Deco style, with clean lines, expanses of wood, and a rich, earthy color scheme. The upscale decor continues into the hallways and guest rooms, which have been refurbished with new carpets, draperies, wall coverings, furniture, and redesigned bathrooms. An underground shopping arcade, open primarily during weekday office hours, is accessible from inside the hotel. The extensive health

Where to Stay

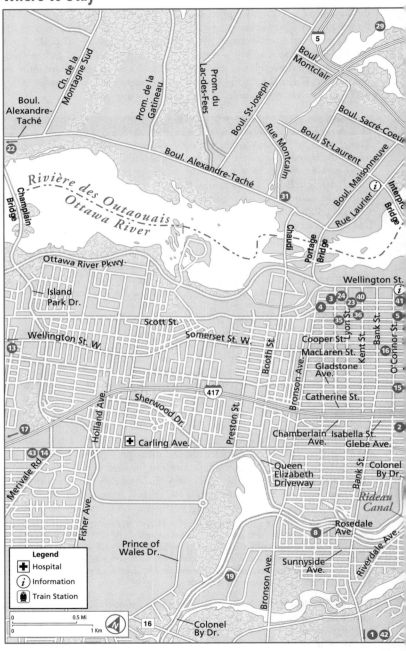

Legend
- ✚ Hospital
- ⓘ Information
- 🚆 Train Station

0   0.5 Mi
0   1 Km

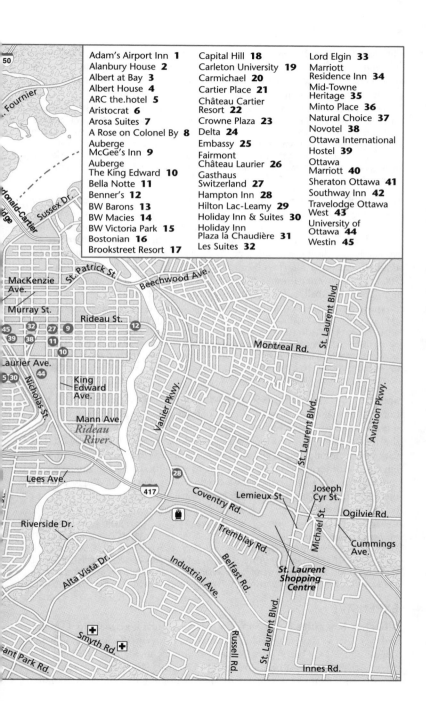

Adam's Airport Inn **1**
Alanbury House **2**
Albert at Bay **3**
Albert House **4**
ARC the.hotel **5**
Aristocrat **6**
Arosa Suites **7**
A Rose on Colonel By **8**
Auberge
McGee's Inn **9**
Auberge
The King Edward **10**
Bella Notte **11**
Benner's **12**
BW Barons **13**
BW Macies **14**
BW Victoria Park **15**
Bostonian **16**
Brookstreet Resort **17**

Capital Hill **18**
Carleton University **19**
Carmichael **20**
Cartier Place **21**
Château Cartier
Resort **22**
Crowne Plaza **23**
Delta **24**
Embassy **25**
Fairmont
Château Laurier **26**
Gasthaus
Switzerland **27**
Hampton Inn **28**
Hilton Lac-Leamy **29**
Holiday Inn & Suites **30**
Holiday Inn
Plaza la Chaudière **31**
Les Suites **32**

Lord Elgin **33**
Marriott
Residence Inn **34**
Mid-Towne
Heritage **35**
Minto Place **36**
Natural Choice **37**
Novotel **38**
Ottawa International
Hostel **39**
Ottawa
Marriott **40**
Sheraton Ottawa **41**
Southway Inn **42**
Travelodge Ottawa
West **43**
University of
Ottawa **44**
Westin **45**

club features a large fitness center, basketball court, outdoor terrace, and saunas. The indoor pool area, nicely set in a light-filled space, has patio doors leading onto a courtyard. Staff are attentive, courteous, and efficient. International cuisine is served in the sophisticated atmosphere of Café 101 & Bar.

101 Lyon St., Ottawa, ON K1R 5T9. (*C*) **800/227-6963** or 613/237-3600. Fax 613/237-2351. www.crowne ottawa.ca. 411 units. From C$119 (US$98) double; C$325 (US$267) 1-bed suite. Weekend packages available. Children 17 and under stay free in parent's room. AE, DC, DISC, MC, V. Valet parking C$23 (US$19), self-parking C$15 (US$12). Pets accepted. **Amenities:** Restaurant; bar; indoor pool; health club; sauna; children's play area; concierge; business center; shopping arcade; 24-hour room service; babysitting; laundry service; dry-cleaning; executive floors. *In room:* A/C, TV w/pay movies, fax, dataport, fridge in some units, coffeemaker, hair dryer, iron.

Ottawa Marriott ★★   Ottawa's downtown Marriott has the distinction of having the only rooftop revolving restaurant in the region, where diners can gaze at an ever-changing view of the nation's capital while enjoying global cuisine highlighted with Canadian products. With the aim of attracting families on weekends and during school holidays, the hotel has expanded its facilities for children, gaining a big thumbs-up from *Child and Youth Friendly Ottawa* in 2004. The Kids Zone features an activity and craft center, game room for teens, mini-golf, basketball half-court, and big-screen movies.

100 Kent St., Ottawa, ON K1P 5R7. (*C*) **800/853-8463** Canada or 613/238-1122. www.ottawamarriott.com. 480 units. C$129–C$234 (US$106–US$192) double; C$295–C$495 (US$242–US$406) 1- and 2-bedroom suites. Children 18 and under stay free in parent's room. AE, DC, DISC, MC, V. Valet parking C$25 (US$20), parking C$15 (US$12). Pets accepted. **Amenities:** 2 restaurants (1 revolving); cafe; indoor pool; health club; Jacuzzi; sauna; children's center; game room; concierge; business center; shopping arcade; limited room service; babysitting; washers and dryers; same-day dry-cleaning/laundry; executive floors. *In room:* A/C, TV w/pay movies, dataport, coffeemaker, hair dryer, iron.

Sheraton Ottawa Hotel ★★   The Sheraton is a classy hotel, as you'll note from the moment you enter the elegant lobby and are greeted by the impeccably dressed doorman. A spiral staircase leads to the second floor, but you can opt for the more conventional elevator. Even the restaurant is posh, furnished with rich, dark wood, gleaming brass, and sparkling chandeliers. Rooms are spacious, with upgraded vanities and ceramic tiles in the bathrooms. The spotless indoor pool complex features a bank of windows at one end to allow natural light to flood the space. If luxurious surroundings are a priority on your vacation, you won't be disappointed here.

150 Albert St., Ottawa, ON K1P 5G2. (*C*) **800/489-8333** or 613/238-1500. Fax 613/235-2723. www.sheraton.com/ottawa. 236 units. C$129–C$260 (US$106–US$213) double; C$350–C$575 (US$287–US$472) executive suite. Children 18 and under stay free in parent's room. AE, DC, DISC, MC, V. Valet parking C$20 (US$16) Sun–Thurs, C$15 (US$12) Fri–Sat. Small pets accepted. **Amenities:** Restaurant; lounge; indoor pool; exercise room; sauna; concierge; business center; room service; babysitting; same-day dry-cleaning/laundry; executive floor. *In room:* A/C, TV w/pay movies, dataport, coffeemaker, hair dryer, iron.

EXPENSIVE

Albert at Bay Suite Hotel ★★ (*Kids*)   This all-suite hotel welcomes families and even goes so far as to provide a free children's program during June, July, and August and March break (usually the second week in March). The kids' club offers a wide variety of supervised activities for kids ages 3 to 12 daily in July and August, from 9am to noon and 1 to 5pm. A bright and sunny exercise room with a Jacuzzi and an adjacent rooftop patio provide a refuge for parents who want to sneak away and relax while the children are busy at the kids' club. An indoor pool is under construction; its expected opening is late 2005. The downtown location is a great base for visitors traveling without children as well. You're within strolling distance of Parliament Hill (3 blocks), the National Arts Centre (7 blocks), and the Rideau Centre (8 blocks). A five-minute walk will take you right down to the pathway along the banks of the Ottawa River. All units have a kitchen with full-size appliances, including a dishwasher; one or two bedrooms; and two TVs. Some suites have two bathrooms.

435 Albert St., Ottawa, ON K1R 7X4. ℂ **800/267-6644** or 613/238-8858. Fax 613/238-1433. www.albertat bay.com. 197 units. C$109–C$159 (US$89–US$130) 1-bedroom suite; C$179–C$259 (US$147–US$212) 2-bedroom suite. Children 16 and under stay free in parent's room. AE, DC, DISC, MC, V. Parking C$12 (US$10). **Amenities:** Restaurant; bar; exercise room; Jacuzzi; sauna; seasonal children's program; business center; limited room service; babysitting; washers and dryers; laundry service; dry-cleaning; executive suites. *In room:* A/C, TV w/pay movies, fax, dataport, kitchen, coffeemaker, iron, in-room safe.

Bostonian Executive Suites ✸

The Bostonian is an all-suite property, converted from an existing high-rise building. Opened in March 2001, the suites have full kitchens and a choice of studio or one-bedroom models. High-speed wireless Internet access, voice mail, 24-hour business support services, ergonomic seating, and long-stay options make the Bostonian an ideal base for business travelers. Families will enjoy the convenience of laundry facilities, grocery delivery, microwave, and dishwasher.

341 MacLaren St., Ottawa ON K2P 2E2. ℂ **866/320-4567** or 613/594-5757. Fax 613/594-3221. www.the bostonian.ca. 116 units. C$99–C$159 (US$81–US$130) studio; C$139–C$189 (US$114–US$155) 1-bedroom suite. Children under 17 stay free in parent's room. Rollaway/cribs free for under 16; C$10 (US$8) 16 and over. AE, MC, V. Parking C$12 (US$10). Pets sometimes accepted. **Amenities:** Exercise room; concierge; business services; washers and dryers; same-day dry-cleaning. *In room:* A/C, TV w/pay movies, dataport, kitchen, coffeemaker, hair dryer, iron.

Carmichael Inn & Spa ✸✸

A quiet oasis in the heart of the busy city awaits guests at the Carmichael Inn & Spa. The inn is a designated heritage site, built in 1901 as the retirement residence of a local businessman. The atmosphere is calm and restful. You may catch the scent of spiced pear as you enter the inn, which is decorated predominantly in soft greens, golds, and browns. Many fine antiques are displayed in public areas and guest rooms. Flowering trees, including a magnolia, shelter the veranda, making it a favorite resting place in spring and summer. When the weather is cold, curl up in an armchair by the lounge fireplace. The inn is best suited to adult guests. The luxurious spa is located on the lower level and offers massages, body wraps, foot treatments, herbal baths, and facials. Locals visit the spa as day guests. Ask for package details. The entire building is nonsmoking.

46 Cartier St., Ottawa ON K2P 1J3. ℂ **613/236-4667**. Fax 613/563-7529. www.carmichaelinn.com. 11 units. C$149–C$189 (US$122–US$155) double. Rates include breakfast. AE, DC, MC, V. Free parking. **Amenities:** Spa on-site; business services; massage; washers and dryers; same-day dry-cleaning/laundry. *In room:* A/C, TV, dataport, hair dryer, iron.

⌇ Tips

If you're visiting on Canada Day, July 1, request a higher-floor room or suite at the **Delta Ottawa,** overlooking the Ottawa River. A few years back we watched a military air display pass over the Parliament Buildings at lunchtime and the fabulous Canada Day fireworks display in the evening through the window of our upper-floor suite.

Delta Ottawa Hotel and Suites ✦✦ *Kids*   Over the past couple of years an extensive refurbishment has brightened up everything from pool tiles and the children's playroom to carpets, wall coverings, and fabrics in the guest rooms. A new business center has been installed, and the lobby and health club have been renovated. Two on-site dining facilities provide above-average fare. Families flock here on weekends, during March break, and over the summer. The giant two-story indoor waterslide is a major hit with kids. In addition to standard guest rooms, the hotel offers studios with kitchenettes (fridge, microwave, sink, and utensils) and one- and two-bedroom suites with balconies and kitchenettes.

361 Queen St., Ottawa, ON K1R 7S9. © **800/268-1133** or 613/238-6000. Fax 613/238-2290. www.delta hotels.com. 328 units. C$99–C$159 (US$81–US$130) double; C$109–C$169 (US$89–US$139) studio; C$129–C$199 (US$106–US$163) 1-bedroom suite; children under 18 stay free in parent's room. AE, DC, DISC, MC, V. Self-parking C$14 (US$12), valet parking C$20 (US$16). Small domestic pets accepted. C$50 (US$41) cleaning charge applies. **Amenities:** 2 restaurants, lounge; indoor pool with adjacent waterslide; exercise room; Jacuzzi; sauna; children's center; seasonal children's program; concierge; business center; salon; limited room service; massage; babysitting; washers and dryers; same-day dry-cleaning/laundry; executive floor. *In room:* A/C, TV w/pay movies, dataport, kitchenette in some units, coffeemaker, hair dryer, iron.

Holiday Inn Hotel & Suites Ottawa ✦   The property is situated at the quiet end of Cooper Street, just steps from the banks of the Rideau Canal and a few blocks west of the shops and restaurants of Elgin Street. One-bedroom suites are equipped with a full kitchen, and a small number have a connecting door to a single room, effectively creating a two-bedroom suite. Some guest rooms include a kitchenette or fridge and microwave. Three luxury Jacuzzi suites are available. A special family guest room featuring a children's play area with a SpongeBob SquarePants theme has been added; maximum occupancy is 2 adults and 2 children. Major renovations were completed in 2004, and all guest rooms have now been redecorated.

111 Cooper St., Ottawa, ON K2P 2E3. © **613/238-1331**. Fax 613/230-2179. 229 units. C$119–C$144 (US$98–US$118) double; C$151–C$211 (US$124–US$173) 1-bedroom suite. Children under 18 stay free in parent's room. AE, DC, DISC, MC, V. Parking C$10 (US$8). Pets accepted. **Amenities:** Restaurant; exercise room; business center; limited room service; massage; babysitting; washers and dryers; same-day dry-cleaning/laundry; executive rooms. *In room:* A/C, TV w/pay movies, dataport, kitchen or kitchenette in some units, coffeemaker, hair dryer, iron.

Lord Elgin Hotel ✦✦   This established hotel, one of Ottawa's landmark properties, features an elegant château-inspired design and admirably preserved and restored 1940s interior detail. The location could not be better as a base for visitors to Ottawa. Directly across the street is Confederation Park, a small but pretty city park that provides a peaceful respite from the dense metropolis of skyscrapers crowding the business district behind the hotel. During the annual Winterlude festival, the park turns into a magical wonderland of sparkling ice sculptures, artistically flooded with colored lights in the evenings. Parliament Hill, the Rideau Canal, ByWard Market, and Rideau Shopping Centre are literally a five-minute stroll away. If you venture south along Elgin Street, you'll find plenty of pleasant eateries, lively pubs, and shops. Two new guest-room wings have been seamlessly added to the property. The massive renovation and expansion included upgrades to the health club and a new indoor lap pool. Room sizes vary, with the units in the new wings larger. Bathrooms have been fitted with dark granite countertops and polished nickel accents. Rooms at the back are quieter, but you lose the view of the park. Staff are formal, courteous, and efficient.

100 Elgin St., Ottawa, ON K1P 5K8. C **800/267-4298** or 613/235-3333. Fax 613/235-3223. www.lordelgin.ca. 355 units. C$122–C$199 (US$100–US$163) std. double; C$152–C$229 (US$125–US$188) executive double on upper floors. Children 17 and under stay free in parent's room. AE, DC, DISC, MC, V. Valet parking C$14 (US$12). Pets accepted. **Amenities:** Restaurant, lounge; indoor pool; health club; bicycle rental nearby; concierge; spa/hair salon next door; hot tub; sauna; business center; limited room service; babysitting; same-day dry-cleaning/laundry; executive floors. *In room:* A/C, TV w/pay movies, fax, dataport, fridge in most rooms, coffeemaker, hair dryer, iron.

Marriott Residence Inn Ottawa ★★

The units in this all-suites hotel are at least 50% larger than those in standard hotels. If you're staying in town longer than a night or two, it's nice to be able to spread out a little in comfort. If you have kids with you, splurge if you can on a two-bedroom suite, which boasts a well equipped kitchen, two full bathrooms, and three TVs. It's well worth the money — and if it's going to push you over budget, take advantage of the grocery service and cook meals in the suite. The pool has a uniform 1.1-m (4-ft.) depth. Expect cheerful faces and friendly greetings from staff whenever you cross their path. Two one-bedroom suites are equipped for guests with disabilities.

161 Laurier Ave. W., Ottawa, ON K1P 5J2. C **800/331-3131** or 613/231-2020. Fax 613/231-2090. www.residenceinn.com. 171 units. C$125–C$165 (US$103–US$135) studio; C$229–C$279 (US$188–US$229) 2-bedroom suite. AE, DC, DISC, MC, V. Parking C$13 (US$11). Pets C$150 (US$99) flat fee. **Amenities:** Lounge serving complimentary breakfast and snacks; indoor pool; exercise room; spa next door; hot tub; sauna; business center; laundry room (some units have washers/dryers); same-day dry-cleaning/laundry. *In room:* A/C, TV w/pay movies, dataport, kitchen (equipment varies with suite size), coffeemaker, hair dryer, iron.

Minto Place Suite Hotel ★★★ *Value*

Beautifully appointed, spacious suites with kitchenettes or full kitchens make Minto Place one of Ottawa's best places to stay — and the property just had a $17-million facelift covering everything from elevators to bathroom fittings, and relocation of the lobby from the second floor to street level. The new in-room safes are even equipped with an electrical socket to recharge your laptop, phone, or camera. Adding to its appeal is direct access to an indoor shopping concourse with a bank, food court, pharmacy, wine store, and 24-hour grocery store. The 19.5-m-long (65 ft.) indoor pool, lit by skylights, is a uniform 1.2-m (4 ft.) deep and sparkling clean. A sundeck leads off the pool area. Vacationing families are welcome and well-catered to; in the summer, your kids can sign up for the fun and games at the kids' club. Staff are courteous, pleasant, and experienced in helping visitors make the most of their stay in Ottawa.

433 Laurier Ave. W., Ottawa, ON K1R 7Y1. C **800/267-3377** or 613/782-2350. Fax 613/232-6962. www.minto-hotel.com. 417 units. C$133–C$160 (US$109–US$131) studio; C$148–C$180 (US$121–US$148) 1-bedroom suite; C$175–C$230 (US$144–US$189) 2-bedroom suite. Children 18 and under stay free in parent's room. AE, DC, DISC, MC, V. Parking C$14 (US$12) Mon–Thurs; C$4 (US$3.25) Fri–Sun. **Amenities:** Restaurant; bar; indoor pool; exercise rooms; Jacuzzi; sauna; children's play area; seasonal children's program; business center; shopping arcade; hair salon; limited room service; massage; babysitting; washers and dryers; same-day dry-cleaning/laundry. *In room:* A/C, TV w/pay movies, dataport, kitchen or kitchenette, coffeemaker, hair dryer, iron, safe.

Tips

Hotel pools do not usually provide lifeguards or other supervisory personnel. It is parents' responsibility to closely supervise their own children in the pool area. Exercise extra caution when the pool is crowded. Enjoy your swim and always follow pool safety rules.

MODERATE

Albert House Inn ✿   This gracious Victorian building has operated as an inn for the past 24 years. It was designed and built by Thomas Seaton Scott, a renowned architect whose work includes the Cartier Drill Hall, the Langevin Block (home of the prime minister's offices), and many other federal buildings. The furnishings and decor enhance the historical atmosphere. Its convenient downtown location is only a short walk from the Parliament Buildings and beautiful pathways for walking and biking along the Ottawa River. A secure storage room for bicycles is provided. The environment is adult-oriented, but older children are welcome.

478 Albert St., Ottawa, ON K1R 5B5. ✆ **800/267-1982** or 613/236-4479. Fax 613/237-9079. www.albertinn.com. 17 units. C$98–C$108 (US$80–US$88) double; C$168 (US$138) king with double Jacuzzi. Rates include breakfast. AE, DC, MC, V. Parking C$8 (US$6.50). **Amenities:** Business center; limited room service; washers and dryers. *In room:* A/C, TV, dataport, hair dryer.

Aristocrat Suite Hotel ✿   With a full kitchen in every unit, the Aristocrat guarantees self-sufficient accommodation. Be prepared to roll up your sleeves, though, because there are no dishwashers. Located in a quieter downtown district, away from the office-block bustle, it's still within walking distance of many downtown attractions — and a short stroll from the banks of the Rideau Canal, which is great for walkers. The bedrooms and living room are a decent size, but the kitchens are a bit short on elbow room. An Italian restaurant on the main floor serves breakfast, lunch, and dinner daily. You can have groceries delivered to your suite to save you the trouble of shopping. An airport shuttle bus is provided. Many suites now have complimentary wireless high-speed Internet.

141 Cooper St., Ottawa, ON K2P 0E8. ✆ **800/563-5634** or 613/236-7500. Fax 613/563-2836. www.aristo cratsuites.com. 216 units. C$99–C$119 (US$81–US$98) studio; C$109–C$145 (US$89–US$119) 1-bedroom suite; from C$159 (US$130) 2-bedroom suite. Pets accepted; C$15 (US$12) per night. Children 18 and under stay free in parent's room. AE, DC, DISC, MC, V. Parking C$11 (US$9). **Amenities:** Restaurant; bar; exercise room; Jacuzzi; sauna; business center; limited room service; washers and dryers; laundry service; dry-cleaning; executive floor. *In room:* A/C, TV w/pay movies, dataport, kitchen, coffeemaker, hair dryer, iron.

Best Western Victoria Park Suites ✿✿   This hotel has comfortable and spacious studios and one-bedroom suites, all with kitchenettes. Parliament Hill is 10 blocks north — a bit far for some folks to walk, but a bus or taxi will whisk you there in no time if you'd rather leave your car in the underground lot. The magnificent Museum of Nature, with its huge dinosaurs (the old dinosaur gallery has been closed, but the new Fossil Gallery, with life-size dinosaur models, is due to open in 2006), creepy insects, and beautiful birds, is right on the doorstep. Nearby Bank Street (to the west) and Elgin Street (to the east) are lined with shops and eateries. Deluxe continental breakfast can be enjoyed on the pretty treed patio in the warmer months. A penthouse fitness center overlooks downtown Ottawa, so you can work out with a view. A new business center is planned for late 2005; all suites have complimentary high-speed wireless Internet. When the kids' club is running at Victoria Park Suites' sister hotel, the Albert at Bay Suite Hotel (see earlier in this chapter), you can take your children there for free, supervised fun and games.

377 O'Connor St., Ottawa, ON K2P 2M2. ✆ **800/465-7275** or 613/567-7275. Fax 613/567-1161. www.victoriapark.com. 123 units. C$99–$C149 (US$81–US$122) studio; C$109–C$159 (US$89–US$130) 1-bedroom suite. Children 16 and under stay free in parent's room. AE, DC, DISC, MC, V. Parking C$11 (US$9). **Amenities:** Breakfast room; exercise room; sauna; free children's program offsite; business services; babysitting; washers and dryers; laundry service; dry-cleaning; executive suites. *In room:* A/C, TV w/pay movies, fax, dataport, kitchenette, fridge, coffeemaker, hairdryer, iron, in-room safe.

Capital Hill Hotel & Suites *(Value)*   This comfortable but far from ritzy hotel offers good value and the advantage of a downtown location. About one-third of the guest rooms are equipped with a kitchenette, including a stove or microwave, a small fridge, dishes, and utensils, but none have dishwashers. The room size is average and bathrooms tend to be small. The price is the same for a double room with or without kitchenette, so if you'd like to do some self-catering, this represents good value. A penthouse suite featuring a fireplace, Jacuzzi, sauna, and kitchen is exceptional value at C$250 (US$205) per night. The entire hotel is being refreshed several floors at a time with a bright, neutral decor, and a brand-new exercise room opened in 2005. Yuk Yuk's Comedy Club is just next door.

88 Albert St., Ottawa, ON K1P 5E9. © 800/463-7705 or 613/235-1413. Fax 613/235-6047. www.capital hill.com. 150 units. C$99–C$119 (US$81–US$98) double with or without kitchenette; C$119–C$136 (US$98–US$112) 1-bedroom suite. AE, DC, DISC, MC, V. Parking C$10 (US$8). Pets accepted. **Amenities:** Restaurant; exercise room; business services; same-day dry-cleaning/ laundry; executive suite. *In room:* A/C, TV w/pay movies, dataport, kitchenette in some units, coffeemaker, hair dryer, iron.

Cartier Place Suite Hotel ★★ *(Kids)*   This suite hotel has wonderful amenities for children, making it an attractive choice for families. Besides the indoor pool, bathed in natural light streaming through glass doors (which are thrown open in the summer and lead onto a sundeck), there is a well-equipped children's playroom and even a preschool-size play structure in the pool area. An outdoor courtyard features a climbing gym and children's play equipment in summer. Redecoration and replacement of kitchen appliances has been ongoing for the past few years, a couple of floors at a time, so many of the suites are fresh and bright. All units are suites with full kitchens and private balconies with garden chairs.

180 Cooper St., Ottawa, ON K2P 2L5. © 800/236-8399 or 613/236-5000. Fax 613/238-3842. www.suite dreams.com. 252 units. C$89–C$132 (US$73–US$108) suite. Children 16 and under stay free in parent's room. AE, DC, MC, V. Parking C$14 (US$12). Small pets accepted C$15 (US$12) per night. **Amenities:** Restaurant/lounge; indoor pool; exercise room; Jacuzzi; sauna; children's playroom; outdoor playground; game room; business center; limited room service; babysitting; washers and dryers; same-day dry-cleaning/laundry. *In room:* A/C, TV w/pay movies, dataport, kitchen, coffeemaker, hair dryer, iron.

Embassy Hotel and Suites   All units in this hotel have a full kitchen with full-size appliances (minus dishwasher). The bathrooms and bedrooms tend to be small, but there is plenty of seating in the living rooms of the suites; the 2-bed executive suites are quite spacious at 90 sq. m (1,000 sq. ft.). The on-site restaurant/coffee shop serves breakfast and lunch only. A children's lending library stocks movies, books, and games; VCR rental available for C$5 (US$4) for 48 hours. Wireless high-speed Internet access.

25 Cartier St., Ottawa, ON K2P 1J2. © 800/661-5495 or 613/237-2111. Fax 613/563-1353. www.embassy hotelottawa.com. 130 units. C$99–C$140 (US$81–US$115) studio; C$109–C$149 (US$89–US$122) 1-bedroom suite; C$130–C$200 (US$107–US$164) 2-bedroom suite. Children under 16 stay free in parent's room. AE, DC, DISC, MC, V. Parking C$8 (US$7). Pets accepted, C$10 (US$8) per night. **Amenities:** Cafe; lounge (weekdays); exercise room; sauna; business center; limited room service; babysitting; washers and dryers; same-day dry-cleaning/laundry. *In room:* A/C, TV, kitchen, coffeemaker, hair dryer, iron.

Mid-Towne Heritage B&B ★★   Built in 1891 as a fashionable Victorian family home, this is one of the most charming bed-and-breakfasts in Ottawa, with original features including fireplaces, stained glass, wood, and plaster. The shade trees and small gardens are set in one of the last remaining private yards in the city core. The owners reckon their home is the closest B&B to Parliament Hill, which is only a 10-minute stroll along Wellington Street. Breakfasts are delightful. This is one of the few B&Bs to offer suites. The second floor offers a choice of two: a one-bedroom suite with ensuite bathroom and private sitting room with adult-size day bed, and a two-bedroom suite with a bathroom accessible from both bedrooms and a private sun porch. The rooms are fresh and pretty, with Victorian decor. The entire building is nonsmoking. As with most B&Bs, the owners accept children at their discretion, and suggest that ages 8 and up are best suited to the tranquil charm of this home. For travelers who conduct their lives at a gentle pace, this will be a lovely base for an Ottawa vacation.

220 Lyon St., Ottawa, ON K1R 5V7. © 888/669-8888 or 613/236-1169. www.amidtowneh.com. 4 units. C$95 (US$78) and up double; C$129 (US$106) double suite; C$149 (US$122) four adults sharing suite, including breakfast. AE, MC, V. Free parking. *In room:* A/C, TV, hair dryer, no phone.

INEXPENSIVE

Arosa Suites Hotel   If your budget is tight, consider the Arosa Suites. The living quarters are compact and the decor may be dated (rooms are being redecorated a few at a time), but the price is right. A maximum of four occupants plus one baby in a crib is the limit to each one-bedroom suite. Some hotel guests, many of them corporate or government employees, are longer-stay occupants, but you'll see more families and other tourists around in the summer. Parking is cheap, but be warned: The parking lot doesn't have room for every vehicle — it's first-come, first-served. Most kitchens have a dishwasher, and all units but three have a private balcony. High-speed Internet access has been installed in all guest rooms.

163 MacLaren St., Ottawa, ON K2P 2G4. © 613/238-6783. Fax 613/238-5080. www.arosahotel.com. 62 units. C$99 (US$81) double 1-bedroom suite; C$104 (US$85) four adults sharing 1-bedroom suite. Children 16 and under stay free in parent's room. AE, DC, DISC, MC, V. Limited parking C$4 (US$3.25). **Amenities:** Exercise room; washers and dryers. *In room:* A/C, TV, dataport, kitchen, coffeemaker.

Natural Choice/4 Nature B&B   If you take a nuts-and-granola kind of approach to life, you'll feel right at home in this vegetarian, nonsmoking B&B facing the Canadian Museum of Nature. The bedrooms are fresh and bright and decorated with original artwork, in keeping with the relaxed, friendly atmosphere. The hosts provide services ranging from massage to yoga classes and weddings. Their flourishing garden has a picnic table for guests' use, as well as a room on the second floor where children can play when meditation and yoga are not in session. Besides the greenspace outside the Museum of Nature, there's a park within walking distance with a children's playground and wading pool. For even more physical activity, get a day pass to the facilities at the YMCA across the street. Breakfasts are vegetarian, using organic ingredients as much as possible.

263 McLeod St., Ottawa, ON K2P 1A1. © 888/346-9642 or 613/563-4399. www.vegybnb.com. 3 units. C$75 (US$62) and up double; C$150–C$175 (US$123–US$144) per family occupying two rooms, depending on number of guests. Rates include breakfast. MC, V. Limited free parking. Pets C$15 (US$12) per night. **Amenities:** Massage and other services available. *In room:* Ceiling fans, no phone.

2 Downtown (East of the Canal)

This downtown sector is bordered by the Ottawa River to the north, the Rideau River to the east, the Queensway to the south, and the Rideau Canal to the west. You'll find the lively and exciting ByWard Market area in this district, as well as a number of large high-rise hotels, Major's Hill Park, Strathcona Park, the

University of Ottawa, the National Gallery, and the Royal Canadian Mint. On the quiet residential streets, embassy residences and B&Bs are interspersed among elegant Victorian and Edwardian homes.

VERY EXPENSIVE

Fairmont Château Laurier ✸✸✸   One of Ottawa's premier landmarks, this grand hotel, built in 1912 in the same Loire Valley Renaissance style as Quebec City's Château Frontenac, has an imposing stone façade and copper-paneled roof. If you're looking for luxury, tradition, and attentive service, this is the place to stay — royalty and celebrities have always been attracted to the Château Laurier's graceful beauty. You'll pay for the pleasure, but the surroundings are exceptional. The spacious public areas display the grandeur of another era, having recently been refurnished with the hotel's original furniture, rescued from a storeroom and meticulously restored. The less expensive rooms are rather small but just as elegant as the larger rooms and suites; nine rooms are equipped for guests with disabilities. The upper floors offer impressive views over the Ottawa River toward the Gatineau Hills. The extensive health club and pool area, built in 1929 in Art Deco style, has been admirably preserved. The two dining rooms, Wilfrid's and Zoe's — named for former prime minister Sir Wilfrid Laurier and his wife, who were the first guests at the hotel — offer a sumptuous dining experience.

1 Rideau St., Ottawa, ON K1N 8S7. ℂ 800/441-1414 or 613/241-1414. Fax 613/562-7032. www.fairmont.com. 429 units. Low season: C$189 (US$155) and up double; C$339 (US$278) and up suite. High season: C$249 (US$204) and up double; C$419 (US$344) and up suite. Children 17 and under stay free in parent's room AE, DC, DISC, MC, V. Valet parking C$29 (US$24), self-parking C$22 (US$18). Pets C$25 (US$21) per night. **Amenities:** Restaurant, outdoor terrace, bar/tea room; large indoor pool; exercise room; sauna; games room; concierge; business center; shopping arcade; 24-hour room service; massage; babysitting; same-day dry-cleaning/laundry; executive floor. *In room:* A/C, TV w/pay movies, dataport, minibar, coffeemaker, hair dryer, iron, safe in some rooms.

The Westin Ottawa ✸✸   The lobby is grand and the staff are obliging and exceedingly well-mannered at this upscale hotel. All rooms feature floor-to-ceiling windows to provide the best possible views of the city. When you're ready for exercise, go for a challenging game of squash on one of the three international standard courts or take a dip in the indoor pool, which has an adjacent outdoor sundeck. The exercise facilities are contained in a branded "Westin Workout Powered by Reebok" gym, and the plate glass windows offer great views of the city. For those who live to shop, the third floor of the hotel provides direct access to the stores and services of the Rideau Centre. Indoor access is also available to the Congress Centre.

11 Colonel By Dr., Ottawa, ON K1N 9H4. ℂ 888/625-5144 or 613/560-7000. Fax 613/560-2707. www.westin.com. 487 units. C$179–C$419 (US$147–US$344) double, C$250 (US$205) and up suite. Children 18 and under stay free in parent's room. AE, DC, DISC, MC, V. Valet parking C$25 (US$20); self-parking C$14 (US$12). Pets accepted. **Amenities:** Restaurant; 2 bars; indoor pool; health club; spa on-site; hot tub; sauna; concierge; shopping arcade; 24-hour room service; massage; same-day dry-cleaning/laundry; executive floors. *In room:* A/C, TV w/pay movies, dataport, minibar, coffeemaker, hair dryer, iron.

EXPENSIVE

Gasthaus Switzerland Inn ✸   A restored heritage property constructed of limestone in 1872, this family owned and operated inn features Swiss-style beds with cozy duvets and Swiss buffet breakfasts. Each room is individually decorated and amenities vary. There are two specialty suites that are popular with couples.

Each suite has a poster canopy bed, double Jacuzzi, CD stereo player, and ensuite bathroom. Efforts have been made to reduce allergens — windows can be opened, hardwood flooring has been used where possible, and non-allergenic duvets can be arranged if requested when making your reservation. The non-smoking rule is strictly enforced throughout the building. The property is best suited for adults and children over age 12.

89 Daly Ave., Ottawa, ON K1N 6E6. ⓒ 888/663-0000 or 613/237-0335. Fax 613/594-3327. www.gasthauss-witzerlandinn.com. 22 units. C$108 (US$89) economy double; C$128–C$168 (US$105–US$138) large double; C$248 (US$203) suite. Rates include breakfast. AE, DC, MC, V. Limited free parking. **Amenities:** Same-day dry-cleaning/laundry. *In room:* A/C, TV, dataport, hair dryer.

Les Suites Hotel Ottawa ⭐⭐ ⓥ*alue*   An all-suite property, Les Suites was originally built as a condominium complex in 1989. As a result, the one- and two-bedroom suites are spacious and well equipped, with a full kitchen in every unit. Elevators are situated away from the rooms, and bedrooms are located at the back of the suites, away from potential hallway noise. For an even quieter environment, ask for a suite overlooking the garden courtyard. The health club and indoor pool on the fifth floor have a panoramic city view and are shared with guests of Novotel Ottawa. The Rideau Centre and the ByWard Market area are on the hotel's doorstep. Executive business suites with separate offices are now available at rates ranging from C$169 (US$139) and up. Upgraded amenities including cordless phones, wireless high-speed Internet, in-room safes, and office equipment are supplied in these suites.

130 Besserer St., Ottawa, ON K1N 9M9. ⓒ 800/267-1989 or 613/232-2000. Fax 613/232-1242. www.les-suites.com. 243 units. C$149–C$179 (US$122–US$147) 1-bedroom suite; C$189–C$229 (US$155–US$188) 2-bedroom suite. Children under 18 stay free in parent's room. AE, DC, DISC, MC, V. Parking C$14 (US$12). Pets C$25 (US$16) one-time fee. **Amenities:** Restaurant; indoor pool; health club; hot tub; sauna; concierge; business services; shopping arcade; limited room service; massage; babysitting; washers and dryers; same-day dry-cleaning; executive suites. *In room:* A/C, TV w/pay movies, kitchen, coffeemaker, hair dryer, iron.

Novotel Ottawa ⭐   This hotel is right in the middle of it all — the Rideau Centre, Parliament Hill, Rideau Canal, ByWard Market, and many of the museums are only a short walk away. Public areas and many of the rooms are decorated in Mediterranean hues of blue, orange, and yellow. The result is striking and sunny. Two floors have recently been refitted as business class; the decor here is neutral earth tones. Upgraded amenities include duvets, in-room safes, and 32-inch wall-mounted LCD televisions. Staff are cheerful and attentive.

33 Nicholas St., Ottawa, ON K1N 9M7. ⓒ 800/668-6835 or 613/230-3033. Fax 613/760-4766. www.novotelottawa.com. 281 units. C$119–C$199 (US$98–US$163) double; C$149–C$229 (US$122–US$188) business-class rooms; C$169–C$249 (US$139–US$204) 1-bed executive suites. Children under 16 stay free in parent's room. AE, DC, DISC, MC, V. Parking C$12–C$14 (US$10–US$12). Pets accepted. **Amenities:** Restaurant; cafe; bar; indoor pool; health club; hot tub; sauna; business services; limited room service; massage; babysitting; same-day dry-cleaning/laundry; executive floors. *In room:* A/C, TV w/pay movies, dataport, minibar, coffeemaker, hair dryer, iron.

MODERATE

Auberge McGee's Inn ⭐   Nestled in the heart of the historical Sandy Hill district on a quiet tree-lined avenue, the inn was built in 1886 as a residence for John J. McGee. The guest rooms are individually decorated and amenities vary. Some rooms have fireplaces; others have private balconies. There are two suites designed for romantic couples — the Egyptian Room and the Victorian Roses Suite, both with fireplaces and double Jacuzzis. The second floor has a laundry room, ironing board and iron, and kitchenette with small stove and microwave for guest use. Complimentary wireless high-speed Internet. In-room coffeemaker supplied on request. The entire inn is smoke-free. Special packages are often available; check the website or call for details.

185 Daly Ave., Ottawa, ON K1N 6E8. Ⓒ **800/262-4337** or 613/237-6089. Fax 613/237-6201. www.mcgeesinn.com. 14 units. C$108–C$148 (US$89–US$121) double; C$168 (US$138) romantic suite. Rates include breakfast. Children under 12 stay free in parent's room. AE, MC, V. Free parking. **Amenities:** Business services. *In room:* A/C, TV, dataport, fridge, hair dryer.

Bella Notte B&B   The hosts of this B&B, located in the historical residential Sandy Hill district, just east of the Rideau Canal, are charming and welcoming. The Victorian property, built in 1868, was originally the home of Sir Alexander Campbell, one of Canada's Fathers of Confederation. Amenities are basic, but the hospitality of the owners and the care and attention given to the preparation and presentation of breakfast are worth experiencing. Bella Notte is well-positioned for reaching downtown on foot.

108 Daly Ave., Ottawa, ON K1N 6E7. Ⓒ **613/565-0497.** www.bellanottebb.com. 3 units. C$98–C$148 (US$80–US$121) double. Rates include breakfast. Limited street parking. *In room:* No phone.

Benner's Bed & Breakfast   A comfortable stroll from the ByWard Market, University of Ottawa, and downtown shopping, Benner's B&B is an elegant Edwardian brownstone house in the historical residential district of Sandy Hill. Guest rooms have been decorated with simple, clean lines and restful colors. This property is best suited to adults; well-behaved children 9 years and older are welcome. Next door, a second B&B operated by the owners' daughter features contemporary decor and a spacious loft suite.

541 Besserer St., Ottawa, ON K1N 6C6. Ⓒ **877-891-5485** or 613/789-8320. Fax 613/789-9563. www.bennersbedandbreakfast.com. 3 units. C$95–C$130 (US$78–US$107) double. Rates include breakfast. AE, DC, MC, V. Free parking. *In room:* A/C, TV, phone in some rooms.

INEXPENSIVE

Auberge "The King Edward" B&B ✪   Conveniently situated close to the Rideau Canal and within easy walking distance of the ByWard Market, the Rideau Centre, and many downtown attractions, the King Edward is a distinguished Victorian home. The front parlor has been turned into a peaceful oasis of tropical plants, accented by a trickling fountain. A second sitting room offers comfortable chairs and sofas, suitable for reading or listening to music. Throughout the home you'll find many period details, including fireplaces, plaster moldings, pillars, and stained-glass windows. The elegant bedrooms, with turn-of-the-century furnishings, are generously proportioned. One room is large enough to accommodate a cot, and two other rooms have private balconies. At Christmas, a 3.6-m-high (12 ft.) tree trimmed with Victorian decorations is a sight to behold, and the owner also displays his extensive collection of Christmas village pieces on the main floor of the property. Children are welcomed at the discretion of the owner.

525 King Edward Ave., Ottawa, ON K1N 7N3. Ⓒ **800/841-8786** or 613/565-6700. www.bbcanada.com/kingedward. 3 units. C$80–C$100 (US$66–US$82) double. Rates include breakfast. MC, V. Free parking. *In room:* A/C, TV, no phone.

Ottawa International Hostel   Before becoming a hostel, the building was the Carleton County Gaol (1862–1972). Guided tours of the former prison are available through Haunted Walks Inc. (see Walking Tours, chapter 6, p. 142). Your bed for the night is a bunk in a jail cell or one of the dorms. Enjoy a quiet night's sleep behind bars — if the ghost of the last prisoner to be publicly hanged in Canada doesn't disturb you. If you are a Hostelling International member, you'll receive a discounted room rate. The cozy TV lounge has leather couches and a big-screen TV. The communal kitchen recently received new appliances, tables, and chairs. Lockers for storing food are available for guests. The dining room is housed in the former prison chapel, and in the summer guests may use the barbecue in the garden. Washroom facilities, with washbasins, toilets, and showers, are unisex (except in single-sex dorm areas). Families may opt for a private room with bunk beds, which accommodates up to five people, but most likely your kids will want to sleep in the jail cells. Although the space is cramped and the beds are narrow, the experience will be authentic.

75 Nicholas St., Ottawa, ON K1N 7B9. ☎ **613/235-2595.** Fax 613/235-9202. www.hostellingintl.on.ca. 154 units. C$26 (US$21) adult, C$13 (US$11) child/youth aged 10–17 in dormitory; C$60 (US$49) private room (max. 5 people); children 9 and under free. AE, MC, V. Parking C$5 (US$4). **Amenities:** Game room; washers and dryers. *In room:* Tabletop fans, no phone.

University of Ottawa Student Residence *Value*   Although availability is limited to May through August this is prime tourist time, so for many visitors staying here will work out just fine. Rooms are available in a variety of student residences, but the one I recommend is the building at 90 rue Université, a recently built, all-suite residence. Each unit has two bedrooms with double beds, a kitchenette with fridge, microwave, sink, and storage, and an ensuite bathroom. The location is perfect for visiting downtown attractions, and daily maid service keeps everything clean, clean, clean. I think it's the best value in the city for those on a limited budget.

90 rue Université, Ottawa, ON K1N 1H3. ☎ **613/564-5400.** Fax 613/654-6530. www.uottawa.ca. 1,200 rooms (across all types of residence). C$99 (US$81) 2-bed suite, max. 4 people. MC, V. Parking C$10 (US$8). **Amenities:** Pool and exercise room on campus for extra fee; games room; washers and dryers. *In suites (dorm rooms may differ):* A/C, TV, dataport, kitchenette.

3 The Glebe & South Central

The Glebe is a trendy, upper-middle-class family neighborhood lined with turn-of-the-century redbrick homes and a number of larger, elegant houses. Although the district's main street, Bank Street, has wonderful restaurants and shops, hotels and motels are scarce. But some of the nicest B&Bs are to be found here, and many people prefer to be on a quiet back street than in the high-rises of downtown. Just south of the Glebe lies another quiet neighborhood, where you'll find the Carleton University campus, bordered by Dow's Lake, Bronson Avenue (one of the main arteries to downtown), and the Ottawa River.

MODERATE

Alanbury House B&B ★★★   Alanbury House is an elegant and welcoming B&B. The owners have meticulously decorated the interior with chic Montreal style and taste. Furnishings and fabrics have been carefully selected to complement this beautiful three-story Victorian home. In the warmer months, a comfortable sunroom is the perfect place to relax and read. When the weather turns cold, snuggle up by the fireplace in the living room. For a romantic getaway, stay in the Willow Room, which features a fireplace, a double Jacuzzi tub in the ensuite bathroom, and a private balcony. If you're traveling as a family or would like a private sitting room, stay in the one-bedroom suite. The adjoining room can be used as a TV lounge or extra bedroom. The property is best suited for adults and children ages 8 and up. Truly an exceptional property.

119 Strathcona Ave., Ottawa, ON K1S 1X5. (*C*) **613/234-8378**. Fax 613/569-5691. www.alanburyhouse.com. 3 units. C$109–C$159 (US$89–US$130) double; C$159–C$179 (US$130–US$147) 1-bedroom suite. Rates include breakfast. AE, DC, MC, V. Free parking. *In room:* A/C, TV, dataport, hair dryer, iron, phone.

A Rose On Colonel By B&B ★★ *Finds*   This cozy Edwardian-style home, built in 1925, is just steps from the Rideau Canal on a quiet residential street. Before becoming a B&B, the property was leased for many years by the American and French embassies as a diplomatic residence. The atmosphere is warm and friendly. The breakfast room is decorated with a collection of blue glass, strikingly displayed along the windowsills to catch the sunlight. The two bathrooms are shared among three guest rooms, but bathrobes have been thoughtfully supplied. A comfy lounge on the second floor is equipped with a fridge, microwave, coffeemaker, and phone. A short walk away is Brewer Park, bordered on its southern edge by the scenic Rideau River. Children are very welcome; the owner of the B&B will even supply you and your children with crusts of bread to feed the ducks and swans on Brewer Pond.

9 Rosedale Ave., Ottawa, ON K1S 4T2. (*C*) **613/291-7831**. www.rosebandb.com. 3 units. C$110 (US$90) double. Rate includes breakfast. AE, MC, V. Free parking. **Amenities:** Washer and dryer. *In room:* Ceiling fans, dataport, no phone.

Carleton University Tour and Conference Centre   The student residences at Carleton are available between early May and late August. There are about 2,000 beds available in several residence buildings. Most bedrooms are either single or double (two single beds) occupancy with shared bathrooms. The newer buildings offer two- and four-bedroom suites, all with double beds and one or two bathrooms per suite; each suite also has a fridge and sink; some units have microwaves. Rates include an all-you-can-eat breakfast in the large cafeteria. Athletic and recreational facilities on campus, available for an additional charge, include an indoor pool, squash and tennis courts, a fitness center with sauna and whirlpool, and a game room and video arcade. You can walk, bike, or in-line skate all the way downtown on canal-side pathways. At nearby Dow's Lake you can rent canoes, kayaks, and bicycles.

1125 Colonel By Dr., Ottawa ON K1S 5B6. (*C*) **613/520-5612**. www.carleton.ca/housing/tourandconf. 2,000 units. C$50–C$70 (US$41–US$57) per person in dorm-style room; C$70–C$90 (US$57–US$74) per person in newer suite building. Rates include breakfast. MC, V. Parking C$8 (US$7) per day Mon–Fri; free on weekends. **Amenities on campus:** Cafeteria, fast-food outlet, food court; indoor pool; health club; tennis courts; hot tub; sauna; watersports/bicycle rental at Dow's Lake; game room; video arcade; washers and dryers. *In room:* A/C in most units.

4 Near the Train Station

For those traveling by train, the hotel listed here is a very short cab ride from the station — you may even wish to walk in summer, although you must use the underpass under the busy Queensway (Highway 417). St. Laurent Shopping Centre, with more than 230 stores and services, is within walking distance. Several family entertainment venues, including the Silver City movie theater and the Gloucester Wave Pool, are within easy reach. Take in a game of AAA baseball at Jetform Stadium in season, right on your doorstep. A couple of minutes' drive north on St. Laurent Boulevard will bring you to the Canada Aviation Museum and the Musical Ride Centre, RCMP Rockcliffe Stables, and a couple of minutes in the opposite direction will take you to the Museum of Science and Technology.

MODERATE

Hampton Inn ⭐ *(Value)*   This hotel, built in 2000, has larger than average guest rooms with high-quality furnishings and oversize bathrooms. Each room is equipped with a kitchenette that includes a microwave, sink, and small fridge (dishes and utensils are supplied on request). The indoor pool area is spotless and spacious. A complimentary continental breakfast is served in the lobby lounge. As a result of its new and comfortable accommodations, indoor pool, and competitive pricing, the Hampton Inn has an edge over other options in the area.

100 Coventry Rd., Ottawa, ON K1K 4S3. ⓒ **877/701-1281** or 613/741-2300. Fax 613/741-8689. www.hamptoninn.com. 179 units. C$135 (US$111) studio. Rate includes breakfast. Children 17 and under stay free in parent's room. AE, DC, DISC, MC, V. Free parking. **Amenities:** Breakfast room/lounge; indoor pool; exercise room; hot tub; business services; babysitting; washers and dryers; same-day dry-cleaning/laundry. *In room:* A/C, TV, dataport, kitchenette, coffeemaker, hair dryer, iron.

5 Ottawa West

The selection of hotels listed here includes a luxurious resort property in Kanata, an Ottawa West suburb, and three hotels a short drive west of downtown that have retail stores and family-style restaurants within walking distance, for those who may find the downtown hotels a little pricey. All are good bets if you want to be closer to the Corel Centre or plan to explore the countryside west and south of Ottawa. Although you'll need to drive to downtown attractions, all of these hotels provide pools and comfortable rooms.

EXPENSIVE

Brookstreet Resort ⭐⭐⭐   Ultra-modern, chic, and sleek sum up Brookstreet Resort, Ottawa's newest addition to the hotel scene. Built in the heart of Silicon Valley North, it was the vision of high-tech giant Terry Matthews, chairman of Mitel Networks Corp. The property exudes luxury at every turn, but with a fresh, modern twist rather than an emulation of the grandeur of ages past. Signature guest-room colors are raspberry and gray, and a minimalist approach gives a boutique-hotel feel to rooms and suites. Although surrounded by low-rise high-tech offices, Brookstreet Resort nestles on the edge of greenspace, overlooking the award-winning The Marshes Golf Club, as well as cycling and walking paths and cross-country ski trails. With a full spa on-site, indoor and outdoor swimming pools, children's wading pool, skating rink, putting green, and new (2005) 9-hole par 3 golf course in addition to the championship course, you will never wonder what to do with your time. The dining facilities are top class; Brookstreet's restaurant, Perspectives, has been awarded several accolades for its cuisine. Check the website for packages, ranging from romantic getaways to golf and spa weekends.

525 Legget Dr., Ottawa ON K2K 2W2. ⓒ **888-826-2220** or ⓒ 613/271-1800. Fax 613/271-1850. www.brookstreetresort.com. 276 units. C$139–C$169 (US$114–US$169) double; C$199–C$229 (US$163–US$188) junior suite; C$399–C$449 (US$327–US$368) master suite. Children 17 and under stay free in parent's room. AE, DC, DISC, MC, V. Free parking above ground, C$10 (US$8) underground. Pets accepted, C$25 (US$20) per night. **Amenities:** Restaurant; bar/lounge; championship golf course; 9-hole golf course; putting green; health club; spa; Jacuzzi; steam room; concierge; car-rental desk; courtesy car; business center; shopping arcade; 24-hour room service; massage; babysitting; same-day dry-cleaning/laundry. *In room:* A/C, TV w/pay movies, dataport, kitchenette in some units, minibar, coffeemaker, hair dryer, iron, in-room safe.

MODERATE

Best Western Barons Hotel   Although the location is a little way from downtown, the family-friendly nature of this hotel makes it a worthwhile option. Its proximity to the Queensway means you can drive in to the city in 15 minutes. A large regional shopping mall, Bayshore, is 5 minutes away (great if you have teenagers in tow), and the Corel Centre is only a 10-minute drive west. Families will enjoy the clean, bright indoor pool. In the summer, a patio and grassy courtyard out back are popular with guests, who are welcome to use the two barbecues or enjoy a picnic under the trees. Rooms are larger than average, and 30 rooms in the back wing have received new granite-lined showers and countertops. Families will find the 1-bedroom suites convenient, since they include a sink, microwave, and small fridge (utensils are available on request). Complimentary high-speed wireless Internet access.

3700 Richmond Rd., Ottawa ON K2H 5B8. © **866-214-1239** or © 613/828-2741. Fax 613/596-4742. www.bestwestern.com/ca/baronshotel. 83 units. C$120–C$140 (US$98–US$115) double. Children 17 and under stay free in parent's room. AE, DC, DISC, MC, V. Free parking. Pets accepted; C$10 (US$8) per night; must be caged if left alone in room. **Amenities:** Restaurant; indoor pool; exercise room; hot tub; sauna; business services; limited room service; washers and dryers; same-day dry-cleaning/laundry. *In room:* A/C, TV w/pay movies, dataport, kitchenette in some units, coffeemaker, hair dryer, iron.

Best Western Macies Hotel   Macies is one of Ottawa's oldest family-run hotels. Now in their third generation of family management and with more than 60 years of hospitality experience, the Macies staff are skilled at dealing with both tourists and business travelers. Enjoy the large outdoor pool in the summer. Westgate Shopping Centre, with around 45 stores and services, is directly opposite the hotel. A 10-minute drive east will take you to the foot of the Peace Tower on Parliament Hill.

1274 Carling Ave., Ottawa, ON K1Z 7K8. © **613/728-1951**. Fax 613/728-1955. www.macieshotel.com. 123 units. C$109 (US$89) and up double. Children 14 and under stay free in parent's room. AE, DC, DISC, MC, V. Free parking. **Amenities:** Restaurant, bar; large heated outdoor pool; exercise room; Jacuzzi; sauna; business services; limited room service; washers and dryers; same-day dry-cleaning/laundry. *In room:* A/C, TV w/pay movies, dataport, coffeemaker, hair dryer, iron, in-room safe.

Travelodge Hotel Ottawa West *(Kids)*   This hotel is a huge magnet for families and traveling sports teams due to its indoor waterpark, featuring wavepool, slide, whirlpool, and children's wading pool. Popular packages include poolview rooms with balcony, complimentary continental breakfast, pizza coupon, and access to the waterpark. A leafy courtyard with a tranquil garden provides a haven from the mayhem; surrounding this quieter section of the hotel are the business-grade and longer-stay rooms.

1376 Carling Ave., Ottawa, ON K1Z 7L5. © **800/267-4166** or 613/722-7600. Fax 613/722-2226. www.travelodgeottawa.com. 196 units. C$99–C$189 (US$81–US$155) std. double to king. Children under 18 stay free in parent's room. AE, DC, DISC, MC, V. Free parking. Small pets accepted; C$50 cleaning charge may apply. **Amenities:** Restaurant, lounge; indoor waterpark; exercise room; games room; business center; limited room service; babysitting; same-day dry-cleaning/laundry; executive floor. *In room:* A/C, TV w/pay movies, dataport, fridge, coffeemaker, hair dryer, iron.

6 The Airport

If you are traveling to Ottawa by air and would like a room close to the airport on arrival or prior to departure, these hotels are both comfortable. The Southway Inn has more amenities for families and business travelers than the Airport Inn.

EXPENSIVE

The Southway Inn   If you're seeking accommodations far from the high-rise jungle of downtown, this property in the south end of the city will suit. There are chain restaurants and services, including a bank and drugstore, nearby, and if you avoid traveling during rush hour it's only a 15-minute drive from the action of downtown Ottawa. The airport is only 5 to 10 minutes away by car. The indoor pool is bright and pleasant. Recent expansion included the introduction of 15 new suites with full kitchens. High-speed Internet access available in all guest rooms.

2431 Bank St. S., Ottawa, ON K1V 8R9. *C* **877/688-4929** or 613/737-0811. Fax 613/737-3207. www.southway.com. 170 units. C$135–C$165 (US$111–US$135) double; C$235 (US$193) suite with kitchen. AE, DC, DISC, MC, V. Free parking. Pets C$15 (US$10) first day, C$5 (US$3) each additional day. **Amenities:** Restaurant/bar; indoor pool; exercise room; hot tub; sauna; business services; limited room service; washers and dryers; same-day dry-cleaning/laundry; executive rooms. *In room:* A/C, TV, dataport, kitchen in some units, fridge, coffeemaker, hair dryer, iron, in-room safes in some units.

INEXPENSIVE

Adam's Airport Inn *Value*   A 7-minute drive from the airport, this hotel is a good bet for a night's rest at either end of your vacation if you're traveling by air, especially if you have a late arrival or early-morning start. The rates are spot-on for what's on offer, which is a clean and comfortable bed, friendly desk staff, and free parking. Just the basics, nicely delivered. Although the building is set back a little way from busy Bank Street, ask for a room at the back overlooking the quiet residential neighborhood. A complimentary continental breakfast and 24-hour coffee are available in the lobby. There is one luxury suite available, with king-size bed and in-room double Jacuzzi at C$135 (US$111), and two king suites with sitting area and coffeemaker at C$95 (US$78).

2721 Bank St., Ottawa, ON K1T 1M8. *C* **800/261-5835** or 613/738-3838. Fax 613/736-8211. 62 units. C$79 (US$49) double; C$89 (US$55) family rate (4 people) in a room with two double beds. AE, DC, MC, V. Free parking. Pets C$20 (US$16) per day. **Amenities:** Exercise room; washers and dryers. *In room:* A/C, TV, dataport, fridge, hair dryer.

7 On the Quebec Side

For some reason, the perception exists that Quebec is "way over there," when in fact you're only a bridgespan away from the major attractions in Ottawa. Gatineau has its share of good-quality places to stay, ranging from B&Bs to upper-end hotel chains. I've listed three here, but you could also consider the **Best Western Hotel Jacques Cartier** *C* **800/265-8550** or the **Four Points by Sheraton** *C* **800/567-9607.** If you're a nonsmoker, remember that you're likely to run into a lot of smokers in hotels, restaurants, and bars on this side of the Ottawa River.

VERY EXPENSIVE

Hilton Lac-Leamy ✦✦✦   This fabulous hotel complements the urban resort of Casino du Lac-Leamy, standing between two bodies of water — Lac Leamy and Lac de la Carrière, with its majestic fountain. The rooms are all larger than standard and you have a choice of view: the Ottawa skyline or the Gatineau Hills. The ostentatious public areas are designed to impress. Extensive use of wood and marble in the interior conveys warmth and luxury. A series of remarkable blown-glass sculptures adorns the lobby and main public areas. The luxurious spa offers a wide range of treatments.

3 boulevard du Casino, Gatineau (Hull Sector), QC J8Y 6X4. (©) **866/488-7888** or 819/790-6444. Fax 819/790-6408. www.hiltonlacleamy.com. 349 units. C$159–C$189 (US$130–US$155) standard double; C$209–C$239 (US$171–US$196) executive double; C$319 (US$262) and up suite. Children 18 and under stay free in parent's room. AE, DC, DISC, MC, V. Free self-parking; valet parking C$15 (US$12). **Amenities:** Restaurant; bar; indoor and outdoor pools; tennis courts; health club; spa; Jacuzzi; sauna; bike/in-line skate rental at nearby Lac Leamy; children's center; theater room; concierge; business center; 24-hour room service; babysitting; same-day dry-cleaning/laundry; executive floors. *In room:* A/C, TV w/ pay movies, dataport, minibar, coffeemaker, hair dryer, iron, safe.

EXPENSIVE

Château Cartier Resort ✮✮✮   A luxuriously comfortable resort set in 62 hectares (152 acres) of rolling countryside on the north shore of the Ottawa River, just a 10-minute drive from downtown Ottawa. The majority of the guest rooms are junior suites, with a comfortable sitting room and separate bedroom with French doors. Leisure and recreational facilities are outstanding. There's an 18-hole golf course on the property, with teaching professionals on hand. Two outdoor tennis courts, indoor racquetball and squash courts, fitness center with top-quality equipment, and full-service spa are just some of the activities available for guests. In the winter, there's a skating rink, tobogganing, tubing, cross-country skiing, snowshoeing, and horse-drawn sleigh rides. Downhill skiing is nearby and seasonal packages range from golf getaways to ski weekends. Public areas and guest rooms are extremely well-appointed and furnished.

1170 chemin Aylmer, Aylmer, QC J9H 5E1. (©) **800/807-1088** or 819/777-1088. Fax 819/777-7161. www.chateaucartier.com. 129 units. C$139–C$199 (US$114–US$163) junior suite. Children under 18 stay free in parent's room. AE, DC, DISC, MC, V. Free parking. **Amenities:** Restaurant/lounge; indoor pool; golf course; 2 tennis courts; health club; spa; Jacuzzi; sauna; bike rental; other sports equipment rental; seasonal children's programs; business center; limited room service; massage; babysitting; same-day dry-cleaning/laundry; executive suites. *In room:* A/C, TV w/pay movies, dataport, fridge, coffeemaker, hair dryer, iron.

Holiday Inn Plaza la Chaudière ✮   A convenient and pretty location opposite a city park where the Theatre de l'Ile (Island Theatre) performs in the summer. A couple of minutes' walk will link you up with bike and walking pathways along the Ottawa River, and you're only a short drive or bike ride away from the entrance to Gatineau Park. RentABike operates an outlet at the hotel, so you can arrange your bike rental right on the premises. Rentals include helmets, locks, and maps. The lobby has a beautiful display of indoor plants and a waterfall. Guest rooms are equipped with high-speed wireless Internet access.

2 rue Montcalm, Gatineau (Hull Sector), QC J8X 4B4. (©) **800/567-1962** (Canada) or 819/778-3880. Fax 819/778-3309. www.rosdevhotels.com. 232 units. C$89–C$149 (US$73–US$122) double; C$150–C$200 (US$123–US$164) 1-bedroom suite. Children under 17 stay free in parent's room. AE, DC, DISC, MC, V. Parking C$10 (US$8). Pets accepted. **Amenities:** Restaurant; lounge; indoor pool; exercise room; Jacuzzi; sauna; bike/in-line skate rental; games room; business center; hair salon next door; limited room service; babysitting; same-day dry-cleaning; executive floors. *In room:* A/C, TV w/pay movies, dataport, minibar, coffeemaker, hair dryer, iron, in-room safe.

5

Dining

Dining out, at its best, is one of life's greatest pleasures — a sensual blend of terrific food, memorable setting, and expert service. And I'm happy to say that yes, it is possible to experience this in Ottawa.

In this chapter, I've listed some of the best places to eat in Ottawa and Gatineau. The multi-ethnic capital region has a large (and sophisticated) enough population to support excellent restaurants that offer a wide range of cuisines.

You can dine by candlelight at a lace-covered table in a traditional dark-wood-and-burgundy room, soak up the lively atmosphere of an Italian *pasticceria* while you sip an espresso, or lounge around in a diner, chomping pancakes and bacon washed down with a bottomless mug of coffee. If you want to kick it up a notch, head for a European-style cafe and order café au lait *dans un bol,* or experience the breathtaking creations of talented local chefs who specialize in using Canadian ingredients. If British afternoon tea, pad Thai, or fresh organic vegetarian dishes are what you have in mind, you'll be well satisfied.

Whenever the weather permits, I urge you to go alfresco, here in Ottawa just as much as anywhere else. Eating outdoors adds another dimension to the experience, whether it's morning coffee on a busy sidewalk, a leisurely lunch on the banks of the Rideau Canal, or a romantic evening under the stars.

I feel obliged to alert out-of-towners who stroll around the city that they will sooner or later come face to face with an Ottawa institution: the chip wagon. Their offerings hold no appeal for me, but I cannot deny their popularity with local folk. As well as the usual deep-fried sliced potatoes, many wagons serve poutine, a Québécois concoction of fries topped with cheese curds and smothered in gravy. As in most Canadian cities, sausage and hot dog carts edge their way onto downtown sidewalks once the weather begins to warm up in the spring.

The following listings are by no means the only places to enjoy good food in the Ottawa area. Rather, the idea is to give you a sampling of the broad range of excellent cuisine that awaits you here. Bon appétit!

DINING NOTES Dining out in Ottawa does not have to be an expensive venture, but be aware that taxes are high. Meals are subject to 8% provincial sales tax and 7% GST, so when you factor in an average tip, a whopping 30% is added to the bill. Tipping is usually left to the diner's discretion, although some establishments add 15% to the bill for parties of six or more. Wine prices in restaurants are quite high — don't be surprised to find your favorite vintage at double the price you'd pay at the liquor store. Save a little money by ordering an Ontario wine; Niagara vineyards produce some distinguished wines that are increasingly gaining international respect. Note that a 10% liquor tax is added to alcoholic beverage purchases.

1 Restaurants by Cuisine

AFTERNOON TEA
Zoe's Lounge at the Fairmont Château Laurier ★★★ (Downtown East of the Canal, $$$, p. 94).

AMERICAN
Hard Rock Cafe ★ (Downtown East of the Canal, $$, p. 94).

ASIAN
Shanghai Restaurant ★ (Chinatown, $$, p. 102).

BAGELS
Kettleman's Bagels (The Glebe, $, p. 99).
Ottawa Bagelshop & Deli (Wellington Street West, $, p. 100–101).

BAKERY
The French Baker/Le Boulanger Français (Downtown East of the Canal, $, p. 96).
Le Moulin de Provence (Downtown East of the Canal, $, p. 96).
Wild Oat Bakery and Natural Foods (The Glebe, $, p. 99).

BISTRO
ARC Lounge & Restaurant ★★ (Downtown West of the Canal, $$$$, p. 89).
The Black Tomato ★★ (Downtown East of the Canal, $$$, p. 94).
Luxe Bistro ★ (Downtown East of the Canal, $$$$, p. 93).
Von's Bistro (The Glebe, $$$, p. 98–99).

BREAKFAST
Eggspectation (Downtown West of the Canal, $$, p. 90).

CANADIAN
BeaverTails (Downtown East of the Canal, $, p. 95).

Domus ★★★ (Downtown East of the Canal, $$$$, p. 92–93).
The Urban Pear ★★★ (The Glebe, $$$$, p. 97–98).

CHINESE
Yangtze (Chinatown, $$, p. 102).

COFFEEHOUSE
Bridgehead (Wellington Street West, $, p. 100).
Café La Brûlerie ★ (Gatineau, $, p. 87 & 105).
Planet Coffee (Downtown East of the Canal, $, p. 97).
Roasted Cherry (Finds) (Downtown West of the Canal, $, p. 92).

CRÊPERIE
L'Argoät ★★★ (Gatineau, $$, p. 105).

DELI
Dunn's Famous Delicatessen (Downtown West of the Canal, $, p. 91).

DESSERTS
Oh So Good Desserts Café (Downtown East of the Canal, $, p. 96–97).

DINER
Elgin St. Diner (Downtown West of the Canal, $, p. 91).

ECLECTIC
Infusion (The Glebe, $$$, p. 98).
Marchélino ★★ (Downtown East of the Canal, $, p. 96).

FRENCH
Bistro 115 ★ (Downtown East of the Canal, $$$, p. 93–94).
Le Pied de Cochon ★★ (Gatineau, $$, p. 104–105).
Le 1908 ★★ (Gatineau, $$$, p. 104).
Signatures ★★★ (Downtown East of the Canal, $$$$, p. 93).

Key to Abbreviations: $$$$ = Very Expensive $$$ = Expensive $$ = Moderate $ = Inexpensive

Ottawa Dining

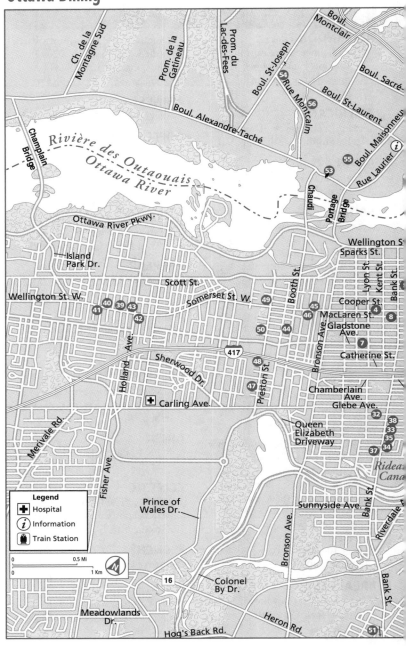

Legend
- ✚ Hospital
- ⓘ Information
- 🚂 Train Station

0 0.5 Mi
0 1 Km

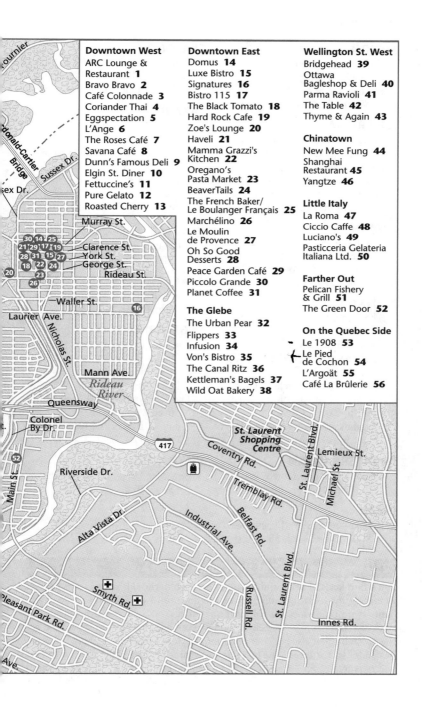

Downtown West
ARC Lounge & Restaurant **1**
Bravo Bravo **2**
Café Colonnade **3**
Coriander Thai **4**
Eggspectation **5**
L'Ange **6**
The Roses Café **7**
Savana Café **8**
Dunn's Famous Deli **9**
Elgin St. Diner **10**
Fettuccine's **11**
Pure Gelato **12**
Roasted Cherry **13**

Downtown East
Domus **14**
Luxe Bistro **15**
Signatures **16**
Bistro 115 **17**
The Black Tomato **18**
Hard Rock Cafe **19**
Zoe's Lounge **20**
Haveli **21**
Mamma Grazzi's Kitchen **22**
Oregano's Pasta Market **23**
BeaverTails **24**
The French Baker/ Le Boulanger Français **25**
Marchélino **26**
Le Moulin de Provence **27**
Oh So Good Desserts **28**
Peace Garden Café **29**
Piccolo Grande **30**
Planet Coffee **31**

The Glebe
The Urban Pear **32**
Flippers **33**
Infusion **34**
Von's Bistro **35**
The Canal Ritz **36**
Kettleman's Bagels **37**
Wild Oat Bakery **38**

Wellington St. West
Bridgehead **39**
Ottawa Bagleshop & Deli **40**
Parma Ravioli **41**
The Table **42**
Thyme & Again **43**

Chinatown
New Mee Fung **44**
Shanghai Restaurant **45**
Yangtze **46**

Little Italy
La Roma **47**
Ciccio Caffe **48**
Luciano's **49**
Pasticceria Gelateria Italiana Ltd. **50**

Farther Out
Pelican Fishery & Grill **51**
The Green Door **52**

On the Quebec Side
Le 1908 **53**
Le Pied de Cochon **54**
L'Argoät **55**
Café La Brûlerie **56**

FUSION

L'Ange ★★ (Downtown West of the Canal, $$, p. 90).

Savana Café ★★ (Downtown West of the Canal, $$, p. 91).

ICE CREAM

Pasticceria Gelateria Italiana Ltd. ★ (Little Italy, $, p. 103).

Piccolo Grande (Downtown East of the Canal, $, p. 97).

Pure Gelato ★★ (Downtown West of the Canal, $, p. 92).

INDIAN

Haveli (Downtown East of the Canal, $$, p. 94–95).

The Roses Café (Downtown West of the Canal, $$, p. 90).

ITALIAN

The Canal Ritz (The Glebe, $$, p. 99).

Ciccio (Little Italy, $$, p. 103).

La Roma ★★ (Little Italy, $$$, p. 102–103).

Mamma Grazzi's Kitchen ★★★ (Downtown East of the Canal, $$, p. 95).

Oregano's Pasta Market (Downtown East of the Canal, $$, p. 95).

MEDITERRANEAN

Bravo Bravo (Downtown West of the Canal, $$$, p. 89).

PIZZA

Café Colonnade ★ (Downtown West of the Canal, $$, p. 89).

SEAFOOD

Flippers (The Glebe, $$$, p. 98).

The Pelican Fishery and Grill ★ (Farther Out, $$, p. 103–104).

TAKEOUT

BeaverTails (Downtown East of the Canal, $, p. 95).

Fettuccine's (Downtown West of the Canal, $, p. 91).

Luciano's ★★ (Little Italy, $, p. 103).

Parma Ravioli (Wellington Street West, $, p. 101).

Thyme & Again ★★ *Finds* (Wellington Street West, $, p. 101).

THAI

Coriander Thai (Downtown West of the Canal, $$, p. 90).

VEGETARIAN

The Green Door ★ *Value* (Farther Out, $, p. 104).

Peace Garden Café (Downtown East of the Canal, $, p. 97).

The Table ★★ *Value* (Wellington Street West, $, p. 101).

Wild Oat Bakery and Natural Foods (The Glebe, $, p. 99).

VIETNAMESE

New Mee Fung ★ (Chinatown, $$, p. 102).

2 Downtown (West of the Canal)

You'll find loads of delightful restaurants tucked in the side streets and squeezed in among the high-rise buildings of the downtown core. Office workers and "suits" with cellphones grafted onto one ear fill these eateries at lunchtime on weekdays, but if you arrive before noon you can not only beat the crowd and get the best table, but also get your order into the kitchen before the hungry hordes descend. Elgin Street is quite lively in the evening because of the plethora of bars and restaurants, but farther west the foot traffic can be pretty light after around 6pm — it can seem too quiet in some spots, although Sparks Street Mall always has a few tourists taking an evening stroll during the summer months. Parking can be a challenge in the downtown core around noon on weekdays as vehicles circle around hunting for the perfect spot, so allow extra time. Public parking is free in this sector of downtown on Saturdays and Sundays.

VERY EXPENSIVE

ARC Lounge & Restaurant ✦✦ BISTRO

ARC the.hotel's sleek restaurant and lounge evoke the same feeling of simple good taste that prevails throughout the hotel. Subdued lighting, rich dark wood, and contemporary decor combine to create a sophisticated yet relaxing atmosphere. Dishes get top marks for presentation, with taste to match. At midday, you may dine on roasted quail fragranced with juniper berries, accompanied by sun-dried tomato risotto and natural jus or sesame-crusted salmon and tuna tataki with lemon aioli and taro chips. If the menu lists pressed duck foie gras, you are indeed a lucky diner. The freshly prepared soups are also divine. For dinner, you may find grain-fed chicken, medallion of caribou, or Brome Lake duck on offer. For a unique dining experience reserve the "Mood Booth," a subtly lit booth flanked by mirrors and featuring constantly changing colors.

140 Slater St. ✆ **613/238-2888.** Reservations recommended. Main courses C$25–C$35 (US$20–US$29). AE, DC, MC, V. Restaurant Mon–Fri 6:30–10:30am breakfast, 11:30am–2pm lunch, 5:30–10pm dinner; Sat 7–11am breakfast, 5:30–10pm dinner; Sun 7–11am breakfast. Lounge Mon–Thurs 10:30am–11pm, Fri 10:30am–1am; Sat 4:30pm–1am.

EXPENSIVE

Bravo Bravo Ristorante & Bar MEDITERRANEAN

The main dining area at the front of this large restaurant is bright and airy, with plenty of space between tables. A warm Mediterranean sunset palette, scuffed wooden floors, and a faux stone archway complete the picture. Check out the display of authentic hand-painted Venetian masks on one of the walls. Creative pasta dishes include fusilli with red onions, garlic, capers, and chilies in a spicy roma tomato sauce, and tagliatelle with veal, prosciutto, artichokes, fresh sage, garlic, dry vermouth, and a touch of cream. After dinner, play a game of pool or sit at the granite bar and sip a drink or two. A narrow alley at the side of the restaurant has been turned into a summer Mediterranean paradise, with bright wall murals and tables for dining. If you want to savor Bravo Bravo at home or in your hotel suite, pick up some antipasto and rich, gooey desserts from the takeout section at the entrance.

292 Elgin St. ✆ **613/233-7525.** Reservations recommended weekends only. Main courses C$13–C$26 (US$11–US$21). AE, DC, MC, V. Mon–Wed 11:30am–2pm and 5–10pm, Thurs–Fri 11:30am–2pm and 5–11pm, Sat 5–11pm, Sun 10am–2pm and 5–10pm.

MODERATE

Café Colonnade ✦ PIZZA

Pizzas almost fly from the oven onto tables or out the door at this place, because Ottawans love Colonnade's pizza. And I agree, because there's a lot to like — thick crust with a sprinkling of cheese around the edge, generous smears of tangy tomato sauce, and gooey mozzarella to hold the toppings in place. Personal pizzas will fill most grown-up tummies or two kids at lunchtime, or you can order a medium or large and let everyone dig in. Although you really should go for the pizza, the menu offers pasta, veal, chicken, manicotti, cannelloni, and other dishes. North American fare, including sandwiches and burgers, is also listed. The dining room is spacious and plainly furnished — the focus is clearly on the food. An outdoor terrace stretches along one side of the building, providing a place to hang out on warm summer days and evenings.

280 Metcalfe St. ✆ **613/237-3179.** Pizza C$7–C$19 (US$6–US$16); main courses C$7–C$11 (US$6–US$9). AE, DC, MC, V. Mon–Thurs 11am–10pm or 11pm; Fri–Sat 11am–11pm or 11:30pm; Sun 11am–9:30pm or 10pm.

Coriander Thai THAI   A tiny restaurant tucked away a couple of blocks from the big hotels and office blocks of downtown, Coriander Thai is a great place to sample a variety of Thai dishes, whether you are a newbie or vet of Thai cuisine. Choose spring rolls, stuffed mussels, pork or chicken satay, or classic Thai soups prepared with fresh lime juice, lemongrass, chilies, coriander, coconut milk, and ginger. Salads, curries, seafood, and vegetable dishes abound. To adjust the heat in any dish, just mention to your server whether you want it turned up or down a notch, and the kitchen will be happy to oblige. The tables are elbow-rubbingly close together, and a lack of background noise makes it uncomfortably easy to eavesdrop on other diners' conversations, but the service is quietly courteous and the food is fresh tasting.

282 Kent St. ℂ **613/233-2828.** Main courses C$10–C$13 (US$8–US$11). AE, DC, MC, V. Mon–Thurs 11:30am–2:30pm and 5–10pm; Fri 11:30am–2:30pm and 5–11:30pm; Sat 5–11pm; Sun 5–10pm.

Eggspectation BREAKFAST/BRUNCH   Throw away your diet for a day and indulge in a real North American breakfast (served all day, of course!). The delish plates may start off as a simple omelet or waffle, but the toppings elevate them to the next level. Think the Normande Omelette with sweet apples and cinnamon, served with potatoes sautéed in butter and brown sugar, or the Brioche Beauty, a buttered grilled pastry served with mixed fresh fruit, plain yogurt, and roasted almonds, drizzled with honey. Pancakes, French toast, and waffles abound. The signature egg dishes cover almost every permutation of traditional breakfast fare. Service is efficient and the two-level dining room is spacious and airy, featuring exposed brick walls.

171 Bank St. ℂ **613/569-6505.** Most breakfast items under C$10 (US$8). Main courses C$8–C$12 (US$7–US$10). AE, DC, MC, V. Mon–Fri 6am–3pm; Sat–Sun 6am–5pm.

L'Ange ✹✹ FUSION   Step into the sunshine and vibrant colors of the south of France in this Sparks Street Mall cafe. Cheerful Provençal tablecloths, warm Mediterranean colors on the walls, and original artwork featuring the landscapes of Provence and Tuscany create an inviting ambience. The open kitchen puts diners on nodding terms with the chef from the moment of arrival. The menu is limited, which I think is always a good indication that dishes are freshly prepared. Certainly, the maple-seared pork tenderloin with sun-dried tomatoes and garlic mashed potatoes that I enjoyed on a dull winter's day was expertly prepared and suitably reflective of classic bistro fare prepared with style. Grilled panini are also a menu feature, with fillings such as portobello mushrooms, zucchini, and walnut thyme pesto. Special events — for example, a recent five-course Arabian dinner for C$46 (US$38) — are held sporadically, and the owner and kitchen staff are constantly working to evolve the restaurant's personality, so it's worth calling them when you're in town to find out what may be scheduled during your stay.

109B Sparks St. ℂ **613/232-8777.** Main courses C$11–C$14 (US$9–US$12). AE, DC, MC, V. Opening hours may vary, please call ahead. Winter generally Mon–Fri 10am–5pm, Sat 10am–3pm; Summer generally Mon–Fri 10am–10pm; Sat 10am–3pm.

The Roses Café INDIAN   I always find East Indian cuisine to be a culinary adventure, because diners can spoon as much or as little of each dish onto their plate as they like. Typically, there are a lot of meatless choices, and vegetables are presented with delicately spiced sauces. The appetizers and accompanying dishes are lots of fun to eat. Try papadums — thin, crispy chip-like disks that melt in your mouth. With a focus on South Indian cuisine, the Roses menu features the *dosa*, a rice and lentil flour crepe filled with a variety of Indian-style vegetables.

Their butter chicken curry is mildly spiced and has earned a well-deserved reputation for excellence. Takeout is available. The success of the Gladstone Avenue location prompted the owners to open another location, Roses Café Also, in the ByWard Market district at 349 Dalhousie St.

523 Gladstone Ave. © **613/233-5574.** Reservations recommended on weekends. Main courses C$6–C$12 (US$5–US$10). AE, DC, MC, V. Mon–Fri 11am–2pm and 5–10pm; Sat–Sun 5–10pm.

Savana Café ★★ FUSION The walls of the Savana Café are warm, vivid, and tropical. Intense Caribbean blue, brilliant green, and exquisite sunset colors put you in the mood for fun, and the food makes you want to sing (reggae, possibly?). Sweet basil shrimp flavored with oyster sauce, soya, orange juice, and Thai basil is an absolutely divine dish. Or try the two-potato fries, coconut rice, pad Thai, satay, or curry chicken roti — there's something for everyone. Servers are enthusiastic and knowledgeable. Don't be shy to ask for the ingredients of a particular dish or request to have the heat turned down if you're not a spicy diner. Come hungry, because the portions are generous and you won't be able to resist cleaning your plate. Savana is a popular spot and fills up quickly on weekdays at lunchtime. A small terrace out front in the shade of mature trees is pleasant in the summer.

431 Gilmour St. © **613/233-9159.** Reservations recommended. Main courses C$14–C$20 (US$12–US$16). AE, DC, MC, V. Mon–Fri 11:30am–3pm and 5–10pm; Sat 5–10pm.

INEXPENSIVE

Dunn's Famous Delicatessen DELI If you want to sample an authentic Montreal smoked meat sandwich without making the 2-hour road trip from Ottawa, dive into Dunn's and sink your teeth into a stack of hand-carved smoked meat brought in fresh from the Dunn's smokehouse in Montreal. Dunn's opened for business in Montreal in 1927, and the first Ottawa restaurant opened in 1990. The decor is a little scuffed around the edges, but that just adds to its comfortable, mom's-kitchen kind of appeal. With customers chattering, dishes clattering, and servers dashing around, it's an unpretentious place. The Elgin Street location never closes, so whether you're hungry for breakfast, lunch, or dinner, Dunn's is ready for you. The Queen Street restaurant, relocated from 57 Bank St. in 2005, keeps more sedate hours.

220 Elgin St. © **613/230-6444.** Most items under C$10 (US$8). AE, DC, MC, V. Daily 24 hours. Also at 203 Queen St. at Bank St. © **613/230-4005.** Mon–Fri 7am–7pm, Sat 7am–2pm.

Elgin St. Diner DINER This is a comfy, neighborhood kind of place where you can saunter in, flop into a chair, and hang out with a coffee while the kids slurp milkshakes and chomp peanut butter and jam sandwiches. The retro breakfast special features two eggs, your choice of bacon, ham, or sausage, home fries, baked beans, toast, and coffee for C$6 (US$5), or you can choose from the variety of omelets or pancakes — with real maple syrup — on the all-day breakfast menu. There are plenty of old-fashioned dinners, including meat loaf, shepherd's pie, and liver and onions. Folks who live for traditional comfort food will feel right at home. Servers are cheerful, and you can drop in any time — they never close.

374 Elgin St. © **613/237-9700.** Most items under C$10 (US$8). AE, DC, MC, V. Daily 24 hours.

Fettuccine's TAKEOUT If you're staying in a downtown suite with kitchen facilities, pay a visit to Fettuccine's and stock your fridge with fresh pasta, sauces, and ready-to-eat salads. Locals swear by the four-cheese cappelletti topped with tomato vodka sauce. I like the spinach and cheese ravioli, chicken parmigiana, and basil pesto. Lasagna, cannelloni, pasta salad, and Caesar salad are also regular menu items. Everything is made on the premises.

280C Elgin St. ⓒ **613/230-4723.** Most items under C$10 (US$8). AE, V. Mon–Sat 11am–8pm, Sun 11am–7pm.

Pure Gelato ⭐⭐ *(Finds* ICE CREAM/CAFE   I always say you can never have too much ice cream, and Pure Gelato is my number-one choice in Ottawa to get the really good stuff. The choice is dizzying, with lots of fruit flavors, more than nine chocolate concoctions, and unusual flavors like ginger, Toblerone, and chestnut. Hot, golden malted Belgian waffles are only C$5 (US$4), and you can add gelato for a buck. Plunk yourself down on a shiny metallic stool at the long counter and enjoy. A European-style bar serves a variety of coffee-based beverages. A seasonal gelato bar operates inside Sugar Mountain at 71 William St. in the ByWard Market.

350 Elgin St. ⓒ **613/237-3799.** Most items under C$10 (US$8). V. Summer daily 11am–midnight; winter Sun–Wed 11am–10pm, Thurs–Sat 11am–11pm.

The Roasted Cherry Coffee House *(Finds* COFFEEHOUSE   This is a corner cafe with a genuine feel-good story to tell. The youth who serve behind the counter and manage the business are university and high school co-op students and marginalized youth. Profits are plowed back into the local community in support of charitable activities associated with youth and education. The Roasted Cherry serves a fine shot of espresso, and food is available in the form of muffins, sandwiches, and other light fare. Settle down at a table and tap in to the wireless Internet service, or sit on a stool in front of the window and people watch.

93 O'Connor St. ⓒ **613/236-1656.** Most items under C$10 (US$8). Mon–Fri 6:30am–4pm.

3 Downtown (East of the Canal)

By far the greatest concentration of restaurants and food shops in Ottawa is in the ByWard Market district — but be warned, not all of them are good. East of the Rideau Canal, the area is officially bordered by Sussex Drive, St. Patrick Street, King Edward Avenue, and Rideau Street. The ByWard Market building and seasonal farmers' market run between York and George streets. Late at night the bar crowd makes its presence known here. If you're a night owl or a party animal, you'll feel right at home in the busy pubs. There are quieter, more romantic and sophisticated venues in which to sip a cocktail or indulge in a good meal as well — the Market district has something for everyone. Parking is plentiful, but because of the popularity of the dining and shopping here, metered spaces are scarce. If you don't luck out on the first or second pass, bite the bullet and park in one of the open-air or underground lots. It may cost a little more, but you're saved the time and stress of driving around in circles, and you can leave your vehicle for hours for a flat fee of C$10 (US$8) or less, whereas most meters in the market allow a maximum of 1 or 2 hours at certain times of the day at a rate of C$2.50 (US$2.05) per hour.

VERY EXPENSIVE

Domus ⭐⭐⭐ CANADIAN   Extremely popular with Ottawans and visitors alike, Domus's chef/owner John Taylor presents menus featuring Canada's freshest available regional, seasonal, and often organic products. You can watch Taylor's team, headed by *chef de cuisine* Simon Fraser, at work in the shiny stainless-steel open kitchen at the rear of this compact restaurant. The decor is simple, with retro butter-yellow and diner-red walls and scuffed wood floors — the message seems to be that the food here is what shines. Lovers of fine cuisine will delight in the menu, which changes daily. At lunch recently, my daughter and I enjoyed Ontario beetroot and Quebec endive salad accompanied by toasted walnuts, soft blue cheese, apple cider reduction and chives, and warm in-house–smoked Atlantic sea trout with Yukon gold potato rosti, pommery mustard crème fraîche, capers, and shaved red onion. Dinner delights may include roasted red pepper bisque, Quebec bobwhite quail, or pan-roasted Plantagenet red deer. Service is friendly and efficient. Next door is the Domus kitchenware store; enter through the restaurant or from the street. It's a gourmet's delight.

87 Murray St. ℂ **613/241-6007.** Main courses C$23–C$28 (US$19–US$23). AE, DC, MC, V. Mon–Sat 11:30am–2pm and 5:30–9:00pm; Sun 11am–2:30pm and 5:30–9pm.

Luxe Bistro ✦ BISTRO   One of the top newer restaurants in Ottawa, Luxe attracts everyone from couples to girls' nights out to men in suits, with the only common theme being a youngish demographic. The club beat of the background music feels strangely at odds with the upscale dining room decor, but patrons don't seem to notice. The menu is extensive and imaginative, covering off the classic bistro dishes and adding in a few fresh ideas. Ravioli filled with duck confit, served with toasted hazelnuts, sun-dried tomatoes, and crisp sage in a brown butter reduction is flavorful and satisfying. Oysters on the half shell, a choice of steaks, and braised lamb shank are but a few of the menu choices. The olive bread is divine, and the kitchen can rustle up a mean crème brûlée. The wine list has won acclaim, and features no fewer than 30 wines by the glass. Wine "flights" — a selection of three 3-oz. glasses—range from C$14 to $C19 (US$12–US$16).

47 York St. ℂ **613/241-8805.** Reservations recommended. AE, DC, MC, V. Main courses C$13–C$40 (US$11–US$33). Daily 11:30am–late. May be closed Sun in winter.

Signatures ✦✦✦ FRENCH   If you seek an exemplary classic French cuisine dining experience, look no further than Signatures, the only Le Cordon Bleu restaurant in North America. The restaurant is located in an elegant, impeccably restored Victorian mansion within Le Cordon Bleu Paris Ottawa Culinary Arts Institute. Expectations are rightfully high, and both the kitchen and the service excel. A truly memorable evening awaits. When I had the pleasure of dining here, I enjoyed langoustines (scampi) with a delicate tomato accompaniment, followed by Atlantic sole — finished in the pan and filleted at tableside — served with Manitoba wild rice and winter-squash cream. A dainty *l'amuse bouche* preceded the meal, and a selection of Québécois cheeses and a light chocolate mousse *mille-feuille* served with flambéed pears completed the meal. I recommend finishing the evening with *petit fours* and coffee.

453 Laurier Ave. E. ℂ **613/236-2499.** Reservations recommended. Main courses C$28–C$41 (US$23–US$34). Table d'hôte (3–7 courses) C$47–C$98 (US$39–US$80).Tues–Sat 5:30–10pm.

EXPENSIVE

Bistro 115 ✦ FRENCH   I think this restaurant, housed in an Edwardian property in the heart of the ByWard Market district, is everything a romantic restaurant should be: dark wood, deep burgundy walls and linens, candlelit tables, lace cloths, and formal, attentive service. In winter, a cozy fireplace adds warmth to the dining room. Summer diners often retreat to the rear courtyard, shaded by grapevines and a maple tree. The food doesn't always have the lively personality that the kitchens in the Black Tomato and Domus inject into their creations, which makes the prices here a bit hard to swallow. Best value is the mid-day *table d'hôte,* which gives you a choice of soup or salad and one of four main courses for C$15 to C$18 (US$12–US$15).

110 Murray St. ℂ **613/562-7244.** Reservations recommended. Main courses C$17–C$28 (US$14–US$23). AE, MC, V. Mon–Sat 11:30am–9:30pm; Sun 10:30am–9pm.

The Black Tomato ✮✮ BISTRO   This is one of the best places to eat in the ByWard Market area, with top marks for the food and the surroundings. The kitchen has heaps of culinary talent, so prepare yourself for a hedonistic meal. When the weather is warm, I escape to the back patio in the picturesque cobblestone courtyard, sip on a microbrew beer, and lazily munch on one of their delightful salads. Arrive early, because the place gets extremely busy, especially in the evening.

11 George St. ℂ **613/789-8123.** Reservations accepted for parties of eight or more only. Main courses C$15–C$28 (US$12–US$23). AE, DC, MC, V. Mon–Sat 11:30am–late; Sun 11:00am–late.

Hard Rock Cafe ✮ AMERICAN   If you're a rock music fan, you'll find the collection of memorabilia from rock's most legendary performers jaw-dropping. Make sure you take the time to stroll around the place, and don't miss upstairs. There are posters, jackets, records, instruments, and other bits and pieces on display. I was impressed by signed guitars from Brian May of Queen and David Bowie, but if your taste in music runs in a different direction you'll get a thrill or two no matter what your age. Rock videos blare from TV screens, and when the restaurant is busy the atmosphere is charged. There are two outdoor patios for summer toe-tapping and tabletop drumming. But stop singing along long enough to eat — burgers, steaks, fajitas, chicken breasts, and pot roast are all menu favorites. And how good is their hot-fudge sundae, made with the Hard Rock Cafe's unbelievably rich signature ice cream? You'll just have to try it for yourself. For Hard Rock Cafe merchandise, including the legendary T-shirts, stop into the shop just inside the entrance on the left.

73 York St. ℂ **613/241-2442.** Main courses C$10–C$27 (US$8–US$22). AE, DC, MC, V. Daily 11:30am–late.

Zoe's Lounge ✮✮✮ AFTERNOON TEA   There is nothing more civilized than afternoon tea, and the Château Laurier does it exceptionally well, from the white linen to the silver tea service and waiters in waistcoats and bow ties. Tea is served in the afternoon in the glass-enclosed atrium, which is   part of Zoe's Lounge (on the east side of the main hotel lobby). Choose among traditional English tea, Canadian high tea, or champagne tea. Each menu has a generous selection of dainty finger sandwiches, Victorian scones with Devonshire cream and strawberry jam, fresh fruit, and cakes and pastries. The Canadian high tea incorporates maple syrup into some recipes and includes a Canadian cheese board. When it's time to choose your tea for drinking, a white-gloved waiter will wheel the tea trolley tableside and invite you to inspect and inhale the aroma from a selection of no fewer than 13 loose teas. This is an indulgence not to be missed.

Fairmont Château Laurier, 1 Rideau St. ℂ **613/241-1414.** Reservations required for afternoon tea. C$24–C$49 (US$20–US$40) for full afternoon tea. AE, DC, MC, V. Afternoon tea Mon–Fri 3–5:30pm. Sat–Sun 2pm–5:30pm.

MODERATE

Haveli INDIAN   Popular with Ottawans, Haveli specializes in authentic Punjab cuisine, prepared by a team of chefs from various regions of India. The dining room reflects traditional Indian decor, with high-backed chairs in intricately carved dark wood, and brass plates on the tables. The buffet, served for lunch on weekdays, allows novice and experienced samplers of Indian cuisine to taste a variety of dishes, from meat curries to tandoori chicken, naan, rice, samosas, vegetables, and salads — plus those little extras that we all love to order: raita, papadums, pickles, and chutneys. Takeout is available.

39 Clarence St. ⓒ **613/241-1700.** Reservations recommended weekends only. Main courses C$8–C$14 (US$7–US$12). AE, DC, MC, V. Mon–Fri 11:45am–2:15pm and 5pm–10pm; Sat 5pm–11pm; Sun noon–2:30pm and 5–9pm. Other location: 194 Robertson Rd. ⓒ **613/820-1700.**

Mamma Grazzi's Kitchen ★★★ ITALIAN   Mamma Grazzi's is one of those rare places that serves up consistently good food in a knockout location. I've been coming here for years and have never been disappointed. Whether you like your pasta dressed with tomato, cream, or olive oil, you'll have several combinations of ingredients to choose from. Their wine-by-the-glass selection, served in chunky tumblers, changes frequently. Housed in a heritage stone building, Mamma Grazzi's is especially delightful in the summer, when you can enjoy the historical cobblestone courtyard out back. The quaint courtyard is flanked by the terraces of a few other eateries, creating a European atmosphere. Because they make everything to order you may have to wait a little, but it's worth it. The entrance to the restaurant is in a little alleyway off George Street, and you'll have to negotiate stairs wherever you eat — up to the second floor, or down to the ground floor or outdoor terrace. Arrive early for lunch or dinner if you want to avoid lineups.

25 George St. ⓒ **613/241-8656.** Main courses C$9–C$16 (US$7–US$13). AE, DC, MC, V. Daily 11:30am–late.

Oregano's Pasta Market ITALIAN   In a historical building in the heart of the market at the corner of William and George streets, Oregano's features a large dining room and two outdoor patios where you can watch the hustle and bustle of the ByWard Market while you eat. As you would expect, there's lots of pasta on the menu, including seashell pasta with shrimp, cannelloni, manicotti, tortellini, and grilled chicken with fettuccine. Servings are generous, and some pasta dishes can be ordered as half-portions (my half-portion of spaghettini Bolognese was sufficiently large to keep hunger pangs at bay for the entire afternoon). Pizzas with traditional toppings hover around C$13 (US$11). The all-you-can-eat Sunday brunch buffet, served between 10:30am and 2:30pm, is an extravagant selection of appetizers, salads, pastas, and pizza.

74 George St. ⓒ **613/241-5100.** Reservations recommended for dinner. Main courses C$13–C$18 (US$11–US$15); buffet C$13 (US$11). AE, DC, MC, V. Mon–Sat 11am–11pm, Sun 10:30am–11pm.

INEXPENSIVE

BeaverTails CANADIAN   This hand-held fast-food treat, first served in 1978 in the ByWard Market, enjoys a loyal following in Ottawa. Beaver Tails are flat, deep-fried pastries shaped like — you guessed it — a beaver tail, with toppings like drizzled chocolate, cinnamon and sugar, garlic, and cheese (but not all on the same tail!). They sell well in all seasons, but our family likes them best outdoors on a cold, crisp, sunny winter day when we've worked up an appetite from skating or skiing (you'll also find locations at Blue Mountain ski resort in Ontario and Mont Tremblant in Quebec). If you're more of an indoor kind of person, the St. Laurent Shopping Centre in Ottawa also has a stall. The opening and closing times are somewhat weather- and crowd-dependent, and may vary by an hour or so from the times listed below.

87 George St. ⓒ **613/241-1230.** Most items under C$10 (US$8). Summer daily 10am–late. Winter Mon–Wed 11am–5:30pm; Thurs–Sun 10am–late.

The French Baker/Le Boulanger Français & Benny's Bistro

BAKERY/CAFE   Reputed to have the flakiest, richest, most buttery croissants in the city, the French Baker also has authentic baguettes and other bread and pastry items. If you venture down the long corridor to the back of the small bakery, you'll find a chic gourmet food shop. Selection is limited but delicious. French and Québécois cheeses are available, and you can sit and sip a coffee or sample the light fare. In 2001, this small space was dubbed Benny's Bistro and began offering lunches and snacks between 8am and 4pm.

119 Murray St. ℂ **613/789-7941** (Bakery), **613/789-6797** (Benny's Bistro). Most items under C$10 (US$8). AE, MC, V. Bakery open Mon–Fri 7am–6:30pm, Sat–Sun 8am–5:30pm. Benny's Bistro Mon–Fri 8–11am and 11:30am–2:30pm; Sat–Sun 8–10:30am coffee & croissants; 10:30am–2:30pm brunch.

Marchélino   ✸✸ ECLECTIC

This unique restaurant, situated just inside the east entrance of the Rideau Centre, offers an eclectic mix of gourmet fast food served up at various market-style stalls. It's an assault on the senses to wander among the colorful displays of fruits, salads, breads, and pastries, and watch the staff at work rolling out dough, baking bread, roasting chickens, sliding pizzas in and out of the stone hearth oven, and assembling sushi. The extensive selection of food to eat in or take out includes chocolate croissants, muffins, cinnamon buns, scrambled eggs with ham and chives, at least seven varieties of soup, custom-made sandwiches with five kinds of bread and a dozen fillings, grain-fed roasted chickens, pizza with classic or adventurous toppings, Yukon gold fries, and pasta. Try the rosti, a Swiss dish of shredded potato, pan-fried golden brown and topped with smoked salmon, chicken, or sour cream. The crepes are highly recommended. Just tell the cook your choice of fillings and toppings — try bananas, vanilla ice cream and chocolate sauce, or fresh strawberries and crème anglaise. Portions are generous. Even the coffee is upscale here — each cup is ground and brewed individually. Since you order items from different stations as you wander around the marché, keep an eye on the purchase price of each selection — I will warn you, everything looks so tempting, you can quickly run up quite a large bill.

50 Rideau St. (in the Rideau Centre, ground floor). ℂ **613/569-4934.** Most items under C$10 (US$8). AE, MC, V. Daily 7:30am–9pm.

Le Moulin de Provence BAKERY/CAFE

At the north end of the ByWard Market building lies this wonderful mix of bakery, cafe, and patisserie. The atmosphere is comfy and cozy. Your only problem will be deciding what to choose from the gleaming display cases of artfully crafted baked goods, pastries, salads, and delicatessen items. Warm your hands around a bowl of café au lait and nibble on a delicate French pastry while you watch the shoppers bustle past the windows in the midst of the market. Then grab some cheese or paté, tuck a baguette under your arm, and head home for lunch in the true European manner.

55 ByWard Market. ℂ **613/241-9152.** Most items under C$10 (US$8). V. Daily 7am–7pm.

Oh So Good Desserts & Coffee House DESSERTS

The delectable desserts are tucked away in a shiny glass showcase toward the rear of the cafe. On the day we visited, we counted 34 different cakes. There's only one serving size, which is huge, so bring a friend along unless you have a hefty appetite. If you order at least one day ahead, you can take the whole cake home. Selections may include raspberry white chocolate cheesecake, Dutch apple pie, lemon meringue torte, and cakes loaded with chocolate. Evenings tend to be busy, since it's a popular spot to hang out after dinner.

25 York St. ✆ **613/241-8028.** Most items under C$10 (US$8). AE, MC, V. Mon–Thurs 2–11pm, Fri 2pm–midnight or 1am, Sat noon–midnight or 1am, Sun noon–11pm.

Peace Garden Café VEGETARIAN   A tiny oasis in the leafy inner court of the Times Square Building, Peace Garden is a great place to retreat when you feel the need to escape from noisy city streets. There are a few small tables in the courtyard next to a tinkling fountain and a counter with stools. If you're hungry, soup, salads, sandwiches, and a variety of Indian, Malaysian, Italian, and Greek specialties will fit the bill. It's also a great place just to sip a spicy Indian chai tea or a cool, fresh mango *lassi* (yogurt drink). To boost your energy after a day of sightseeing, ask the server to recommend one of their power juices. Closing hours sometimes vary seasonally.

47 Clarence St. ✆ **613/562-2434.** Most items under C$10 (US$8). AE, MC, V. Thurs–Tues 9am–8pm; Wed 9am–6:30pm.

Piccolo Grande ICE CREAM   Dream up any flavor of gelato and the folks at Piccolo Grande will do their best to make it for you, although you may have to give them a few days to work on it. If it's one of their regular flavors (they have almost 80, so they can't keep them all in the store at once) and you'd like a liter (quart) or more, they will try to get it for you within 48 hours. Of course, they may already make your ultimate ice cream. Close your eyes and think of amaretto, mochaccino, pear, or zabaglione. If you want to appeal to your inner child, there's caramel chocolate chip, banana peanut butter, pumpkin, cinnamon, or strawberries and cream. Like fruit? Try apple, grape, or tangerine sorbet, or cranberry, mango, or honeydew melon sherbet. You can eat a tasty and inexpensive lunch here, too. Homemade soups, salads, and Italian sandwiches are all available to eat in or take out. There are only 40 seats inside, and lunchtime can get very busy. The lunch menu is available only on weekdays between 11am and 3pm. You can order Piccolo Grande's wonderful products for dessert at three restaurants — Vittoria Trattoria, at 35 William St.; Bravo Bravo, at 292 Elgin St.; and Pub Italia at 434½ Preston St. Grande's ice cream is also on the shelf at Nicastro's Groceteria, at 1558 Merivale Rd. Now start dreaming.

55 Murray St. ✆ **613/241-2909.** Most items under C$10 (US$8). AE, MC, V. Summer Mon–Sat 9am–midnight, Sun 9am–11pm. Winter Sun–Wed 9am–5pm; Thurs–Sat 9am–10pm.

Planet Coffee COFFEEHOUSE   Tucked away from the bustle of the ByWard Market district in Clarendon Lanes, this is a nice place to hang out and write all those postcards home or curl up on the padded banquettes and indulge in dessert — try the lunar lemon squares, cosmic carrot cake, or molasses cookies. Funky, casual urban decor, centred on buttermilk yellow, tangerine, and slate gray.

24A York St. ✆ **613/789-6261.** Most items under C$10 (US$8). Mon 7am–9pm; Tues–Fri 7am–10pm; Sat 7:30am–10pm; Sun 9am–7pm.

4 The Glebe

Strung along Bank Street between the Queensway and the Canal lies the trendy shopping and dining district known as the Glebe. Have your plastic ready, because there will be lots of treasures to tempt you. When you need a break from all that frenzied shopping, take refuge in a cafe, restaurant, or gourmet food shop until your energy levels begin to rise once more.

VERY EXPENSIVE

The Urban Pear ✸✸✸ CANADIAN   Once in a while, you find a restaurant where everything speaks to you, from the philosophy of the chef/owners right down to the china — a place where, in another life, you would do things in exactly the same way if you were a restaurateur. The Urban Pear is that place for me. The menu changes daily, depending on which fresh, local ingredients the chefs select. All vegetables are local and organic in the summer months, and meat and fish are exclusively Canadian. As you might expect, the pear appears frequently throughout the menu, and not only as dessert. The decor is simple, the space intimate (only 40 seats), and the service intuitive. On my lucky day, I dined on baked St. Paulin cheese and wild organic mushroom compote in filo pastry, garnished with black olive tapenade and arugula, and pan-seared East Coast scallops with fresh orange and pea shoot salad. Love it.

151 Second Ave. (© **613/569-9305.** Reservations recommended. Main courses C$22–C$31 (US$18–US$25). AE, DC, MC, V. Mon–Fri 11:30am–2pm and 5:30–9pm; Sat 5:30–9pm; Sun 11am–2pm and 5:30–9pm.

EXPENSIVE

Flippers ★ SEAFOOD Find the discreet doorway at 819 Bank St., next to Von's Bistro (see below), and climb the stairs to a fresh fish restaurant that has been serving Ottawans since 1980 — a long time in the fickle restaurant business. Seafood-restaurant staples (bay scallops, salmon, shrimp, and mussels) are treated with respect and prepared with style. Specials include Alaskan king crab legs, Arctic char, and bouillabaisse. For the less adventurous, the menu includes English-style fish and chips, grilled Atlantic salmon, and pasta. A papier-mâché mermaid perches in one corner of the room, and glass fish mobiles hang from the ceiling.

819 Bank St. (Fifth Avenue Court). (© **613/232-2703.** Reservations accepted only for parties of 6 or more. Main courses C$14–C$23 (US$12–US$19) and up. AE, DC, MC, V. Mon 5–10pm; Tues–Fri 11:30am–2pm and 5–10pm; Sat 5–10pm; Sun 5–9pm.

Infusion ★★ ECLECTIC Infusion has heaps of talent in the kitchen. Their objective is to carefully turn the spotlight on individual flavors and aromas in their dishes, rather than rushing the cooking process to serve diners quickly. Happily, they score high marks for exceptional presentation as well, making a meal at Infusion a very satisfying experience. The imaginative menu stimulates the appetite. Dishes include portobello, shiitake, and oyster mushroom strudel with Gruyère and fresh herb cream sauce, grilled lamb and baby spinach salad, and house-made Jamaican jerk pork tenderloin. The scrumptious weekend brunch is excellent value, with a choice of ten entrees at C$10 (US$8) a plate. No bacon and eggs here; these dishes will blow your taste buds away. If you like seafood, what about blue crab, ice shrimp, and Nova Scotia lobster with mascarpone cheese and fresh chives? Or for a little sophistication, order the sautéed chicken, leeks, and mushrooms with champagne Dijon velouté and wild rice pilaf. If you have a sweet tooth, you just can't pass on the baked French toast stuffed with roasted bananas, pecans, and mascarpone cheese, dipped in Kahlúa batter and served with fresh fruit. Close to heaven!

825 Bank St. (© **613/234-2412.** Reservations recommended. Main courses C$10–C$25 (US$8–US$21). AE, DC, MC, V. Mon 5–9pm, Tues–Thurs 11:30am–10pm, Fri 11:30am–11pm, Sat 10am–11:30pm, Sun 10am–9pm.

Von's Bistro BISTRO Local residents are fond patrons of this centrally located Glebe eatery. The subdued, neutral decor with caramel walls, bisque tablecloths, and an abundance of dark wood is accented with chalkboard-covered pillars adorned with amusing and thought-provoking quotations. Lunch fare is light and quick — bagels, wraps, pasta, quiches, and omelets. In the evening, indulge in homemade ravioli, grain-fed chicken, *moules et frites* (mussels and french fries) with a choice of broths, or red snapper.

819 Bank St. © **613/233-3277.** Reservations accepted only for parties of 6 or more; reservations not accepted for weekend brunch. Main courses C$16–C$25 (US$13–US$21). AE, DC, MC, V. Mon–Fri 11:30am–3pm and 5–10pm; Sat–Sun 8:30am–3pm and 5–10pm.

MODERATE

The Canal Ritz ✿ ITALIAN   With its converted boathouse setting, the Canal Ritz offers a constantly changing view of the Rideau Canal. In summer, boats sail past the tables on the spacious terrace, and in winter, skaters glide past on the world's longest skating rink. For lunch, try the Canal Ritz salad with fresh salad greens, herb-marinated shrimp, feta, cucumber, and tomatoes. The bread here is wonderful — loaves are satisfyingly dense, with a hint of sweetness and a crisp but not crumbly crust. Thin-crust designer pizza offers a choice of funky toppings such as pears and brie, smoked salmon, and asparagus. The restaurant perches on the edge of the canal, with the Queen Elizabeth Driveway sweeping past the front door. You'll find the parking lot on the southwest corner of Fifth Avenue and Queen Elizabeth Driveway, directly opposite the restaurant.

375 Queen Elizabeth Dr. © **613/238-8998.** Reservations recommended. Main courses C$10–C$18 (US$8–US$15). AE, DC, MC, V. Daily 11:30am–10:30pm.

INEXPENSIVE

Kettleman's Bagels BAGELS   I like to come here as much for the entertainment of watching the bakers at work as for the Montreal-style bagels. From the mounds of dough, bakers cut off strips, hand-roll them into circles, and slide them into the open wood-burning oven on long planks. The freshly baked bagels are delicious simply spread with cream cheese, but Kettleman's doesn't stop there. There's a choice of more than a dozen sandwiches, including two classics — smoked salmon, cream cheese, tomato, and onion, and the house special with hot Montreal smoked meat and sweet mustard. There are two additional locations: Carling Avenue in the west end and Place d'Orléans Drive in the east end. They never close, so you can satisfy hunger pangs at any time of the day or night.

912 Bank St. © **613/567-7100.** Most items under C$10 (US$8). Daily 24 hours. Other locations: 2177 Carling Ave. © **613/722-4357;** 1222 Place d'Orléans Dr. © **613/841-4409.**

Wild Oat Bakery and Natural Foods BAKERY   If you're into whole foods, health foods, or anything in between, you must drop in here if you're in the Glebe. The bakery, grocery shelves, and takeout sections are in the original location on the corner of Bank Street, and a casual, funky healthy-eating restaurant has opened in the space next door, with a connecting doorway between the two. Ready-to-eat small pizzas, samosas, soups, crepes, or chili make a good light lunch, and you can follow them with brownies, squares, or one of the large cookies lined up in wicker baskets on the counter — I've sampled the chocolate chip, peanut butter, ginger, maple and hemp seed, and oatmeal raisin and haven't found a dud among them. Wheat-free, yeast-free, and naturally sweetened baked goods are available. Browse the shelves for organic pasta, 100% organic fresh produce, and other healthy food items.

817 Bank St. © **613/232-6232.** Most items under C$10 (US$8). Mon–Fri 8am–8pm (9pm in summer), Sat–Sun 8am–6pm.

Coffee Break

Old-fashioned coffee and donut shops still abound in small-town Ontario, but in the big cities chains with a more sophisticated (and expensive!) twist dominate downtown street corners. In Ottawa, **Second Cup** and **Starbucks** are the names you're most likely to see downtown. The coffee-based drinks in these trendy cafes tend to be tasty, but by the time you've downed your double decaf mocha latte with extra foam and a biscotti, the bill for your much-needed jolt of caffeine may be a little hard to swallow. Keep your eyes open for **Tim Hortons,** a more down-to-earth chain in terms of coffee selection and prices. There are a couple of downtown locations, but most branches are out in the suburbs, where they attract drive-through business in droves. Tim's serves great donuts and reliable drip-filter coffee, as well as inexpensive sandwiches, soups, and chili. Another trend in the coffeehouse biz is the enthusiastic promotion of humanitarian and environmental values. Local coffee-house **Bridgehead,** with four Ottawa locations, prides itself on serving exclusively organic, fair trade, shade-grown coffee, although not all their food and beverage products are organic. Other coffeehouses are beginning to offer similar products, as the image of coffee drinking continues to strengthen its link with social responsibility.

5 Wellington Street West

This residential neighborhood west of downtown is quieter than the Glebe, but there are also unique little shops to be found here (see chapter 8, "Shopping"). Spend some time strolling the street and refuel at the eateries below. Watch for the seasonal farmers' market on Parkdale Avenue, where you can browse for local fresh produce daily from April to September.

INEXPENSIVE

Bridgehead COFFEEHOUSE   This is one of four local coffeehouses operated by Ottawa-based Bridgehead, a company that strives to put social responsibility first through its philosophy of doing business with small-scale farmers and purchasing only fairly traded, organic, and shade-grown coffees. So feel free to soothe your conscience while sipping your favorite brew. Spice, pumpkin, and clay tones are the predominant decorating colors. The cafe is a wireless network hotspot — laptops are welcome table companions. Light fare in the form of sandwiches, scones, oatmeal cookies, and carrot cake are served up alongside the usual array of urban coffee-based drinks. If you're a chai fan, you can get a better than average version here.

1277 Wellington St. W. ℂ **613/725-5500.** Most items under C$10 (US$8). MC, V. Mon–Sat 6:30am–10pm; Sun 8am–9pm.

Ottawa Bagelshop & Deli BAGELS   Here, you'll find bagels and much, much more. This is a food retailer of many hats — bakery, deli, cafe, and gourmet food shop. The food shop is a warren of shelves jam-packed with a bewildering variety of ethnic goodies. Venture toward the back and you'll discover the bagel counter, where you can buy bags of many-flavored bagels to take home. Turn right and up the steps to enter the eat-in section. A European coffee counter, a buffet table with hot and cold food, and a sandwich counter round off the simple eatery. Try the cheese blintzes — they're light and creamy with just a touch of sweetness. The place is a true neighborhood haunt, catering to everyone from schoolchildren to mothers with babies to seniors.

1321 Wellington St. W. ⓒ **613/722-8753.** Most items under C$10 (US$8). AE, MC, V. Mon–Thurs and Sat 6:30am–7pm, Fri 6:30am–8pm, Sun 6:30am–6pm.

Parma Ravioli TAKEOUT   With its spacious open kitchen behind the retail counter, Parma Ravioli is an entertaining place. You're likely to see something different each time you visit. Cooks in white jackets and tall hats knead dough, mix pasta fillings, and assemble ravioli right before your eyes. After you've finished watching the show, take home oodles of Italian goodies — bread, rolls, foccacia, fresh pasta, ravioli, lasagna, manicotti, pasta sauces, and Italian desserts.

1314 Wellington St. W. ⓒ **613/722-6003.** Most items under C$10 (US$8). Mon–Wed 9am–6pm, Thurs–Fri 9am–6:30pm, Sat 9am–6pm, Sun 10am–5pm.

The Table ★★ *Value* VEGETARIAN   In a large, bright cafeteria-style dining room with a generous number of country kitchen pine tables and chairs, you can eat for health and still enjoy the food. The Table has a wide selection of tasty vegetarian dishes arranged buffet-style. Grab a tray and sample soups, salads, meatless main courses, baked goods, and more. Vegan and gluten-free items are available. Organic ingredients are used whenever possible. Whole grains are emphasized, and maple syrup, molasses, and honey are used in place of refined sugar. You can also fill takeout containers if you fancy a picnic or want to stock up your fridge.

1230 Wellington St. W. ⓒ **613/729-5973.** Also at 261 Dalhousie St. ⓒ 613/244-1100. Price by weight C$18 (US$15) per kg (2.2 lb.). AE, MC, V. Daily 11am–9pm..

Thyme & Again ★★ *Finds* TAKEOUT/CAFE   Thyme & Again is a delightful place to browse, shop, and debate over which scrumptious dishes to take home and enjoy. At the front of the shop there's a small but select display of gifts and home accessories. If you're visiting during the Christmas season, you must drop in to see their unique selection of decorations. The take-home menu changes weekly and features a choice of seasonal soups, three salads, five side dishes, six main courses, and a dip and vinaigrette of the week. The list reads like a fine-dining menu — baked eggplant salad with sweet peppers and honey-cumin dressing, green beans with pesto butter and pine nuts, grilled beef tenderloin with sun-dried-cherry port-rosemary jus, and baked fillet of salmon with grapefruit and mint. Dreamy desserts include white chocolate cranberry velvet tart, chocolate hazelnut mousse cake, and praline cheesecake. You can also savor the pleasure of an espresso and biscotti at one of the tiny tables tucked into the front corner of the shop. When skies are clear, sunlight streams through the windows. A very pleasant spot to while away the time.

1255 Wellington St. W. ⓒ **613/722-6277.** Most items under C$10 (US$8). AE, DC, MC, V. Mon–Fri 8am–8pm, Sat 9am–6pm, Sun 10am–5pm.

6 Chinatown

Ottawa's Asian community has settled primarily around Somerset Street West. The main street is lined with Asian grocery stores and restaurants. Highlighting just a few eateries is a difficult task because there are so many good places to find Asian food in the city, and not all are in Chinatown.

MODERATE

New Mee Fung ✸ VIETNAMESE   Meticulous attention to detail in the composition and presentation of the dishes results in a memorable dining experience. This small restaurant is clean, simply furnished, and casual. Lots of finger foods, dishes that require assembly (you can roll up your chicken in semi-transparent rice pancakes), and chopsticks to master. Each dish on the extensive menu is coded: just jot down the numbers on the scrap of paper the smiling server gives you and wait for a splendid feast to arrive. Many dishes feature grilled chicken, beef, and pork, and there's a good selection of soups, spring rolls, salads, and noodles. Our grilled marinated chicken was accompanied by fresh mint, basil, and lettuce; soft, paper-thin disks made from rice flour for wrapping morsels of food; glass noodles sprinkled with chopped peanuts, carrots, bean sprouts, and cucumber salad; and delicately flavored dipping sauce. Takeout is available.

350 Booth St. ✆ **613/567-8228.** Main courses C$5–C$12 (US$4–US$10). MC, V. Wed–Mon 10am–10pm.

Shanghai Restaurant ✸ ASIAN   Serving a mixture of Cantonese, Szechuan, and Asian dishes, Shanghai is one of the top restaurants in Ottawa's Chinatown. You'll find some familiar Canadian-Chinese dishes on the menu, but allow yourself to be tempted by spicy Thai chicken with sweet basil, ginger teriyaki vegetable fried rice, Shanghai crispy beef, or shrimp with bok choy and roasted garlic. The coconut-curry vegetables in a spicy peanut sauce go well with a bowl of steamed rice. On Thursday evenings after 8pm the menu switches to finger foods and light snacks as a twentysomething crowd moves in to listen to a DJ spin tunes until 1am. Occasional Karaoke nights. Takeout is available.

651 Somerset St. W. ✆ **613/233-4001.** Reservations recommended weekends only. Main courses C$7–C$15 (US$5–US$10). AE, MC, V. Tues–Wed 11:30am–2pm and 4:30pm–11pm, Thurs–Fri 11:30am–2pm and 4:30pm–1am, Sat 4:30pm–1am, Sun 4:30–10:30pm.

Yangtze CHINESE   Both Cantonese and Szechuan cuisine are served in this spacious dining room. Large, round tables will seat 8 to 10 comfortably, and a Lazy Susan in the center of the table allows everyone to help him- or herself from the communal dishes. Families and groups are welcome here for all-day dining. Many dishes familiar to North American diners are on the menu — kung po shrimp, sweet-and-sour chicken, broccoli with scallops, beef with snow peas, chow mein, and fried rice. House specialties include chicken in black-bean sauce, pepper steak, and Imperial spareribs. Takeout is available.

700 Somerset St. W. ✆ **613/236-0555.** Reservations recommended. C$12–C$16 (US$10–US$13). AE, DC, MC, V. Mon–Thurs 11am–midnight, Fri 11am–1am, Sat 10am–1am, Sun 10am–midnight.

7 Little Italy

Preston Street, also known as Corso Italia, is the heart of Ottawa's Little Italy. Food is the soul of Italy, and when you stroll up one side of Preston Street and down the other you'll pass by plenty of *ristorantes, trattorie,* and *caffès.* Many of them have outdoor patios, and all offer a warm Mediterranean welcome. I've selected a formal fine-dining restaurant, a smart-casual restaurant with a summer terrace, a neighborhood cafe, and a pasta shop to give you a taste of Corso Italia. Explore on your own and you'll discover many more treasures.

EXPENSIVE

La Roma ✸✸ ITALIAN   A well-established Preston Street *ristorante,* La Roma has a solid reputation for good-quality traditional Italian cuisine. The elegant ivory and burgundy dining room is sophisticated and charming. Service is impeccable. Choose from a wide variety of chicken, veal, pasta, and other Italian specialties, accompanied by Italian bread. The all-Italian wine list is impressive in both its length and variety. I recommend the breast of chicken with lemon sauce, with a light, creamy, and dreamy tiramisu to follow and a robust espresso as the grand finale.

430 Preston St. ℂ **613/234-8244.** Reservations recommended. Main courses C$13–C$23 (US$11–US$19). AE, DC, MC, V. Mon–Thurs 11:30am–2pm and 5–10pm, Fri 11:30am–2pm and 5–11pm, Sat 5–11pm, Sun 5–10pm.

MODERATE

Ciccio Caffé ITALIAN   Ciccio takes pride in its traditional Italian menu featuring fresh pasta (lasagna, cannelloni, and linguine) and desserts made on the premises. Traditional Italian dishes include rabbit with mushrooms in white wine, *osso buco,* and roast veal. In the summer, patrons love the ambience of the outdoor terrace.

330 Preston St. ℂ **613/232-1675.** Reservations recommended. Main courses C$10–C$19 (US$8–US$16). AE, DC, MC, V. Sun–Thurs 11am–10pm; Fri 11am–11pm; Sat noon–11pm.

INEXPENSIVE

Luciano's 👫👫 TAKEOUT   Near the top of Preston Street, just north of Somerset Street West, you'll find Luciano's. Park behind the building (enter the parking lot off Somerset) and stock up on ravioli, agnolotti, and tortellini stuffed with yummy fillings like sun-dried tomato, spinach and ricotta, and butternut squash. Choose fresh spaghetti, fettuccine, linguine, or rigatoni and homemade sauces — Bolognese, clam, tomato, putanesca, mushroom, pesto, or roasted red pepper. Buy oven-ready portions of lasagna or cannelloni, a baguette, olive oil, balsamic vinegar, and a tub of gelato, and you have an instant Italian dinner — home-cooked meals should always be so easy! Next door to the take-home food shop you'll find Luciano's Italian supermarket.

106 Preston St. ℂ **613/236-7545.** Most items under C$10 (US$8). MC, V. Mon 1–6pm, Tues–Thurs 9am–6pm, Fri 9am–7pm, Sat 9am–5:30pm.

Pasticceria Gelateria Italiana Ltd. 👫 ICE CREAM/CAFE   A decidedly European atmosphere prevails in this mix of pastry shop, ice-cream store, and neighborhood cafe. You'll hear Italian spoken as older-generation local residents come for the social hour to exchange news over their espressos. The beautifully sculpted Italian pastries are a feast for the eyes as well as the stomach. For a filling and inexpensive lunch, the hot pasta bar is only C$7.50 (US$6); price includes a panini roll. The homemade gelato is superb — try the mandarin orange. In fine weather, you can while away an hour or two on the large sheltered terrace.

200 Preston St. ℂ **613/233-6199.** Most items under C$10 (US$8). MC, V. Mon–Sat 7:30am–10pm, Sun 8am–10pm. Closes at 11pm daily in summer.

8 Farther Out

Here are two more places to try. They're no more than a 10- or 15-minute drive from downtown.

MODERATE

Pelican Fishery & Grill 👫 SEAFOOD   You know the fish is fresh at this place — you walk right by the eye-catching display of fresh fish and seafood on the way to your table. The premises operate as a fishmonger on one side and restaurant on the other. Decor is simple and casual. The menu changes every day, depending on what's available. Grilled trout with wasabi and dill cream sauce accompanied by herbed potatoes and mixed vegetables was featured the day we were there, and the fish was expertly cooked. In the evening, main courses are a little fancier. Paella, steamed sea bass, broiled scallops, and cedar-roasted Atlantic salmon fillet are often listed.

1500 Bank St. (in the Blue Heron Mall). ℰ **613/526-0995.** Reservations recommended. Main courses C$11–C$20 (US$9–US$16). AE, DC, MC, V. Mon–Sat 11:30am–3:30pm, 4:30–9pm; Sun 5–8:30pm.

INEXPENSIVE

The Green Door ⭐ VEGETARIAN   This casual eatery has tables set up cafeteria-style and a U-shaped buffet with a dessert station in the middle. Grab a tray and wander past hot vegetable stir-fries, tofu dishes, pastas, salads, breads, fresh fruits, cakes, and pies. If you're not a dedicated vegetarian but you've always wanted to try tofu or soy milk, here's your chance. A lot of the offerings are certified organic. You won't see meat anywhere, and if dishes contain dairy products there's a sign to let you know. Pricing is easy — just hand your plate to the cashier and you'll be charged by weight. With prices set at C$17.50 (US$14) a kilogram (2.2 lb.), your stomach will be full before your wallet is empty. If you're heading out to a park, put together a picnic lunch. Servers will supply takeout containers and paper bags.

198 Main St. ℰ **613/234-9597.** C$17.50 (US$14) per kg (2.2 lb.). AE, DC, MC, V. Tues–Sun 11am–9pm.

9 On the Quebec Side

While you may find the hotels pretty much the same on one side of the Ottawa River as the other, if you have a fondness for French cuisine you really must cross over to the Quebec side. I've singled out four places here: a traditional *crêperie,* a solid example of authentic French-country cooking, a small cafe serving European-style beverages, and a classy bistro. You may also like to try the following places for French cuisine: **Café Henry Burger** ℰ **819/777-5646** (fine dining in elegant surroundings), **Café Jean Sébastien** ℰ **819/771-2934** (romantic setting), **Laurier sur Montcalm** ℰ **819/775-5030** (French regional cuisine), and **Le Tartuffe** ℰ **819/776-6424** (formal fine dining).

EXPENSIVE

Le 1908 ⭐⭐ FRENCH   When you enter Le 1908, you'll find a small wine bar overlooking the large sunken dining room. The ceiling in the main dining area is extremely high, making the room open and spacious. Wood is everywhere: cherry trim, blond wood floors, functional wooden chairs. Crisp white table linens complete the picture. Diners can watch the chefs at work in the open kitchen at the rear; a huge chalkboard listing the day's specials hangs above. Classic French dishes include *boeuf bourguignon, steak tartare,* braised lamb shank, and cassoulet with duck confit. For dessert, sample profiteroles or *tarte au fromage.* There is a pay parking lot next door to the restaurant. Service is commendable.

70 promenade du Portage, Gatineau (Hull Sector). ℰ **819/770-1908.** Reservations recommended. Main courses C$16–C$27 (US$13–US$22). AE, DC, MC, V. Mon–Wed 11:30am–10pm, Thurs 11:30am–11pm, Fri 11:30am–midnight, Sat 5:30–11pm.

Le Pied de Cochon ⭐⭐ FRENCH   Begin with a simple green salad, *moules marinière,* or rabbit terrine. Progress to roast leg of lamb, grilled steak with tarragon, or veal medallions with chanterelles. Complement the remainder of your bottle of wine with a fine selection of cheese. Indulge in a fine, rich, crème brûlée — and above all, linger. For francophones, eating is a serious business and must not be rushed. The decor is comfortable but unremarkable and the atmosphere is smart-casual. Service is satisfyingly attentive: your needs will be anticipated, but the intimacy of your meal is not intruded upon. Free parking is available beside the restaurant. In summer, there is a terrace in front. Book ahead to avoid disappointment.

248 rue Montcalm, Gatineau (Hull Sector). ℭ **819/777-5808.** Reservations recommended. Main courses C$19 (US$16); three-course table d'hôte from C$29 (US$24). AE, DC, MC, V. Tues–Fri 11:30am–2:30pm and 6–10pm, Sat 6–10pm.

MODERATE

L'Argoät ✪✪✪ CREPERIE   The owner's ancestry is Breton (the Brittany region of France), and this authentic *crêperie,* from its French-country decor to the old prints on the walls and the Breton cider served in bowls, is a fine tribute to the old country. The menu has a satisfyingly long list of "galettes" (savory crepes made with buckwheat flour) and filled with delectable combinations such as Camembert and potatoes, or venison, wild mushroom, and sautéed onions. Toppings for the sweet crepes, which are made with white flour, include caramelized apples flambéed with Calvados, sweet chestnut purée and whipped cream, or preserved oranges and chocolate sauce. Aside from crepes, a limited choice of beef, chicken, or fish of the day is offered. But trust me, the crepes rule here. And the service is charming.

39A rue Laval, Gatineau (Hull Sector). ℭ **819/771-6170.** Main courses C$5–C$17 (US$4–US$14). Mon–Fri 11:30am–2pm and 5:30–10:30pm; Sat 5:30–10:30pm.

INEXPENSIVE

Café La Brûlerie ✪ COFFEEHOUSE   For expertly prepared European-style coffee-based drinks, pay a visit to La Brûlerie. More than three dozen beans and blends are available, and they are roasted onsite. Take home whole beans or have them ground to your specifications. Specialty teas, *cafetières,* and coffee mugs also for sale. Soups, sandwiches, and salads are available daily until 6pm. Chocolate-dipped biscuits and cakes go well with a latte or café au lait.

152 rue Montcalm, Gatineau (Hull Sector). ℭ **819/778-0109.** Most items under C$10 (US$8). MC, V. Daily 7:30am–11pm.

Gourmet on the Go

Ottawa must have a lot of enthusiastic resident foodies, because the number of top-quality upper-end food retailers and specialty shops is satisfyingly high. For visitors looking for a quick but delicious meal to take home to their hotel suite, or for portable food for a picnic, this is good news. The obvious place to head to first is the **ByWard Market Square.** In spring, summer, and fall, local farmers proudly sell their produce. The quality is exceptional. An abundance of fresh flowers in season adds color and fragrance to the market atmosphere. Inside the ByWard Market building are a number of specialty food shops, including the delightful **Tea Store** ℭ **613/241-1291,** which has an abundance of all things tea. **Godiva Chocolatier Inc.** in the Rideau Shopping

Centre, adjacent to the ByWard Market ✆ **613/234-4470,** has exquisite chocolate confectionery. You'll pay dearly for the experience, but it's worth every penny. **A Culinary Conspiracy,** 541 Rideau St. ✆ **613/241-3126,** offers gourmet food on the go in a renovated Victorian house. Their constantly changing menu is innovative and delectable. **Epicuria Fine Food Store and Catering,** 419 Mackay St. ✆ **613/745-7356,** also has an imaginative and ever-changing selection of take-home soups, side dishes, main courses, and desserts. **Thyme & Again** at 1255 Wellington St. W. ✆ **613/722-6277** is a take-home food shop and catering establishment. You can choose soups, salads, side dishes, main courses, and desserts from an ever-changing menu. **Le Cordon Bleu Ottawa Culinary Arts Institute,** at 453 Laurier Ave. E. ✆ **613/236-2433,** offers a variety of cooking classes, or you can dine in the gastronomic restaurant featuring fine French cuisine. The **LCBO (Liquor Control Board of Ontario)** has an incredible retail outlet at 275 Rideau St. ✆ **613/789-5226,** including two floors of wines, beers, and liquors from around the world. Gifts and accessories are also available. Educational programs and demonstrations include Tuscan cuisine, tutored Scotch tastings, wine appreciation, and cocktail preparation. **Loblaw's Vanier Market,** 100 McArthur Ave. ✆ **613/744-0705,** opened in 2001. This is your best bet in the downtown area for grocery staples. **Luciano's,** at 106 Preston St. ✆ **613/236-7545,** has a wide range of homemade pasta and delectable sauces. Oven-ready lasagna and cannelloni, plus gelato, olive oil, bread — it's a gourmet must-go. If you're a fan of fresh fish and seafood, pay a visit to **Pelican Fishery** (also a restaurant) at 1500 Bank St. in the Blue Heron Mall ✆ **613/526-0995.**

What to See & Do

The nation's capital and the surrounding region have so many activities both indoor and outdoor — including major attractions, national museums, parks, pathways, and festivals — you could build a jam-packed itinerary for every day of your vacation in Ottawa and still not see and do everything. But take a deep breath and make a list of your personal must-see priorities. It's much better to spend your time visiting a few attractions than to dash madly around trying to experience it all. Plan a return visit during a different time of year — each season in Ottawa has a unique personality and activities to match.

Visit some of the world-class attractions and experience Ottawa's greenspace in one of the area's many beautiful parks. You can run, walk, bike, or in-line skate along the network of pathways throughout the region (see chapter 7, "Active Ottawa"). In winter, lace up your skates and glide along the canal. If you like to shop, stroll along the famous Sparks Street pedestrian mall downtown, experience the funky neighborhood shopping districts, or head for a large suburban indoor mall (see chapter 8, "Shopping").

If you're only in Ottawa for a short break, concentrate your sightseeing in and around the downtown area. You'll find that many of the major attractions are within walking distance of each other along Wellington Street and Sussex Drive, or on streets leading off these two roads. Visit www.virtual museum.ca for a listing and brief description of some of Ottawa's museums and heritage attractions.

Don't forget that Ottawa hosts a wide variety of festivals and events, ranging from Winterlude in February to the Canadian Tulip Festival in May, to Canada Day celebrations and lots of summer festivities. See chapter 2, "Planning a Trip to Ottawa," for a list of annual events.

If this is a family vacation, keep in mind that many museums put on special programs and workshops for children and families on weekends and during school holidays (one week in mid-March, the months of July and August, and two weeks surrounding Christmas and New Year's Day). Call the **Capital Infocentre** © **800/465-1867** or © 613/239-5000 for exact dates, as they vary from year to year.

SUGGESTED ITINERARIES
If You Have 1 Day

In the summer, start the day with a parade. Head for the **Changing of the Guard** parade route along Elgin Street north of Laurier Avenue, then west on Wellington Street to **Parliament Hill** if you want to watch them march past. If your priority is watching the ceremonial guard change rather than the parade, stake your place on Parliament Hill by 9:45am (the ceremony starts at 10am). While you're there, drop by the Info Tent on the Hill and reserve a spot on a **free tour of the Centre Block of the Parliament Buildings** for later in the day. The rest of the day will have to be planned around your allocated tour time. The interior of the Parliament Buildings and the accompanying commentary are highly recommended, but if you really don't want the rest of your day's plans revolving around returning to the Hill you can forgo the tour. After the Changing of the Guard is over, head east on Wellington Street. Stop on the north side of **Plaza Bridge** and look down to view the **Ottawa Locks.** You may be lucky enough to watch a boat or two making its way through the lock system. Continue east to the magnificent **Fairmont Château Laurier Hotel.** If you're interested in period architecture and design, take a few minutes to peek inside the lobby and other public areas on the main level. Turn left along MacKenzie Avenue and take a stroll around **Major's Hill Park.** Head to the **ByWard Market district** for an early lunch at one of the dozens of restaurants. Using the pedestrian walkway, cross the **Alexandra Bridge** over the **Ottawa River** to reach the **Canadian Museum of Civilization.** Take in the spectacular view of the Parliament Buildings, the Ottawa skyline, and the Ottawa River. Explore the main exhibition halls, which will take at least a couple of hours — seeing the entire museum can take a full day. Enjoy an evening meal in one of **Gatineau/Hull's excellent French-cuisine restaurants** (reservations recommended), or head back across the Alexandra Bridge and browse the ByWard Market district, which is packed with boutiques, restaurants, and cafes.

In the winter, begin the day with a **guided tour of the Centre Block of the Parliament Buildings** (prior reservations usually not required in the winter). Take a cab to the **Canadian Museum of Civilization** or walk if you're dressed warmly. For lunch, the **Café du Musée** in the museum offers fine dining and an impressive view of the Ottawa

River and Parliament Hill. Reservations, which are recommended, can be made by calling © **819/776-7009. Café Henry Burger,** an elegant fine-dining restaurant © **819/ 777-5646,** is directly opposite the museum. Reservations are recommended. After lunch, head for the new **Canadian War Museum** (via taxi) or the **National Gallery of Canada.** The architecture of both buildings is absolutely stunning and each museum is an admirable example of the finest in its category. Later in the afternoon, lace up a pair of rental skates and take a spin on the **Rideau Canal Skateway.** If you'd rather shop, wander the **ByWard Market district** or head for the **Rideau Centre** (an indoor shopping mall).

If You Have 2 Days

On the first day, follow the itinerary above. On day 2, in the summer buy a day pass for a city tour bus — either a **double-decker bus** or **an old-fashioned trolley bus.** The buses run approximately hourly and a day pass allows you hop-on-and-off privileges along the route. Allow a couple of hours to explore one of the following: the new **Canadian War Museum,** the **National Gallery of Canada,** the **Museum of Nature,** the **Aviation Museum,** or the **Museum of Science and Technology.** Step back on the bus and enjoy an alfresco lunch at one of the many restaurants in the **ByWard Market.** In the afternoon, take a **boat tour on the Ottawa River or a Rideau Canal cruise.** If you have energy to burn, **rent in-line skates or bikes** and follow the multi-use pathways along the banks of the Rideau Canal (see the bike tours listed in chapter 7). In the winter, visit one or more of the museums recommended above or explore the Glebe shopping district along Bank Street — just make sure you wrap up well in cold weather.

If You Have 3 Days

On your third day in the Capital Region, check out any of the suggested destinations in day 1 and 2 that you haven't had time to fit in yet. If you'd rather get out of the city, head for **Gatineau Park.** You can hike, swim, and bike in the summer, enjoy the autumn leaves in September and October, or ski and snowshoe in the winter.

If You Have 4 Days or More

With a longer visit, you can build in a couple of **day trips.** Enjoy a day out on the **Hull–Chelsea–Wakefield Steam Train,** explore the towns and villages of the **Rideau Valley,** drive out to the **Diefenbunker Cold War Museum,** or head to Quebec for **downhill skiing, waterparks, or golf,** depending on the season. Chapter 10, "Exploring the Region," contains lots of ideas for active days out.

If You Have Kids with You

See the section "Especially for Kids" later in this chapter for suggestions for different age groups from toddlers to teens.

1 The Top Attractions

PARLIAMENT HILL ★★★

The **Parliament Buildings,** with their grand façade of steeply pitched copper roof panels, multiple towers, and sandstone-block construction, are an impressive sight, especially on first viewing. In 1860, Prince Edward (later King Edward VII) laid the cornerstone for the buildings, which were finished in time to host the inaugural session of the first Parliament of the new Dominion of Canada in 1867. As you enter through the main gates on Wellington Street and approach the **Centre Block** with its stately central **Peace Tower** you'll pass the Centennial Flame, lit by then–prime minister Lester B. Pearson on New Year's Eve 1966 to mark the passing of 100 years since Confederation. In June, July, and August, you can meet the **Royal Canadian Mounted Police** (affectionately called the Mounties) on Parliament Hill. They're friendly — and love to have their photo taken. If you're visiting the capital between mid-May and early September, your first stop on Parliament Hill should be the **Info Tent,** where you can pick up free information on the Hill and **free same-day tickets for tours of the Parliament Buildings.** Tickets are limited, though, and there is no guarantee in the busy summer months or weekends in spring and fall that you will get tickets for your first choice of time, or even day. If you arrive between 9 and 10am, you can usually select a tour time of your choice. Between September and May, get same-day tickets from the Visitor Welcome Centre, directly under the Peace Tower. All visitors to the buildings are required to go through a security screening system similar to that used in airports.

Where to eat: Parliament Hill is in the center of downtown Ottawa on Wellington Street, so stroll along Sparks or Elgin streets or visit the ByWard Market area for a variety of restaurants; all of these districts are no more than a 5- to 15-minute walk. From late June to early September, the West Block Courtyard is open for light refreshments (weather permitting).

Tips

During the busy summer months, drop by the information tent on the lawn in front of the Parliament Buildings between 9 and 10am. You can reserve a spot on the free tour of the Centre Block for later in the day and avoid the long lineups.

Ottawa Attractions

The Top Attractions
Parliament Hill **1**
Canadian Museum
of Civilization **2**
National Gallery **3**
Canadian Museum
of Nature **4**
Canada Science &
Technology Museum **5**
Canada Aviation Museum **6**
RCMP Rockcliffe Stables **7**
Canadian War Museum **8**
Canada Agriculture
Museum & Central
Experimental Farm **9**

Ottawa's Waterways
Rideau Canal **10A**
Rideau River **10B**
Rideau Falls **10C**
Ottawa River **10D**
Dow's Lake **10E**
Ottawa Locks **10F**
Hartwells Locks **10G**
Hog's Back
Locks & Falls **10H**

Museums & Galleries
Canada and
the World Pavilion **11**
Canadian Museum of
Contemporary Photography **12**
Canadian Postal Museum **13**
Canadian Children's
Museum **14**
Canadian Ski Museum **15**
Currency Museum
of the Bank of Canada **16**
Logan Hall, Geological Survey
of Canada **17**
National Library of Canada/
National Archives **18**
Royal Canadian Mint **19**
Lester B. Pearson Building **20**
Supreme Court of Canada **21**

Heritage Attractions
Billings Estate Museum **22**
Bytown Museum **23**
ByWard Market **24**
Laurier House **25**
Rideau Hall **26**
Turtle Island
Aboriginal Village **27**

Historic Churches
Cathedral Basilica
of Notre-Dame **28**
Christ Church Cathedral **29**
St. Andrew's
Presbyterian Church **30**

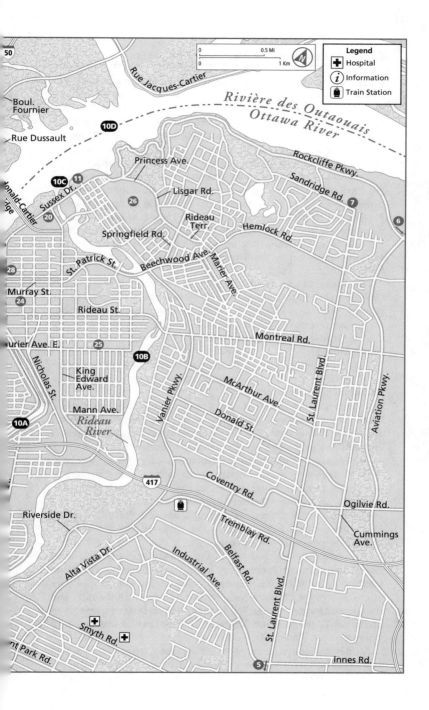

Legend
Hospital
Information
Train Station

Rivière des Outaouais
Ottawa River

Rue Jacques-Cartier

Boul. Fournier

Rue Dussault

10D

Princess Ave.

Rockcliffe Pkwy.

Sandridge Rd.

7

6

10C 11

Sussex Dr.

Lisgar Rd.

26

20

Rideau Terr.

Hemlock Rd.

Springfield Rd.

St. Patrick St.

Beechwood Ave.

Marier Ave.

28

Murray St.

24

Rideau St.

urier Ave. E.

25

Montreal Rd.

St. Laurent Blvd.

Nicholas St.

10B

King Edward Ave.

Vanier Pkwy.

McArthur Ave.

Aviation Pkwy.

Mann Ave.

Rideau River

Donald St.

10A

417

Coventry Rd.

Ogilvie Rd.

Riverside Dr.

Tremblay Rd.

Cummings Ave.

Alta Vista Dr.

Industrial Ave.

Belfast Rd.

St. Laurent Blvd.

nt Park Rd.

Smyth Rd.

Innes Rd.

5

Canada's Government: The Basics

Canada functions as a parliamentary democracy, which means its government consists of elected representatives chosen by its citizens. Based upon the British structure of federal government that was established when Canada became self-governing, the **Parliament of Canada** consists of the head of state (**Queen Elizabeth II,** who is represented by the **Governor General**), the **Senate** (the equivalent of the British House of Lords), and the **House of Commons.**

The parliamentary duties of the **Governor General** include summoning **Parliament** following each general election, announcing the current government's objectives at the beginning of each session of **Parliament** through the Speech from the Throne, and approving all bills passed by the **Senate** and the **House of Commons.** The **Senate** is made up of 105 **Senators,** who represent regions and provinces. They are appointed by the **Governor General** on the advice of the **Prime Minister.**

The **House of Commons** has 308 seats. **Members of Parliament (MPs)** are elected to represent their constituents in each of these 308 **ridings,** or political districts, for up to five years. The party that wins the greatest number of seats in the House of Commons in a federal election usually forms the government, and the party's leader becomes **Prime Minister.**

The Prime Minister appoints **Cabinet Ministers,** who are responsible for a specific portfolio, for example, health, finance, industry, the environment, or immigration.

A Parliament is made up of one or more sessions during its lifetime. Parliament sits about 27 weeks of the year, beginning in September and usually lasting until June. Breaks are scheduled to allow **Senators** and **MPs** to spend time working in their regions and ridings.

The **Senate** and the **House of Commons** each meet on a regular basis to deal with issues of national concern and to debate bills (legislative proposals) that are introduced by **Cabinet Ministers, Senators,** or **private Members. Question Period** is often the most lively part of each sitting day. During **Question Period, Cabinet Ministers** are held accountable for their department's activities and also for the policies of the **government.**

To oversee the proceedings of the **Senate** and the **House of Commons,** to maintain order, and to enforce parliamentary rules and traditions, each House has a **Speaker,** who sits on a ceremonial chair at one end of the Chamber, with the **Government** on the right and the **Opposition** on the left. The **Speaker of the Senate** is appointed on the advice of the **Prime Minister.** The **Speaker of the House of Commons** is a current **MP,** elected by peers.

Besides the federal government, whose seat is Ottawa, Canada's 10 provinces and 3 territories elect representatives to deal with matters of provincial and territorial concern. The provinces and territories combine to make a federation in which the power is distributed between the **federal government** and the **provincial legislatures.**

Tips

When Parliament is in session, you can watch the proceedings from the public galleries in both the Senate Chambers and the House of Commons. Parliament sits between September and June, although breaks are scheduled to allow members to attend to business in their constituencies and perform other duties. Call the National Infocentre at ℂ **800/465-1867** or visit www.parl.gc.ca to view the calendar of sitting days.

THE PARLIAMENT BUILDINGS ⍟⍟

Centre Block, East Block, and West Block   The Parliament Buildings consist of three blocks of buildings — the Centre Block, with its central Peace Tower, and the flanking West Block and East Block. This is the heart of Canadian political life — the workplace of the House of Commons and the Senate. When the House of Commons is sitting, you can sit in the public gallery and observe the 308 elected members debating in their grand green chamber with its tall stained-glass windows. Parliament is in recess usually from late June until early September and occasionally between September and June, including the Easter and Christmas holidays. Otherwise, the House usually sits on weekdays. The 105 appointed members of the Senate sit in a stately red chamber. A fire destroyed the original Centre Block in 1916; only the Library of Parliament was saved. The West Block, containing parliamentary offices, is closed to the public except for the Courtyard, which serves light refreshments in the summer months. You can tour the East Block, which has four historic rooms restored for public viewing: the original governor general's office, restored to the period of Lord Dufferin (1872–1878); the offices of Sir John A. Macdonald and Sir Georges-Étienne Cartier (the principal fathers of Confederation); and the Privy Council Chamber with anteroom.

Library of Parliament ⍟⍟   A glorious 16-sided dome hewn from Nepean sandstone, supported outside by flying buttresses and paneled inside with Canadian white pine, the library is designed in the Gothic Revival style and was opened in 1876. Inside, a variety of textures, colors, and hand-crafted detail is evident. The floor is an intricate parquet design of cherry, walnut, and oak. The pine paneling features thousands of carved flowers, masks, and mythical beasts. The center of the room is dominated by a white marble statue of the young Queen Victoria, created in 1871. The library has been closed to the public since 2002 to enable a large-scale conservation, rehabilitation, and upgrade project to be carried out. The project has taken great care to respect the integrity of this significant historical building; work is scheduled to be completed in 2005. Call ℂ **800/465-1867** to find out whether the Library will be open during your visit.

The Peace Tower ⍟⍟   The imposing 92-m (302-ft.) campanile of the Peace Tower is one of the most easily recognizable Canadian landmarks and dominates the Centre Block's façade. It houses a 53-bell carillon, a huge clock, an observation

Fact

There are hundreds of gargoyles, grotesques, bosses, and other unusual figures carved into the sandstone of the outer walls of the Parliament Buildings. Keep your eyes open for these entertaining sculptures.

> **Fact**
>
> One of the most laborious tasks of the renovation and repair of the Library of Parliament has been the replacement of the copper roof. The new roof will look "new" for only a couple of weeks; it will turn brown quite quickly, but it will be approximately 30 years before it achieves its final green colour. The old copper panels have been incorporated into the interior walls of the new Canadian War Museum.

deck, and the Memorial Chamber, commemorating Canada's war dead. A 10.5-m (35-ft.) bronze mast flying a Canadian flag is on top of the tower. When Parliament is in session, the tower is lit. The elevator in the tower is unusual. See if you can sense the 10-degree angle off vertical that the elevator travels for the first 29m (98 ft.) of the journey. It's well worth the trip — the views from the Observation Deck are marvelous in every direction.

Guided Tour of Centre Block ⭐⭐ Free guided tours of the **Centre Block,** which may include the **House of Commons,** the **Senate,** the **Hall of Honour,** and the **Library of Parliament,** are available in English and French all year. Guides tell animated stories and interesting anecdotes about the buildings and the people who have worked there. When Parliament is sitting, the tours do not visit the House of Commons or the Senate, but visitors are invited to sit in the public galleries and watch the proceedings. Please note that the **Library of Parliament** closed in 2002 to allow extensive restoration and repair work to be carried out. It is scheduled to reopen in 2005, but call ahead if you want to know whether the Library will be open during your visit. Centre Block tour times vary throughout the year; call the **Capital Infocentre** at ✆ **800/465-1867** or 613/239-5000 for information.

Self-Guided Tour of the Grounds With the help of an outdoor self-guiding booklet called **Discover the Hill,** available from the **Capital Infocentre** across the street from the Parliament Buildings, you can wander around Parliament Hill and explore the monuments, grounds, and exterior of the buildings on your own. Stroll the grounds clockwise around the Centre Block — they're dotted with statues honoring such prominent historical figures as Queen Victoria, Sir Georges-Étienne Cartier, William Lyon Mackenzie King, and Sir Wilfrid Laurier. Behind the building is a promenade with sweeping views of the river. Here too is the old Centre Block's bell, which crashed to the ground shortly after tolling midnight on the eve of the 1916 fire. At the bottom of the cliff behind Parliament Hill, a pleasant pathway leads along the Ottawa River. The pathway is also accessible from the Ottawa Locks at the foot of the Rideau Canal, where it meets the Ottawa River. In July and August you may be lucky enough to meet one or more of the costumed interpreters who represent historical characters from early Confederation times and exchange a word or two with them.

> **Tips**
>
> Visit the Peace Tower and enjoy the view from the Observation Deck, but be aware the tower closes half an hour before the last Centre Block tour of the day.

Fact

Concerts of the 53-bell Carillon of the Peace Tower are presented weekdays in July and August at 2pm (1-hour concert). From September to June, there is a 15-minute noon concert most weekdays.

Guided Outdoor Walking Tour   Between late June and early September, you can get free same-day tickets at the Info Tent for a guided tour of the Parliament Hill grounds. Visitors will get an introduction to some of the historical figures who have shaped Canada's past and present.

Changing of the Guard ⊛   On Parliament Hill's lawn, a colorful Canadian ceremony is held every morning (weather permitting) between late June and late August. Two historical regiments — the Governor General's Foot Guards and the Canadian Grenadier Guards — make up the Ceremonial Guard of the Armed Forces. The daily parade includes 125 soldiers in busbies and scarlet tunics. The Guard assembles at Cartier Square Drill Hall, 2 Queen Elizabeth Dr. (near the corner of Laurier Avenue by the Rideau Canal) at 9:30am and marches north on Elgin Street, sweeping west along Wellington Street and timed to reach Parliament Hill at 10am. On arrival at the Hill the Ceremonial Guard splits, with the old and new guard positioning themselves on opposite sides of the lawn. The dress and weaponry of both groups are inspected. The colors are then marched before the troops and saluted, and the guards present arms to each other. In true military fashion, sergeant-majors bark commands that prompt the soldiers to perform their synchronized maneuvers. The final symbolic act is the transfer of the guardroom key to the incoming guard commander, signifying that the process has been completed. The relieved unit marches down Wellington Street and back to the Drill Hall to the beat of the military band.

Sound and Light on the Hill   Every evening between early July and early September, Canada's history unfolds and the country's spirit is revealed through music, lights, and giant images projected on the Parliament Buildings. This dazzling half-hour display of sound and light is free of charge, and limited bleacher seating is available.

Test Your Knowledge of Parliament Hill

1. How many female speakers of the House of Commons have there been?
2. How tall is the Peace Tower?
3. How was the Library saved during the terrible fire of 1916 that destroyed the rest of the Parliament Buildings?
4. What color is the carpet in the Senate Chamber?
5. What or who stands in the center of the Parliamentary Library?
6. How many bells are there in the Carillon of the Peace Tower?
7. When was Canada's now-familiar red-and-white flag raised for the first time on the Peace Tower?
8. Who carved the frieze in the House of Commons foyer that depicts the History of Canada, and how long did it take to complete?

9. What stone is primarily used on the exterior and interior of the Parliament Buildings?

10. What images can be seen in the stained-glass windows of the House of Commons?

11. Who lit the Centennial Flame in 1967?

12. How long does it take for the copper roof panels to turn green?

ANSWERS: 1. Two. 2. 92.2m (302.5 ft.). 3. A quick-thinking employee closed the iron doors to prevent the fire from spreading there. 4. Red. 5. A white marble statue of Queen Victoria. 6. 53. 7. February 15, 1965. 8. Sculptor Eleanor Milne took 11 years to create the beautiful stone frieze. 9. Nepean sandstone from Ontario is used on the exterior and Tyndall limestone from Manitoba is used inside. 10. The floral emblems of Canada's provinces and territories. 11. Prime Minister Lester B. Pearson. 12. About 30 years.

CANADIAN MUSEUM OF CIVILIZATION ✹✹✹

The largest of Canada's cultural institutions, the Canadian Museum of Civilization (CMC) is a combination of permanent and temporary exhibits that explore human history with special, although not exclusive, reference to Canada. The museum is located on the north shore of the Ottawa River in Gatineau, its stunning award-winning architecture clearly visible from downtown Ottawa. The building's flowing curves appear to have been sculpted by the forces of nature. Inside the museum, the impressive design continues to delight visitors as they make their way around the exhibition halls. Added attractions within the building are the Canadian Children's Museum, the Canadian Postal Museum, and the IMAX Theatre.

You'll enter the building at street level, where you can buy your museum entrance tickets and IMAX tickets and access the Canadian Children's Museum. You can register for a 45-minute guided tour of the Grand Hall or the Canada Hall for an extra C$2.50 (US$1.70) per person, or just wander on your own. Before you begin your exploration of the museum, be sure to drop off coats, umbrellas, and other outdoor gear at the complimentary cloakroom and collect a stroller or wheelchair if needed. There is pay underground parking with an inside entrance to the museum. You could easily spend the whole day here, especially if you take in an IMAX show. For visitors with disabilities, there are designated bays on level 1 of the parking arcade, elevator access to all floors, and access ramps installed where necessary. Spaces are reserved for wheelchairs in the IMAX Theatre and the performance/lecture theater.

Where to eat: There is a fine-dining restaurant, **Café du Musée,** and a spacious cafeteria on-site. Both facilities enjoy a spacious spectacular view of the Ottawa River and Parliament Hill. Reservations recommended at **Café du Musée;** call ℂ **819/ 776-7009.** If the weather's nice you can take a picnic to Jacques-Cartier Park, which is on the banks of the Ottawa River right beside the Canadian Museum of Civilization.

Tips   **Buy Two and Save**

If you want to see an **IMAX** presentation (about 45 minutes in length) the same day, buy your tickets when you pay the museum entrance fee at the **Canadian Museum of Civilization.** You'll save a few dollars and also ensure you get a seat in the theater. **IMAX** shows often sell out in advance of showtime, particularly in the peak tourist season.

Grand Hall ✶✶ From the street-level lobby, descend the escalator to the museum's showpiece — the magnificent Grand Hall. This enormous exhibition hall features a display of more than 40 totem poles, representing the culture of the Native peoples of Canada's Pacific Northwest Coast. Six Native house façades have been constructed in the hall, based on architectural styles of different coastal nations over the past 150 years. The Grand Hall also has a performance stage where storytelling sessions, demonstrations, and performances are held regularly. At the far end of the Hall, a forest setting has been created in a room displaying pre-historic artifacts and articles from the Tsimshian people of British Columbia.

Canada Hall ✶✶✶ This impressive exhibit, set under a dramatically lit 17-m-high (56 ft.) dome, takes visitors on a journey through 1,000 years of Canada's social, cultural, and material history. The Canada Hall is a presentation of full-scale tableaux and buildings that have been constructed in the architectural style of specific periods in history using materials (solid wood beams and planking, plaster, stucco, stone, and so on) and methods in use at the time. The sights and sounds of the country's past unfold before you, beginning with the landing of the Norsemen on Newfoundland's coast in A.D. 1000. As you move through the hall, you go west through the country and forward in time. Look below-deck in a full-scale stern section of a 16th-century Basque whaling ship, see the crude process of rendering whale blubber into oil in a Labrador whaling station, and peer into a farmhouse in the St. Lawrence Valley in 18th-century New France. You'll walk into the public square of a town in New France and have the liberty of opening doors and peeking through windows into the lives of the inhabitants. You may be lucky enough to meet one of the colorful historical characters who roam the exhibits from time to time, interacting with the public and adding a new dimension to the museum experience. A lumber camp shanty, a Conestoga wagon, and the main street of a small Ontario town in the Victorian era are a few more sights you'll see during your exploration of Canada's heritage.

Kids   **Let Them Play**

If you have children with you when you visit the **Canadian Museum of Civilization,** I recommend visiting the **Children's Museum** first. Let them run around, play, and let off steam in there, take a break for a drink and a snack or lunch (you can choose from formal dining or a cafeteria; both offer spectacular views over the Ottawa River toward the Parliament Buildings, or brownbag it in the Lunch Box), and then walk through the **main exhibition halls.**

Value

Admission to the **Children's Museum** is included with the main entrance ticket for the **Canadian Museum of Civilization,** although the hours may vary slightly from the main museum hours. You can visit just the Children's Museum if you wish, but the price will be the same.

First Peoples Hall This large and impressive collection showcases the cultural, historical, and artistic accomplishments of Aboriginal peoples in Canada, and contains more than 2,000 artifacts. Various aspects of First Peoples' identity are explored, from the earliest origins to present-day contributions and challenges. Exhibits include an Art Gallery dedicated to contemporary Aboriginal art.

Special Exhibitions Several distinct exhibition spaces are dedicated to short-term displays encompassing all museum disciplines — archeology, ethnology, folk culture, and history. Call the museum to see what's on in the special exhibitions galleries, mezzanine, and salons, or just drop in and be surprised.

Canadian Postal Museum This museum is housed within the Canadian Museum of Civilization and admission is included with the main museum ticket. Discover the story of postal communications from coast to coast and around the world. Interactive displays and a high-tech station teach visitors about the world of stamps. All kinds of memorabilia are on display, from toys and quilts to mailboxes and mailbags. A permanent exhibition shows the role the post has played in Canada's history and features a complete post office from Quebec. Temporary exhibits range from an introduction to stamp-collecting and an opportunity to design your own stamp to displays of postage stamps from around the world, with specimens from the Canadian Museum's International Philatelic Collection.

Canadian Children's Museum 🎭🎭 Kids absolutely love to play in this hands-on, just-for-kids museum. Every exhibit is child-size and the layout strongly encourages exploration. Hands-on activities and programs use real materials from the museum's collection. Visitors touch, climb, build, manipulate, move, and create. Through this highly interactive learning, children explore the world and its many cultures. For example, they can step inside a child-size Japanese family home. In the *tatami* (straw-matting) room, kids are invited to try the art of origami (Japanese paper folding) or write their own haiku poetry in the garden. Other exciting adventures include exploring an Egyptian pyramid, crawling into a Bedouin tent, putting on an Indonesian shadow puppet show, sitting astride a camel, driving a Pakistani tour bus, or building a brick wall. Because of the scale of the interactive buildings and stations, kids immediately feel comfortable here and they do tend to zip around from place to place like an out-of-control pinball if you don't exercise a little parental guidance. Kids from 0 to 14 are the target group, but the kids who will get the most out of the museum (and may want to stay all day) are probably 4- to 11-year-olds. Programs, workshops, and theater performances are scheduled all year around. Call ahead to find out about upcoming special events. During the summer months, you get double the fun because the outdoor exhibition park Adventure World is open. Play chess on a giant chessboard, hop along with hopscotch, or shoot some marbles. The Art-rageous Adventure exhibit area hosts visual arts activities

Fact

Did you know that Ottawa has the highest concentration of museums in Canada?

for children. The Waterways exhibit has a boat-making yard where you can design, build, and launch your own model watercraft. Kids can climb on a log-pulling tugboat or take an imaginary tour in the floatplane.

Where to eat: See Canadian Museum of Civilization above.

100 Laurier St., Hull, QC. Within the Canadian Museum of Civilization (CMC). ℂ **819/776-8294**. Admission included with CMC ticket. For directions see complete listing information for Canadian Museum of Civilization below.

IMAX Theatre ⭐⭐ This amazing theater combines the technology of IMAX and IMAX DOME. The feeling is one of being wrapped in sight and sound. The IMAX screen is amazing enough — it's seven stories high and ten times the size of a conventional movie screen. To experience the full effect, a 23-m-diameter (76 ft.) hemispheric IMAX DOME moves into place overhead once the audience is seated — the seats tilt back to give the audience a comfortable and clear view of the dome. Not all films use the entire screening system. Advance ticket purchase is recommended, as shows often sell out. Tickets can be purchased in person at the museum box office (there's a discount if purchased with a museum entrance ticket). All ages admitted. Plan to arrive 20 minutes before show time, as latecomers will not be admitted. Films are approximately 45 minutes in length.

100 Laurier St., Hull, QC. ℂ **800/555-5621** or 819/776-7000. www.civilization.ca. IMAX Theatre information and tickets available at museum box office or call ℂ **819/776-7010**. Museum admission (prices subject to change) C$10 (US$8) adult, C$7 (US$6) senior, C$6 (US$5) student, C$4 (US$3.30) child, C$22 (US$18) family (max. 4 members). Half price every Sunday, Museums Day weekend (mid-May), and Heritage Day (February 20). Free every Thurs 4–9pm, Canada Day (July 1), and Remembrance Day (Nov 11). Admission free for members. IMAX tickets sold separately. May 1–June 30 daily 9am–6pm, Thurs until 9pm (Children's Museum closes 7pm). July 1 to first Tues in Sept, Sat–Wed 9am–6pm, Thurs and Fri 9am–9pm. First Wed in Sept to second Tues in Oct daily 9am to 6pm, Thurs until 9pm (Children's Museum closes at 6pm). Second Wed in Oct to April 30, Tues–Sun 9am–5pm, Thurs until 9pm (Children's Museum closes at 5pm). IMAX Theatre hours may differ from museum hours. Pay parking on-site in underground lot with inside access to museum. From the Ottawa River Parkway or Wellington Street downtown, take the Portage Bridge to Gatineau (Hull) and turn right onto rue Laurier. The museum is on your right, just a couple of minutes' drive. From the east side of the canal, take Sussex Drive and cross the Alexandra Bridge. The museum is on your immediate left as you exit the bridge.

CANADIAN WAR MUSEUM ⭐⭐⭐

I had the extraordinary privilege of touring this facility just prior to its grand opening and I must say I was amazed at every turn. The architecture is stunning; the vision for the design of the exhibits is nothing less than astounding. What else can I say? You must make this destination a priority during your visit to Ottawa.

The new **Canadian War Museum,** which held its opening ceremonies on May 8, 2005 — the 60th anniversary of VE (Victory in Europe) Day and the 125th anniversary of the Canadian War Museum — delivers an unforgettable visitor experience. Expect to be emotionally moved and intellectually engaged at this spectacular facility. The **permanent galleries** have made full use of leading-edge museum-design theories and techniques to bring to life Canada's role in conflicts and war, emphasizing how military events have affected Canadians at a

---

(*Tips*

The **Canadian Virtual War Memorial** serves as an electronic tribute to the Canadians and Newfoundlanders who have lost their lives in major conflicts since 1884. The website also serves as a searchable database so people can look for men and women in their own families who have given their lives for their country. Canadians are invited to submit digital images of photos, letters, postcards, medals, and other war memorabilia. Visit **www.virtualmemorial.gc.ca** for instructions on how to add your family's war memorabilia to the Virtual War Memorial.

---

personal, national, and international level. The story of war and its consequences is told through the stories, artifacts, and memories of ordinary Canadians, with a view to presenting the human story rather than simply a display of objects and artifacts. The **permanent galleries** are **Pre-Contact to Permanent European Settlement ca. 1600; Wars for Empire, ca. 1600–1774; Wars for Canada, 1774–1885; Costly Road to Autonomy, 1885–1931; A Nation Forged in Fire, 1931–1946; Cold War, Hot Peace, 1946–1993; The Challenge of Uncertainty, 1993–present;** and **The Royal Canadian Legion Hall of Honour.** In addition to the impressive permanent exhibit galleries, there are spaces for **special exhibitions,** an **art gallery** featuring one of the best collections of **war art** in the world, and two extraordinary halls: **Memorial Hall** and **Regeneration Hall. Memorial Hall,** with its spare interior, is designed as a sanctuary for personal remembrance. A single window has been placed in such a manner that each November 11 at precisely 11am the sun will illuminate the Tombstone of the Unknown Soldier, which originally marked the grave in France and has been donated to the Canadian War Museum. **Regeneration Hall** is the final stop on the museum tour. It is a dramatic space flanked by expansive angled walls. The message here is hope — for the future and for remembrance of the past. "Lest we forget" and "N'oublions jamais" are projected on one wall in Morse Code by sunlight streaming through a series of dots and dashes on the opposite wall. The museum is located at **LeBreton Flats,** a greenspace area about 2km (1.25 miles) west of **Parliament Hill.** Although the east face of the building features a sharply angled presentation, the bulk of the building is low-profile, literally uniting with the surrounding earth — the gently sloping vegetation-covered roof is actually a pedestrian walkway, easily accessible from ground level. The website gives much insight into the extensive innovative and highly imaginative planning that went into creating the museum.

Where to eat: There's a cafeteria on-site and plans are underway to offer grill fare on the patio in summer. The Trans-Canada Trail follows the Ottawa River on the north side of the Museum and provides greenspace for picnics and relaxation.

1 Vimy Place, Ottawa. ⓒ **800/555-5621** or 819/776-8600. www.warmuseum.ca. Admission C$10 (US$8) adult, C$7 (US$6) senior, C$6 (US$5) student, C$4 (US$3.25) child 3–12, C$22 (US$18) family (4 people, max. 2 adults). Half-price Sundays, Heritage Day weekend (third weekend in February) and Museums Day weekend (mid-May). Free every Thursday 4–9pm, July 1, and Nov 11. Early May–June 30 daily 9am–6pm, Thurs until 9pm. July 1 to first Monday in September daily 9am–6pm, Thurs–Fri until 9pm; First Tues in Sept–mid-Oct daily 9am–6pm, Thurs until 9pm; Mid-Oct–April 30 Tues–Sun 9am–5pm, Thurs until 9pm. Closed one week in early–mid January for annual maintenance. Pay parking on-site with inside access to museum. From Wellington Street in downtown Ottawa, head west past Booth Street traffic lights until you reach Vimy Place. Turn right into the Canadian War Museum. Note there is no access to the museum when heading north on Booth Street toward Quebec.

Tips

The Canadian Museum of Civilization Corporation launched a new admission package in 2005 called "2+2." For a special rate, visitors can visit both the Canadian War Museum and the Canadian Museum of Civilization. For example, a visitor purchasing a 2+2 ticket on a Monday in one museum has until end of day on Wednesday to visit the other museum. Admission package subject to change.

NATIONAL GALLERY OF CANADA ✪✪✪

One of the most attractive buildings in the city, the National Gallery glitters and gleams from a promontory overlooking the Ottawa River. Moshe Safdie, who designed the Habitat apartment block and Musée des Beaux-Arts in Montreal, was the architect for the building, which is the permanent home of the largest collection of Canadian art in the world. The public entrance to the Grand Hall is along a cavernous sloped-glass concourse that offers splendid views of Parliament Hill. Ingeniously designed shafts with reflective panels maximize the amount of natural light that floods the galleries. Regularly on display are more than 800 paintings, sculptures, and decorative works by Canadian artists, a sampling of the 10,000 works in the permanent collection. Among the highlights are a comprehensive collection of works by Tom Thomson and the Group of Seven, early Québécois artists, and Montreal Automatistes. European masters are also represented, from Corot and Turner to Chagall and Picasso, and contemporary galleries feature pop art and minimalism, plus abstract works from Canadian and American artists. Advance tickets may be purchased for some exhibitions — if you particularly want to see a certain one, get tickets ahead to avoid disappointment. Families can visit the Artissimo kiosk weekends and during school vacations, where kids age 3 and up accompanied by an adult can create their own masterpieces. Family workshops are designed for parents and kids to learn more about art, its interpretation, and its origins. Artissimo is a drop-in program, but registration is required for workshops and vacation activities programs ✆ **613/ 998-4888.** Programs are also available for guests with special needs, including practical workshops for intellectually impaired visitors and tours for visually impaired visitors. Free guided tours of the permanent collections are held for the public daily at 11am and 2pm. Facilities include a cafeteria, a cafe, and a gift and bookstore, which is well worth a visit. Wheelchairs available.

380 Sussex Dr. ✆ **800/319-2787** or 613/990-1985. www.national.gallery.ca. Admission to permanent collection C$6 (US$5) adult, C$5 (US$4) senior and student, C$3 (US$2.50) youth, free for children under 12, C$12 (US$10) family (max. 2 adults and 3 youths). Additional variable admission price for special exhibitions. May 1–mid-Oct daily 10am–5pm, Thurs until 8pm. Mid-Oct–end of Apr Wed–Sun 10am–5pm, Thurs until 8pm. From the Queensway, take Nicholas St. exit (exit 118). Turn left on Rideau St., right onto Sussex Dr. The Museum is on your left. Pay parking available on-site in underground lot with inside entrance to museum.

CANADIAN MUSEUM OF NATURE ✪✪✪

The wonders of the natural world are featured at the Canadian Museum of Nature, housed in the Victoria Memorial Museum Building, which was officially recognized for its national historical significance in 2004. The architecture of the historical building is remarkable. Built of local sandstone, the Tudor Revival design includes towers, arched windows, a crenellated roofline, magnificent stained-glass windows, and a grand central staircase.

Please note: A major five-year renovation project began in 2004. The museum is open during this period, but exhibitions will close in their turn as the work progresses. In 2005, Birds in Canada, Mammals in Canada, Creepy Critters Gallery, Animals in Nature Gallery, and Plant Gallery & Nature's Pharmacy are open; the earth gallery and dinosaur gallery are closed. A new fossil gallery is scheduled to open in 2006. Focusing on a critical period in the earth's history — from 85 to 35 million years ago — the new gallery will contain two true-to-life dioramas, life-size dinosaur models, and numerous multimedia stations. A new Nature of Humans Gallery, set to open in 2007, will explore what it means to be human and how humans connect with nature and the environment. A new Water Gallery will show visitors the importance of water and its interrelationships with life on earth. The Viola McMillan Mineral Gallery and Activity Centre is also closed; a new mineral gallery will open in 2008.

The **Creepy Critters Gallery** is alive with insects, rodents, and reptiles. It's not for the squeamish — only a pane of glass separates you from the hundreds of crawling, scurrying, and slippery creatures. See cockroaches, slugs, rats, snakes, leeches, spiders, and toads in habitats that replicate their natural living conditions. If you prefer cuddly, furry creatures, pay a visit to the galleries on the second floor east, which display preserved specimens of **Canadian birds and mammals** in highly detailed dioramas. Learn how animals communicate with each other and interact with their environment in the **Animals in Nature Gallery.** The **Plant Gallery** has hundreds of living plants, everything from ferns and mosses to coniferous plants and flowers. Between June and September, a colony of bees collect pollen to make honey. An exhibit on obtaining medicines from plant sources rounds out the "green" gallery.

Highly entertaining and educational nature documentaries are on show in the high-definition electronic cinema, the highest-quality digital television and video technology available. Daily shows, usually 30 to 45 minutes long, are screened in both official languages. Admission is included with museum entrance fee.

Where to eat: The cafeteria is closed during renovation, but there are vending machines and a brown-bag lunch room in the basement of the museum. The YMCA on nearby Argyle Avenue has a quick-serve cafeteria, and Elgin Street has lots of places to grab a bite to eat. Keep your entrance ticket stub to allow readmission to the museum after your break.

Victoria Memorial Museum Building, 240 McLeod St. ℭ **800/263-4433** or 613/566-4700. www.nature.ca. Please note admission prices are likely to vary for the duration of the renovation project. Admission at the time of printing was half-price, as follows: C$4 (US$3.25) adult, C$3.50 (US$3) senior/student, C$1.75 (US$1.40) child 3–12, children 2 and under free. Free admission Sat before noon. Mid Oct–Apr Tues–Sun 10am–5pm, Thurs until 8pm. May–mid-Oct 9:30am–5pm, Thurs until 8pm. Located at the corner of Metcalfe and McLeod St., one block west of Elgin St.

(*Fun Fact*

Do you know how the head gardener at the Museum of Nature keeps the plants looking so green and lush? Look up at the ceiling. When the museum is closed, these lights are switched on to simulate bright daylight at a greater intensity than would be possible naturally in the relatively dark conditions of the museum during the day.

> **Fun Fact**
>
> Following the fire that destroyed the Parliament Buildings in 1916, emergency quarters were set up for the government in the building that is now the home of the Canadian Museum of Nature. The House of Commons sat in the Auditorium for four years, and the Senate occupied the Hall of Invertebrate Fossils (no pun intended). In 1919, the body of Sir Wilfrid Laurier lay in state in the Auditorium.

OTTAWA'S WATERWAYS ✫✫

Ottawa's origins are inextricably linked to its waterways, since it was the settlement that grew up around the canal construction site that eventually became Ottawa. Modern-day Ottawa enjoys the canal and river primarily for leisure and pleasure. The city's beauty is enhanced by the extensive network of parkways, pathways, and parks that follow the shores of the **Rideau Canal, Rideau River,** and **Ottawa River.**

Rideau Canal ✫ The **Rideau Canal,** a National Historic Site, is actually a continuous chain of beautiful lakes, rivers, and canal cuts, stretching 202km (125 miles) between Ottawa and Kingston, and often described as the most scenic waterway in North America. Parks Canada has the responsibility of preserving and maintaining the canal's natural and historic features and providing a safe waterway for boats to navigate. The canal and locks that link the lakes and rivers of the **Rideau Valley** were constructed between 1826 and 1832 to provide a secure route for the military to travel between Montreal and Kingston in the wake of the War of 1812. Colonel By, the British engineer in charge of the project, had the foresight to build the locks and canal large enough to permit commercial traffic to access the system rather than building the canal solely for military use. As things turned out, the inhabitants of North America decided to live peaceably. The canal became a main transportation and trade route and communities along the canal grew and thrived. With the introduction of railroads in the mid-19th century, commercial traffic subsided and the canal gradually became a tourist destination due to its beauty and tranquility. The locks have operated continuously since they first opened. In the winter, the canal freezes over and turns into the world's longest and most famous skating rink, the **Rideau Canal Skateway.** The season usually runs from late December to late February or early March. For current information on ice conditions during the season, call the Skateway Hotline ✆ **613/239-5234.** Heated shelters, skate and sled rentals, boot-check and skate-sharpening services, rest areas, food concessions, and toilets are located at various points along the Skateway. Main access points are by the **National Arts Centre, Fifth Avenue** and **Queen Elizabeth Driveway,** and **Dow's Lake.**

Rideau River The Ottawa section of the **Rideau River** bisects the city, with the **Rideau Canal** running roughly parallel for the final 8km (5 miles) leading to the **Rideau Falls.** The **Rideau River** is part of the **Rideau Waterway,** a collective name for the entire system of lakes, rivers, and canal cuts that make up the route between Ottawa and Kingston. Many city parks are located along its banks, including Rideau Falls Park, New Edinburgh Park, Strathcona Park, Rideau River Park, Brewer Park, Vincent Massey Park, Hog's Back Park, and Mooney's Bay Park.

Rideau Falls ✫ Located just off Sussex Drive where the **Rideau River** empties over a cliff into the Ottawa River, **Rideau Falls** is surrounded by a beautifully

Tips **Tiptoe Through the Tulips**

The tulip beds in Confederation Park at the northern tip of Dow's Lake attract thousands of visitors during the Canadian Tulip Festival in May. An amazing 300,000 bulbs bloom in the park, making it the largest tulip display in the region.

landscaped park, and a footbridge spans the **Rideau River. Canada and the World Pavilion,** a seasonal attraction celebrating the achievements of Canadians on the international scene, is located here in the park.

Ottawa River Historically, the **Ottawa River** was a major transportation corridor for moving people and goods. When the Europeans settled in the area, the water was harnessed to generate power for the lumber industry. This majestic river is now enjoyed by canoeists, whitewater enthusiasts, and other outdoor adventurers. **Whitewater rapids** are about an hour's drive north of Ottawa. See chapter 10, "Exploring the Region," for whitewater outfitters and excursions.

Dow's Lake ✯ The pretty lake that adjoins the **Rideau Canal** in central Ottawa was once a mosquito-infested swamp, and outbreaks of malaria were common among canal construction workers in the early 1800s. No one wanted to cut a canal through the swampland. Colonel By, the British engineer in charge of the canal construction, solved the problem by damming a branch of the **Rideau River** that used to run where Preston Street is now, and flooded the swamp. If you visit **Dow's Lake** when the water levels are low, you may see tree stumps here and there. These stumps are all that remain of the old white pines that grew in the area before the basin was flooded. **Dow's Lake** is a popular site in the summer. Paddleboats, canoes, kayaks, and rowboats are available for rental at the fully operational marina at the Pavilion site; call ✆ **613/232-1001.** The **Pavilion** has restaurants with terraces overlooking the lake. In winter you can rent skates and go for a twirl on the ice.

Get on the Water

There are several companies operating river and canal tours. Reservations are recommended for all of them. **Ottawa Riverboat Company** (✆ **613/562-4888**) offers a one-hour tour on the 305-passenger *Sea Prince II,* the largest tour boat in Ottawa. Bilingual guides provide commentary as you tour past famous buildings and landmarks as seen from the Ottawa River. **Paul's Boat Lines** (✆ **613/225-6781**) cruises the Ottawa River and the Rideau Canal. On the Ottawa River, the 150-passenger *Paula D* takes visitors on a 90-minute cruise, with spectacular views of the Parliament Buildings, Rideau Falls, and other sites. On the canal, you can glide along in one of three low-profile tour boats for a 75-minute cruise. Small ticket booths for both tour companies are located in the area of Confederation Square and Plaza Bridge during the boating season; you can usually buy same-day tickets. If what appeals to you is nothing more than just "messing around in boats," then rent a **paddleboat or canoe at Dow's Lake**. For more detailed information on boat tours, see "On the Water" later in this chapter.

Locks ✫ Rivers often have rocky sections with shallow, fast-flowing water. Naturally this presents a challenge to navigation, and locks were devised to enable boats to safely move uphill and downhill through the water in a controlled manner. There are **45 locks** manned by 24 lock stations along the main channel of the 202-km (125-mile) **Rideau Canal.** The waterway rises a total of 50m (164 ft.) from Kingston on Lake Ontario to Upper Rideau Lake, then drops 83m (273 ft.) to the Ottawa River in Ottawa, ending in the 30-m (98-ft.) **Rideau Falls.**

The **Rideau Canal** joins the **Ottawa River** with a series of eight locks just east of the **Parliament Buildings.** The canal winds south for approximately 8km (5 miles), opening out into **Dow's Lake** roughly two-thirds of the way along, and eventually joins the **Rideau River** at **Mooney's Bay** on the west side of Riverside Drive at Hog's Back Road. The canal is bordered by Prince of Wales Drive and Queen Elizabeth Driveway on the west side and Colonel By Drive on the east side. The **Rideau River** follows a similar course to the east of the canal.

In Ottawa there are three places where you can watch the locks in action. The best spot to view one of the lock systems is in downtown Ottawa right at the point where the first locks were built. If you stand on the north side of the Plaza Bridge (between Parliament Hill and Château Laurier) and look over the side, you'll have a wonderful view of the eight **Ottawa Locks,** which connect the canal to the Ottawa River, a drop of 24 m (80 ft.). Travel time for water traffic through the locks is about 1^1/$_2$ hours. To get down to the level of the locks, go down a stairway beside the bridge (or descend a ramp from the south side of the bridge if you need universal access). *Note:* If you have children with you, be extremely careful to keep them away from the sides of the locks, because there are no safety barriers next to the water. The **Bytown Museum** is alongside the locks. Upstream along the canal, the next two locks are **Hartwells Locks,** which take about half an hour to navigate. The road entrance to the locks is off **Prince of Wales Drive** south of **Dow's Lake.** The **Central Experimental Farm** borders this section of the canal and there's an extensive network of paved and gravel bike paths. A little farther upstream are the **Hog's Back Locks**, reached by road at 795 Hog's Back Rd. An interpretive trail links the locks with Hog's Back dam. There's a bonus at Hog's Back — a **swing bridge** is part of the lock system, designed to accommodate vessels requiring a clearance greater than 2.8m (9.4 ft.). The bridge swings on demand except during peak traffic periods on weekdays. The parkland in this area surrounds the spectacular **Hog's Back Falls,** situated at the point where the **Rideau Canal** meets the **Rideau River.** They're named after rocks that are said to resemble the bristles on a hog's back. A refreshment pavilion, parking, and washroom facilities are available.

CANADA SCIENCE & TECHNOLOGY MUSEUM ✫✫✫

This excellent museum has eye-catching interactive exhibits at every turn. Plan a half-day visit here. One of the most intriguing long-term exhibits is **Canada in Space.** Discover the story of Canada's role in space. Various tools such as Radarsat, MSAT, the Canadarm, and the International Space Station Alpha can be explored. A space flight simulator will take you on a virtual voyage in a six-seat cinema pod that moves to the action on the huge screen. Separate tickets at a cost of C$3 (US$2.50) are required; it's simplest to purchase these when you arrive at the front desk. Take note of the ride time so you don't miss your trip to outer space. The **Locomotive Hall** holds four huge steam locomotives, meticulously restored and maintained. You can climb in the cabs of some of them and you can also see a caboose, business car, and old number boards, and hear sound effects that give you the feeling of riding in a live locomotive. A major **exhibition on communications** is one of the largest of its kind in Canada and illustrates the history of electric and electronic communications in Canada. **Innovation Canada** celebrates great Canadian inventions. More than 100 artifacts are on display, including the Bombardier snowmobile and a replica of Jacques Plante's hockey goalie mask. Lively, short demonstrations on various science and technology topics are held frequently during the day; ask for show times and topics when you arrive and take in an entertaining show or two during your visit. Lots of programs and workshops are scheduled, so call ahead if you want to take part. In the summer, have a picnic in the Technology Park in front of the museum — kids will be fascinated to take a close-up look at the Cape North Lighthouse, radar antenna, pump jack, Convair Atlas rocket, telescope, windmill, and steam locomotive. There's also a cafeteria serving light meals and snacks. The museum's science/technology/educational–themed gift shop, located close to the main entrance, is an intriguing place to shop. The museum is fully wheelchair accessible and parking is free.

Where to eat: There's a cafeteria on-site. In front of the museum there is a small park with picnic tables. On St. Laurent Boulevard there are a number of family restaurant chains.

1867 St. Laurent Blvd. ℂ **613/991-3044.** www.sciencetech.technomuses.ca. Admission C$6 (US$5) adult, C$5 (US$4) senior/student, C$3 (US$2.50) children 4–14, children 3 and under free, C$14 (US$12) family (max. 2 adults and 3 children). Simulator ride C$3 (US$2.50) per person. Summer daily 9am–5pm. Winter Tues–Sun 9am–5pm. From the Queensway (Hwy 417) take the St. Laurent Blvd. South exit. Go south on St. Laurent Blvd. to Lancaster Rd. and turn left. The museum entrance is on your left.

CANADA AVIATION MUSEUM ✯✯

One of the best collections of **vintage aircraft** in the world is on display here. Whether you're young or old, you'll find something to catch your interest as you stroll through the huge exhibition hall and trace the history of aviation from its beginning to the jet age. You can come close (but not close enough to touch; aircraft are fragile machines) to more than 50 aircraft inside the building and a number of others are displayed outside in the summer months; the total number of aircraft in the collection has risen to approximately 130. A Silver Dart hangs from the ceiling as you enter. From that point, as you move through the museum, you'll see such famous aircraft as the Sopwith Camel, Messerschmitt, Spitfire, and Lancaster Bomber. The postwar exhibits include manufacturers such as Lockheed, deHavilland, and Sikorsky. Examples of the Beaver and Otter bush planes are on display, and in the post-1960 section there are aircraft from the jet age. Video terminals dot the hall, showing short documentaries about aspects of flight. Several interactive displays designed to teach the principles of flight are simple enough for children to operate and understand. Workshops for kids are offered, ranging from five-week mid-afternoon preschooler sessions to daily 2-hour sessions for kids aged 6 to 13. Entertaining demonstrations are scheduled throughout the day — everything from understanding wind tunnels to flying a Cessna 150. If you're looking for something a little different, try an evening program with scheduled events and dinner, or an overnight stay where you can explore the museum by flashlight and sleep under the wings of an airplane. If you are an aviation buff, or just love to fly, take advantage of a rare opportunity and splurge on a vintage aircraft flight, available from May to autumn. A 15-minute ride in an open cockpit biplane or a two-seater deHavilland Canada Chipmunk — with a canopy that allows clear views as you soar in the sky — costs

C$75 (US$62). When you're back on terra firma, don't forget to take a turn through the Aeronautica Boutique, which stocks scale models of aircraft, books, posters, prints, toys, clothing, and kites. Free strollers and wheelchairs are available at the front entrance, plus a thoughtful addition: motorized wheelchairs for visitors with physical disabilities and seniors. There's also a library specializing in the history of aviation, with an emphasis on the Canadian experience. The library is primarily open by appointment for visitors with a special interest in aviation. A new collection storage wing and library, archives, and administration wing were completed in early 2005. With the 100th anniversary of Canadian powered flight approaching in 2009, the museum is focusing on its next major project — a large restoration facility to support the work of preserving Canada's aerospace heritage.

Where to eat: There is a small snack bar on-site and an outdoor picnic area. Nearby St. Laurent Boulevard has a number of family restaurant chains.

11 Aviation Pkwy. (Rockcliffe Airport). ℂ **800/463-2038** or 613/993-2010. www.aviation.technomuses.ca. Admission C$6 (US$5) adults, C$5 (US$4) seniors and students, C$3 (US$2.50) children 4–15, children under 4 free; C$14 (US$12) family (1 or 2 adults with children). Admission free daily 4–5pm only. May 1–Labour Day (first Mon in Sept) daily 9am–5pm. After Labour Day to April 30 Tues–Sun 10am–5pm. Closed Mon and Tues in winter except holidays and school breaks. From downtown, travel northeast on Sussex Dr. (changes name to Rockcliffe Pkwy.) to Aviation Pkwy. Follow signs; museum is on the left.

RCMP MUSICAL RIDE AND STABLES ✮✮

The Mounties are beloved by Canadians and renowned the world over for their courage, integrity, and poise. They are also well known for their personable manner with the public, and this courtesy extends to their open invitation to the public to visit the Training School and Stables of the RCMP Musical Ride. The Musical Ride is a visual display by specially trained officers and horses who perform intricate riding drills and figures set to musical accompaniment. Free tours are available all year around. In the summer months, you'll find larger groups and more frequent tour schedules. In the winter, it's advisable to call ahead and set up a time with the coordinator, although it's not essential. When we called to ask about tours, we found out that there was a full dress rehearsal scheduled for the indoor arena in two days' time. We had the rare treat of watching the complete Musical Ride from a comfortable glassed-in gallery — in the company of the Irish Ambassador and his family, no less, which was an unexpected pleasure. We also had a tour of the stables and met several horses, including one who pulls the Queen's carriage when she's in town. Tour guides are friendly and willing to answer questions about the Musical Ride or the Mounties in general. If you happen to visit on a day when a practice isn't in session, or if the Ride isn't away on tour across Canada (which happens often during the summer), try to get tickets to one of their shows. They're always in Ottawa for the annual Sunset Ceremonies in late June/early July, and they perform their Musical Ride on Parliament Hill on July 1 (Canada Day). Between May and October they're on tour, but there are always some Eastern Ontario venues. In 2005, the tour schedule included appearances in Washington State and Arizona. There's a boutique at the Stables, open in the main tourist season, which stocks a variety of Mountie souvenirs.

Where to eat: St. Laurent Boulevard has a number of family restaurant chains, or head back downtown for a wider range of eateries.

Corner of Sandridge Rd. and St. Laurent Blvd. ℂ **613/998-8199.** www.rcmp-grc.gc.ca/musicalride/home_e.htm. Free admission. Donations accepted. May–Oct daily 9am–4pm. Nov–Apr Mon–Fri 10am–2pm. From downtown, follow Sussex Dr. (changes name to Rockcliffe Pkwy.) to Aviation Pkwy. Follow signs; the Musical Ride Centre is at the northeast corner of Sandridge Rd. and St. Laurent Blvd.

All About the Mounties

The Royal Canadian Mounted Police (RCMP) is Canada's national police force, providing a total federal policing service to all Canadians, and provincial and territorial policing to all areas except Ontario and Quebec, which operate their own independent provincial police forces. The RCMP is unique in the world because it provides policing services at the national, federal, provincial, and municipal levels. Their mission is to preserve the peace, uphold the law, and provide quality service in partnership with the communities they serve.

The idea of a mounted police force was conceived by Sir John A. Macdonald, Canada's first prime minister and minister of justice. In order to open the western and northern frontiers of the young country for settlement and development in an orderly manner, law enforcement officers were needed. In 1873, the North-West Mounted Police was created, inspired by the Royal Irish Constabulary and the mounted rifle units of the United States Army. A year later, approximately 275 officers and men were dispatched to northwestern Canada.

Over the years, the force expanded and developed into the present-day organization, which numbers around 22,200 employees in total. Today the RCMP's role is multifaceted. Here's a list of the programs and services.

- Prevent and investigate crime
- Maintain order
- Enforce laws
- Contribute to national security
- Ensure the safety of state officials, visiting dignitaries, and foreign missions
- Provide vital operational support services to other police and law-enforcement agencies.

RCMP Musical Ride: Facts & Figures

- The choreography of the Musical Ride is based upon traditional cavalry drill movements.
- The horse, scarlet tunic, and lance of the Ride are symbols of the Force's early history.
- The first Musical Ride was performed at Regina Barracks in Saskatchewan in 1887.
- The Ride is performed by 32 regular member volunteers (male and female) who have at least two years' police experience and who have taken a training course to qualify for the Ride.
- When on tour, the Ride team consists of 36 horses, 36 constables, 1 farrier, a technical production manager, and 3 officers.
- The requirements for the horses' eligibility are very specific. They must be black, 16 to 17.2 hands high, and weigh between 523kg

(1,150 lbs.) and 725kg (1,600 lbs.). Stallions must be registered Thoroughbred and broodmares are part Thoroughbred.

- Young horses, called remounts, begin training at 3 years of age. At 6 years old, they begin training specifically for the Musical Ride and take their first trip with the Ride.
- The saddle blankets feature the Force's regimental colors (blue and yellow) and bear the fused letters MP.
- The maple leaf pattern you can see on the horses' rumps is made with a metal stencil. Using a damp brush, the horses' hair is brushed across its natural lie to make it stand up.

CANADA AGRICULTURE MUSEUM & CENTRAL EXPERIMENTAL FARM ★★ Kids

The **Canada Agriculture Museum,** which charges a modest entrance fee, features animal barns, special exhibits, and a chance to experience a traditional farm in action. The Museum is one of four public areas within the **Central Experimental Farm,** a large (400 hectares; 1,000 acres) tract of farmland in the heart of south central Ottawa. The major tenant of the CEF, occupying more than three-quarters of the property, is a crop research center, part of the federal government department of Agriculture and Agri-Food Canada. In addition to the Canada Agriculture Museum, the public can visit the **Dominion Arboretum, Ornamental Gardens,** and **Tropical Greenhouse;** all three have free admission. The Agriculture Museum offers city slickers (and country bumpkins, for that matter) a chance to get up close and personal with all things agricultural. The 2-hectare (5-acre) site is a unique blend of modern working farm and museum. Several heritage buildings are on the site, including a dairy barn. The small-animal barn houses goats, sheep, pigs, and poultry. There's always something going on at the Agriculture Museum, whether it's a festival, special exhibit, day camp, or demonstration. If you're planning a visit, call ahead so you can catch one of the special days on the farm. Activities are planned with kids in mind and everyone from babies to grandparents will enjoy meeting the animals and learning about the farm. Programs and special events focus on how science and technology mesh with modern agriculture and show visitors the processes by which Canadians get their food, fibers, and other agricultural products.

Where to eat: Bring a picnic in summer and enjoy your lunch in the extensive grounds of the Central Experimental Farm. Dow's Lake Pavilion and Preston Street (Little Italy) are close by if you have a car.

Corner of Experimental Farm Dr. and Prince of Wales Dr. ✆ **613/991-3044.** www.agriculture.technomuses.ca. Admission to Arboretum, Ornamental Gardens, and Tropical Greenhouse free. Admission to exhibits and animal barns of Agriculture Museum C$6 (US$5) adult, C$5 (US$4) students and seniors, C$3 (US$2) children 3–15, children under 3 free, C$13 (US$11) family (max. 2 adults and 3 children). Animal barns daily 9am–5pm except Dec 25; exhibits and barn boutique daily 9am–5pm Mar 1–Oct 31. Take Prince of Wales Dr. and follow the signs. The museum is just west of Prince of Wales Dr. between Carling Ave. and Baseline Rd.

Fun Fact

The Mounties do not, in fact, use horses for regular duties today. The last patrol on horseback was around 1936.

Green Thumbs Up

Gardeners are well known for their passion for touring other people's gardens. The Ottawa area has several lovely gardens open to the public. At the **Central Experimental Farm,** the **Arboretum** covers about 35 hectares (88 acres) of rolling land near the Prince of Wales Drive roundabout. Open from sunrise to sunset daily, the Arboretum is a popular place for families to picnic and play in the summer. In the winter, the hills are used for tobogganing. Well over 2,400 distinct species and varieties of trees and shrubs grow here, with some dating from the 1880s. A donor tree program provides local residents and visitors with a means of contributing to the continued growth of the Arboretum. More than 700 trees have been donated since 1991. The 3.2-hectare (8-acre) **Ornamental Gardens** are a must-see. They were created by the government in the late 19th century to assist European immigrant farmers to test imported flowers, shrubs, and trees in the Canadian environment. There is a perennial collection, annual garden, rose garden, sunken garden, and rock garden. The rose collection includes the "Explorer" series of winter-hardy roses. Some of the specimens in the hedge collection date from 1891. Approximately 100 types of iris and 125 strains of lilac are on display. The **Tropical Greenhouse,** relocated from Major Hill's Park in the 1930s, holds 500 different plants and is open daily 9am to 4pm. There is also a **Demonstration Organic Garden** adjacent to the Experimental Farm parking lot just off Prince of Wales Drive. The garden, maintained by volunteers, features companion planting, a perennial bed, a bee and butterfly bed, a fragrance bed, a herb bed, a rockery, fruit trees and bushes, vegetable beds that include heirloom varieties, and a composting area. **Maplelawn** is a historical Victorian walled garden located at 529 Richmond Rd. in Ottawa's west end. Dating from 1831, the garden has been preserved and rehabilitated by a volunteer group, using historical documents to aid preservation of the original design. Stroll the grounds of historic **Rideau Hall,** residence of the Governor General, and view the **Heritage Rose Garden.** The **Mackenzie King Estate,** located within beautiful **Gatineau Park,** features formal flower beds, a hidden rock garden, a collection of picturesque ruins from Canada and abroad, and forest trails. And last but not least — don't forget the magnificent displays of **tulips in mid-May** throughout the city of Ottawa.

2 Museums & Galleries

MUSEUMS

Canada and the World Pavilion Designed to celebrate and demonstrate achievements of individual Canadians on the international scene, this 1,104 sq. m (12,000 sq. ft.) pavilion opened as a permanent exhibition in 2001. Discover the unique stories of Canadians who have made an impact on the world in the fields of sports, the arts, international relations, and science and technology.

Learn about filmmakers, comedians, the game of hockey, Olympic athletes, and the International Space Station. Operate a myoelectric arm or maneuver a wheelchair just like Rick Hansen's. Find out what Canadians are doing throughout the world to promote social justice, sustainable development, and basic human rights. Located in Rideau Falls Park on Sussex Drive, only a short walk from downtown. Free admission and on-site parking. While you're there, visit Rideau Falls (also in Rideau Falls Park) and Rideau Hall, whose main entrance is just a 3-minute walk east along Sussex Drive on your right.

50 Sussex Dr. (in Rideau Falls Park). For information call the Capital Infocentre at © **800/465-1867** or 613/239-5000. Free admission. May–late June daily 9:30am–5pm; late June–Labour Day (first Mon in Sept) daily 10am–6pm; Labour Day–late Oct daily 9:30am–5pm. Parking on-site. From downtown, travel northeast along Sussex Dr. The Pavilion is adjacent to Rideau Falls on your left.

Canadian Museum of Contemporary Photography This museum is an affiliate of the National Gallery and the collection complements that of Canada's premier art gallery. On show is the best of documentary and art photography produced by Canada's most dynamic photographers, changing on a regular basis. The museum also organizes traveling exhibitions and educational programs. Wheelchairs and strollers are available for visitors. The museum building is a former "tunnel" of the Grand Trunk Railway, and measures 166 m (545 ft.) long by 17m (56 ft.) wide. The exterior blends comfortably with its historical surroundings, featuring limestone walls and stone balustrades. A glass and steel pavilion entrance on Wellington Street leads visitors down into the lobby, adjacent to the Ottawa Locks.

1 Rideau Canal. © **613/990-8257.** http://cmcp.gallery.ca. Admission C$4 (US$3.25) adult, C$3 (US$2.50) senior/student; C$2 (US$1.65) youth 12–19; free for children under 12; C$8 (US$7) family (max. 2 adults & 3 children). Free admission Thursdays after 5pm. May–Oct daily 10am–5pm, Thurs until 8pm. Oct–May Wed–Sun 10am–5pm, Thurs until 8pm. The museum is sandwiched between the Ottawa Locks and the Fairmont Château Laurier, just east of the Parliament Buildings.

Canadian Postal Museum Tracing the history of mail delivery across the vast landscape of Canada, the Postal Museum is housed within the Canadian Museum of Civilization. For details, see the Canadian Museum of Civilization entry earlier in this chapter.

Canadian Ski Museum Winter sports enthusiasts will enjoy a visit to the Canadian Ski Museum to learn about the history of skiing and how it evolved into the high-tech, high-speed sport of today. A large collection of photographs, memorabilia, and ski equipment is on display, aiming to preserve the memory of Canada's skiing history. The evolution of downhill skiing is explained, with credit for the world's first ski tow going to an enterprising Quebecer in the 1930s. Handmade wooden skis with strips of sealskin on the base to prevent back-slipping are a long way from the parabolic skis of today. After visiting the museum, you can browse the outdoor adventure equipment and supplies in Trailhead, the retail store on the main floor of the building. There are a number of other outdoor stores in the neighborhood of Westboro to explore as well — Bushtukah at 206 Richmond Rd., Mountain Equipment Co-op at 366 Richmond Rd., and The Expedition Shoppe at 369 Richmond Rd. The Canadian Ski Museum entrance is at the side of the "Trailhead" timber frame building on the south side of Scott Street..

1960 Scott St. © **613/722-3584.** www.skimuseum.ca. Free admission. Mon–Sat 9am–5pm, Sun 11am–5pm. Guided tours are available.

Currency Museum of the Bank of Canada Tracing the development of money over the past 2,500 years, the Currency Museum offers eight galleries to wander through and a spacious, light-filled atrium in the entrance hall of the center block of the Bank of Canada on Wellington Street, a couple of minutes' walk from Parliament Hill. Some unusual articles have been used as currency, including teeth, grain, cattle, glass beads, shells, fish hooks, and cocoa beans. Six of the galleries are devoted to history, the seventh holds special exhibits, and the eighth showcases the most comprehensive display of Canadian numismatic material in the world. The collection puts particular emphasis on Canadian currency and its history. You can visit on your own or join a guided tour held twice daily in the summer months.

245 Sparks St. ℂ **613/782-8914.** www.currencymuseum.ca. Free admission. May–Labour Day (first Mon in Sept) Mon–Sat 10:30am–5pm, Sun 1–5pm; Labour Day–April Tues–Sat 10:30am–5pm, Sun 1–5pm.

Library and Archives Canada This federal agency describes itself as an innovative knowledge institution. It combines the collections, services, and staff of the former National Library of Canada and National Archives of Canada. Millions of documents of all types — diaries, artwork, maps, films, treaties, journals, and more — that pertain to Canada's cultural, social, and political development are accessed through this agency. In addition, the Library focuses on the collection and preservation of works in all subjects written by, about, or of interest to Canadians. Anyone who registers at the Library can use the resources to find information on Canadian literature, music, history, genealogy, literary manuscripts, artists' books, and rare books. There are also tapes, records, and CDs in the music collection and personal papers and memorabilia in the literary manuscript collection. Exhibitions and displays are staged regularly. Lectures, book launches, readings, films, storytelling workshops, musical concerts (featuring pianists, medieval ensembles, folksingers, and cellists), and other events are held throughout the year.

395 Wellington St. ℂ **866/578-7777** or 613/996-5115. www.collectionscanada.ca. Admission free; some events require tickets and fee. General hours Mon–Fri 8:30am–5pm; reading room daily 8am–11pm.

Logan Hall, Geological Survey of Canada Logan Hall serves as an exhibition hall for a selection of the Geological Survey of Canada's vast collection of Canadian rocks, minerals, fossils, meteorites, and ores. Interactive displays and videos test visitors' knowledge of geology and even teach you how to pan for gold. An extensive fossil collection shows examples of bacteria, plants, and invertebrate and vertebrate animals, as well as fossils of specific historical interest. Logan Hall is named after Sir William Logan, who founded the Geological Survey of Canada in 1842 and was its first director.

601 Booth St. ℂ **613/996-3919.** Free admission. Mon–Fri 8am–4pm.

Royal Canadian Mint ✦ Established in 1908 to produce Canada's circulation coins, the Royal Canadian Mint enjoys an excellent reputation around the world for producing high-quality coins. Since 1976, when a plant was built in Winnipeg, Manitoba, for the high-speed, high-volume production of circulation coins, the Royal Canadian Mint has concentrated on producing numismatic (commemorative) coins. The Royal Canadian Mint is also the oldest and one of the largest gold refineries in the Western Hemisphere and is known and respected around the globe as a premier gold refinery. Just gaining entry to the building is an experience at the Royal Canadian Mint. First you peer into the ticket booth beside a huge pair of iron gates to buy your tour tickets (you can also visit the boutique without taking the tour). As a security guard watches the entrance (also equipped with a surveillance camera), one of the gates swings open momentarily to allow you to step inside the compound, and then clanks shut behind you. When you enter the stone "castle," you find yourself in a foyer with a set of stairs leading upward on your left and an elevator straight ahead. Both will take you to the boutique, which displays the many coins and souvenirs available for purchase in well-lit glass showcases around the room. When it's time for the tour, you're ushered into a small theater to watch a short film on a selected aspect of the mint's activities. Next your guide accompanies you to the viewing gallery, which winds its way through the factory. There is a lot to see here, and the tour guide outlines the process of manufacturing coins as you move along the corridor above the factory floor. The process is fascinating, from the rollers that transform the cast bars into flattened strips, to tubs of blanks that have been punched from the strips, to workers hand-drying the blanks after washing, right to the final inspection and hand-packaging of the finished coins.

Where to eat: The ByWard Market area is your best bet for somewhere to grab a snack or meal. It's only a short walk southeast of the Mint.

320 Sussex Dr. ✆ **800/276-7714** or 613/993-8990. www.mint.ca. Admission C$5 (US$4) adults; C$3 (US$2.50) children 4–15; children under 4 free; C$13 (US$11) family (max. 2 adults and 4 children). Weekends reduced rate. Victoria Day (third Mon in May)–Labour Day (first Mon in Sept) Mon–Fri 9am–8pm, Sat–Sun 9am–5:30pm. Rest of the year daily 9am–5pm. Call for advance reservations for guided tours. From the Queensway, take the Nicholas St. exit (118). Turn left on Rideau St. and right onto Sussex Dr. The Mint is on your left.

FEDERAL BUILDINGS

Lester B. Pearson Building This building, with its award-winning granite-aggregate-covered tiered towers, is the home of the federal department of Foreign Affairs and International Trade. More than 7,000 people work for this department globally to manage Canada's relations with the world; 3,000 of them work within this building. You are welcome to enter the main lobby and view the flags of more than 170 countries on display. Former prime minister Lester B. Pearson's Nobel Peace Prize medal, which he was awarded for his peacekeeping efforts during the Suez crisis in 1956, is also on display. Canada and the World Pavilion and Rideau Falls are just a few steps farther along Sussex Drive.

125 Sussex Dr. Lobby accessible to the public during normal business hours; some exceptions may apply. From the Queensway, take the Nicholas St. exit (118). Turn left on Rideau St. and right onto Sussex Dr. The Lester B. Pearson Building is on your right, just past the Macdonald–Cartier bridge to Quebec.

Supreme Court of Canada The Supreme Court is a general court of appeal for both criminal and civil cases and is the highest court of appeal in the country. Three sessions per year, each lasting three months, are held between October and June. When the Court is in session it sits Monday through Friday, usually hearing two appeals a day. Law students take members of the public on free guided tours, which take about half an hour and are recommended for all ages. From May to August, tours are held daily on a continuing basis, and the rest of the year tours are available by prior arrangement on weekdays. The architecture of the building is impressive to behold and the grand entrance hall is magnificent. If you'd like the experience of witnessing an appeal, take a seat in the public gallery when court is in session.

301 Wellington St. ✆ **613/995-4330**. www.scc-csc.gc.ca. For tour reservations, call ✆ **613/995-5361**. May–Aug daily 9am–5pm, Sept–Apr Mon–Fri 9am–5pm.

GALLERIES

Carleton University Art Gallery The collection focuses on three main areas: Canadian art, particularly post-1942, when the university was founded, European art, especially prints and drawings created between the 16th and 19th centuries, and Inuit art, encompassing sculptures, textiles, drawings, and prints.

1125 Colonel By Dr., St. Patrick's Building, Carleton University Campus. ✆ **613/520-2120.**

Gallery 101 This nonprofit, artist-run center focuses on professional presentation of visual and media art from Canadian and international contemporary artists.

236 Nepean St. ✆ **613/230-2799.**

Ottawa Art Gallery The Ottawa Art Gallery is an independent nonprofit public art gallery showing contemporary visual art from the local arts community. Programs include exhibitions, tours, and talks.

Arts Court Building, 2 Daly Ave. ✆ **613/233-8699.**

Ottawa School of Art Gallery The Ottawa School of Art holds courses and workshops by professional artists for all levels of students. The school gallery features work by students in addition to special exhibitions of professional artists.

35 George St. ✆ **613/241-7471.**

SAW Gallery This contemporary art center focuses on new media arts, performance visual art that reaches beyond traditional forms of expression, and art that openly declares its political and social position.

67 Nicholas St. ✆ **613/236-6181.**

3 Heritage Attractions

Ottawa has an unusually high number of designated heritage properties and districts. This is partly due to a keen interest in local architecture and history expressed by citizens and politicians. The sophisticated system of heritage planning that protects many of Ottawa's most interesting and beautiful structures is a relatively recent phenomenon, however. It began in 1975, the year that the Ontario government passed the *Ontario Heritage Act,* which gave power to municipal governments to designate properties of heritage significance. As a result of efforts by the Local Architectural Conservation Advisory Committee, the City of Ottawa's official policy on encouragement of heritage preservation was accepted in 1995. Approximately 3,000 properties in Ottawa are designated under the *Ontario Heritage Act.* About 10% of these have individual designation; the rest lie within 15 heritage conservation districts.

If you're looking for a stroll through a heritage district, wander the streets in the following neighborhoods, easily accessible from downtown: ByWard Market and Lowertown (bounded by Sussex Drive, Bolton Street, King Edward Avenue, and Rideau Street), or Sandy Hill between Waller Street, Besserer Street, Cobourg Street, and Laurier Avenue. Centretown (bounded by Kent Street, Lisgar Street, Elgin Street, and Arlington Avenue), although a heritage district, is not as pleasant for walking, since there is a lot of road traffic and there are high-rise buildings on the major roads. Somerset Village, a stretch of Somerset Street between Bank and O'Connor streets, is characterized by a cluster of redbrick historical buildings. You can also enjoy the leafy residential streets of the Glebe. Streets leading off Bank Street between the Queensway and the Rideau Canal are lined with Victorian and Edwardian homes. The village of Rockcliffe Park, a residential neighborhood just northeast of Rideau Hall, has numerous gracious properties, many of which have been transformed into ambassadors' residences. If you are interested in learning more about Ottawa's heritage buildings, visit www.heritageottawa.org.

MUSEUMS & ATTRACTIONS

Aboriginal Experiences On historical Victoria Island in the Ottawa River, just west of Parliament Hill, Turtle Island Tourism Company operates an award-winning Aboriginal village in the summer months. Choose your "experience" package upon arrival at the site. Packages range from a 1-hour interpretive learning tour of the village at a cost of C$7 (US$6) adult and C$4 (US$3.25) child to craft workshops, Native lunches, and overnight tipi camping retreats in the Gatineau Hills at a cost of C$149 (US$122) per person, inclusive of camping supplies and food. Live demonstrations of traditional and contemporary Native singing, drumming, and dancing are staged daily. Listen to an ancient legend or story in an authentic tipi, enjoy traditional Aboriginal foods, and visit the cultural displays. On show are tipis, birch bark canoes, totem poles, and Cree Hunt Camps. Fun for all ages. The Trading Post craft shop stocks arts and crafts made by the local Aboriginal community. You can reach Victoria Island from the Chaudières Bridge by car or via the Portage Bridge if you're walking or cycling.

Victoria Island (**877/811-3233** or 613/564-9494. www.aboriginalexperiences.com. Late June–early Sept daily 11am–6pm. Victoria Island is just west of the Parliament Buildings, and lies below the Chaudières and Portage bridges.

Billings Estate Museum This historical Georgian estate home, which was completed in 1829, is one of Ottawa's oldest properties. Built for Braddish and Lamira Billings, who settled on the land in 1813, the Billings Estate includes several outbuildings on the 3.4-hectare (8.4-acre) site and was home to five generations of the Billings family, spanning two centuries. Browse the collections of family heirlooms, furnishings, tools, paintings, and documents on your own or take a guided tour. Hands-on activities, special events, and workshops are scheduled on a regular basis. Stroll the lush lawns, colorful flower beds, wooded slopes, and old pathways. Enjoy tea on the lawn in the summer months, served several afternoons each week.

2100 Cabot St. (**613/247-4830.** Admission C$2.50 (US$2) adult, C$2 (US$1.65) senior, C$1.50 (US$1.25) child. May–Oct, Tues–Sun noon–5pm. Hours subject to change; call ahead.

Bytown Museum Housed in Ottawa's oldest stone building (1827), which served as the Commissariat during the construction of the Rideau Canal, this museum is operated by the Historical Society of Ottawa. Articles belonging to Lieutenant-Colonel By, the canal's builder and one of Ottawa's (then known as Bytown) most influential citizens, are on display. In addition, artifacts reflect the social history of local pioneer families in four period rooms and a number of changing exhibits. The rooms depict an 1850s Bytown kitchen, a French-Canadian lumber camp shanty, a Victorian parlor, and an early toy store. The museum is situated beside the Ottawa Locks, sandwiched between Parliament Hill and the Fairmont Château Laurier Hotel.

Beside Ottawa Locks. (**613/234-4570.** Admission C$5 (US$4) adult, C$3 (US$2.50) senior/student; C$2 (US$1.65) child 4–12. Children under 4 free. Apr–mid-May Mon–Fri 10am–2pm. Mid-May–mid-Oct Mon–Fri 10am–5pm; Sat–Sun 10am–4pm; Mid-Oct–Nov Mon–Fri 10am–2pm.

History of the ByWard Market

The ByWard Market area is the oldest part of Ottawa. Following the War of 1812, the British were looking for an alternative navigable waterway between Montreal and Kingston as a precaution against renewed hostilities with the Americans. The Rideau River was chosen, despite the fact that a canal would have to be built to bypass the Rideau Falls, the only point of contact between the Ottawa and Rideau Rivers. Wrightsville was a thriving lumber town on the north shore of the Ottawa River, but a settlement was needed for canal workers on the south shore adjacent to the construction site. Accordingly, a shantytown grew up in the area between the Rideau River and the canal and came to be known as Lowertown, which has today's ByWard Market district as its heart. The opening of the Rideau Centre shopping mall adjacent to the Market led residents and visitors to rediscover the district, and the ByWard Market is now one of the trendiest places in Ottawa for shopping, dining, and entertainment.

ByWard Market ✿✿ In a compact area bordered by St. Patrick Street on the north, King Edward Avenue on the east, Rideau Street on the south, and Sussex Drive on the west, there is a lively district known as the ByWard Market. In the heart of the area, one block east of Sussex Drive between York and George streets, lies the ByWard Market building and the outdoor stalls of the farmers' market, where you can buy outstanding fresh local produce, flowers, and other products such as maple syrup. Outdoor markets are wonderful places to stroll. The activity and bustle of the market and the fun of choosing a selection of fresh fruit and vegetables to take home and enjoy are a world away from trudging up and down supermarket aisles. To complement the fresh produce, you'll find gourmet food vendors inside the Market building. There are dozens of excellent food retailers in the district, and I urge you to venture inside and taste what's on offer. Here are a few places to keep a lookout for, just to get you started: Bottega Nicastro, 64 George St.; Le Boulanger Français/The French Baker, 119 Murray St.; Chilly Chilies, 55 ByWard Market; House of Cheese, 34 ByWard Market; International Cheese & Deli, 40 ByWard Market; Lapointe Fish, 46 ByWard Market; Le Moulin de Provence, 55 ByWard Market; and the Tea Store, 55 ByWard Market. Throughout the year, the ByWard Market hosts family-oriented events on weekends as a thank-you to their customers and to make the community surrounding the market a little brighter. Events include a Mother's Day celebration with special restaurant menus, an outdoor fashion show, a jazz band, free hayrides, and farm animals on display. On the first Sunday in June, a display of 150 vintage, classic, and high-performance cars is held. Annual events later in the year include Bytown Days when 19th-century Ottawa is revisited, a search for the world's biggest pumpkin, and an old-fashioned Christmas with carolers serenading visitors to the Market district as they ride in horse-drawn carriages adorned with sleigh bells.

From the Queensway, exit at Nicholas St. (exit 118). At Rideau St., turn right and then left on King Edward Ave. From King Edward Ave., turn left onto George, York, Clarence, or Patrick streets. Or you can turn left onto Rideau St., right on Sussex Dr., and then turn right onto George, York, Clarence, or Murray streets.

Laurier House   This fine Victorian residence, built in 1878, has been home to two prime ministers and is a designated National Historic Site. A tour of this home helps to put a human face on Canada's politics and history. Prior to 1896, there was no official residence provided for the prime minister. Sir Wilfrid Laurier, Canada's first French-Canadian prime minister, was the first resident of Laurier House, purchased by the Liberal Party to house their leader. Several rooms contain furnishings and mementos of Laurier's, but the majority of the house is restored to the era of William Lyon Mackenzie King, Canada's longest serving prime minister and the second occupant of the house. Apparently King held seances in the library, and his crystal ball is on display. The Pearson Gallery contains former prime minister Lester B. Pearson's study, which was moved here from his home in Rockcliffe Park. The gallery displays photographs and artifacts from the Pearson years, including a replica of Pearson's Nobel Peace Prize medal, which he was awarded for his role in the 1956 Suez crisis. Wander over to Strathcona Park after visiting the museum. It's just a couple of minutes' walk east along Laurier Avenue. Stroll the pathways in summer and watch the swans glide along the Rideau River. If you have children with you, take them to the delightful playground.

335 Laurier Ave. E. *©* **613/992-8142.** Admission C$3.75 (US$3) adult, C$3.25 (US$2.70) senior, C$2.25 (US$1.85) youth 6–16, free for children 5 and under. Apr–mid-May Mon–Fri 9am–5pm; Mid-May–mid-Oct Mon–Sat 9am–5pm, Sun 1–5pm. Closed mid-Oct–Mar except for group tours by reservation only. From the Queensway, take the Nicholas St. exit (exit 118). Turn right on Laurier Ave. E. The museum is on your left.

The Role of the Governor General

The governor general's role is to represent the Crown in Canada, promote Canadian sovereignty, celebrate Canadian excellence, and encourage national identity, national unity, and moral leadership. Canada is both a parliamentary democracy and a constitutional monarchy. Since Canadians recognize Her Majesty Queen Elizabeth II as the Head of State, a representative of the Queen is required in Canada. This is one of the roles of the governor general — to carry out Her Majesty's duties in Canada on a daily basis.

Various trophies and awards, including the Stanley Cup, Grey Cup, and the Governor General's Literary Awards, have been created by past governors general and serve to recognize and celebrate Canadian achievements.

Governors general are appointed by the Queen on the advice of the prime minister.

The current governor general of Canada is Her Excellency the Right Honourable Adrienne Clarkson.

Rideau Hall   Rideau Hall has been the official residence and workplace of Canada's Governor General since 1867 and is considered to be the symbolic home of all Canadians. The public is welcome to wander the 32 hectares (79 acres) of beautiful gardens and forested areas and visit the greenhouse. Outdoor concerts and cricket matches are held in the summer, and there's ice-skating on the pond in winter. Free guided tours of the staterooms of the residence are offered; hours vary throughout the year, although in the peak tourist season in the summer there are self-guided tours every morning and guided tours in the afternoons, approximately 45 minutes long. The Governor General's Awards are presented here annually, honoring Canadians for extraordinary accomplishments, courage, and contributions to science, the arts, and humanity. Two major events are held annually for the public — a Garden Party in June or July and a Winter Celebration. The Ceremonial Guard is on duty at Rideau Hall during July and August. The first Changing of the Guard Ceremony, held in late June, features a colorful parade led by a marching band. Relief of the Sentries is a ceremony performed hourly 9am to 5pm during the summer. The Visitor Centre, operating daily between May and October, has family activities, a play structure, and hands-on activities for children. The Governor General's Summer Concerts are held on the beautifully landscaped grounds. Set up your lawn chair, spread out the picnic blanket, and enjoy the sunshine. Wheelchairs, washroom facilities, and picnic tables are available at Rideau Hall.

1 Sussex Dr. *(C)* **800/465-6890** or 613/991-4422. www.gg.ca. Admission to all tours and activities is free. Grounds are generally open daily 8am–one hour before sunset; subject to change without notice. From the Queensway, take the Nicholas St. exit (exit 118), turn left on Rideau St., right on Sussex Dr. The entrance to Rideau Hall is on your right, just after you cross the Rideau River.

The Lives and Times of Canada's PMs

As you tour around the city, you will notice public buildings, streets, and bridges named after some of Canada's most prominent past political leaders. There are plenty of places to visit where you can learn more about the country's prime ministers and how they shaped Canada's identity, political structure, and social fabric.

You can visit the office of **Sir John A. Macdonald,** Canada's first prime minister, in the East Block of the Parliament Buildings. His statue stands on the Hill between Centre Block and East Block. A visit to **Laurier House** at 334 Laurier Ave. E. will give you a glimpse into the lives of three prime ministers. **Sir Wilfrid Laurier** was the first prime minister to reside there. Several rooms contain items pertaining to Laurier, but the majority of the house has been restored to the era of **William Lyon Mackenzie King,** who inherited the house from the Lauriers. Churchill and Roosevelt both visited King at this residence. King had an estate in the midst of **Gatineau Park,** which was bequeathed to the Canadian people upon his death in 1950. It's open from mid-May to mid-October. Also at Laurier House is **Lester B. Pearson's** study, which was moved here from his home in Rockcliffe Park. On Parliament Hill, Laurier's statue stands at the southeast corner of East Block, King at the northwest corner of East Block, and you'll find Pearson just north of West Block. To learn more about the times of **John Diefenbaker,** take a tour of the **Diefenbunker Cold War Museum,** an underground bunker built to shelter the Canadian government in the event of nuclear attack during the period of the Cold War. Diefenbaker's statue stands on the northeast corner of West Block. A memorial in the form of a larger than life–size statue, to be carved from light grey granite by Canadian artist John Douglas Batten, will commemorate the life of the late **Pierre Elliott Trudeau.** The statue will stand in Andrew Haydon Park, 15 minutes west of downtown Ottawa on the banks of the Ottawa River. Finally, if you want to catch a glimpse of Canada's current head of government, Prime Minister **Paul Martin,** keep your eyes open around the **Langevin Block** at 50 Wellington St., across from Parliament Hill. The offices of the prime minister are housed in this magnificent olive sandstone building. You can also drive or stroll past the gates of **24 Sussex Drive,** the official residence of the prime minister.

PLACES OF WORSHIP

Cathedral Basilica of Notre-Dame ✛ The splendid Notre-Dame Cathedral Basilica is Ottawa's oldest church. A wooden structure was first erected on the site in 1832, and construction of the current building began in 1841. The exterior stonework has a plain, flat facade but this is offset by the magnificent French-Canadian tin steeples that house the church bells. The late-Victorian interior is typically ornate. Details include two vaulted ceilings, side galleries, extensive carved woodwork, carved altars, and 30 life-size carved figures. A 3-m-high (10 ft.) wooden gilded statue of the Madonna and Child, created by Italian sculptor Cardona in 1865, stands above the apex of the front facade gable between the two steeples.

385 Sussex Dr.

Christ Church Cathedral The original church on this site was completed in 1833. In 1872, the growing congregation required a larger church, and a new building was constructed on the site between 1872 and 1873. When the Diocese of Ottawa was formed in 1896, Christ Church became the seat of the Anglican bishop of Ottawa. The architectural style is that of English Gothic Revival and the building's exterior has survived in its original form. Some changes have been made to the interior over the years. A number of state funerals have been held here, including those of governor general Vincent Massey, prime minister John Diefenbaker, and prime minister Lester B. Pearson.

439 Queen St.

St. Andrew's Presbyterian Church St. Andrew's predates Christ Church as the oldest Protestant congregation in Ottawa, with worship held on the site since 1828. When the construction of the new Christ Church began in 1872, it prompted St. Andrew's, which was also suffering from overcrowding, to build a new church on the site. Also constructed in Gothic Revival style, the new St. Andrew's was built of rock-faced gray limestone, which distinguished it from the golden sandstone of Christ Church. Then–prime minister Mackenzie King attended services at St. Andrew's. During World War II, when the Dutch Royal family was in exile in Ottawa, the daughter of Queen Juliana of the Netherlands was baptized at this church.

82 Kent St.

Other downtown churches you may like to visit, which all date from the 19th century and are designated heritage properties, include St. Patrick's Basilica, 240 Kent St.; First Baptist Church, 140 Laurier Ave. W.; St. Alban the Martyr Church, 125 Daly Ave.; St. Paul's–Eastern United Church (originally St. Paul's Presbyterian Church; the United Church was not created until 1925), 90 Daly Ave.; St. Paul's Evangelical Lutheran Church, 210 Wilbrod St.; All Saints Anglican Church, 315–317 Chapel St.; and Eglise Ste-Anne, 528–530 Old St. Patrick St.

4 Organized Tours
ON WHEELS

Grayline Sightseeing Tours ✸ Choose an open-top double decker bus or vintage trolley bus. Tours officially start at the corner of Sparks and Metcalfe streets, but you can step on or off the bus any time you wish at these stops: Parliament Hill, Museum of Civilization, Notre-Dame Basilica, Rideau Hall, RCMP Rockcliffe Stables, Canada Aviation Museum, National War Museum, Royal Canadian Mint, National Gallery of Canada, ByWard Market, Rideau Canal, Dow's Lake, Central Experimental Farm, Museum of Nature. Tours operate from May to October. Tickets are valid for two days and prices are reasonable — a family of four can get a two-day, on-off-privilege ticket for C$80 (US$66).

For departure locations and times and other information call Grayline ℰ **800/297-6422** or 613/565-5463. Seasonal.

The Terry Fox Statue: A Symbol of Hope and Courage

Across from the Centre Block of Parliament Hill, in front of the Capital Infocentre, stands a proud memorial to a courageous young Canadian. In 1977, 18-year-old **Terry Fox** was given the devastating news that he had bone cancer and his right leg would have to be amputated six inches above the knee. Terry wanted to do something to give hope to people living with cancer, and he decided to run across Canada to raise money for **cancer research.** After many months of training, during which he ran more than 5,000km (3,000 miles), Terry dipped his artificial leg in the Atlantic Ocean on April 12, 1980 and began his **"Marathon of Hope."** He traveled courageously through six provinces and over 5,370km (3,330 miles) before being forced to retire near Thunder Bay, Ontario. The cancer had spread to Terry's lungs and he was flown home to British Columbia. Ten months later, in June 1981, Terry died at the age of 22. The country was in mourning.

An annual fundraising event was established in his memory and the first **Terry Fox Run,** held at more than 760 sites across Canada and around the world in 1981, raised C$3.5 million. By the year 2004, the total amount of money raised in Terry's name was close to C$360 million. Terry is a true Canadian hero and has become a symbol of hope and courage to people living with cancer and their families and friends.

Take Time for a Scenic Drive

Enjoy a leisurely drive along Ottawa's parkways and scenic driveways. **HEADING EAST** Head east on Wellington Street past **Parliament Hill,** through Confederation Square. You'll pass the grand **Fairmont Château Laurier** on your left. Turn left at the lights (north) onto Sussex Drive. After passing the **American Embassy** on your left, glorious views open up across the islands.

Continue along Sussex Drive to St. Patrick Street, turning left into **Nepean Point.** Here you can share a fine view of the river with a statue of French explorer **Samuel de Champlain,** one of the first Europeans to arrive in the region almost 400 years ago. Adjacent to Nepean Point is **Major's Hill Park,** where there are wonderful views of the canal locks, the Ottawa River, and the striking architecture of the **National Gallery.** Rejoin Sussex Drive, traveling northeast. You'll cross the Rideau River via Green Island. **Rideau Falls** are on your left. The road passes **24 Sussex Drive,** the **residence of the prime minister,** which is not open to the public. Just ahead on your right is **Rideau Hall.** Tours of the grounds and the interior public rooms are available. Continuing, the drive becomes **Rockcliffe Parkway,** a beautiful route along the Ottawa River and through **Rockcliffe Park.** Watch for a right fork to Acacia Avenue, which leads to the **Rockeries,** which are carpeted with colourful blooms in the spring. If you wish, continue along the Parkway to the **Musical Ride Centre, RCMP Rockcliffe Stables,** and the **Aviation Museum,** or return to the Parkway and head west toward downtown Ottawa.

HEADING WEST Head west on Wellington Street, past **Parliament Hill,** the **Supreme Court of Canada,** and the **Library and Archives Canada** on your right. The road opens up into the **Ottawa River Parkway,** passing the new **Canadian War Museum.** Continue through the parkland to **Island Park Drive** and turn left. This road will take you under the Queensway (Hwy 417) and through the grounds of the **Experimental Farm and Arboretum.** When you reach a European-style "roundabout," you have two choices. Turn **right,** taking **Prince of Wales Drive** to **Hog's Back Road.** Turn left here, by the locks and **Hog's Back Falls.** Turn left again onto **Colonel By Drive** and follow this picturesque route along the east bank of the **Rideau Canal** back downtown. If you decide to turn left (north) at the roundabout, you'll take a slightly shorter but just as pretty route back downtown along **Queen Elizabeth Driveway,** on the west bank of the **Rideau Canal.**

ON FOOT

Aside from the tours listed here, see the walking tours described in chapter 7, "Active Ottawa."

Art Walk (Self-Guided) The National Capital Commission has produced a guide, called *Street SmART,* describing seven public art walking tours in Ottawa and Hull. You will see statues of prominent historical figures, contemporary sculptures made of wood, stone, papier-mâché, metal, and fiberglass, war memorials, statues of Canadian heroes, totem poles, murals, and monuments. Tours vary from 35 minutes to 1 hour in length.

Available free from the Capital Infocentre, 90 Wellington Street ℂ **800/465-1867.**

Haunted Walks Inc. ★ I highly recommend joining Haunted Walks Inc. for an evening's entertainment. Follow a black-cloaked storyteller, lantern in hand, through the city streets and hear the darker side of Ottawa's history. They welcome families on the tours (with the exception of the Naughty Ottawa Pub Tour, which as you might expect is for adults only), and claim that many of their fans are in fact children. There aren't any nasty surprises or theatrical incidents on the tour — the guides prefer to tell the stories and take you to the sites of hauntings and ghost sightings, and leave the rest up to your imagination. The ghost stories have been meticulously researched using local and national archives, old newspapers, and books, and by interviewing folks who have had first-hand experiences with the hauntings. The walks take place mostly out of doors, so dress for the weather. Several tours are available, including a tour of the old Carleton County Jail (death row and the gallows are disconcertingly eerie), the Fairmont Château Laurier, and the Original Haunted Walk of Ottawa. Tours last between 1 and 2¹/₂ hours and the maximum distance covered is about 1.6km (1 mile). Call for information on French-language tours and Halloween tours.

The Haunted Walks Inc. ticket booth is at the corner of Sparks St. and Elgin St.; some tours depart directly from there, others from the Farimont Château Laurier or the Old Carleton County Jail. ℂ **613/232-0344.** Tickets C$10–C$14 (US$8–US$12) adult, C$5–C$7 (US$4–US$6) child, depending on the tour. Tours daily throughout the year, but times and frequency change with the season. Please call for current tour schedule.

Ottawa On Foot/Original Ottawa Walking Tour Follow an enthusiastic tour guide in the steps of Ottawa's colorful history on a 1-hour (1.4-km, 1-mile) or 2-hour (2.6-km, 1¹/₂-mile) walk around the city sights. Inspired by the European city walking tours experienced by the young owners of this tour company, the tours have a strong historical bias, delivered in an engaging and entertaining manner.

Tours start from the corner of Metcalfe St. and Wellington St. in front of the Capital Infocentre and are generally twice daily. ℂ **613/447-7566.** Purchase tickets directly from tour guide ten minutes before tour. Tour times: Tues–Sun 11am and 1:45pm. Call to confirm, since times subject to change. Tickets C$7–C$11 (US$7–US$9) adult, C$5–C$9 (US$4–US$7) senior/student, C$5 (US$4) child 10 and under.

Parliament Hill Walking Tours A free booklet available from the Capital Infocentre gives a detailed description of a self-guided outdoor walking tour of Parliament Hill — and from late June to early September there is a guided outdoor walking tour called "In the Footsteps of Great Canadians" that takes place daily. Same-day free tickets are available from the Info-Tent on Parliament Hill. See the entry under "Parliament Hill" earlier in this chapter for more information.

ON THE WATER

Ottawa Riverboat Company ★ Take a one-hour narrated tour on the 305-passenger *Sea Prince II,* the largest tour boat in Ottawa. Refreshments are available on board. Reservations recommended. Cruise tickets available at the ticket booth in Confederation Square, Ottawa Riverboat Dock (at the foot of the Ottawa Locks just west of the Fairmont Château Laurier Hotel), Jacques-Cartier Park and Marina in Gatineau, and selected hotels. A family-oriented Sunday brunch tour is offered late June to early September. Evening cruises with dinner and dancing are also offered in the summer. Reservations are required for brunch and dinner cruises.

(Kids) Cruises for Kids

If you have young children (under age 10 or so), then an Ottawa River cruise is the better choice. You can stroll around the deck or have a snack, and the open design is perfect on a hot summer's day, as you can catch the cool breeze off the water. In contrast, the canal boats have a single enclosed deck and are more confined.

335 Cumberland St., Suite 200. ✆ **613/562-4888.** www.ottawariverboat.ca. Tickets for 1-hour tour C$16 (US$13) adult, C$14 (US$12) senior/student, C$8 (US$7) child 6–12, under 6 free, C$38 (US$31) family (max. 2 adults and 2 children). Three to six departures daily in season from Ottawa dock at the foot of the Ottawa Locks and from the Jacques-Cartier Park marina in Hull; call for departure times and information on brunch and dinner cruises.

Paul's Boat Lines ✪ Paul's Boat Lines cruises the Ottawa River and the Rideau Canal. On the Ottawa River, the 150-passenger *Paula D* takes visitors on a 90-minute cruise, with spectacular views of the Parliament Buildings, Rideau Falls, and other sites. The *Paula D* has an open-air upper deck shaded by an awning and an enclosed lower deck with a small snack bar, tables, and chairs. On the canal, you can glide along in one of three tour boats for a 75-minute cruise that takes you past the National Arts Centre, the University of Ottawa, Lansdowne Park, Carleton University, the Experimental Farm, and Dow's Lake.

219 Colonnade Rd. ✆ **613/225-6781** (office), 613/235-8409 (summer dock). Tickets for River Cruise: C$16 (US$13) adult, C$14 (US$12) senior/student, C$9 (US$7) child 5–15, free for child under 5, C$38 (US$31) family (max. 2 adults and 2 children). Canal cruise slightly lower rates. Four to 7 departures daily in season from Ottawa dock at the foot of the Ottawa Locks, from the Jacques-Cartier Park marina in Hull, and from the Conference Centre on the Rideau Canal; call for departure times.

IN THE AIR

Hot Air Ballooning If you fancy floating in the sky at a leisurely pace with the city spread out below you and you're not afraid of heights, you might like to splurge on a trip in a hot air balloon. For many people it's a once-in-a-lifetime experience. There may be restrictions on the minimum age for passengers, so call ahead. Or go to a launching and just watch as the balloons are prepared for flight and then take off. Everyone from babies to grandparents will enjoy the sight of the huge, colorful silken spheres as they gracefully rise into the sky. In the Ottawa area, the main operators are High Time Balloon Co. Inc. ✆ **613/521-9921,** www.hightimeballoon.com; Skyview Ballooning ✆ **613/724-7784,** www. skyviewballooning.com; Sundance Balloons ✆ **613/247-8277,** www.sundance balloons.com; and Windborne Ballooning ✆ **613/739-7388,** www.magmacom. com/windborneballooning.

Private Small Aircraft Year-round sightseeing tours over Ottawa and Gatineau are offered by West Capital Aviation, Carp Airport, 3257 Carp Rd., Carp, west of Ottawa ✆ **613/296-7971.**

5 Spectator Sports

Ottawa Lynx Take me out to the ball game! For fun and affordable family entertainment, visit JetForm Park, where the Ottawa Lynx, Ottawa's Triple-A affiliate of the Baltimore Orioles, play more than 70 home games from April to September. JetForm Park, which opened in 1993, is a state-of-the-art building that combines the old-time ballpark experience with modern facilities and services. The stadium boasts an award-winning natural grass and clay field, comfortable seats, and excellent sightlines. The open-air stands hold 10,000 spectators, most of whom are families. Facilities include a picnic area, barbecue terrace, and parking for 800 cars. Since the team's inception in 1993, the Ottawa Lynx Baseball Club has set two attendance records in the league and has won the International League Championship. JetForm Park is close to Highway 417 (the Queensway), at the corner of Vanier Parkway and Coventry Road. Tickets are available at the park or by phone.

300 Coventry Rd. ⓒ **613/747-LYNX (5969)**. www.ottawalynx.com. Tickets C$9–$11 (US$7–$9); C$7–$9 (US$6–US$7) seniors and children 14 and under.

Ottawa Renegades Ottawa resurrected its CFL (Canadian Football League) team in the 2002 season after an eight-year absence following the collapse of the Ottawa Rough Riders at the end of the 1996 season. The Ottawa Renegades' home field is at Frank Clair Stadium, located at Lansdowne Park, a multi-event site on Bank Street in the south end of the Glebe, just north of where the Rideau Canal crosses Bank Street. The season runs from June to October.

Frank Clair Stadium at Lansdowne Park, 1015 Bank St. ⓒ **613/231-5608** (general information and tickets); for tickets only visit CapitalTickets.ca ⓒ 613/599-3267. Tickets C$36–$92 adult; 20% discount for youth under 18 or with a valid student card.

Ottawa Senators Experience all the excitement of true National Hockey League (NHL) action at the Corel Centre, home of the Ottawa Senators — well, except during the 2004/2005 season, which was cancelled due to a salary dispute. Current ticket prices were not available when we went to press, but you can visit them online or call the Sens Customer Service & Information line at ⓒ **800/444-SENS (7367)** or ⓒ 613/599-0300. For meals, snacks, or suds before or after the game, check out the Senate Club, Marshy's Bar-B-Q and Grill, the Penalty Box Sandwich Bar, Frank Finnigan's, Club Scotiabank, Rickard's Pub, or the Silver Seven Brew House. For all your Sens souvenirs visit Sensations, the official merchandise outlet of the Ottawa Senators Hockey Club (in the Corel Centre at Gate 1).

1000 Palladium Dr. ⓒ **800/444-SENS (7367)** or 613/599-0300. www.ottawasenators.com. For tickets, visit CapitalTickets.ca ⓒ 613/599-3267 or the general numbers listed above. Ticket prices unavailable at time of printing.

Ottawa 67's For up-close and personal Ontario Hockey League (OHL) action, visit the Civic Centre in Lansdowne Park, home of the Ottawa 67's since their inception in — not coincidentally — 1967. With a seating capacity of almost 10,000 and 47 luxury suites, it is reputed to be one of the best homes in Junior hockey. On-site parking available.

1015 Bank St. ⓒ **613/232-6767** general information. For game-day tickets ⓒ **613/755-1166** or Ticketmaster (www.ticketmaster.ca). Tickets C$13 (US$11) adults, C$12 (US$10) senior/student, C$10 (US$8) child 12 and under.

University Sports Teams Check out the variety of varsity sports at Carleton University (ⓒ **613/520-7400;** www.carleton.ca), including basketball, fencing, field hockey, golf, Nordic skiing, rowing, rugby, soccer, swimming, and water polo. The University of Ottawa (ⓒ **613/562-5700**; www.uottawa.ca) has inter-university teams for basketball, cross-country, football, hockey, rugby, soccer, skiing, swimming, and volleyball.

6 Especially for Kids

When you're traveling with children, if you can put their needs first when planning your itinerary and include activities that all ages will enjoy then everyone will have a more pleasant vacation. Be sure to schedule plenty of time for relaxation (and naps, if your children are very young). The best advice you can follow is not to overschedule. Don't expect your kids to act like adults — young children have short attention spans. When they start to wiggle and fidget, let them have half an hour to blow off steam in a playground, sit with them on a park bench and lick ice-cream cones, or take them to a movie. Here's a lineup of the best things for kids to see and do in the Ottawa area. Please don't feel restricted by these lists. The intention is to guide you to the best attractions for these age groups. No matter what their ages, your kids will still enjoy visiting places not mentioned under their age group (and so will you!). You should also check out chapter 7, "Active Ottawa," and chapter 10, "Exploring the Region," for other family-oriented activities.

All Ages Museum of Nature, Museum of Science and Technology, Changing of the Guard, Aviation Museum.

5 and under Children's Museum, Agriculture Museum.

6- to 9-year-olds Children's Museum, Agriculture Museum, Musical Ride Centre, RCMP Rockcliffe Stables, Canadian Museum of Civilization, Rideau Skateway and bike paths, Rideau Hall grounds.

9- to 12-year-olds Canadian Museum of Civilization, Canadian War Museum, Children's Museum, Agriculture Museum, Musical Ride Centre, RCMP Rockcliffe Stables, Rideau Skateway and bike paths, Changing of the Guard, Rideau Hall grounds and tour of the residence.

Teens Canadian Museum of Civilization, Canadian War Museum, National Gallery, Parliament Hill tours, Musical Ride Centre, RCMP Rockcliffe Stables, Rideau Skateway and bike paths, ByWard Market, Diefenbunker Cold War Museum, Rideau Hall grounds and tour of the residence.

7 For Visitors with Special Interests

Adventure Downhill skiing, snowboarding, caving, whitewater rafting and kayaking, and even bungee jumping are all within driving distance of Ottawa. Have a look at **chapter 10, "Exploring the Region."**

Animals To see farm animals at close range and perhaps get a chance to handle small ones, or even to help milk a cow or shear a sheep, visit the **Canada Agriculture Museum.** A tour of the **Musical Ride Centre, RCMP Rockcliffe Stables** takes you right into the stables, where you can pat the horses' noses and feed them carrots. At the **Museum of Nature** most of the creatures are of the preserved variety, but they are extremely well displayed.

First Nations The **Canadian Museum of Civilization** has excellent exhibits on Native peoples and an impressive collection of giant totem poles. For a first-hand experience and the opportunity to meet First Nations people at work and play, visit Victoria Island in the summer months to experience an **Aboriginal summer village** operated by Turtle Island Tourism Company, complete with tipis, canoes, storytelling, and Native foods, or the **Odawa Annual Pow Wow,** held at Ottawa Municipal Campground in late May.

Fitness   You can bike, hike, jog, walk, in-line skate, snowshoe, ski, and probably a few other things on the trails and pathways in Ottawa and Gatineau's extensive greenspace. Skate on the longest ice rink in the world, the **Rideau Canal.** Experience the beauty of the wilderness in **Gatineau Park.** Join in one of the annual events, such as the **Keskinada Loppet cross-country ski competition** or the **National Capital Race Weekend** that features a world-class 42-km (26-mile) **marathon**.

Flight   The obvious choice here is the **Canada Aviation Museum,** where you can get close to dozens of real aircraft and sit in cockpit sections, fly a hang glider simulator, or go up for a ride in a vintage airplane. Visit the **Ottawa Airport's Observation Deck** and watch the big guys take off and land. And every Labour Day weekend (first weekend in September), there's the **Gatineau Hot Air Balloon Festival.** For commercial flights in small aircraft and hot air balloons, see "In the Air" earlier in this chapter.

Food & Wine   Head first for the **ByWard Market.** Also worth a visit is the extensive **Liquor Control Board of Ontario** (LCBO)'s two-level retail outlet at the corner of Rideau Street and King Edward Avenue. See also **"Gourmet on the Go"** in chapter 5, "Dining," for more food destinations. And don't forget to have at least one meal at a **French restaurant** across the river in **Quebec.**

Ghosts   Those with nerves of steel can visit the ghost of **Watson's Mill** in Manotick or the ghost that haunts the **Ottawa International Hostel** (the site of Canada's last public hanging in this former jail). Enjoy an evening of entertainment on the **Haunted Walk of Ottawa** or check out the gravestones in **Beechwood Cemetery,** the final resting place of many famous Canadians, including politicians, writers, poets, and 12 Hockey Hall of Fame members. You'll find Beechwood Cemetery in the Vanier neighbourhood of Ottawa, east of the Rideau River, bordered by Beechwood Avenue, Hemlock Road, and St. Laurent Boulevard.

History   Visit the **Canadian Museum of Civilization, Canadian War Museum, Library and Archives Canada, Billings Estate Museum, Bytown Museum, Laurier House, Rideau Hall,** and the **Diefenbunker Cold War Museum.**

The Military   The new **Canadian War Museum** is an absolute must-see destination. Watch the colorful **Changing of the Guard** ceremony at Parliament Hill in the summer.

Music   The **National Arts Centre** features live musical performances all year around. Popular musical artists appear at the **Corel Centre, Centrepoint Theatre,** and the **Civic Centre. Theatre du Casino du Lac-Leamy** focuses on musical entertainment. There are dozens of live music venues as well: bars, clubs, and restaurants, some of which are listed in chapter 9, "Ottawa After Dark." Summer music festivals include the **Ottawa Chamber Music Festival, Ottawa International Jazz Festival, Bluesfest,** and the **Ottawa Folk Festival.** Concerts are also held throughout the year at various downtown churches.

Numismatics   Visit the **Royal Canadian Mint** where you can purchase commemorative coins and take a guided tour of the factory along an enclosed walkway above all the action. Check out the **Currency Museum** in the center block of the Bank of Canada on Wellington Street.

Philately   The **Postal Museum,** housed within the Canadian Museum of Civilization, traces the history of Canadian postal communications.

Photography For the most comprehensive showing of works by contemporary Canadian photographers, the **Canadian Museum of Contemporary Photography** is the place to go. The museum also runs workshops on topics related to photography. There are also some photographs exhibited in the **National Gallery.**

Politics/Law In addition to the obvious **(Parliament Hill),** pay a visit to the **Supreme Court of Canada.** If you'd like to learn more about Canada's past prime ministers, see the special section earlier in this chapter, "The Lives and Times of Canada's PMs."

Rocks and Minerals For those with an interest in rocks, minerals, fossils, meteorites, and ores, the small museum at **Logan Hall** is a good choice to spend an hour or two. The **Ecomuseum** in Gatineau (Hull Sector) and the **Museum of Nature** also have excellent displays of rocks and minerals, although please note that the Museum of Nature is undergoing extensive renovations and the Mineral Gallery is closed; the new Mineral Gallery is scheduled to open in 2008.

Science and Nature Best bets for the sci-and-tech crowd are the **Canada Museum of Science and Technology** and the **Canadian Museum of Nature.** They'll be occupied for hours.

Trains Train buffs will enjoy the locomotive collections at the **Museum of Science and Technology** and the **Smiths Falls Railway Museum.** If you want to really blow their whistle, take eager train-spotters for a trip on the **Hull–Chelsea–Wakefield Steam Train** (see chapter 10, "Exploring the Region" for more details).

Visual Arts The **National Gallery** has an impressive collection of art, with an emphasis on Canadian artists. Plan to spend several hours here if you have a passion for art. The new **Canadian War Museum** has an extensive collection of **war art** on display. You'll also enjoy the **Canadian Museum of Contemporary Photography.** Local galleries always have something of interest — see the listings earlier in this chapter under "Museums & Galleries."

7

Active Ottawa

Ottawa is one of the greenest capital cities in the world. Expertly groomed city parks are complemented by vast expanses of protected wilderness, and peaceful waterways flow with grace through the center of the city and along its northern borders.

Much of the credit for the establishment of Ottawa's natural beauty goes to Jacques Grüber, a French urban planner, and former prime minister William Lyon Mackenzie King. In the late 1930s, King invited Grüber to Ottawa initially as an advisor for the planning of the War Memorial and Confederation Square. World War II interrupted these plans, but following the war Grüber returned and prepared a visionary report that proposed extensive urban renewal.

The National Capital Greenbelt, a swath of greenery that circles the city like an emerald necklace, can be largely attributed to Grüber's design. Stretching from Gatineau Park in Quebec across the Ottawa River, through Nepean in the west end, around the southern city limits, through Gloucester, and back up to the Ottawa River in the east, the Greenbelt surrounds Canada's capital.

It's no accident that the logo, flag, and coat of arms created for the newly expanded City of Ottawa, which was established in 2001, feature green and blue. The colors were chosen to represent the city's abundant greenspace and picturesque waterways and to symbolize the connection between the natural environment and quality of life that citizens of Ottawa enjoy.

Ottawans appreciate the beauty of their surroundings, as you will soon see when you witness the hustle and bustle as they cycle, walk, jog, in-line skate, ice skate, and cross-country ski their way to work or school and then do it all over again as they enjoy the outdoors in their leisure time. In fact, Ottawa residents have one of the highest participation rates in the country for golf, skiing, and cycling. With the expanse of waterways that meander around the city, boating, hanging out on the beach, and playing water sports are popular as well.

Since Ottawa is a major urban center, there are also more citified ways to be physically active. You can splash in a wave pool, scale a rock-climbing wall, or experience the thrill of high-tech arcade games. If you enjoy sports, you'll find plenty of places to play tennis or golf, go skiing, or swim.

1 City Strolls

So many of Ottawa's famous landmarks, museums, and attractions are located within walking distance of each other in the downtown areas east and west of the **Rideau Canal** that you are bound to spend a fair amount of time on foot when you visit the city. The three walking tours in this section will cover most of the places of interest in the center of the city. The fourth tour takes you on a cycling route along designated bike pathways next to the **Rideau Canal** and offers several options for the return journey, making an enjoyable morning or afternoon outing. There are other pleasant areas of the city to wander at leisure. The leafy residential streets leading off **Bank Street** in the **Glebe** are fairly quiet. The area bounded by **King Edward Avenue, Rideau Street, Laurier Avenue, and Charlotte Street** has some interesting older properties, and the streets are reasonably traffic-free during the day. The extensive grounds of **Rideau Hall** welcome visitors looking for a place for a leisurely stroll.

Active Ottawa Maps

To take full advantage of Ottawa's parks, pathways, and waterways, get hold of some specialized maps that clearly mark routes for cycling, walking, skating, or skiing. Some maps have suggested routes with information on the length and the level of difficulty. Good hunting grounds for maps are the **Capital Infocentre,** 90 Wellington St. (℗ **800/ 465-1867** or 613/239-5000); **Place Bell Books,** 175 Metcalfe St. (℗ **613/ 233-3821**), which specializes in maps, travel guides, and travel literature; and **A World of Maps,** 1235 Wellington St. (℗ **800/214-8524** or 613/724-6776), which carries topographic maps, nautical maps, and travel guides for the local region and the rest of the world. **Bushtukah: Great Outdoor Gear** at 203 Richmond Rd. ℗ **888/993-9947** or 613/ 792-1170 carries local maps for cycling, hiking, and canoeing/kayaking. For maps of **Gatineau Park,** including highly detailed trail maps, visit the **Gatineau Park Visitor Centre,** 33 Scott Rd., Chelsea (℗ **800/465- 1867** or 819/827-2020).

Here's a rundown of a few maps to get you started. **Explore the Recreational Pathways of Canada's Capital Region,** produced by the National Capital Commission, details pathways in **Gatineau Park** and other sites in Quebec, as well as pathways in Ottawa. There are 17 routes marked on the map, ranging from 1.5 km (1 mile) to 31 km (20 miles) in length. Descriptions of the terrain, level of difficulty, and points of interest are listed for each route. Five tours are highlighted. Maps of the **Rideau Corridor,** detailing routes along the 202-km (125-mile) waterway between Ottawa and Kingston, can be obtained by contacting **Parks Canada** at their **Rideau Canal Office,** 34a Beckwith St. South in Smiths Falls ℗ **800/230-0016** or 613/283-5170. If you are taking a more adventurous tack and plan to do some boating on the Rideau River or Canal, **Rideau Navigational Charts** can be obtained from **Friends of the Rideau,** 1 Jasper Ave., Smiths Falls ℗ **613/ 283-5810.** One of the **Gatineau Park** maps available at the Gatineau Park Visitor Centre is a scale map that includes hiking trails, cycling paths, bridle paths, seasonal trails, and sections of the Trans Canada Trail. A winter trail map for Gatineau Park includes contour lines, magnetic north, and exact drawings of ski trails, winter hiking trails, and snowshoe trails, with huts and shelters also marked. For trails in the **National Capital Greenbelt,** which encircles Ottawa from Kanata in the west, along the entire southern edge of the city, and around to Cumberland in the east, refer to the **Greenbelt All Seasons Trail Map.** The **National Capital Commission** produces a map of the **Capital Pathway,** 170km (106 miles) of recreational multi-use pathways that are great for cycling, walking, running, and in-line skating. Visit the **Outaouais Tourism Office** at 103 Laurier St., Gatineau, Quebec (©) **800/265-7822** or 819/778-2222 for many of the above maps, and also a map of snowmobile trails.

WALKING TOUR 1   THE HEART OF IT ALL

Start:	Ottawa Locks
Finish:	Canadian Museum of Civilization or Jacques-Cartier Park
Distance:	Approximately 2.5–4.5km (1.5–3 miles); 1–2 hours
Best Time:	Anytime when the weather is reasonably fine.
Worst Time:	It won't be much fun crossing Alexandra Bridge if the weather is very cold, windy, or wet. Rush-hour traffic will also detract from the pleasure of this walk.

This tour will take you past symbols of Ottawa's history from its earliest days to modern-day national endeavors. Begin your tour at the site of Ottawa's birth — the Ottawa Locks.

1 Stand on the north side of the **Plaza Bridge** and look down onto the eight **Ottawa Locks,** which connect the canal to the Ottawa River, a drop of 24m (80 ft.). Travel time through the locks for canal traffic is about 1¹/2 hours. You can walk down a stairway beside the bridge (or cross to the south side of the street and go down a ramp that will take you under the roadway) right to the level of the locks and watch them in operation. The public are allowed to cross the narrow lock gates when they are in the closed position and no boating traffic is present. If you have small children or non-swimmers with you, take extra care because there are no barriers along the perimeter of the locks. Next make your way to the old stone building on the west side of the locks, the **Commissariat.**

2 **The Bytown Museum** is housed in the Commissariat, the oldest building still remaining from the original settlement of Bytown. **Lieutenant-Colonel John By** had the Commissariat built in 1827 to be used as offices during the construction of the **Rideau Canal.**

Articles belonging to Colonel By are displayed here, as are artifacts reflecting the social history of the pioneer families of the area. Opening hours vary; they are longer in summer, limited in winter. (©) **613 /234-4570**.

3 South of **Plaza Bridge** lies **Confederation Square,** a triangular concrete pedestrian precinct bound on each side by several lanes of traffic, but graced with the **National War Memorial,** inaugurated by King George VI in 1939. From the Rideau Canal, a broad set of stairs leads up to the center of the Square. Every year, crowds gather in the Square on November 11, Remembrance Day.

4 Walk south on the east side of **Elgin Street,** passing the **National Arts Centre** on your left and the **British High Commission** and the elegant **Lord Elgin Hotel** on your right.

5 Stroll through **Confederation Park.** Rest on a park bench or wander past the sculptures and artwork on display. The central **fountain** is a belated tribute to **Colonel John By,** who met with disapproval upon his return to England because of overspending on the construction of the Rideau Canal. Consequently, during his lifetime Colonel By did not receive

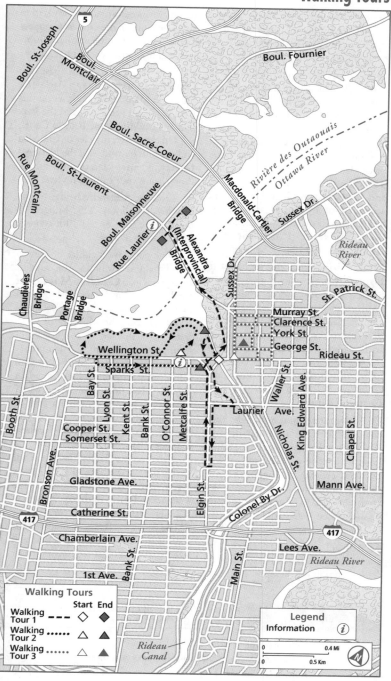

Walking Tours

	Start	End
Walking Tour 1	◇	◆
Walking Tour 2	△	▲
Walking Tour 3	△	▲

Legend

Information (i)

0		0.4 Mi
0		0.5 Km

Rideau Canal

the credit he deserved for his monumental achievement. On a hot day, the misty spray from the fountain will cool you off nicely.

⑥ Leave the park at the south end and walk east along **Laurier Street** until you see **Cartier Square Drill Hall** on your right. This is the oldest armory in Canada still in use and also the starting point of the **Changing of the Guard** ceremony, which takes place daily in the summer months. The Governor General's Foot Guards and the Canadian Grenadier Guards, accompanied by drums and a brass military band, march up **Elgin Street**, timed to reach **Parliament Hill** promptly for the 10am ceremony.

⑦ Walk back along **Laurier Street** to **Elgin Street.** If you're ready for a break, walk farther south along Elgin until you reach the beginning of the commercial district, where you will find plenty of options for relaxing with a cup of tea, a cold drink, or fortification with a stronger beverage. Otherwise, head north on Elgin and cross over Rideau Street to the **Château Laurier.**

⑧ Admire the imposing facade, then enter the lobby and wander through the main public areas on the ground floor. Rich wood paneling and opulent decor is evident throughout. For a special treat, make reservations for afternoon tea at **Zoe's,** the elegant glass-enclosed cafe visible above the main entranceway.

⑨ As you leave the hotel, you will see the distinctive columns of the old Union Station on the opposite side of the street, once the main railway station and now home of the **Ottawa Congress Centre,** host of conventions, exhibitions, and government conferences.

⑩ Turn immediately left past the **Château Laurier** (along Mackenzie Street) to **Major's Hill Park.** From this park you'll get great views of the **Parliament Buildings,** the **Rideau Canal,** the **Ottawa River,** the city of **Gatineau** and the hills beyond, and the **National Gallery.** If you're a fan of tourist snapshots, bring your camera up here.

⑪ Cross the **Alexandra Bridge** on the pedestrian walkway. This bridge was built at the turn of the 20th century for two railway lines.

⑫ Now you have a choice of how to spend the next few hours. You can visit the spectacular **Canadian Museum of Civilization,** Canada's national museum of human history, or enjoy **Jacques-Cartier Park.** The Museum of Civilization, completed in 1989, features impressive permanent and temporary exhibits, as well as the **Canadian Children's Museum,** the **Canadian Postal Museum,** and the **IMAX Theatre.** There is a cafeteria and an upscale dining room on-site. If you decide to wander through **Jacques-Cartier Park,** you can follow the pathway of the **Trans Canada Trail** along the north shore of the **Ottawa River,** eventually linking with the **Gatineau River Pathway. Jacques-Cartier Park** has been designated "Mile 0" of the **Trans Canada Trail,** a multi-use recreational trail that will eventually link Canada from coast to coast.

WALKING TOUR 2	PARLIAMENT HILL AND WELLINGTON STREET

Start:	Capital Infocentre
Finish:	D'Arcy McGee's pub, Capital Infocentre, or Ottawa Locks
Distance:	3–3.5km (2 miles); 1½ hours

Best Time:	Weekdays during the day, when there are plenty of walkers on the river trail and Sparks Street is filled with pedestrians. Early August during the Sparks Street Mall International Busker Festival. December when more than 300,000 lights shine in celebration of the beginning of winter and the Christmas season.
Worst Time:	Evenings or weekends November to March, Christmas and Winterlude excepted. Once the office workers go home for the day at this time of year, the district is very quiet.

Begin your outdoor exploration of Parliament Hill and historic Wellington Street at the Capital Infocentre, 90 Wellington Street. If you stand in the square in front of the building and look north, you're facing the Parliament Buildings' Centre Block with its central Peace Tower.

1 You will also see a statue of a courageous young Canadian, **Terry Fox,** who attempted to run across Canada despite having lost his right leg to bone cancer. Every year, in memory of this brave young man, Canadian schoolchildren take part in a sponsored run/walk to raise funds for cancer research.

2 Cross **Wellington Street** and enter **Parliament Hill** through the gates. Note the elaborate stone and iron **Parliamentary Fence,** built between 1872 and 1874. Some modifications have been made over the years to accommodate changes in traffic flow, but its characteristics have changed little since its construction.

3 At the foot of the central pathway leading to the **Centre Block** is a fountain with a natural gas flame, the **Centennial Flame,** which burns through the water flowing over the bronze shields of Canada's provinces and territories. Former prime minister Lester B. Pearson lit the flame at one second after midnight on January 1, 1967, to commemorate Canada's 100th birthday — and the flame has been burning ever since.

4 The building to your right is the **East Block** of the **Parliament Buildings.** Its architecture is an outstanding example of Gothic Revival design. Several rooms, including Sir John A. Macdonald's office, have been restored to resemble their original state.

5 In front of the **East Block,** turn south and look across the street to admire the **Langevin Block** at 62 Wellington St. It was built in the Second Empire style, similar to the New Louvre, built in Paris in 1852. The Langevin Block was constructed to accommodate the growing number of politicians and civil servants on the Hill, and today the offices of the prime minister are located here.

6 After circling the **East Block** building, walk north along the pathways to the rear of **Centre Block.** Here you will discover the imposing **Library of Parliament.** The library's design is based on the round medieval chapter house. The building features massive flying buttresses and the exterior is primarily local Nepean sandstone. The Library was closed in February 2002 for extensive restoration and repair work, with a reopening scheduled for the summer of 2005.

7 As you continue along the pathways on the west side of Centre Block and past the West Block, which houses government offices and is not open to the public, you will pass by many statues and monuments. For a detailed description of these tributes to Canadian people and events, obtain a free copy of **"Discover the Hill,"** published by the National Capital Commission and available at the Capital Infocentre.

⑧ Walk west on **Wellington Street** to number 128, the **Union Bank** building. This building, made of olive-colored New Brunswick sandstone, is the only surviving bank building of its era on Wellington Street, which was once the banking center of the city.

⑨ Farther west, between Bank Street and Kent Street, stands the **Bank of Canada** building. Originally constructed in 1937, a glass-towered addition appeared in the mid-1970s. The **Currency Museum** can be found inside.

⑩ As you cross Kent Street, you'll see **St. Andrew's Presbyterian Church** on the southwest corner, constructed of Ottawa Valley limestone between 1872 and 1874.

⑪ On the north side of Wellington just past Kent Street stands the impressive architecture of the **Supreme Court of Canada.** The plain, smooth-cut sandstone topped by the château-style roofing similar to the Parliament Buildings and the Château Laurier makes a dramatic impression as you approach the building. The court is in session between October and June. Free half-hour guided tours of the building are available year-round, on a continuing basis between May and August, and by pre-arrangement during the remainder of the year. It's worth

taking a peek at the grand entrance hall, even if you don't take a tour.

⑫ Next you will come to the **National Library and National Archives of Canada.** The Library is responsible for collecting and preserving Canada's published heritage. The National Archives holds a huge collection of maps, diaries, films, journals, official records, photographs, and documentary art. There are washrooms and a snack bar in the library.

⑬ At this point, you can decide whether to return to your starting point via the **Trans Canada Trail** along the south shore of the Ottawa River, or stroll back through **Sparks Street Mall,** Canada's first pedestrian mall. If you walk back along the river, you will end up at the **Ottawa Locks** and you can ascend the stairs or ramp to **Plaza Bridge** (where Wellington Street becomes Rideau Street). If you walk back along pedestrianized **Sparks Street,** you can turn left on Metcalfe to return to the **Capital Infocentre,** or continue along Sparks Street to Elgin Street. On the corner of Elgin and Sparks you will find a jovial pub, **D'Arcy McGee's,** where you can reward yourself with a fine pint of draught Guinness after your long walk.

WALKING TOUR 3	SUSSEX DRIVE AND BYWARD MARKET DISTRICT

Start:	Junction of Rideau St. and Sussex Dr.
Finish:	Clarendon Court
Distance:	2–4km (1.25–2.5 miles), depending on how many streets you wander up and down in the ByWard Market district; 1–2 hours or more.
Best Time:	This area always offers something interesting to see and do. It's a great place to stroll almost any time.
Worst Time:	Late at night when the bar crowd is out and about.

Sussex Drive is Ottawa's "other" famous roadway, aside from Wellington Street where the Parliament Buildings are located. Originally named Sussex Street, it was once the commercial center of Ottawa and was lined on both sides with handsome limestone buildings.

❶ Walk north on **Sussex Drive** on the left-hand side of the road so you can see the restored limestone and brick commercial buildings on the east side of the street. One of the finest remaining examples of these properties is 541 Sussex Dr., on the northeast corner of Sussex Drive and George Street.

❷ Next you'll pass by **York Street,** which has a number of designated heritage properties along its length. Some buildings (on York Street as well as many other city streets) have a bronze plaque that gives a brief bilingual description of the heritage significance of the property.

❸ Continuing north, keep an eye out for an original carved wooden signpost hanging on **449 Sussex Drive.** The former Castor Hotel (*castor* is French for "beaver") depended on this sign to attract their illiterate customers. Other businesses in the area used the same strategy during the mid-1800s — the local hardware store, jeweler, shoe store, and tobacco shop all sported wooden symbols.

❹ As you approach **Murray Street,** you'll see the roadway sweep to the left across **Alexandra Bridge** to the city of Gatineau, across the river in Quebec. On a concrete island in the center of the traffic lanes stands the **Peacekeeping Monument,** erected in 1992.

❺ The magnificent glass and stone **National Gallery of Canada** stands on the northeast corner of Sussex Drive and Patrick Street. At this point, you might like to visit the gallery, or walk a few steps farther north on Sussex Drive to the **Royal Canadian Mint.**

❻ If these attractions are scheduled for another day of your trip, cross Sussex Drive to **Notre-Dame Cathedral Basilica,** the oldest church in Ottawa. The exterior of this Roman Catholic church is rather plain on the front facade, contrasting with the ornate and elaborately detailed late-Victorian interior. Vaulted ceilings, side galleries, intricately carved woodwork, and 30 life-size figures are some of the most impressive features of the Basilica's interior.

❼ Turn left (south) upon exiting the Basilica until you reach **Murray Street.** This is a most charming street on which to while away an hour or so. Unique retailers, restaurants, and cafes can be found here. One of the most picturesque buildings is the block at **47–61 Murray Street,** the former **Martineau Hotel.** The rounded arched openings you can see once led to stable yards at the rear.

❽ Continue along Murray Street and turn right (south) onto **Dalhousie Street,** the easternmost border of the ByWard Market, as defined for heritage district purposes in 1991.

❾ Now, you can wander at will in the area bordered by Murray Street, Dalhousie Street, Rideau Street, and Sussex Drive. Within these few city blocks, there are dozens of shops, bars, cafes, and restaurants. At the heart of the district lies the **ByWard Market Building.** There has been a market on this site since the 1830s, but three market buildings were destroyed by fire before the current one was built in 1927. Between May and October, the outdoor farmers' market clusters around the perimeter of the building, located between York Street, George Street, William Street, and a lane known as ByWard Market.

❿ Your final glimpse into the colorful history of this district is experiencing the charm of two courtyards. **Tin House Court** is situated between York and Clarence streets and originally served as a tradesman's entrance to properties on Sussex Drive. Tin House Court is characterized by the preserved facade of an early Edwardian tinsmith's house, which has been mounted on one of the limestone walls enclosing the courtyard. **Clarendon Court** can be reached through a narrow alleyway on the north side of George Street, just east of Sussex Drive. This cobblestone courtyard is a romantic spot on a summer evening. Several restaurants have terraces facing into the courtyard, and the atmosphere is decidedly European.

CYCLING TOUR   CANAL, LAKE, AND LOCKS

Start:	Ottawa Locks
Finish:	Ottawa Locks
Distance:	Minimum 16km (10 miles); maximum 24km (15 miles) if you take the longest route back.
Best Time:	When tulips are in bloom in May; on a warm day when you can enjoy boating on Dow's Lake; in midsummer when you can enjoy the beach at Mooney's Bay.
Worst Time:	Morning and evening rush hour in the event you decide to do some road travel; also there is more noise and fumes from adjacent roadways at those times.

Begin your tour at the head of the Ottawa Locks. There's a pathway under Plaza Bridge (the bridge overlooking the locks) that leads you to the **Rideau Canal Western Pathway.**

❶ The first landmark you pass is the **National Arts Centre,** one of the largest performing arts complexes in Canada. A wide variety of performances can be seen on its four stages, including English and French theater, dance, music, and community programming.

❷ Next you'll pass by the edge of **Confederation Park,** site of many summer festivals and a popular spot during warmer weather for office workers and tourists to relax on the benches or stretch out on the grass.

❸ The pathway continues alongside the canal, with **Queen Elizabeth Driveway** on the west side. Keep an eye out for drinking fountains stationed along this stretch.

❹ At the intersection of **Queen Elizabeth Driveway** and **Fifth Avenue,** you'll see the **Canal Ritz.** Open 11:30am to 11pm daily, you can enjoy a drink, snack, or full meal. Sit on the terrace and watch the boats on the canal.

❺ **Dow's Lake** is a couple of kilometers (about 1.25 miles) farther along. There are restaurants, washroom facilities, and boat rentals here. **Dow's Lake** is adjacent to **Commissioner's Park,** which in the spring has the largest display of tulips in the capital — an amazing 300,000 bulbs burst into bloom in a colorful display.

❻ Continue past Dow's Lake for about 1km (just over half a mile) until you reach **Hartwells Lock Station.** At this point you have several options:

- **The shortest tour, about 16km total (10 miles):** Cross over the canal and return to **Ottawa Locks** at the head of the Rideau Canal via the **Rideau Canal Eastern Pathway.** This pathway has the canal on its west side and **Colonel By Drive** on its east side.

- **A longer tour, about 20km (12.5 miles):** Turn west along the

Cycling Tours

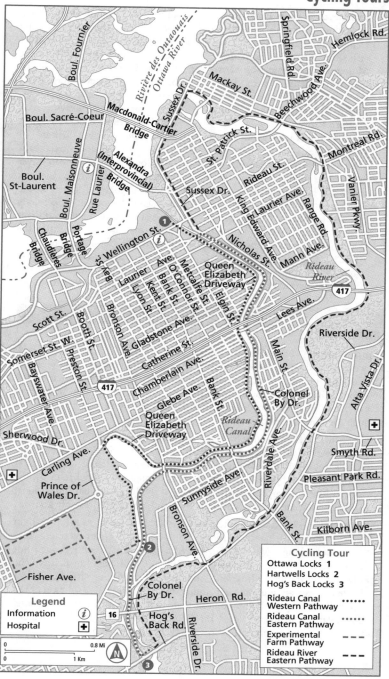

Cycling Tour

Ottawa Locks **1**
Hartwells Locks **2**
Hog's Back Locks **3**

Rideau Canal
Western Pathway ••••••

Rideau Canal
Eastern Pathway ••••••

Experimental
Farm Pathway – – –

Rideau River
Eastern Pathway – – –

Legend

Information *i*

Hospital ✚

0   0.8 Mi
0   1 Km

Experimental Farm Pathway and cycle through wooded and open scenic natural areas. If you wish, visit the **Canada Agriculture Museum, Arboretum,** and **Ornamental Gardens.** Return downtown on the **Rideau Canal Eastern Pathway** or **Rideau Canal Western Pathway.**

• **Another longer tour, about 20km (12.5 miles):** Continue past **Hartwells Lock Station** for another 2km (1.25 miles) until you reach **Hog's Back Falls.** This is the point where the Ottawa section of the Rideau Canal begins, stretching northward through downtown Ottawa to the Ottawa River. Refreshments and washroom facilities are available here. Enjoy the picturesque waterfalls,

and, if there's any boating traffic, you can watch the locks and swing bridge in operation. A little farther along on the east bank of the **Rideau River** you can enjoy the beach at **Mooney's Bay Park.** Return to your starting point via one of the canal pathways.

• **A different route back from Hog's Back Falls — about 24km (15 miles):** If you wish, cycle back downtown via the **Rideau River Eastern Pathway,** which takes you on an entirely different route through numerous city parks along the east banks of the **Rideau River** and across the bridge next to the **Rideau Falls.** From that point, you need to cycle west on **Sussex Drive** (which does not have a designated bike lane) to return downtown.

2 Green Ottawa

URBAN PARKS

Commissioner's Park Situated along Dow's Lake, Commissioner's Park attracts thousands of visitors during the **Canadian Tulip Festival** with the largest tulip display in the region. An amazing 300,000 bulbs bloom in the park flowerbeds. Bring your camera and snap away. After the tulips fade in late May or early June, the beds are filled with colorful annuals to delight visitors all through the summer season.

Confederation Park Major festivals, including **Winterlude,** are held in this downtown park at the intersection of Elgin Street and Laurier Avenue. There are memorials to Canadian history here, including a fountain that originally stood in Trafalgar Square in London and has been dedicated to **Colonel John By,** the British engineer who supervised the building of the Rideau Canal. The colonel was a major influence in establishing Bytown, as Ottawa was formerly known.

Major's Hill Park Ottawa's oldest park, established in 1874, is tucked in behind the Fairmont Château Laurier. A statue of Colonel John By stands close to the site of his house, which was destroyed by fire. This park offers outstanding views of the Parliament Buildings, the Rideau Canal, the Ottawa River, the city of Gatineau and the hills beyond, and the National Gallery. It's also a major site for many festivals and events, including the Tulip Festival. At the tip of the park, you'll find **Nepean Point.** You can share the view with a statue of **Samuel de Champlain,** who first explored the Ottawa River in 1613. The **Astrolabe Theatre,** a venue for summer concerts and events, is located here.

Fun Fact

The astrolabe (a 17th-century navigational instrument) held by the statue of Samuel de Champlain at Nepean Point was unwittingly placed upside down by sculptor Hamilton McCarthy. You can view the original astrolabe at the **Canadian Museum of Civilization.**

Rockcliffe Park Travel east along Sussex Drive just past the prime minister's residence to reach this pretty park, complete with a picnic site and stone shelter. You can take a scenic drive through the park and catch a glimpse of the grand residences in the area.

Rockcliffe Rockeries Continue a little farther east along Rockcliffe Parkway and you'll reach the Rockeries, with their gorgeous show of flowers from spring to fall. The best time of year to view the Rockeries is in May when the fruit trees are in blossom, adding their delicate pink and white flowers to the hundreds of thousands of daffodils in bloom.

Rideau Falls Park Located just off Sussex Drive where the Rideau River empties into the Ottawa River, this park is beautifully landscaped. A footbridge spans the Rideau River and the 30-m (98-ft.) falls are illuminated in the evening. **Canada and the World Pavilion,** a summer season attraction that showcases Canadian achievements on the international stage, is located in the park.

Garden of the Provinces Opposite the National Library and National Archives of Canada at the intersection of Wellington and Bay streets, the Garden of the Provinces commemorates the union of Canada's provinces and territories. The display features two fountains and all the provincial coats of arms and floral emblems.

Hog's Back Park The parklands in this area surround the spectacular Hog's Back Falls, situated at the point where the Rideau Canal meets the Rideau River. The falls are named after rocks in the river that are said to resemble the bristles on a hog's back. A refreshment pavilion, parking, and washroom facilities are available.

Vincent Massey Park Located on Heron Road, west of Riverside Drive and just north of Hog's Back Park, Vincent Massey Park is a popular place for family reunions and other large gatherings. Amenities include ball diamonds, horseshoe pits, a bandstand, picnic tables, fireplaces, a refreshment pavilion, playing fields, recreational pathways, drinking fountains, and public washrooms. A parking fee is charged from May to October.

Mooney's Bay Park South of Vincent Massey Park and Hog's Back Park along Riverside Drive, you'll find Mooney's Bay. There's a supervised, sandy swimming beach, a playground, shade trees, a refreshment pavilion, and public washrooms. Cross-country skiing is available in the winter, on 5km (3 miles) of groomed, well-lit trails. A parking fee applies in the summer months.

Strathcona Park On the banks of the Rideau River, beautiful Strathcona Park beckons. Relax on a bench under the huge shade trees and watch the royal swans lazily swim past on a sunny summer afternoon. Odyssey Theatre

Parks & Greenspaces

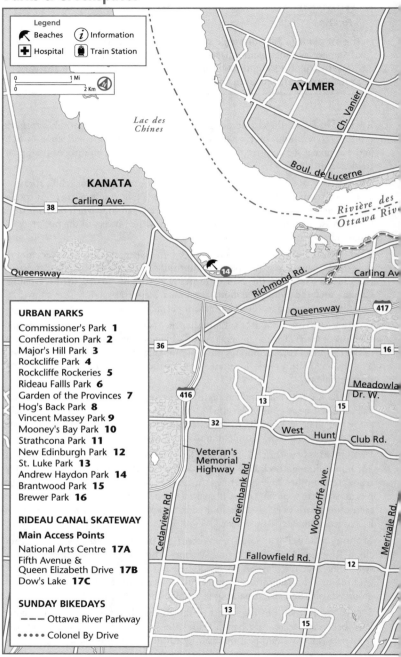

Legend
- Beaches
- (i) Information
- Hospital
- Train Station

0 — 1 Mi
0 — 2 Km

Lac des Chines

AYLMER

Ch. Vanier

Boul. de Lucerne

KANATA

Carling Ave.

38

Rivière des Ottawa River

Queensway

14

Richmond Rd.

Carling Av

Queensway

417

36

16

Meadowla
Dr. W.

416

13

15

32

West Hunt Club Rd.

Veteran's
Memorial
Highway

Cedarview Rd.

Greenbank Rd.

Woodroffe Ave.

Merivale Rd.

Fallowfield Rd.

12

13

15

URBAN PARKS

Commissioner's Park **1**
Confederation Park **2**
Major's Hill Park **3**
Rockcliffe Park **4**
Rockcliffe Rockeries **5**
Rideau Fallls Park **6**
Garden of the Provinces **7**
Hog's Back Park **8**
Vincent Massey Park **9**
Mooney's Bay Park **10**
Strathcona Park **11**
New Edinburgh Park **12**
St. Luke Park **13**
Andrew Haydon Park **14**
Brantwood Park **15**
Brewer Park **16**

RIDEAU CANAL SKATEWAY

Main Access Points
National Arts Centre **17A**
Fifth Avenue &
Queen Elizabeth Drive **17B**
Dow's Lake **17C**

SUNDAY BIKEDAYS
- – – Ottawa River Parkway
- • • • Colonel By Drive

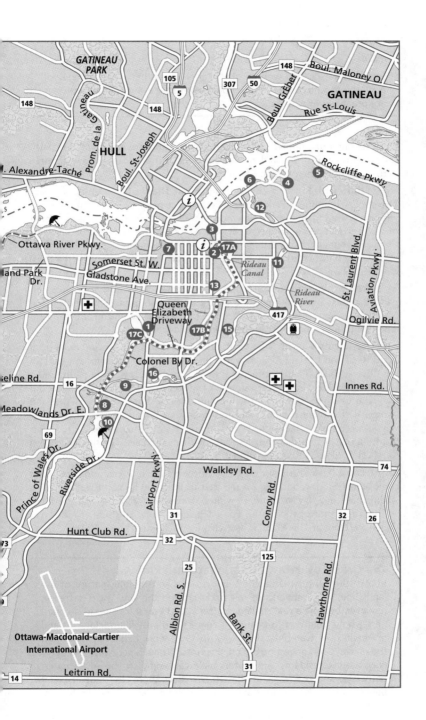

> **Kids**
>
> Strathcona Park has a wonderful play area for children. The wading pool, playground, and castle ruins, complete with a slide and animal statuettes, are great fun to explore.

holds its outdoor summer performances here. There are paved walking paths for easy stroller pushing and an elegant water fountain. If you have children with you, this is the place to be.

New Edinburgh Park On the east side of the Rideau River, south of Sussex Drive, New Edinburgh Park provides yet another peaceful refuge from the city within a few minutes' drive of downtown. Walking trails weave along the banks of the river, and because much of the park has been preserved in its natural state there's an abundance of wildlife, including groundhogs, turtles, muskrats, butterflies, and blue herons. Bring binoculars — and insect repellent. There's also a children's playground.

St. Luke's Park At the intersection of Elgin Street and Gladstone Avenue, this park is a great place to hang out after a bout of shopping on Elgin. Sugar Mountain (candy heaven) and Pure Gelato (Italian ice cream) are close by. There's a paddling pool, playground, and picnic tables.

Andrew Haydon Park West of the downtown core, at the intersection of Acres Road and Carling Avenue, you'll find this park on the southern bank of the Ottawa River. There are picnic sites with barbecues, walking paths, and a small artificial lake. Lots of diversions for younger children: water sprinklers and jets, sand to dig in, and play structures, including a ship with rope ladders and swings. Refreshment pavilions and washrooms are on-site. A project is underway to erect a memorial statue portraying the Right Honourable Pierre Elliott Trudeau, one of Canada's most respected parliamentarians. The site was chosen to reflect Trudeau's love of the outdoors.

Brantwood Park Turn east on Clegg Street off Main Street, and you'll soon come across Brantwood Park, on the west bank of the Rideau River. There's a wading pool and play structure. In winter, skaters can weave through a series of skating rinks joined by ice paths. For a delicious vegetarian snack or meal, visit the Green Door at 198 Main St. (see chapter 5, "Dining," page 104).

The Origin of Ottawa's Parkways and Pathways

In the 19th century, Ottawa's railways were an essential feature of the landscape. Vast networks of rail tracks crossed the city. Their existence, however, became a real challenge after World War II for the urban planners whose goal was to beautify Canada's capital while reclaiming and preserving the waterway shorelines. In 1950, work began on relocating the railway and converting old rail lines into Ottawa's parkways and pathways. Today, residents and visitors alike can enjoy the beautiful parks, pathways, and roadways of the Ottawa River shore, the Rideau Canal banks, and Dow's Lake. Most pathways are smooth asphalt on flat terrain, so they're easy to negotiate for all ages.

Brewer Park Bordering the Rideau River and Bronson Avenue, Brewer Park is a good site for feeding waterfowl on the river, so bring along some crusts of bread. There's a children's waterpark in the summer, with water sprays, jets, and slides. Three play structures, each one catering to 2 different age group, a pool, an arena, baseball diamonds, picnic areas, and pathways along the river complete the scene. In the winter, an outdoor skating rink and a speed-skating oval are open to the public.

SUBURBAN & RURAL GREENSPACE

Gatineau Park This beautiful wilderness area, covering 361 sq. km (141 sq. miles) in the Gatineau Hills of Quebec, is under the care of the National Capital Commission. The south entrance to the park is located just across the Ottawa River in the city of Gatineau, a few minutes' drive from downtown Ottawa. Hiking trails, cycling pathways, mountain-bike trails, cross-country ski trails, sandy beaches, and campgrounds are all located within the park. Your first stop should be the **Gatineau Park Visitor Centre,** at 33 Scott Rd. in Chelsea (© 800/465-1867 or 819/827-2020), open every day of the year. For more information on **Gatineau Park,** see chapter 10, "Exploring the Region."

The Greenbelt The **National Capital Greenbelt** covers 200 sq. km (77 sq. miles) of crescent-shaped land bordering Ottawa to the west, south, and east. A mix of forests, agricultural land, and natural areas, the **Greenbelt** has several sectors open to the public and accessible from major highways. Moose, beavers, chipmunks, foxes, raccoons, deer, pygmy shrews, rabbits, and squirrels all call this wilderness area home. For directions to specific sites, call the Capital Infocentre (© 800/465-1867 or 613/239-5000). Better yet, pick up a copy of the Greenbelt All Seasons Trail Map, available at the Infocentre opposite Parliament Hill, or downloadable from the National Capital Commission's website at **www.canadascapital.ca**. If you're venturing into the Greenbelt during bug season (May to September), protect yourself with insect repellent or use a bug jacket. Always respect the Greenbelt rules — place all litter in the waste bins provided in parking areas, keep your dog on a leash and pick up after it, and don't walk or snowshoe on cross-country ski tracks in winter.

The **Pine Grove Forest** is a large urban forest with a mixture of natural woods and plantations extending southeast from Hunt Club and Conroy roads. Along the wide, level trails are interpretive panels to help visitors identify more than 20 species of native trees and to explain the principles of modern forest management. **Stony Swamp Conservation Area** has been designated a provincially significant wetland and contains more than 700 species of plants and many types of animals. A recently constructed 5-km (3-mile) section of the **Trans Canada Trail** runs through **Stony Swamp.** The **Rideau Trail,** a 300-km (185-mile) footpath between Ottawa and Kingston, also passes through this sector. In the summer months, the **Sarsaparilla Trail** in Stony Swamp is **universally accessible.**

The **Mer Bleue Conservation Area** on the southeastern edge of Ottawa is a unique ecological environment protected by an international treaty. The area contains a large peat bog more than 5m (16 ft.) deep and a northern boreal forest, a type of forest that is typically found much farther north. If you visit on a cool morning in the spring or fall, you may be lucky enough to witness a bluish-tinged mist hanging over the bog, which gave the area its name (*mer bleue* is French for "blue sea"). There are several trails crossing the area, but the easiest one to negotiate is the **Mer Bleue Interpretative Trail,** a walk of just over 1km

---

(Kids) For Active Families: Where to Play Indoors

Since Ottawa is a major urban center, there are lots of indoor entertainment venues where kids can run, jump, and play. You can splash in a wave pool, scale a rock-climbing wall, or experience the thrill of high-tech arcade games. Many museums have organized activities for children and families on weekends and during school vacation periods, so you'll always have an answer when your kids get into one of those "There's nothing to do!" moods.

Gloucester Splash Wave Pool has a sloping entry, so running in and out of the waves is almost as exciting as being on a natural beach. There's a 34-m-long (112 ft.) water slide with its own landing pool, a separate toddler pool, solarium, and plenty of deck chairs. Located at 2040 Ogilvie Rd. in Ottawa's east end; (✆) **613/748-4222.** For information on municipally owned and operated **indoor pools** around the city call (✆) **613/580-2400.** If you're looking for a place to tire out a high-energy kid or two, go to **Cosmic Adventures,** one of Canada's largest indoor playgrounds. Kids ages 12 and under can bounce, crawl, slide, climb, and swing in a four-level soft-play structure filled with tunnels, mazes, obstacle courses, ball pits, and slides. Located in east Ottawa at 1373 Ogilvie Rd. (✆) **613/742-8989.** At **Fun Junction,** 1399 Triole Ave. near the St. Laurent Shopping Centre (✆) **613/745-1881,** kids ages 5 to 85 can play laser tag, experience an M4 simulator, play video arcade games, or climb the rock-climbing wall. Across the road from the Canada Science and Technology Museum you'll find **Midway Family Fun Park,** at 2370 Lancaster Rd. (✆) **613/526-0343.** There's nine-hole mini golf, a jungle gym, bowling lanes, arcade games, and a toddler play center.

(^{2}/₃ mile) with a **boardwalk** and information panels. To reach the Interpretive Trail, follow Innes Road to Anderson Road, then go south to Borthwick Ridge Road and follow the signs. Elsewhere in the Greenbelt, during the winter you can go **cross-country skiing** on the trails and recreational pathways. All trails are suitable for beginner or family outings. Volunteer groups from local ski clubs machine track-set some of the trails. For family **tobogganing** fun, visit **Conroy Pit** (Parking Lot 15, south of Hunt Club Road on Conroy Road). The hill at Conroy Pit is lit from 4pm to 11pm. Please note the speed limit along the access road is a cautious 20km (12.5 miles) per hour. You can also visit Bruce Pit (Parking Lot 12, Cedarview Rd. off Hwy. 416 at Hunt Club Road) and Green's Creek Conservation Area (off St. Joseph's Boulevard, Parking Lot 24).

3 Sports & Games

BEACHES

Along the banks of the **Ottawa River** and the **Rideau River,** there are a number of beaches where you can cool off on a hot summer's day. Sandy shores abound, and there are usually washrooms, changing rooms, and snack bars nearby.

Supervised swimming is available at **Britannia Bay, Mooney's Bay,** and **Westboro** beaches in the city of Ottawa. Beaches are open from late June until the end of August. Water quality is checked daily and beaches may occasionally be closed for a brief period, usually after heavy rainfall. For water-quality updates

Tips

Each person should wear a life jacket while boating. If you are renting a boat, ask the rental facility to provide life jackets for everyone in your party. Be aware that Dow's Lake, the Rideau Canal, and Rideau River are unsupervised waterways and you use these waterways at your own risk.

---

call ☎ 613/244-5678. You can get to **Britannia Bay,** on the Ottawa River, by following Richmond Road to Britannia Road or by traveling on the Ottawa River bike path. For **Mooney's Bay Park,** on the banks of the Rideau River, drive along Riverside Drive just north of Walkley Road, or take the Colonel By Drive bike path to Hog's Back, cross Meadowlands Drive, and take the path through the marina. You'll find **Westboro Beach** on the south shore of the Ottawa River, off the Ottawa River Parkway at Kitchissippi Lookout (west of the Champlain Bridge).

Just a short drive from the city you can visit **Baxter Conservation Area,** south of Kars on Dilworth Road (☎ 613/489-3592), which has a beach on the Rideau River. The refreshing lakes of **Gatineau Park** (☎ 819/827-2020) are open for public swimming from mid-June to early September. The park has five public beaches, located at Philippe, Meech, and La Pêche lakes. Lifeguards are on duty daily from 10am to 6pm; swimming in the park is prohibited at other times. Swimming is also available in **Lac Beauchamp,** at Parc du Lac Beauchamp, 745 Maloney Est blvd., Gatineau, QC (☎ **819/669-2548**).

BOATING

If you want to spend a lazy summer afternoon drifting around in a boat, visit **Dow's Lake Pavilion,** 1001 Queen Elizabeth Dr. ☎ **613/232-1001.** A fully operational marina at the pavilion site on Dow's Lake rents out paddleboats, canoes, kayaks, and rowboats. Dow's Lake is an artificial lake that provides a quiet place for water recreation away from the main traffic in the Rideau Canal. In **Gatineau Park,** boat rentals are available at **Philippe Lake** and **La Pêche Lake** (☎ **819/827-2020** to check opening hours for the rental booths). If you like your outdoor activities wet'n'wild, check out the white-water rafting adventure companies listed in chapter 10, "Exploring the Region."

CROSS-COUNTRY SKIING

You're spoiled for choice for cross-country skiing in the Ottawa area. If you want to use the trails throughout the extensive **Greenbelt,** consult the **Greenbelt All Seasons Trail Map.** All trails are suitable for beginner and family outings. Many of the trails pass through wooded areas. Or come to **Mooney's Bay Cross-country Ski Centre**, 2960 Riverside Dr. (☎ **613/247-4883**) and ski on 5km (3 miles) of groomed and well-lit trails. Classic and skate skiing are available for a mere C$2

Fun Fact

Did you know that there are more than 370km (230 miles) of major bike routes and 273km (170 miles) of minor routes in the City of Ottawa? Designated recreational pathways in the National Capital Region account for 170 km (106) miles of this total.

(US$1.60) per day or C$28 (US$18) for a season's pass. Across the Ottawa River in the city of **Gatineau,** you'll find **Parc du Lac Beauchamp** at 745 boul. Maloney ℭ **819/669-2548.** Winter activities in the park include outdoor ice skating and 15km (9 miles) of cross-country ski trails. Equipment rental is available.

For the ultimate cross-country ski experience, visit **Gatineau Park.** The park has earned a reputation as one of the best ski-trail networks in North America due to its remarkable 200km (125 miles) of trails, which are well maintained using the latest technology. The level of difficulty is marked on each trail, enabling skiers of all abilities to enjoy the meadows, valleys, and forests of the park. Both skiing styles are accommodated throughout the park, so you can glide along in classic Nordic fashion or burn up energy with the skate-skiing technique. There are eight heated shelters where you can stop to rest and refuel with a snack from your backpack. Gatineau Park ski patrollers are on watch to assist skiers in difficulty. When you arrive at the park, you can buy a day pass at any of the 16 parking lots, which give direct access to the ski trails, or at the Gatineau Park Visitor Centre, 33 Scott Rd., Chelsea, QC (ℭ **819/827-2020**), open throughout the year daily from 9am to 5pm. Daily pass prices for cross-country ski trails are C$9 (US$7) for adults, C$6 (US$5) for seniors, students, and youths, free for children 12 and under, and C$20 (US$16) per family (2 adults and 3 teens).

Always carry a map when in wilderness areas. When you arrive at the park, pick up the **Gatineau Park official winter trail map** from the visitor center for C$5 (US$4). Depicted on this highly detailed map — drawn using GIS technology — are ski trails, winter hiking trails, snowshoeing trails, huts, and shelters. Because skiing and weather conditions change frequently, Gatineau Park reviews and updates ski condition information three times daily. The trail conditions hotline is open 24 hours daily ℭ **819/827-2020.**

Sunday Bikedays

In the summer, Sunday mornings present a real treat for lovers of the outdoors in Ottawa. No less than 52km (32 miles) of parkways in Ottawa and Gatineau Park are reserved exclusively for walking, running, cycling, in-line skating, and other non-motorized recreational activities. Motor traffic is banned. In Ottawa the motor-free period runs from 9am to 1pm. In Gatineau Park, there are 30km (19 miles) of hilly roadways to hike, bike, or skate from 6 to 11am, plus one route that is designated motor-traffic-free until 1pm. **Sunday Bikedays** are sponsored by local businesses. Many local organizations provide volunteers to supervise start and end points and crossings every Sunday morning during the event.

In Ottawa, there are three motor traffic–free areas for the event, all of which are fully accessible to people with disabilities. The westbound lanes of the **Ottawa River Parkway,** located on the south side of the Ottawa River just west of downtown, have a 5.5km (3.5 mile) stretch beginning at Island Park Drive and continuing to Carling Avenue. If you drive to this section, park your vehicle at the Lincoln Fields Shopping Centre at Carling Avenue. Beginning at the Laurier Bridge, you can enjoy **Colonel By Drive** as it winds its way along the east side of the

Rideau Canal to Hog's Back Bridge, a total distance of 8km (5 miles). Park your car on one of the side streets to access Colonel By Drive. **Rockcliffe Parkway** is another choice for the Sunday morning excursion. Just east of downtown, and running along the southern shore of the Ottawa River, is an 8 km (5 mile) section between the Canada Aviation Museum and St. Joseph Boulevard. Parking is available at the Canada Aviation Museum.

In **Gatineau Park**, the majority of the parkways (27km, 17 miles) cover quite hilly terrain. The section north of Lac–Meech Road, accessible from Parking Lot 8, is recommended for families with young children.

For more information about the Sunday Bikeday program, visit the **Capital Infocentre** at 90 Wellington St. (*©* **800/465-1867** or 613/239-5000), or call the **Gatineau Park Visitor Centre** (*©* **819/827-2020**).

CYCLING AND IN-LINE SKATING

Ottawa and its environs offer a comprehensive network of pathways and parkways where people can bike and in-line skate through beautiful natural scenery. In addition, there are designated bicycle lanes on a number of city streets. No wonder Ottawa has the highest per capita population of cyclists in Canada.

If you didn't bring your own equipment, **Rent-A-Bike** (on the east side of the Rideau Canal at Plaza Bridge, next to Paul's Boat Lines *©* **613/241-4140**) has all kinds of bikes, including standard hybrid bikes designed for comfortable, leisurely touring, standard light-trail mountain bikes, on-road and off-road performance bikes, and on-road tandems. You can add a two-seat trailer for infants and toddlers or a one-seat trail-a-bike for 3- to 5-year-olds to your rental bike. In-line skates are also available. Daily bike rentals start at C$8 (US$7) per hour or C$20 (US$16) for four hours. Escorted tours for groups of six or more are available. **Cyco's**, at 5 Hawthorne Ave. (by the canal at Pretoria Bridge; *©* **613/567-**8180), also rents out bicycles and in-line skates. You can rent mountain bikes and bike trailers in **Gatineau Park** at Philippe Lake campground general store. Rental includes helmets and locks and prices range from C$8 (US$7) per hour to C$35 (US$29) for a 24-hour period.

OC Transpo, Ottawa's public transit system, has installed bike racks on more than 150 buses — most buses on routes 2, 95, and 97 have racks. Each rack holds two bikes and is designed to make loading and unloading quick and easy. There's no cost to use the rack, other than regular bus fare. The program runs from spring through fall. You can also take your bike on the O-Train and on routes 1, 4, 7, 14, 85, 96, and 118. Lock up your bike for the day at all O-Train stations

---

(*Tips*

The Capital Infocentre carries a map that marks the Capital Pathway Network in Ottawa and in Quebec, including Gatineau Park. The "Sunday Bikedays" routes are also marked. Parking lots for vehicles, drinking fountains, washrooms, picnic areas, and information centres are also marked on this map, called "Biking Country — Canada's Capital Region."

> **Tips**
>
> Want to rent cross-country ski equipment? **Gerry & Isobel's** at 14 Scott Rd., Chelsea ⓒ **819/827-4341** and **Greg Christie's Ski & Cycle Works,** 148 Old Chelsea Rd., Chelsea ⓒ **819/827-5340** are close to the main entrance to **Gatineau Park.** In **Ottawa,** try **Fresh Air Experience,** 1291 Wellington St. ⓒ **877/722-3002** or 613/729-3002, or **Trailhead** at 1960 Scott St. ⓒ **613/722-4229.**

and most Transitway stations. Use common sense when riding your bike or in-line skating, and be sure to follow the specific rules for cyclists. All cyclists under age 18 must wear a bicycle helmet under Ontario law. Cyclists cannot ride on the sidewalk and must not exceed speeds of 20kmph (12.5 mph) on multi-use pathways. Pass only when it is safe to do so, and use your bell or voice to let others know you're about to pass. Be considerate of other road or pathway users, and always keep to the right, whether you're skating or cycling.

If you're in the vicinity of the Rideau Centre and the ByWard Market, you can park your bike at a **supervised facility.** Located at **Rideau and William streets,** the facility operates daily from Victoria Day until Labour Day weekend (third Saturday in May to first Monday in September). For maps of the pathways and more information, head to the **Capital Infocentre,** opposite Parliament Hill at 90 Wellington St. (ⓒ 800/465-1867 or 613/239-5000).

FISHING

Fishing with a **Quebec** provincial permit is allowed in the **Gatineau Park** lakes (Philippe Lake, Meech Lake, and La Pêche Lake). Mulvihill Lake, near the Mackenzie King Estate, has a fishing jetty designed to accommodate wheelchairs. Gatineau Park's waters are home to 40 species of fish, including trout, yellow perch, pike, and bass. Quebec fishing permits can be purchased at Canadian Tire, 355 boul. de la Carrière, Gatineau ⓒ **819/770-7920.** To fish in **Ontario,** you need an Ontario provincial license. Ontario residents, other Canadian residents, and nonresidents all receive different licenses. **Access Ontario,** in the Rideau Centre (ⓒ **613/238-3630**), provides licenses as well as a list of Ottawa-area merchants that sell them. Please do not fish on Dow's Lake, since the fish stocked in this area do not respond favorably to catch-and-release.

GOLF

There are dozens of golf courses within an hour or so's drive of Ottawa, in both Ontario and Quebec. The varied countryside in the region provides excellent sites for courses. Most are open to the public. Green fees vary enormously, dependent upon the season, day of the week, time of day, and other factors. Fees for 18 holes generally fall into the C$25 to $75 (US$20–US$62) range. See individual listings in chapter 10, "Exploring the Region."

HIKING

Besides the pathways and trails through many of the **city parks** and the **Greenbelt** area, as discussed earlier in this chapter, you might wish to explore **Gatineau Park,** the **Rideau Trail,** and parts of the **Trans Canada Trail,** particularly if you're looking for more challenging, longer routes.

The **Rideau Trail** is a cleared and marked hiking trail approximately 300km (185 miles) long that links Ottawa with the city of Kingston, on the shores of

The Trans Canada Trail

The **Trans Canada Trail,** currently under construction, is a recreational trail that will link Canada from coast to coast. At approximately 18,078km (11,300 miles) in length when completed, it will be the longest trail of its kind in the world.

Where practical, the trail is designated as a shared-use pathway with five core activities permitted: walking, cycling, horseback riding, cross-country skiing, and snowmobiling. Wherever possible, existing trails are used, provided they can accommodate these multiple uses. In addition, some provincial and federal park property, Crown land, abandoned railway lines, and rights-of-way on private land will become part of the trail.

The trail truly belongs to Canadians. Local organizations in communities across the country own, operate, and maintain their own segments, and more than 1.5 million volunteers are taking part in the project.

About half of the trail is already accessible, and it's expected that it will be substantially complete by late 2010. In some areas it's virtually completed, but other sections still require a significant amount of work, so you won't find a final set of maps yet. Atlantic Canada's trail network is quite advanced and this has been the first region to be mapped. Available from the Trans Canada Trail website for C$6 (US$4), this map details the route through the Atlantic provinces and includes points of interest along the way. Eventually, maps will be produced for each region of the country.

In the Ottawa area, you'll find sections of the trail in **Gatineau Park, Hull,** the **National Capital Greenbelt,** and the **Ottawa River Parkway** — you can spot them by the trail markers with the Trans Canada Trail logo. For more information on the Trans Canada Trail, call ✆ **800/465-3636** or visit **www.tctrail.ca**.

Lake Ontario. The trail path is indicated by orange triangular markers. To distinguish the two directions, Kingston-bound markers have yellow tips. The path crosses varied terrain, ranging from gentle agricultural land to the rugged Canadian Shield. The trail is designated for walking, cross-country skiing, and snowshoeing. You can pick up a comprehensive guide book with maps and a description of the trail for C$30 (US$25) from the **Rideau Trail Association,** P.O. Box 15, Kingston, ON K7L 4V6 (✆ **613/545-0823**), or order online at **www.rideautrail.org**. You'll also find the guide book in major outdoor expedition stores in Ottawa, at the Scout Shop, 1345 Baseline Rd. (✆ 613/224-0139), and

Fun Fact

Canadians are being asked to help build the Trans Canada Trail by contributing toward the cost of construction. Each meter costs C$50, and donors can sponsor a meter or more of trail in any province or territory. In return they can have their name or the names of anyone they designate inscribed on the trail in one of the Trail Pavilions.

at A World of Maps, 1235 Wellington St. (☏ 613/724-6776). (See chapter 8, "Shopping," for details on these and other stores.) Call the store of your choice before you make a special trip, as they may not always have the book on hand.

The **Trans Canada Trail** is a recreational trail currently under construction that will traverse Canada from coast to coast, crossing every province and territory. In the Ottawa area, sections of the Trans Canada Trail can be found in Gatineau Park, Hull, the National Capital Greenbelt, and the Ottawa River Parkway. The trail is signposted with trail markers featuring the Trans Canada Trail logo. For more information, call ☏ 800/465-3636 or visit **www.tctrail.ca**. For information on hiking in **Gatineau Park,** see "Hull, Gatineau & the Outaouais Hills" in chapter 10, "Exploring the Region."

ICE SKATING

The number-one place to skate in the nation's capital is the world-famous **Rideau Canal.** If you visit Ottawa during the skating season, you must take everyone for a glide along the canal — it's an experience not to be missed. The **Rideau Canal Skateway** is the world's longest skating rink, offering almost 8km (5 miles) of continuous skating surface. The ice is usually ready in late December, and the season lasts until late February or early March. During the first three weekends in February, the Rideau Canal becomes the heart of **Winterlude,** Ottawa's winter festival. Skating is free. Heated shelters, skate and sled rentals, boot-check and skate-sharpening services, rest areas, food concessions, and toilets are located at various points along the Skateway. There are many access points along the canal for skating, so it's easy to get on the ice. To find out about ice conditions on the Rideau Canal, call the Skateway Hotline at ☏ **613/239-5234.**

For a special treat, visit the grounds of **Rideau Hall,** residence of the Governor General, and skate on the historic outdoor rink built by Lord and Lady Dufferin in 1872. The rink is open to the public on weekends from noon to 5pm and reserved for organized groups only on weekdays from noon to 8pm and weekends from 5 to 8pm. The rink opens in early January each year (weather permitting). The skating schedule may vary depending on weather conditions.

Across the Ottawa River in the city of **Gatineau,** you'll find **Parc du Lac Beauchamp.** Winter activities in the park include outdoor ice skating and cross-country skiing. For information on Lac Beauchamp call ☏ **819/669-2548.**

More than 70 outdoor skating rinks are scattered throughout the city of Ottawa. Pleasure skating, lessons, carnivals, and hockey are enthusiastically enjoyed at these sites. In **Brewer Park,** accessible from Hopewell Avenue near

---

Fun Fact

Community outdoor skating rinks in the City of Ottawa are classified as follows:

Puddle: A small ice surface without boards.

Puddle with end boards: A small ice surface with boards at both ends of the rink.

Rink: A single ice surface with full boards surrounding the ice.

Rink with puddle: Two ice surfaces at the same location; one with full boards and one small surface without boards.

Double surface: Two ice surfaces, separated by a snow bank.

Oval: A 400m (1300 ft.) speed-skating oval.

Kids   The Rideau Canal Skateway

- The Skateway is visited by more than 1 million skaters every year.
- Staff work around the clock to maintain the ice surface.
- Many residents use the Skateway to commute to work and school every day.
- The Skateway ice surface area is equivalent to 20 Olympic-size ice rinks.
- The average length of the skating season on the canal is 52 days.
- The shortest season to date was 30 days, and the longest was 90 days.
- There is a flag system for ice conditions. Green flags indicate the Skateway is open; red flags indicate the Skateway is closed.

Bronson Avenue, there's a speed-skating oval that is open to the public, as well as two rinks and a "puddle" (see "Fun Fact," page 170). **Brantwood Park,** at 120 Clegg St., has two ice surfaces. For the outdoor rink closest to you, and to find out the times for family recreational skating at indoor arenas throughout the region, call the **City of Ottawa Client Service Centre** ℭ **613/580-2400.**

SWIMMING

You have a choice of riverbank beaches, municipal pools, and state-of-the-art wave pools. See "Beaches" earlier in this section and "Where to Play Indoors" earlier in this chapter.

TENNIS

The following courts are open to the public — call ahead to book a court time. **Elmdale Tennis Club** is located close to downtown at 184 Holland Ave. ℭ **613/729-3644.** The **Ottawa New Edinburgh Club** provides affordable sporting facilities for its members and the community. Seven European-style, red clay courts and four hard courts are available. The club is located at 504 Rockcliffe Pkwy. ℭ **613/746-8540.** Public tennis courts can also be found at the **RA Centre,** 2451 Riverside Dr. ℭ **613/733-5100.** The **West Ottawa Tennis Club** is located in Britannia Park at the corner of Pinecrest Road and Carling Avenue (ℭ **613/828-7622**). During the summer season (May 1 to September 30), ten clay courts and three hard courts are open. The rest of the year, play is available on six covered clay courts. Instruction for all levels is available.

Tips

For loads of winter fun right in the city, visit **Carlington Snowpark,** at 941 Clyde Ave. ℭ **613/729-9206.** Go tubing or snowboarding and get a comfortable ride back up the hill. There are 10 slides to choose from, with night illumination and machine grooming. Hourly passes are available. Good toboggan hills can also be found at **Mooney's Bay Park** and **Vincent Massey Park.**

8

Shopping

As a capital city with a regional population topping 1.1 million, Ottawa's shopping facilities are excellent. Whether you're a mall rat dazzled by multi-story, glass-and-steel shopping centers, a city sophisticate who thinks heaven is a neighborhood street lined with funky boutiques and hip cafes, or a minivan-driving aficionado of big-box discount stores, Ottawa delivers. Slip on a pair of comfortable shoes, rev up your plastic, and get ready to shop 'til you drop.

HOURS   Most stores in the Ottawa area are open Monday through Saturday from 9:30 or 10am to 6pm, and many have extended hours one or more evenings a week. Sunday opening hours are generally from noon to 5pm, although some malls open at 11am and some independent stores are closed. You should call ahead if you have a specific destination in mind.

TAXES   Sales taxes add a hefty chunk to your bill. The provincial retail sales tax in Ontario is 8% for most items — two exceptions are basic groceries and children's clothing, which are exempt. The federal Goods and Services Tax (GST) is 7%.

Tips   **Visitor Tax Rebate**

Visitors to Canada (non-residents) can apply for a tax refund. The accommodations tax and provincial (8%) and federal (7%) sales taxes on non-disposable items that will be exported for use can be recovered. Keep all your receipts. For details, see "Taxes" under "Fast Facts: Ottawa" in chapter 3.

---

1 The Shopping Scene

GREAT SHOPPING AREAS

BANK STREET PROMENADE

You'll find 15 blocks of stores and services in this area, beginning at Wellington Street in the heart of downtown and stretching south to Gladstone Avenue. About 500 businesses operate on this stretch of Bank Street, ranging from small, locally owned retailers, bargain stores, and souvenir shops to restaurants, bars, and cafes. Some of the shops are rather colorful. As the name suggests, the major banks established their first local offices on this street — in fact, the district is one of the city's oldest shopping areas.

BYWARD MARKET ✸✸

More than 100 boutiques jostle for position with restaurants, pubs, services, and food retailers in the warren of side streets that make up the vibrant ByWard Market area, bordered by Sussex Drive, St. Patrick Street, King Edward Avenue, and Rideau Street. Head for this district to be entertained, excited, and delighted by what's on offer in the diverse collection of shops, cafes, restaurants, pubs, and clubs. The ByWard Market building, located on the original site where farmers and loggers met to carry out their business in the 1800s, was restored in 1998 and now houses gourmet food shops and the wares of local and regional artisans. Excellent-quality local fruit, vegetables, flowers, and other farm products are available at outdoor stalls surrounding the market building between April and October. Cheese shops, butchers, bakeries, and other food retailers complete the mix.

DOWNTOWN RIDEAU

The stores and restaurants continue seamlessly as you stroll from the ByWard Market toward the Rideau Centre, the major downtown shopping mall, so you won't notice that you've stepped into the shopping area known as Downtown Rideau. Bordered by the Rideau Canal, King Edward Avenue, George Street, and the Mackenzie King Bridge, this 23-block section of the city is promoted as the city's arts and theater district — Arts Court, the National Arts Centre, and the Canadian Museum of Contemporary Photography are in the vicinity, in addition to many national chain retailers and unique independent stores.

THE GLEBE ⟨★⟩⟨★⟩

Farther south on Bank Street, between the Queensway and the Rideau Canal, is a stretch of trendy, higher-end stores, services, and eateries serving the upscale middle-class neighborhood known as the Glebe. It's well worth spending a morning or afternoon strolling up one side of the street and down the other. If you begin at the north end, take a break near the canal before making your return journey. Brown's Inlet and Park are tucked a couple of blocks west of Bank Street, north of Queen Elizabeth Drive. If you start at the canal end, take a break in Central Park, which straddles Bank Street in the vicinity of Powell Avenue and Clemow Avenue. For winter strolling, take refuge in the atrium at Fifth Avenue Court, about midway down this section of Bank Street.

SPARKS STREET MALL

Canada's oldest permanent pedestrian shopping street, Sparks Street Mall runs between Elgin and Lyon streets, one block south of Parliament Hill. Although it's busy during the working day because of the many office blocks that surround it, Sparks Street can seem deserted on evenings and weekends. In summer, restaurants set up patio tables and chairs, and there's an annual busker festival (see chapter 9, "Ottawa After Dark").

WELLINGTON STREET WEST ⟨★⟩

Not to be confused with Wellington Street in the downtown core, which runs in front of the Parliament Buildings, Wellington Street West is actually a continuation of Somerset Street West in the stretch between Parkdale Avenue and Island Park Drive, where it then changes name to Richmond Road. There's an interesting mix here, with fine-dining restaurants, neighborhood cafes, interior decorating retailers, and antiques, collectibles, and second-hand shops squeezed in beside the usual main street businesses.

WESTBORO VILLAGE

This traditional city neighborhood west of downtown has enjoyed a revitalization since the late 1990s. The addition of Richmond Road Mountain Equipment Co-op spurred retail growth in the west end of Westboro's commercial ribbon, and the area has become somewhat of a sports-equipment and outdoor-gear mecca. There is hope that the area will eventually link with Wellington Street West to form a shopping district much like the ByWard Market and the Glebe.

WHERE TO BROWSE THE BIG-BOX STORES Strategically placed clusters of big-box retailers have muscled into the Ottawa area, just as in other Canadian cities. Especially popular with consumers hunting for big-ticket items like electronics, furniture, and appliances, the big boxes attract shoppers with their promise of lower prices and wider selection of goods. Multi-screen movie theaters and popular chain restaurants are often located within the complexes. The Centrum in Kanata (take the Terry Fox exit from the Queensway) and South Keys (Bank Street north of Hunt Club Road) are two of the largest big-box sites. Bells Corners and Merivale Road in Nepean and Ogilvie Road in Gloucester are also worth a look, if you're a big-box fan.

MAJOR MALLS

Bayshore Shopping Centre In Ottawa's west end, close to the Queensway, Bayshore Shopping Centre has three floors of shops and services, and five anchor stores — The Bay, Zellers, Sports Experts, Old Navy, and Winners, a discount/end-of-line store carrying clothing and household goods. Around 200 retailers await you. Women's wear is well represented here, and there are a number of better quality shoe stores. The customer service center, on the first level near Gap Kids, offers car unlocking, battery boosting, and other services in addition to stroller, wheelchair, and walker rental. A playcare center, operated by YMCA/YWCA, provides a supervised play area for children aged $2^1/2$ to 7 years. 100 Bayshore Dr. 𝒞 613/829-7491. Mon–Sat 9am–9pm; Sun 10am–6pm. Free parking.

Carlingwood Shopping Centre Carlingwood offers one-floor shopping, which is a boon if you're a young parent or a shopper with physical disabilities. Anchored by Sears and Loblaws, this mall has a number of special services for families, plus coat and parcel check, free stroller and wheelchair use, and a lounge area where you can take a break. There's a good range of shoe stores here and almost two dozen women's wear stores. Retailers number around 130. 2121 Carling Ave. 𝒞 613/725-1546. Mon–Fri 9:30am–9pm; Sat 9:30am–6pm; Sun 10am–6pm. Free parking.

Place d'Orléans Follow Highway 417 to 174 east to the suburb of Orléans and you'll find this large mall just on the edge of the highway, about a 15-minute drive from downtown. Anchored by The Bay, The Bay Home Store, SportChek, and Wal-Mart, Place d'Orléans offers two levels of shops and services. With a large family demographic, Place d'Orléans provides facilities for parents and children, including changing tables and private breastfeeding rooms. On the second floor, there's an indoor playground and playcare center run by the YMCA/YWCA. Stroller and wheelchair usage are free. Unisex clothing stores include American Eagle Outfitters, Eddie Bauer, Gap, Roots, Urban Planet, and West 49°. There are about a dozen home furnishings and accessories stores, including The Bay Home Store, English Butler, Kitchen Sense, McIntosh & Watts, and The Home Company. 110 Place d'Orléans Dr. 𝒞 613/824-9050. Mon–Sat 9:30am–9pm; Sun 11am–5pm. Free parking.

Rideau Centre In the heart of downtown, with direct access from the Ottawa Congress Centre and the Westin Hotel, the four-level Rideau Centre has more than 170 stores, including services, restaurants, and cinemas. You'll find a good selection of jewelers, leather goods stores, and better quality casual clothing. This mall is a good bet for gifts and souvenirs — Mastermark Pewter, Ottawa

Souvenirs & Gifts, Swarovski, WIX, and Oh Yes Ottawa! are all worth a look. Higher-end food outlets include Marchèlino, Café Supreme, and Godiva Chocolatier (chocolate is one of the recommended major food groups for healthy eating, isn't it?). Free stroller and wheelchair usage and a nursing room are available. 50 Rideau St. ℭ 613/236-6565. Mon–Fri 9:30am–9pm; Sat 9:30am–6pm; Sun 11am–5pm.

St. Laurent Shopping Centre   Situated at the junction of the Queensway and St. Laurent Boulevard, this mall has recently opened Rainbow Cinemas, a five-theater movie complex. Almost 200 stores and services, most of them on ground level, make it an easy mall to negotiate. Guest services include free stroller and wheelchair use, parcel check, and car battery boosts. Anchor stores are The Bay, Sears, Sportchek, and Toys "R" Us. A Friendly Corner Centre serves the local community, with activities, seminars, and social opportunities for people of all ages. If you've experienced a BeaverTail in the ByWard Market or along the side of the Rideau Canal in winter and crave another, you can find one to munch on here. 1200 St. Laurent Blvd. ℭ 613/745-6858. Mon–Sat 9:30am–9pm; Sun 11 am–5pm. Free parking.

OTHERS   Downtown, several smaller, upscale indoor malls serve office workers and tourists alike, although their opening hours tend to reflect a 9-to-5 mentality. **L'Esplanade Laurier,** at the corner of Bank Street and Laurier Avenue, features women's fashions, gift shops, banking, and postal services. At the corner of Sparks and Bank streets, **240 Sparks Shopping Centre** has a large food court and is anchored by Holt Renfrew, which stocks designer-label men's and women's clothing and stays open until 7:30pm on Thursday and Friday; Sunday hours are noon to 5pm. **World Exchange Plaza,** at the corner of Metcalfe and Albert streets, combines movie theaters, services, and a cafe catering to the office crowd.

2 Shopping A to Z
ANTIQUES & COLLECTIBLES

There are a number of fine antiques dealers and a host of collectibles shops in the city, but if you want to hit a few places in a single neighborhood then head south on Bank Street to Ottawa's very own antiques alley.

The Antique Shoppe   This store has a wide range of English furniture from the Georgian, Regency, and early Victorian periods. In addition, there is an eclectic mix of Continental, American, and Canadian furniture pieces in a variety of styles. 750 Bank St. ℭ 613/232-0840.

Bloomsbury & Co Antiques   With interests that include antique and period furniture, silver, prints, china, pottery, and decorative items, this store at the corner of Bank and Sunnyside is always on the lookout for antique and period pieces to add to their inventory. 1090 Bank St. ℭ 613/730-1926.

Champagne dit Lambert Antiques   This high-end Glebe antiques dealer specializes in fine furniture, particularly mahogany, and also silver completion, china, and decorative items. They have a strong reputation in the city for their attractive window displays. An annex known as the "Warehouse" stocks teak furniture and other objects for young urban collectors. 1130 Bank St. ℭ 613/730-1181.

Ottawa Antique Market   Just south of the Glebe, more than 40 antique dealers display their wares daily in this indoor market. 1179A Bank St. ℭ 613/730-6000.

Yardley's Antiques   On dry days, you'll see the pavement in front of this shop crammed with articles for sale. There's something for everyone here. Antiques rub shoulders with country pine furniture, old light fixtures, and pop memorabilia. 1240 Bank St. ℭ 613/739-9580.

BOOKS

Basilisk Dreams Books   Specializing in classic and contemporary science fiction, horror, and fantasy, this store is a must for fans of these genres. Book signings and monthly meetings held. 857B Bank St. ℭ 613/230-2474.

Books on Beechwood   This independent store carries general fiction and nonfiction. Emphasis is on literary fiction rather than pulp. Also a large children's and young adult section, a number of British and military history books, and a small but select mystery section. 35 Beechwood Ave. ℭ 613/742-5030.

Chapters   Gaining a presence on city street corners as well as participating in big-box suburban commercial sprawl, Chapters has become a familiar name and favored destination for Canadian shoppers. There are three locations to choose from in the Ottawa area, offering an extensive selection of books and magazines. Larger stores carry CDs and a growing selection of giftware. 47 Rideau St. ℭ 613/241-0073; 2735 Iris St. ℭ 613/596-3003; 2210 Bank St. ℭ 613/521-9199.

Collected Works   This independent store stocks general fiction and nonfiction, with an emphasis on literary fiction and children's books. It offers a cozy browsing atmosphere, augmented with comfy chairs and a small coffee bar. 1242 Wellington St. ℭ 613/722-1265.

Leishman Books Ltd.   This independent store carries general fiction and nonfiction and French-as-a-second-language books. There's a large children's section at the back of the store. Westgate Shopping Centre. ℭ 613/722-8313.

Librairie du Soleil   The new location of Librairie du Soleil lives up to its name — the sun streams into the interior. Come here for the most extensive selection of French-language books in Ottawa. A good choice of French/English dictionaries is on hand. Calendars, TinTin memorabilia, and other nonbook items also available. Bilingual staff. 33 George St. ℭ 613/241-6999.

Nicholas Hoare ★   Specializing in British authors and publishers, this shop also offers a comprehensive children's section and a good selection of Canadian fiction. The atmosphere is restful and the background music soothing. Floor-to-ceiling bookshelves line the walls and elegant library ladders glide on rails to allow access to the top shelves. Enjoy the selection of literature, popular fiction, art books, hardcover coffee table books, travel books, and cookbooks. 419 Sussex Dr. ℭ 613/562-2665.

Octopus Books   The focus at Octopus is on books which encourage analytical thinking about the economic, political, and social world. Many of the recommended texts for social and political science courses at Carleton University and the Universty of Ottawa are stocked here. Canadian and international fiction also feature prominently on the shelves. 116 Third Avenue. ℭ613/233-2589.

Patrick McGahern Books Inc.   A delightful collection of used and rare books — Canadiana, Arctica, voyages and travel, medicine, Irish history and literature, and more. Ladders available to access those tempting titles just out of reach. A must to include on a stroll along Bank Street in the Glebe. 783 Bank St. ℭ 613/230-2275.

Perfect Books   An independent bookseller carrying general fiction and nonfiction, Perfect Books has a strong literary fiction section, plus a good chunk of politics and current events. Higher-end cookbooks are also stocked. 258A Elgin St. ℭ 613/231-6468.

Place Bell Books   Specializing in travel books and maps, this bookstore has a hefty selection of titles on vacation destinations around the world. Local guide books and books featuring scenic photography of the Ottawa region are also on hand, as are general interest titles. In the Place Bell mall, entrance on Metcalfe Street. 175 Metcalfe St. ✆ **613/233-3821**.

Prime Crime Books   As you just may have deduced, this bookstore specializes in crime and mystery fiction. Frequented by local authors and mystery fans. 891 Bank St. ✆ **613/238-2583**.

Singing Pebble Books ★ *Finds*   Those with an interest in and passion for subjects leaning toward the esoteric will find themselves at home here. Think metaphysics, Eastern and Western spirituality, alternative health and healing, women's studies, psychology, and philosophy. You could lose yourself for hours as you discover title after fascinating title. 202A Main St. ✆ **613/230-9165**.

CANADIAN FINE ARTS

The Carlen Gallery   Work by almost 200 contemporary Canadian artisans is featured at this Bank Street showroom, right in the heart of "Antiques Alley." Clay, glass, metal, and wood pieces, fine arts, textiles, sheepskin products, occasional furniture, and whimsical decorative items can all be found here. The gallery is exclusively Canadian. 1171 Bank St. ✆ **613/730-5555**.

Galerie d'Art Vincent   This gallery, located in the elegant Edwardian Fairmont Château Laurier Hotel, features Canadian historical and contemporary art. Exquisite, unique sculptures, 20th-century Canadian paintings, and original Inuit carvings and prints.1 Rideau St. (inside Château Laurier Hotel). ✆ **613/241-1144**.

Northern Country Arts   The work of almost 40 Canadian Inuit artists is featured in this ByWard Market district gallery. Carvings, jewelry, artwork, crafts, and rugs are among the offerings. Sculpture materials include stone, whalebone, and muskox horn. Northern Country Arts owns and operates three major galleries; this location is the only one outside the Arctic. Most pieces are purchased directly from the artists, who live and work in communities across Canada's north. 21 Clarence St. ✆ **613/789-9591**.

Snapdragon Gallery   The front window display of this Glebe shop is a work of art in itself, featuring a variety of pieces by both emerging and established Canadian artists. Step inside and you'll find jewelry, ceramics, glass, wood, leather goods, Inuit sculpture, and copper etchings. 791 Bank St. ✆ **613/233-1296**.

The Snow Goose Limited   This fine arts and crafts shop specializes in Canadian, Inuit, and Native works from the Arctic and the West Coast in every price range. You'll find clothing, sculptures, prints, masks, pottery, quill boxes, totems, leather goods, and jewelry. Conveniently located on Sparks Street Mall close to the Parliament Buildings. 83 Sparks St. ✆ **613/232-2213**.

CDs, MUSIC

Larger shopping malls have at least one store specializing in CDs and DVDs, although they tend to limit their selection to mainstream best sellers and charge full price. The two big chain stores in the Ottawa area are **HMV Canada** and **Music World**. The alternative is to hunt down a used music store — they often carry new as well as used CDs and DVDs, with lower prices than the malls. Some also deal in cassette tapes and vinyl records.

Record Runner A good selection of new music at discounted prices, right in the heart of downtown Ottawa. This store specializes in underground, punk, and electronic music, and welcomes special orders. A great destination for alternative music. Some used vinyl records and CDs. Lots of DVDs in stock. 212 Rideau St. ℂ 613/241-3987.

The Turning Point Two floors of used music will keep music fans occupied for hours. A wide range of genres, including rock, blues, jazz, hip-hop, dance, classical, pop, folk, world, and more. They are a buy-sell-trade enterprise, so the selection is always changing. Used vinyl and CD prices are low. 411 Cooper St. ℂ 613/230-4586.

Vertigo This music store, located across the street from Record Runner, has a huge selection of vinyl records and new and used CDs. Collectors and music buffs will enjoy browsing the music accessories, which include headphones, record players, and collector sets. Special orders are accepted. 193 Rideau St. ℂ 613/241-1011.

CAMERAS & ELECTRONICS

Canadian Camera Service Centre Inc. Sales and repairs to all makes of cameras. Also stocks lenses, binoculars, projectors, and photographic equipment. One-hour photo service and free estimates on repairs. 250 Albert St. ℂ 613/238-4892.

Ginn Photographic Co. This store sells and rents new and used photographic equipment and supplies, plus darkroom equipment and supplies. They also provide digital equipment sales and service and imaging services. 433 Bank St. ℂ 613/567-4686.

Radio Shack Offering the latest in home electronics, computers, phones, and lots of neat accessories, Radio Shack has almost a dozen locations in the city; check out the Yellow Pages. 286 Bank St. ℂ 613/238-6889; Rideau Centre, 1st floor ℂ 613/563-1156 and 3rd floor ℂ 613/241-2981; other locations.

CHOCOLATES & SWEETS

Godiva Chocolatier Inc. Go ahead, indulge in top-quality chocolate confections. This shop is highly recommended if you want to treat a loved one or yourself. Rideau Centre. ℂ 613/234-4470.

Laura Secord This chocolatier has been a Canadian favorite for more than 85 years. The chocolates and truffles are quite delicious. Try the white chocolate almond bark and the butterscotch lollipops. 85 Bank St. ℂ 613/232-6830; Billings Bridge Plaza ℂ 613/737-5695; Place d'Orléans Shopping Centre ℂ 613/837-7546; Rideau Centre ℂ 613/230-2576; St. Laurent Shopping Centre ℂ 613/741-5040.

Rocky Mountain Chocolate Factory This British Columbia–based company has lots of goodies — chocolate (of course!), cookies, fudge, candy apples, and other sweet treats. Located inside the ByWard Market building at the south end. 55 ByWard Market. ℂ 613/241-1091.

Sugar Mountain Kids love this place. Adults are also known to be frequent visitors. Walls are lined with clear plastic bins at the right height for scooping the most outrageous colors and flavors of sugar-loaded confections into loot bags. Islands of boxed and wrapped candy and chocolates fill the two-level store. Looking for retro candy? Thrills gum (why *does* it taste like soap?), black licorice pipes, sherbet fountains, pink popcorn, and Curly Wurlys have all been spotted here. The selection changes frequently and there's often a good variety of British sweets. Get ready for a major sugar rush. 71 William St. (ByWard Market district) holds the title of the world's largest Sugar Mountain store. ✆ **613/789-8428**. Also at 286 Elgin St. ✆ **613/ 230-8886**. A third Ottawa location is scheduled to open on Bank Street in the Glebe early in 2005.

CHRISTMAS STORES

Christmas in the Capital Inc.   High-quality Christmas ornaments and beautifully decorated trees fill the store. Popular collectibles are stocked, and keepsake ornaments, gifts, angels, nativity scenes, Santas, and snowmen abound. Seasonal and holiday decorations for other festivals throughout the year are displayed at appropriate times. 231 Elgin St. ✆ **613/231-4646**.

DEPARTMENT STORES

The Bay   Established in the Canadian north more than 300 years ago as a fur-trading post known as The Hudson's Bay Company, The Bay carries standard department-store collections of fashions and housewares. Sales and promotions are frequent and merchandise is good quality. The Bay occupies an anchor spot at four large Ottawa area malls — Bayshore Shopping Centre, Place d'Orléans Shopping Centre, Rideau Centre, and St. Laurent Shopping Centre.

Sears Canada Inc.   Offering a comprehensive range of consumer goods, Sears anchors Carlingwood Shopping Centre, Rideau Centre, and St. Laurent Shopping Centre. Like The Bay, sales and promotions are offered on an ongoing basis.

DRUGSTORES (24 HOURS)

Shopper's Drug Mart   Shopper's Drug Mart has a dispensary for prescription medicines and an extensive front shop with toiletries, books and magazines, groceries, greeting cards, gifts, vitamins, and over-the-counter medicines. You'll see their distinctive signs — white letters on a red background — all over the city, and many locations are open until midnight. They have one 24-hour location, at 1460 Merivale Rd. (at Baseline Rd.) ✆ **613/224-7270**.

FASHION, CHILDREN'S

Gap Kids   Kids from grade 1 to high school and beyond still want to be seen in the perennially popular Gap sweaters. Gap Kids clothes are practical, the styles are fun, the colors are usually great, and they wash and wear well. Bayshore Shopping Centre ✆ **613/828-8131**; Rideau Centre ✆ **613/569-4110**; St. Laurent Shopping Centre ✆ **613/746-8787**.

Glebe Side Kids   If you don't want to dress your kids in the same gear as your friends and neighbors, step into Glebe Side Kids for designer clothing in eye-catching colors and styles. You'll find casual and dressy clothing for boys and girls in sizes from infants to teens. Lines include Bleu and Deux Par Deux from Quebec and imports from Germany and France. High quality — and prices to match. 793 Bank St. ✆ **613/235-6552**.

Gymboree   This store provides colorful, sturdy clothing and helpful staff, plus a play area at the back of the store. Prices can be on the high side, but the store has frequent sales. Bayshore Shopping Centre ✆ **613/829-7236**; Rideau Centre ✆ **613/565-3323**; St. Laurent Shopping Centre ✆ **613/842-4716**.

Jacob Jr.   This fashion-forward store sells clothing in scaled-down versions of adult styles, including separates and underwear for girls who just want to have fun. Particularly favored by the 11 to 14 crowd. Bayshore Shopping Centre ✆ **613/ 828-2470**; St. Laurent Shopping Centre ✆ **613/746-7095**.

Northern Getaway   Younger school kids all seem to have something from Northern Getaway in their wardrobes. This is strongly themed clothing for boys (sports, wild animals; strong, dark colors) and girls (flowers, puppies; lilacs and pinks). Kids like the clothes and the prices are middle-of-the-road. Sales come up often. Colors are coordinated each season so that separates mix and match throughout the store. Bayshore Shopping Centre ℭ **613/829-0385**; Carlingwood Shopping Centre ℭ **613/722-6107**; Place d'Orléans ℭ **613/834-2377**.

Please Mum   Browse the bright, coordinated separates for active kids. Bayshore Shopping Centre ℭ **613/820-5145**; Place d'Orléans Shopping Centre ℭ **613/830-1366**; St. Laurent Shopping Centre ℭ **613/820-5145**.

Roots Canada Ltd.   This casual clothing, in infant to adult sizes, washes and wears well. Only selected stores carry kids' merchandise; in Ottawa, that's at Place d'Orléans and St. Laurent Shopping Centre. There's also a factory outlet location in the south end of the city; prices are slashed but the selection varies. Place d'Orléans ℭ **613/841-7164**; South Keys Factory Outlet 2210 Bank St. ℭ **613/736-9503**; St. Laurent Shopping Centre ℭ **613/288-1492**.

R.W. Kids   Ottawa's OshKosh store has perhaps Canada's best selection of OshKosh clothing. Most parents are familiar with OshKosh quality — kids just can't seem to wear it out and outfits still look good handed down to a second or even third child. The store is well laid out, with cascading hangers lining the walls so that styles and sizes are easy to find, and it's easy to navigate with a stroller. There's a playroom at the back and a rack of gently used OshKosh consignment clothing on display. An annual membership for a small fee entitles you to a 15% discount on all regular-price items. Kushies, Robeez, and Avent products also in stock. They will ship merchandise anywhere in Canada. Hampton Park Plaza, Carling and Kirkwood avenues. ℭ **613/724-4576**.

Tickled Pink   This effervescent collection features lines from three Ottawa designers. Bright, intense colors, practical styling, and fun patterns. Yummy Mummy maternity wear from Toronto, locally made sheepskin hats, gloves, and slippers, and dress-up clothes (fairies, ballerinas, princesses). Worth a visit. 55 ByWard Market. ℭ **613/562-8350**.

West End Kids   If you're tired of mall wear, head here for top-quality upscale clothing for infants to teens. Labels include Mexx, Columbia, Tommy Hilfiger, Deux Par Deux, and Fresh Produce. 373 Richmond Rd. ℭ **613/722-8947**.

FASHION, MENS & WOMENS

Buckland's Fine Clothing   Clothing and accessories for well-heeled clients. Top brand names and designer labels include Anne Klein, Tommy Hilfiger, Arnold Brant, and Cambridge Suits. 722 Bank St. ℭ **613/238-2020**.

Club Monaco   Favoring young styling with simple lines and neutral tones, mixed with black and white separates, Club Monaco attracts urban sophisticates. Bayshore Shopping Centre ℭ 613/596-4030; St. Laurent Shopping Centre ℭ **613/745-0583**; Rideau Centre ℭ **613/230-0245**.

Guess   Brand-name casual wear for young men and women. Rideau Centre ℭ **613/231-6669**.

Holt Renfrew   Men's and women's fashions and accessories in the upper price range. Many designer labels. 240 Sparks St. ℭ **613/238-2200**.

Mexx   Men's and women's casual clothing and separates for work or play. Young, classy, European, and stylish. Well worth checking out. Rideau Centre ℭ **613/569-6399**.

Roots Canada Ltd.   Although Roots has been a well-known Canadian label for many years, their sponsorship of the Nagano Winter Olympics several years ago catapulted their coats, sweaters, and caps into the world spotlight. Demand has grown for their clothing line since that time, particularly in the U.S. This casual clothing, in infant to adult sizes, washes and wears well. Only selected stores carry kids' merchandise. In Ottawa, that's at Place d'Orléans and St. Laurent Shopping Centre. There's also a factory outlet location in the south end of the city; prices are slashed but the selection varies. Roots has expanded their product line to include fragrances, jewelry, leather goods, and shoes. 787 Bank St. ✆ 613/232-3790; Bayshore Shopping Centre ✆ 613/820-4527; Place d'Orléans ✆ 613/841-7164; Rideau Centre ✆ 613/236-7760; South Keys Factory Outlet 2210 Bank St. ✆ 613/736-9503.

FASHION, MEN'S

E.R. Fisher Ltd.   Dress and casual wear from a fine men's clothier, established in 1905. Custom-made shirts, tailored to measure, and formal-wear service. Lines include Cambridge, Hardy Amies, Cutter & Buck, and Cline. 115 Sparks St. ✆ 613/232-9636.

Harry Rosen   Pay a visit to this upper-end men's clothiers for top-quality service and the finest in menswear designers. Choose from Hugo Boss, Brioni, Versace, and others. Rideau Centre ✆ 613/230-7232.

Moores   Mid-price-range clothing for the average man on the street — although their sizes run from extra short to extra tall and oversize. Some of their merchandise is Canadian made and includes suits, sport coats, and dress pants as well as a good selection of casual wear. In addition to the downtown store at Bank Street, there's one in the west end and one in the east. 162 Bank St. ✆ 613/235-2121.

Morgante Menswear   Fine clothing from formal wear rental to casual and sportswear, with lines by Canali, Jeans Couture, Versace, and Hugo Boss. Professional tailoring available, and alterations while you wait. 141 Sparks St. ✆ 613/234-2232.

FASHION, WOMEN'S

Anik Boutique   High-end women's fashion retailer carrying top lines including Boss, Versace, Marc Cain, AJ Armani, and Ferre. 334 Cumberland St. ✆ 613/241-2444.

Eclection   Exclusively stocking Canadian designers hailing from Toronto through Quebec, Eclection has fascinating and unusual women's separates and accessories. Jewelry, hats, and scarves available. Check out their line of medieval street clothing. 55 ByWard Market. ✆ 613/789-7288.

Richard Robinson   This exciting Ottawa-based fashion designer has a ready-to-wear collection available at the boutique next to the Richard Robinson Academy of Fashion Design. 447 Sussex Dr. ✆ 613/241-5233.

Sable Classics   Women's fashions and accessories, with an emphasis on dresses and sportswear. One of the featured designers is Canadian Linda Lundstrom. 206 Sparks St. ✆ 613/233-8384.

Shepherd's   Canadian, American, and European designers are featured at this local boutique. Lines by Helen Kaminski and Linda Lundstrom. Good selection of accessories, including jewelry, handbags, belts, and purses. Bayshore Shopping Centre ✆ 613/596-0070; Rideau Centre ✆ 613/563-7666.

FOOD

Lovers of fine wines and good food can check out the recommendations in "Gourmet to Go" in chapter 5, "Dining."

GIFT SHOPS

Abington's Animals   This store features many lines of collectibles, especially figurines. For kids, there are Beanie Babies, Beanie Kids, and Harry Potter merchandise. St. Laurent Shopping Centre. ✆ **613/744-7094.**

Burapa Asian Perspective   An intriguing collection of home accessories, personal wear (silk, Pashmina, and cashmere), jewelry, old-teak furniture, and gift items from Thailand, Nepal, Burma, Laos, and Vietnam. 91 Murray St. ✆ **613/789-0759.**

Canada's Four Corners   Fine crafts and quality Canadian souvenirs share space with a gallery of framed and matted prints. 93 Sparks St. ✆ **613/233-2322.**

Dilemme   Making a decision on what to buy in this store full of neat and unusual gifts and trinkets is indeed a dilemma. A wide range of clothing, gifts, and jewelry with an exotic flavor fill the space. 785 Bank St. ✆ **613/233-0445.**

Giraffe African Arts   Authentic art from Africa. Handmade masks, statues, fabric wall hangings, jewelry, ebony, soapstone, musical instruments, and pottery that reflect traditional and contemporary art forms. 19 Clarence St. ✆ **613/562-0284.**

Hard Rock Café   This retail outlet in the restaurant sells souvenir Hard Rock Cafe merchandise featuring their logo, including T-shirts, caps, jackets, and pins. 73 York St. ✆ **613/241-2442.**

Mon Cadeau   Next door to the delicious Ma Cuisine, Mon Cadeau specializes in unique, personal gift items. 261 Dalhousie St. ✆ **613/241-4438.**

O'Shea's Market Ireland   Family owned and operated for more than 25 years, O'Shea's is packed with goods imported from the Emerald Isle. Popular items include Celtic jewelry and woolen goods — especially sweaters, cardigans, blankets, and throws. Hundreds of family crests and coats of arms on hand. Expansion is planned for 2005 to accommodate a larger range of goods from Scotland in addition to the Irish merchandise. 91 Sparks St. ✆ **613/235-5141.**

Oh Yes Ottawa!   This terrific Canadian-made souvenir clothing line also has an airport location. Rideau Centre. ✆ **613/569-7520.**

Ottawa Souvenirs and Gifts   Browse the selection of T-shirts, sweatshirts, mugs, plaques, spoons, and maple syrup products. Rideau Centre. ✆ **613/233-0468.**

The Snow Goose Limited   This Canadian arts and crafts shop specializes in Inuit and Native works in every price range. You'll find clothing, sculptures, prints, masks, dreamcatchers, soapstone carvings, totems, and jewelry. 83 Sparks St. ✆ **613/232-2213.**

3 Trees   Specializing in spiritual items from faraway lands, 3 Trees is a browser's heaven. Imported spiritual tools from Nepal, India, and Thailand include bowls, statues, meditation cushions, candles, incense, and chimes. Imported clothing, jewelry, gifts, and home decor accessories complete the merchandise. 202 Main St. ✆ **613/230-0304.**

HOBBY & CRAFT STORES

Dynamic Hobbies   Model enthusiasts will love the radio-controlled model cars, airplanes, helicopters, and boats, on-site indoor and outdoor tracks, and the 45 m (150 ft.) slot car track. 21 Concourse Gate, Unit 6. ✆ **613/225-9634.**

Hobby House Ltd.   This store offers a wide variety of hobby supplies, including plastic model kits, model trains and accessories, military and aviation books, modelers' tools and supplies, rockets, kites, die-cast models, wooden ship kits, and puzzles. 80 Montreal Rd. ℰ 613/749-5245.

Lewiscraft   Lots of materials and supplies for artistically inclined kids and grown-ups, plus knowledgeable and helpful staff. Carlingwood Shopping Centre ℰ 613/729-8428; Place d'Orléans ℰ 613/834-9039; Rideau Centre. ℰ 613/230-7792.

Lilliput   A delightful collection of dollhouse furniture, fixtures, and accessories is beautifully displayed. Dollhouse kits in several styles are available, with some completed models on show. 9 Murray St. ℰ 613/241-1183.

Michael's Arts and Crafts   Taking up the big-box challenge of trying to carry everything under one roof, Michael's has aisle upon aisle filled with shelves simply groaning with arts and crafts supplies for the home crafter and decorator, including kid-friendly supplies and seasonal decorations for every major annual festival. Especially good hunting ground at Easter, Halloween and Christmas. 2210F Bank St. ℰ 613/521-3717; 2685 Iris St. ℰ 613/726-7211.

The Sassy Bead Co.   Browse the colorful jars, trays, and boxes filled with beads of every description. Make your selection, then sit at a table and create your own jewelry right in the shop. Creative staff are on hand seven days a week to help with design and assembly. There's also a good selection of unique ready-made items. Workshops and kids' birthday parties are available. The Bank Street location carries a line of Sassy clothing for teens and women. 757 Bank St. ℰ 613/567-7886; 11 William St. ℰ 613/562-2812.

HOME DECOR

Belle de Provence   This store is deliciously French in its merchandise and atmosphere. Exquisite toiletries, linens, books, and items for the home. A delightful shop. 80 George St. ℰ 613/789-2552.

Casa Luna   Featuring furniture and home accessories with a Southern flavor, Casa Luna carries Mexican-made furniture, among others. Many unusual and one-of-a-kind items. Carved reproduction Spanish and French pieces and lots of wrought iron. Shop for the dining room, kitchen, bedroom, and bathroom. 1115 Bank St. ℰ 613/730-3561.

Ikea   They advise you to wear comfortable shoes, and they mean it. This Swedish store has about 75 life-size rooms displaying their home furnishings, including kitchens, bedrooms, offices, and living rooms. Most furniture comes flat-packed and requires assembly at home, but many of Ikea's customers are in the family minivan category, so it's easy for them to load up their purchases. The fresh, young, urban image draws big crowds, especially on Saturdays. Free stroller rental, a baby-care room for feeding and changing, and a kids' play area will make parents happy. On-site restaurant. Catalog available. Pinecrest Shopping Centre, 2685 Iris St. ℰ 613/829-4530.

La Cache   Beautiful classic floral linens for dining rooms and bedrooms. 763 Bank St. ℰ 613/233-0412.

Linen Chest   A big-box store that will make filling your bridal registry list a breeze. Aisle upon aisle of china, dinnerware, cutlery, housewares, linens, crystal, kitchenwares, and gifts. After the honeymoon, go back for another visit to stock up on baby bedding, furniture, and accessories. Pinecrest Shopping Centre, 2685 Iris St. ℰ 613/721-9991.

McIntosh & Watts Ltd.   Established in 1906, McIntosh & Watts deals in fine china, crystal, flatware, and giftware. You'll find branches at Bayshore Shopping

Centre ℂ **613/828-9174**, Place d'Orléans Shopping Centre ℂ **613/834-8442**, and Rideau Centre ℂ **613/560-5311**.

Varia   Home and kitchen boutique filled with accessories and gifts. Look here for table linens, candle holders, vases, teapots, and much more. 521 Sussex Dr. ℂ **613/244-1130**; 775 Bank St. in the Glebe ℂ **613/238-1130**.

JEWELRY

Birks   Founded in 1879, Birks is a respected Canadian jewelry retailer. Carries a wide range of silver, crystal, and china as well as top-quality jewelry. Popular for engagement rings. Bayshore Shopping Centre; Rideau Centre. ℂ **800/682-2622**.

Davidson's   Serving customers from their Glebe store since 1939, Davidson's is a full-service jeweler, offering design, repairs, appraisals, and gem prints. Member of the Canadian Jewellers Association. Stockist of Canadian diamonds, Fabergé, Lladro, Movado, and other top brands. 790 Bank St. ℂ **613/234-4136**.

Howard   This family owned downtown business specializes in jewelry design, and there's an artist on staff. Their diamond-ring collection features platinum, 18K, and 14K gold settings. Wristwatches by Tag Heuer, Gucci, Da Vinci, and Rolex. Repairs and appraisals available. 200 Sparks St. ℂ **613/238-3300**.

La Maison d'Or   In the Place d'Orléans Shopping Centre, this jeweler specializes in diamonds from around the world, including Canadian diamonds. Rings can be custom designed, then set right in their own studio. They also buy and sell estate and antique jewelry. Place d'Orléans Shopping Centre ℂ **613/837-1001**.

KITCHENWARE

Ottawa is blessed with fine kitchenware stores, and culinary enthusiasts will love the following five retailers. They're all at the top of their class; you'll just have to visit them all.

C.A. Paradis   Located near a gaggle of antique stores on Bank Street south of the Glebe, C.A. Paradis has some very classy merchandise. If a chef craves it, this place probably has it. Check out their cellaring equipment, tasting supplies, and Reidel stemware too. 1314 Bank St. ℂ **613/731-2866**.

Domus   It's a real dilemma — do you eat first in the delectable Domus restaurant (see chapter 5, "Dining") and shop afterward in the kitchen store, or vice versa? Both are outstanding. Enjoy. 85 Murray St. ℂ **613/241-6410**.

Glebe Emporium   It's extremely tough to browse and not buy in this shop. You're bound to see something you just can't resist owning for yourself or buying as a gift for someone else. Kitchen gadgets, everyday dinnerware, table linens, gifts, and more. 724 Bank St. ℂ **613/233-3474**.

J. D. Adam Kitchen Co.   Walk slowly around this compact Glebe shop so that you don't miss anything. Space is at a premium here, but they make good use of every inch. Great merchandise and helpful staff. 795 Bank St. ℂ **613/235-8714**.

Ma Cuisine   Spacious and gracious, Ma Cuisine has chic dinnerware, a good selection of glassware, pans, gadgets, cookbooks, linens, and lots more. Staff are courteous and welcoming. 269 Dalhousie St. ℂ **613/789-9225**.

LEATHER

Danier Leather   Leather clothing and accessories for men and women. In addition to the three mall locations listed here, there are factory outlet stores at 2210

Bank St. in the south end of Ottawa and in Kanata. Bayshore Shopping Centre ℂ 613/828-4200; Rideau Centre ℂ 613/230-1307; and St. Laurent Shopping Centre ℂ 613/746-7993.

Mix Mix Leather   Leather and suede clothing for men and women. Washable suede and leather available. Carlingwood Shopping Centre ℂ 613/798-1999; St. Laurent Shopping Centre ℂ 613/748-9876.

Ottawa Leather Goods   In the Sparks Street Outdoor Pedestrian Mall one block south of Parliament Hill. A wide range of leather goods, including over-the-shoulder bags designed to reduce back strain. ℂ 613/232-4656.

LINGERIE

Femistique   In the shopping center at the corner of Sparks and Bank streets, this upscale boutique carries high-fashion lingerie and a selection of fragrances, jewelry, and other feminine gifts. 240 Sparks St. ℂ 613/235-8306.

La Senza   Lots of pretty undergarments, sleepwear, and gifts. Carlingwood Shopping Centre ℂ 613/729-4481; St. Laurent Shopping Centre ℂ 613/748-7611.

La Vie en Rose   Feminine lingerie and a good selection of sleepwear. Bayshore Shopping Centre ℂ 613/828-8383; Rideau Centre ℂ 613/563-2959.

MAGAZINES/NEWSPAPERS

For a great variety of international publications, visit **Globe Mags & Cigars** (57 William St. in the ByWard Market; ℂ **613/241-7274**), **Mags & Fags** (254 Elgin St.; ℂ 613/233-9651), or **Planet News** (143 Sparks St.; ℂ 613/232-5500).

MAPS/TRAVEL BOOK STORES

Place Bell Book Store   Specializing in city, country, and worldwide maps, including Michelin, Rand McNally, British Ordinance Survey, and Canadian Topographical, this shop also offers a wide selection of travel guides and literature. 175 Metcalfe St. ℂ 613/233-3821.

A World of Maps   Situated where else but at the geographical center of Ottawa, A World of Maps is both a retailer and a mail-order company. They're a regional distributor for all Canadian government maps and charts produced by the Canada Map Office. Topographical, aeronautical, nautical, international, and world maps, atlases, globes, travel books, and other map-related items are available here. 1235 Wellington St. W. ℂ 800/214-8524 or 613/724-6776.

MARKETS

ByWard Farmers' Market   The quality of the produce is outstanding at this thriving outdoor farmers' market, with about 200 vendors. In spring and early summer, flower stalls abound. Lots of family-oriented events are scheduled on weekends throughout the year. 55 ByWard Market Square. May–Oct daily 6am–6pm, Nov–Apr daily 9:30am–5:30pm.

Ottawa Organic Farmers' Market   For fresh market produce grown without pesticides or other chemicals, head on down on a Saturday all year around between 10am and 2pm. The market, which was established in 1988, has had more than one home, so call ahead. Operated at Ecole Parsifal Waldorf School, Bank Street at Heron Road (behind the Canadian Tire store). Around a dozen vendors. For more information, call ℂ 613/256-4150.

Parkdale Farmers' Market   This small, open-air farmers' market, with 20 vendors on average, offers fresh, high-quality produce and operates daily 7am to 6pm between April and December. Parkdale Ave. at Wellington St. ℂ 613/244-4410.

MUSICAL INSTRUMENTS

Ottawa Folklore Centre   They repair, buy, sell, consign, trade, rent, and appraise just about any instrument you can think of — from guitars to amps, banjos, fiddles, Celtic harps, mandolins, recorders, folk flutes, hand drums, autoharps, accordions, and dulcimers. 1111 Bank St. ℂ 613/730-2887.

Song Bird Music   Dealing in new, used, and rental instruments, Song Bird Music has guitars, woodwinds, percussion, brass, keyboards, amps, and more. They outgrew their original store and had to open a second location across the street. 388 Gladstone Ave. ℂ 613/594-5323.

OUTDOOR STORES

Bushtukah Great Outdoor Gear   This store is well stocked with tents, camping gear, sleeping bags, and other assorted outdoor equipment. 203 Richmond Rd. ℂ 613/792-1170.

The Expedition Shoppe   In the outdoor enthusiast shopper's corner of Ottawa, along with Bushtukah, Mountain Equipment Co-op, and Trailhead, this store sells clothing and outdoor equipment for travel, hiking, and camping as well as guide books and maps. 369 Richmond Rd. ℂ 613/722-0166; 43 York St. ℂ 613/241-8397.

Irving Rivers   If you like the great outdoors, hike over to this outdoor emporium, stuffed with rain gear, camping clothing, travel appliances, backpacks, heavy-duty footwear, and everything else for a back-to-nature vacation. 24 ByWard Market Sq. ℂ 613/241-1415.

Mountain Equipment Co-op   While you're browsing the outdoor adventure stores in the area, stop in here for sound advice on good-quality outdoor gear. Mountain Equipment Co-op has been in operation since 1971. 366 Richmond Rd. ℂ 613/729-2700.

The Scout Shop Camping Centre   You can't miss the huge totem pole on the front lawn. Housed in the Scouts Canada Headquarters building, the Scout Shop has lots of practical, neat, and useful camping accessories, plus books, Scout uniforms, and small toys. 1345 Baseline Rd. ℂ 613/224-0139.

Trailhead   Another outdoor adventure and hiking store, conveniently situated close to most of the others above and not far from the bridge to Gatineau Park. Come here for canoes, kayaks, skis, snowshoes, travel clothing, and accessories. 1960 Scott St. ℂ 613/722-4229.

SHOES

Armstrong Shoes   Better quality footwear can be found here. 240 Sparks St. ℂ 613/230-7840; Bayshore Shopping Centre ℂ 613/829-8282.

Dack's   Dack's has been supplying high-quality men's footwear to customers in the Ottawa area since 1834. 240 Sparks St. ℂ 613/233-4377.

Kiddie Kobbler   For casual and dress shoes, boots, sandals, slippers, and dance shoes for your child. Place d'Orléans ℂ 613/834-8876; or St. Laurent Shopping Centre ℂ 613/746-6411.

Letellier   Specializing in walking and comfort shoes, Letellier is a well-established shoe retailer in Ottawa, serving customers since 1897. A large selection of widths and sizes in both men's and women's footwear, with lines from Clarks, Rockport, Ecco, Mephisto, and more. 146 Rideau St. ℂ 613/241-6557.

Sports 4   Brand-name footwear includes New Balance, Birkenstock, Nike, Reebok, and more from this athletic and casual footwear specialist. A large range of widths and sizes available. 149 Bank St. ℭ **613/234-6562**; also in Kanata.

SPORTS EQUIPMENT & CLOTHING

Cyco's   Specializing in rental and sales of in-line skates, ice skates, bikes, and clothing and accessories for both sports, this store also sells used sports equipment. Next-day turnaround on most repairs. 5 Hawthorne Ave. (beside Rideau Canal) ℭ **613/567-8180.**

Figure 8 and Hockey One Skate Specialists   Whether you're skating in competitions or just gliding along the canal, Figure 8 has a skate for you. They offer new, used, and rental skates, as well as expert sharpening and skate mounting and hockey-skate blade replacement. 1408 Bank St. ℭ **613/731-4007.**

Fresh Air Experience   This is the store for bicycles (mountain, hybrid, road, and children's), cross-country skis, and specialty clothing. 1291 Wellington St. W. ℭ **613/729-3002.**

Kunstadt Sports   These ski, bike, snowboard, tennis, and hockey specialists offer equipment, clothing, and service. They also buy and sell used sports equipment. 1583 Bank St. ℭ **613/260-0696**; 462 Hazeldean Rd. ℭ **613/831-2059.**

Pecco's   In the heart of the ByWard Market district, Pecco's does bikes — road, hybrid, MTB, cyclocross, touring, and children's. 86 Murray St. ℭ **613/562-9602.**

Ritchie's Sports-Fan Apparel Shop   Sports fans will love the wide selection of licensed souvenirs, caps, and jerseys for all the major sports — hockey, baseball, football, basketball, and soccer. 134 Sparks St. ℭ **613/232-6278.**

Running Room Canada   Come here for footwear and apparel for running, walking, swimming, and fitness. 901 Bank St. ℭ **613/233-5617**; 260 Centrum Blvd. ℭ **613/830-7539**; 160 Slater St. ℭ **613/233-5165**; 1568 Merivale Rd. ℭ **613/228-3100.**

Sensations   If you're looking for Sens gear, this is the place to go. The official merchandise outlet of the Ottawa Senators Hockey Club is located in the Corel Centre at Gate 1 and is stocked with hats, jerseys, jackets, pucks, sweaters, shirts, T-shirts, and sticks. Corel Centre, 1000 Palladium Dr. ℭ **888/688-7367** or 613/599-0333.

Tommy & Lefebvre   One of the city's best-known sporting goods retailers, in business since 1958, Tommy & Lefebvre has an extensive selection of goods for adults and children. Ski, board, bike, golf, in-line skates, and more. Lift tickets and transportation arranged for area ski resorts. 464 Bank St., 2206 Carling Ave., and locations in Orleans and Gatineau ℭ **888/888-7547.**

STATIONERY

Paper Papier   A peek inside this little store will reward you with the discovery of unusual and inspiring gift wrap, pens, greeting cards, stationery, journals, and other paper-related items. 18 Clarence St. ℭ **613/241-1212.**

The Papery   This store sells delicate, pretty, and funky things made of paper — cards, wrapping paper, ribbons, invitations, stationery, journals, albums, and pens. During the holiday season, check out their selection of elegant Christmas crackers, remarkable gift wrap, and exquisite table-top angels. 850 Bank St. ℭ **613/230-1313.**

TOYS

The Disney Store   All kinds of products to thrill your little ones, ranging from videos to dress-up costumes, baby and preschool clothing, beach towels, and stuffed Disney character toys. You can even buy passes to Disney theme parks here. Staff love children, and the customer service is good. Rideau Centre ℂ 613/569-5500; Bayshore Shopping Centre ℂ 613/721-4155.

Ikea   In addition to home furnishings especially for younger family members, Ikea has a great selection of European-style toys, including puppets, dollhouses, musical instruments, bean bags, and china tea sets. Of course, they have lots of toy storage, cushions, tables, and chairs, too. See "Home Decor," earlier in this chapter.

Lost Marbles   Grown-ups and kids alike will find this store fascinating. Where else would you find a plush moray eel, a build-your-own set of shark's jaws, a table with human legs, or 16 different kinds of dice? 315 Richmond Rd. ℂ 613/722-1469; 809 Bank St. ℂ 613/594-3325.

Mrs. Tiggywinkles   This store stocks a wide variety of educational and high-quality toys and games for infants to teens. It's a great place to browse. There's a two-floor emporium in the Glebe and several mall locations. A new location on Richmond Road in Westboro Village is now open. 809 Bank St. ℂ 613/234-3836; Bayshore Shopping Centre ℂ 613/721-0549; Place d'Orléans ℂ 613/834-8988; Rideau Centre ℂ 613/230-8081, 313 Richmond Rd. ℂ 613/761-6055.

Playvalue Toys   This is a full-line dealer for Little Tikes, Step 2, Brio, Playmobil, Lego, and other quality toys. 1501 Carling Ave. ℂ 613/722-0175.

Scholar's Choice Retail Store   This store carries educational and high-quality toys for infants and up, as well as elementary teachers' resources. 2635 Alta Vista Dr. ℂ 613/260-8444.

Toys "R" Us   This big-box retailer has a large selection of mainstream toys and other products for children. If your kids have seen it on TV, this is the place to get it. 1683 Merivale Rd. ℂ 613/228-8697; 1200 St. Laurent Blvd. ℂ 613-749-8697.

TRAVEL GOODS

Capital City Luggage   Luggage, garment bags, computer bags, trunks, travel accessories, and briefcases. Repairs to handles, zippers, and locks. 1337 Wellington St. W. ℂ 613/725-3313.

Ottawa Leather Goods   Travel accessories, luggage, business cases, handbags, and small leather goods. Repair shop on premises. 179 Sparks St. ℂ 613/232-4656.

VIDEOS & DVDS

Two major video stores in the Ottawa area are **Blockbuster Video** and **Rogers Video,** both with more than a dozen locations. DVD and VHS movies and games are available for sale and rental. Rental requires a membership. Check out "CDs, Music," earlier in this chapter for listings for used and new DVDs at discount prices. You'll also find DVDs for sale at **Music World** and **HMV Canada;** both stores are common in major malls.

Bestsellers   Just as the name says, you'll find the most popular videos and DVDs here, plus a small selection of the latest paperbacks. They also stock classic films, British humour, Westerns, war movies, and popular musicals. Carlingwood Shopping Centre ℂ 613/728-0689.

Glebe Video International   Foreign, independent, and hard-to-find videos and DVDs are the specialty of this store. Movies from the world's major film festivals are available here. 2–779 Bank St. © 613/237-6252.

WINE & SPIRITS

Most of Ontario's wine, some beer, and all spirits are purchased through the provincial government–owned **Liquor Control Board of Ontario** retail stores. There are locations all over the city. Individual winery boutiques are also licensed to sell wine, but you can't buy alcoholic beverages in a grocery or convenience store in Ontario. If you cross the Ottawa River into Quebec, however, you can buy beer and wine at corner stores and grocery stores, although the selection is better at the provincial government–owned **Société des alcools du Québec (SAQ)** outlets. Beer is also available at The Beer Store, a provincially owned and operated business with about 20 locations in Ottawa. Opening hours vary by individual store. The **LCBO's flagship retail store** is at 275 Rideau St. © **613/789-5226.** This large store has two floors of fine products from around the world, as well as an extensive **Vintages** section with a wide range of fine wines. Wine accessories are available, and seminars and tastings are regularly scheduled.

9

Ottawa After Dark

Bytown, Ottawa's original settlement, had a dubious reputation as a rough and rowdy lumber town. But as middle-class merchants and white-collar civil servants gradually changed the face of the city's population during the last century, the city became decidedly more genteel. An upswing in the energy of Ottawa's nightlife has definitely been noted in the past decade or two, helped along by the influx of young techies to "Silicon Valley North" and the efforts of the local tourism industry and members of Ottawa's arts community.

Ottawa's **Arts and Theatre District** is bordered by the Rideau Canal, George Street, King Edward Avenue, Besserer Street, Waller Street, the Mackenzie King Bridge, and Elgin Street. There are dozens of arts and culture organizations within this zone of 23 city blocks. You'll find the **National Arts Centre, Canadian Museum of Contemporary Photography, Odyssey Theatre, Ottawa Little Theatre,** and **Arts Court** here. Retail stores, restaurants, clubs, bars, galleries, theaters, attractions, hotels, and services — it's all here, ready to entertain you.

The lion's share of annual events and festivals takes place during the summer months, when the weather is warm and the number of visitors peaks. All year round, however, you can take in theater productions, spectator sports, a variety of films, live musical performances, dance clubs, pubs, and the spectacular **Casino du Lac-Leamy.**

FINDING OUT WHAT'S ON For current live music, theater, and film — particularly for the under-40 crowd — your best bet for finding out what's happening and where is to pick up a copy of Ottawa's *Weekly Xpress,* a free publication distributed each Thursday, or visit online at www.ottawaxpress.ca. *Where Ottawa/ Gatineau,* a free monthly tourist guide listing entertainment, shopping, and dining, is available at hotels and stores in the city. *Voir* is a French-language weekly arts and entertainment paper that lists some venues and events in Gatineau as well as Ottawa.

Visiting families should keep an eye out for *Capital Parent,* a free monthly newspaper. *The Ottawa Citizen* has a comprehensive Arts section on Fridays with an emphasis on films, and a special Going Out section on Saturdays, which lists upcoming live entertainment events. Two free publications aimed at the younger demographic are *Trenz,* a modern living magazine, and *Hipster and Poser,* a monthly magazine that celebrates the distinct culture of young and youngish urban Ottawa. For news and information about regional arts events and activities, drop in to **Arts Court,** 2 Daly Ave. (© 613/ 564-7240; www.artscourt.ca), which is home to the Ottawa Art Gallery, SAW Gallery, the Arts Court Theatre, and more than 30 local arts organizations representing performing, visual, literary, and media arts. Another source is the **Council for the Arts in Ottawa** (CAO) © 613/569-1387, www.arts-ottawa.on.ca.

GETTING TICKETS Tickets to events at the **Corel Centre** and the **National Arts Centre** are sold at the on-site box offices or through **Ticketmaster** (Sportsline ℂ 613/755-1166; other events ℂ 613/755-1111; www. ticketmaster.ca). You can also visit the Ticketmaster box office at 112 Kent St. Ticketmaster handles ticket sales for numerous venues. Also see the individual listings in this chapter.

SPECIAL EVENTS Ottawa frequently hosts large sports and entertainment events, so check with the Ottawa Tourism and Convention Authority (www.ottawatourism.ca) or the National Capital Infocentre, 40 Elgin St., Ottawa ON, K1P 1C7 (800/465- 1867 or 613/239-5000; www.canadas capital.gc.ca) for special events scheduled during your visit. It's worth having a word in your hotel concierge's ear if you want tickets for a show; they may be able to oblige.

1 The Performing Arts

Because Ottawa serves two masters — the Canadian population as the national capital and the local citizens of the city of Ottawa — the arts and entertainment field includes a major federal arts presence and a vibrant and energetic local arts community. If you want to find out in depth about the local arts scene, drop in to **Arts Court** at 2 Daly Ave. ℂ 613/564-7240, Ottawa's center for performing, visual, media, and literary arts.

THEATER AND PERFORMANCE VENUES

Centrepointe Theatre Featuring a unique blend of community and professional programming, Centrepointe Theatre is home to the productions of many community groups, including the Nepean Choir, the Canadian Showtime Chorus, the Nepean All-City Jazz Band, Les Petits Ballets, the Nepean Concert Band, the Savoy Society of Ottawa, and the Orpheus Musical Theatre Society — Liona Boyd, Christopher Plummer, and Peter Ustinov have all stood in the Centrepointe's spotlight. Four places are reserved for guests in wheelchairs on the orchestra level, and you can make special arrangements to accommodate larger groups. An audio-loop system for the hearing impaired is also available. To arrange for special seating, please specify your needs to the box-office attendant when purchasing tickets. Plans are underway to build a new presentation space, the Centrepointe Studio, with approximately 200 retractable seats. Parking is free. The theater is one block from the OC Transpo Baseline Station. Ben Franklin Place, 101 Centrepointe Dr. ℂ **613/580-2700**. www.centrepointetheatre.com.

The Corel Centre This 18,500-seat multipurpose sports and entertainment complex, formerly known as the Palladium, opened its doors in January 1996. Home of the Ottawa Senators National Hockey League (NHL) team, this complex hosts various sporting and entertainment events. The facility was purpose-built as a hockey venue, so there's not a bad seat in the house. There are dozens of concession stands on the two public concourses, plus the Senate Club, Marshy's Bar-B-Q and Grill, the Penalty Box Sandwich Bar, Frank Finnigan's, Club Scotiabank, Rickard's Pub, and the Silver Seven Brew House. Official Ottawa Senators merchandise can be purchased at Sensations, located at Gate 1. OC Transpo (ℂ 613/741-4390) provides direct bus service from Transitway stations across the city to all Senators games and most other events. Free parking is provided at five Park & Ride lots. For smaller events, the WordPerfect Theatre provides seating for 2,500 to 7,400 people. An automated retractable curtain system divides the arena in half. For sports and concert tickets call CapitalTickets.ca at **613/599-3267** or visit the Corel Centre box office (Gate 1). 1000 Palladium Dr. ℂ **613/599-0100**. www.corelcentre.com.

Lansdowne Park This large facility hosts hundreds of events annually, including trade and consumer shows, family entertainment, rock concerts, Junior hockey tournaments, national and international athletic competitions, and the Central Canada Exhibition. On-site you'll find the 10,000-seat Ottawa Civic Centre, home of the Ontario Hockey League Ottawa 67's; the Frank Clair Stadium, home of the Canadian Football League (CFL) team Ottawa Renegades; and the Lansdowne Park Convention Centre. 1015 Bank St. ℂ **613/580-2429** for general information; ℂ **613/232-6767** for information on the Ottawa 67's; and for the Ottawa Renegades call ℂ **613/231-5608**.

Maison de la culture de Gatineau The 847-seat Odyssée Hall is located here. Patrons enjoy francophone theater, music, comedy, and dance performances. 855 La Gappe Blvd., Gatineau. ℂ **819/243-2525**.

National Arts Centre Situated in the heart of the city across from Confederation Square and Parliament Hill, the NAC is one of the largest performing-arts complexes in Canada. Home to the internationally acclaimed classical-sized **National Arts Centre Orchestra,** this center also stages a wide variety of performances including English and French theater, dance, music, and community programming. Three performance halls are housed within the unique multi-level structure. **Southam Hall,** the largest of the three performing halls with more than 2,300 seats, hosts Broadway musicals, ballets, operas, musical acts, lectures, ceremonies, films, orchestral music, and other entertainment and corporate events. Mega-musicals such as *Phantom of the Opera* and *Les Miserables* have been staged in Southam Hall. **Theatre Hall,** with just under 900 seats — ideal for plays, musicals, seminars, conferences, films, chamber music, and other musical events — also presents numerous Stratford Festival productions. Musicals such as *Crazy for You* have been showcased in Theatre Hall. **Studio Hall** is a versatile venue that has a capacity of 250 to 300 depending on the seating arrangement, and hosts performances, corporate seminars, and presentations. **The Fourth Stage** is a multipurpose performance space for community programming, including dance, music, storytelling, choral singing, and theater. The Fourth Stage can accommodate various stage configurations and seats up to 150. The NAC's restaurant, **Le Café,** has views over the Rideau Canal, an outdoor terrace for summer dining, and a good local reputation for its cuisine. Enjoy lunch, pre-performance dinner, *table d'hôte* after 8pm, or post-theater dessert and coffee. The NAC is fully accessible to guests with disabilities and provides special tickets for patrons in wheelchairs. Underground parking is available; parking entrances are located on Elgin Street (at the corner of Slater Street) and on Albert Street. 53 Elgin St. ℂ **613/947-7000**. www.nac-can.ca. For tickets visit the NAC box office or call Ticketmaster at ℂ **613/755-1111**.

Ottawa Congress Centre This meeting facility hosts large-scale conventions and trade and consumer shows. The center includes the 6,000 sq. m (66,000 sq. ft.) Congress Hall and the Colonel By Salon, with floor-to-ceiling windows overlooking the Rideau Canal. Rooftop terraces also offer views of downtown Ottawa. Direct access to the Rideau Centre is provided. 55 Colonel By Dr. ℂ **613/563-1984**. www.ottawacongresscentre.com.

Theatre du Casino du Lac-Leamy   This state-of-the-art theater has been designed as an intimate space despite the 1,001 seating capacity. Opened in 2001, the theater is adjacent to Casino du Lac-Leamy. The entrance is separate from the Casino to allow theater patrons of all ages to enjoy performances. 1 Casino Blvd., Gatineau (Hull sector). ✆ 819/772-2100; www.casino-du-lac-leamy.com.

THEATER COMPANIES AND SMALLER THEATERS

Astrolabe Theatre   In the summer months, this outdoor theater on Nepean Point, built as part of the Centennial celebrations, stages entertainment for the whole family. Contact the National Capital Infocentre at ✆ 800/465-1867 or 613/239-5000 for more information, or visit www.canadascapital.gc.ca.

A Company of Fools   Founded in 1990, the company's aim is to make Shakespeare entertaining and accessible. Initially, the troupe rehearsed and acted out Shakespearean scenes on the street. Audiences respond to their unique brand of high-energy performance, classical text, and modern slapstick. Successful shows include performances at the Ottawa Fringe Festival and "Shakespeare Under the Stars," featuring scenes, sonnets, and songs in various parks in the Ottawa region, beneath the night sky. Performing at various locations. ✆ 613/863-7529; www.fools.ca.

Dramamuse   Since 1989, this resident theater company in the Canadian Museum of Civilization has been entertaining visitors. Actors perform short plays and play colorful historical characters who mingle with visitors and "interpret" the museum exhibits. Dramamuse brings the museum to life for young and old. Performing at the Canadian Museum of Civilization, 100 Laurier St., Gatineau (Hull sector). ✆ 819/776-7000.

Great Canadian Theatre Company   The GCTC has provided bold, innovative, and thought-provoking theater to Ottawa audiences for more than a quarter of a century. The season runs from September to March. Performing at 910 Gladstone Ave. ✆ 613/236-5196. Tickets C$20–C$40 (US$16–US$32). www.gctc.ca.

Kanata Theatre   This community theater group was established in 1968. Since then, they have staged more than 110 major productions in their own theater in Kanata. 1 Ron Maslin Way ✆ 613/831-4435. Tickets C$15 (US$12). www.kanatatheatre.com.

NAC English Theatre   The NAC English Theatre develops, produces, and presents an English-language theater program locally, as well as co-producing plays with theater companies in other Canadian centers. The season consists of a five-play Mainstage series; a three-play alternative Studio series; special presentations; family, youth, and education activities; and a new play development program. The plays that make up the season range from the classics to new Canadian works. The Family Theatre Series presents three plays in the studio with matinee and evening performances on weekends. NAC French Theatre features a variety of French-language productions, including performances for children ages 4 to 11. Performing at the NAC, 35 Elgin St. ✆ 613/947-7000. For tickets visit the NAC box office or call Ticketmaster at ✆ 613/755-1111. Ticket prices vary.

Odyssey Theatre   This professional summer theater company is noted for its imaginative use of masks, dance-like movement, and original music. Its open-air productions are based on Italian Renaissance street theater, known as *commedia dell'arte*. Odyssey specializes in productions of classic comic texts and original works. For 5 weeks in late summer, they perform in Strathcona Park on the banks of the Rideau River, close to downtown Ottawa. For youth and family audiences, the troupe also stages one-hour versions of the summer production, with demonstrations and a question-and-answer period. Performing in Strathcona Park. Office at 2 Daly Ave. ℂ **613/232-8407**. www.odysseytheatre.ca.

Orpheus Musical Theatre Society Orpheus has been entertaining Ottawa audiences with their musical performances since 1906. The company performs three fully staged musical shows per season. Recent shows include *Crazy for You*, *Damn Yankees*, and *Oliver!* Performing at Centrepointe Theatre, 101 Centrepointe Dr. ℂ **613/580-2700**. Tickets C$12–C$26 (US$10–US$21).

Ottawa Little Theatre Since 1913, this amateur community theater has been producing plays in Ottawa. The comfortable 510-seat auditorium was redesigned after the original building was destroyed by fire in 1970. The company stages eight productions, with one per month from September through May. Productions range from comedies to dramas, mysteries, farces, and musicals, and include the works of William Shakespeare, Agatha Christie, and Neil Simon. Performing at 400 King Edward Ave. ℂ **613/233-8948**. Tickets C$18 (US$15). www.o-l-t.com.

Salamander Theatre Founded in 1993, the Salamander Theatre for Young Audiences presents professional performances at festivals and in schools and local communities. Office at Arts Court, 2 Daly Ave. ℂ **613/569-5629**. www.salamandertheatre.ca.

Savoy Society The Savoy Society of Ottawa is an organization of people who share a common interest in performing the comic operas of Gilbert and Sullivan. The society staged its first production, *The Pirates of Penzance*, in 1976 and now presents one play annually, running seven public performances (including a Sunday matinee). You can obtain information on the society by calling ℂ 613/825-5855. Performing at Centrepointe Theatre, 101 Centrepointe Dr. ℂ **613/727-6650** for tickets. Tickets C$10–C$22 (US$8–US$18). www.savoysociety.org.

Sock'n'Buskin This theater company is student-run and community-based, performing at the 444-seat Alumni Theatre on the campus of Carleton University. 1125 Colonel By Dr. ℂ **613/520-3770**.

The Tara Players The Tara Players stage classic, modern, and contemporary dramas and comedies from and about Ireland and written by playwrights of Irish heritage. Three productions are staged per season, from October to May. Performing at The Bronson Centre, 211 Bronson Ave. ℂ **613/7461410**. Tickets C$9–C$12 (US$7-US$10). http://taraplayers.ncf.ca.

Theatre de l'Ile This French-language theater actually is on an island in a beautiful park setting in the downtown Hull sector of Gatineau. There is always a summer production, and other performances are scheduled at various times throughout the year. 1 Wellington St., Gatineau (Hull sector). ℂ **819/595-7455**.

DANCE

Anjali Anjali (Anne-Marie Gaston) is a classically trained East Indian dancer, choreographer, teacher, lecturer, and photographer. Performances consist of East Indian temple dances and innovative, contemporary choreography based on traditional forms. Recitals are performed against a backdrop of images of temples, goddesses, and remote corners of Bhutan and the Himalayas. Call for performance schedule and venues. ℂ **613/745-1368**.

Le Groupe Dance Lab At the forefront of choreographic research, Le Groupe Dance Lab is an international center that focuses on the process of creating dance rather than the production of finished pieces of choreography.

The group holds interactive public presentations of works-in-progress each season. 2 Daly Ave. ℂ **613/235-1492.**

NAC Dance Productions   Throughout the year, the NAC hosts a variety of dance performances, ranging from classical ballet to contemporary dance. Guest dance companies include Les Grands Ballet Canadiens de Montreal, Toronto Dance Theatre, Iceland Dance Company, Ballet British Columbia, Brazilian Dance Theater, National Ballet of Canada, and Royal Winnipeg Ballet. 35 Elgin St. ℂ **613/947-7000.** For tickets visit the box office or call Ticketmaster at ℂ **613/755-1111.** Ticket prices vary.

Les Petits Ballets   Les Petits Ballets, a nonprofit organization, was founded in 1976 to develop youth ballet talent. Professional guest dancers and young local talent share the stage in full-length ballets, including *Coppelia* and *Cinderella*. Performances are held twice yearly. Performing at Centrepointe Theatre, 101 Centrepointe Dr. ℂ **613/580-2700** tickets, or 613/596-5783 studio.

CLASSICAL MUSIC, CHORAL MUSIC & OPERA

Cantata Singers of Ottawa   One of the region's most popular choirs, the Cantata Singers perform regularly with the NAC Orchestra and also have their own annual concert series. Call ℂ **613/798-7113** for more information.

NAC Orchestra   Offering more than 100 performances a year, this vibrant, classical-size orchestra draws accolades at home and abroad. In 1998, Pinchas Zukerman became the fifth conductor to lead the orchestra. The NAC Orchestra performs with Opera Lyra Ottawa and frequently accompanies ballets, including regular performances in Ottawa by Canada's three major ballet companies — the National Ballet of Canada, the Royal Winnipeg Ballet, and Les Grands Ballet Canadiens. The Pops Series combines popular songs and light classical music. NACO Young Peoples Concerts are directed to 7- to 11-year-olds and feature music, storytelling, animation, and audience participation. Performing at the NAC, 35 Elgin St. ℂ **613/947-7000.** For tickets visit the box office or call Ticketmaster at ℂ **613/755-1111.**

Opera Lyra Ottawa   Ottawa's resident opera company performs at the NAC, staging three operas between September and April. Recent main-stage productions include *Salome* and *La Bohème*. Performing at Centrepointe Theatre and the NAC. www.operalyra.ca. For tickets call Ticketmaster at ℂ **613/755-1111** or Opera Lyra Office at ℂ **613/233-9200.** Ticket prices vary.

Ottawa Chamber Music Society Concert Series   Some of Canada's most accomplished chamber music artists perform in downtown Ottawa churches from September to March. A 2-week summer festival is also held. Performing at various locations. ℂ **613/234-8008.** Tickets C$25 (US$20) and up adult. www.chamberfest.com.

Ottawa Choral Society   This 100-voice symphonic chorus performs major works from every period of the choral repertoire. They perform regularly with the NAC Orchestra, Ottawa Symphony Orchestra, and Thirteen Strings. Call ℂ **613/725-2560** for more information.

Ottawa Symphony Orchestra   With 90 musicians, the Ottawa Symphony Orchestra is the National Capital Region's largest orchestra. A series of five concerts is held at the NAC from September to May, featuring the music of the 19th and early 20th centuries. Performing at the NAC, 35 Elgin St. ℂ **613/947-7000.** For tickets visit the box office, call the OSO office at ℂ **613/231-2561,** or call Ticketmaster at ℂ **613/755-1111.** Tickets C$21–C$57 (US$17–US$47).

Thirteen Strings One of Canada's foremost chamber music ensembles, Thirteen Strings has an annual subscription series of six concerts at St. Andrew's Presbyterian Church in Ottawa and performs a wide range of music for strings from the 15th to the 20th centuries. Performing at St. Andrew's Presbyterian Church, 82 Kent St. 𝄐 613/738-7888. www.thirteenstrings.ca. Advance tickets at Ticketmaster 𝄐 613/755-1111. Tickets at the door C$25 (US$20) adults, C$5 (US$4) ages 18 and under.

2 The Club & Live Music Scene

Dance clubs, bars, and live entertainment venues are by nature constantly evolving, as they try to keep up with or keep ahead of their patrons' latest passions in terms of music and drinks. By the time you visit some of the venues listed here, they may have changed the type of music they offer, the decor, the beer, or even their name. Your best bet for finding out what's happening, and where, is to pick up a copy of Ottawa's *Weekly Xpress*, a free publication distributed each Thursday. The *Ottawa Citizen* publishes a hefty Arts section on Fridays and a special section, Going Out, on Saturdays. *Voir* is a French-language weekly arts and entertainment paper that lists some venues and events in Hull and Gatineau as well as Ottawa. You can take potluck as well if you're willing to gamble on what you might stumble upon. Ottawa's live music scene is extensive, and there are lots of pubs and bars offering live music on one or more evenings a week — too many to list here. Drop by for a pint or two at one of Ottawa's watering holes and you just might be surprised.

COMEDY CLUBS

Absolute Comedy On Wednesday to Saturday nights, the Absolute Pub features Absolute Comedy. Prices range from C$5 (US$4) to C$12 (US$10). The pub offers food, pool, shuffleboard, and sports TV. 412 Preston St. 𝄐 613/233-8000. www.absolutecomedy.ca.

Yuk Yuk's Stand-up comedians are featured in this club, which has a bar and restaurant service. Shows are generally Wednesday to Saturday evenings and last about 2 hours. Admission C$6 (US$5) for new-talent night on Wednesdays; other evenings generally $C17–C$25 (US$14–US$20). 88 Albert St. 𝄐 613/236-5233. www.yukyuks.com.

ECLECTIC

Barrymore's Music Hall Whatever your musical preferences, sooner or later you'll find a band scheduled to play here that you just have to see. Rock, pop, blues, punk, alternative rock, metal, Celtic, swing, retro — just about everybody hits the stage at Barrymore's. On nights when there isn't a live band, resident DJs get everyone dancing up a storm. 323 Bank St. 𝄐 613/233-0307.

Zaphod Beeblebrox This Ottawa institution is a combination of live music venue and dance club. Famous for their Pan Galactic Gargleblaster cocktail. Past performers include Alanis Morissette, Jewel, Ashley MacIsaac, and The Tea Party. The headline act is usually over by 11pm, and then a DJ spins tunes until very late. 27 York St. 𝄐 613/562-1010.

FOLK & CELTIC

Rasputin's Rasputin's is a small but perennially popular venue featuring lots of variety — in addition to traditional and contemporary folk, you'll find Cajun country, Maritime tunes, storytellers, Celtic jams, and open-mike nights. 696 Bronson Ave. 𝄐 613/230-5102.

JAZZ & BLUES

Jazz music is a natural accompaniment to dining, and several area restaurants feature live jazz on one or more evenings weekly. Try Vineyards Wine Bar & Bistro at 54 York St. ✆ **613/241-4270.**

Bayou Blues & Jazz Club   They play it like the name says — jazz and blues. Past bands include Mississippi Delta blues sensation Big Jack Johnson & The Oilers and metal–blues fusion with The Frank James Project. Swing nights. 1077 Bank St. ✆ **613/738-1709.**

Bourbon Street   In Ottawa's west end, in the Baseline Road/Greenbank Road area, this music hall and bar features blues, jazz, rock, and rhythm & blues. 2557 Baseline Rd. ✆ **613/726-3838.**

Café Paradiso   Live jazz every Thursday, Friday, and Saturday evening. Bistro-style dining is available. Reservations are recommended. In the summer, they fling the large windows wide open and the jazz music floats out into the summer night. 199 Bank St. ✆ **613/565-0657.**

The Rainbow Bistro   A reputation as Ottawa's legendary home of the blues, The Rainbow has had the honor of opening the stage to Dan Ackroyd, Jim Belushi, and Matt Murphy, who performed their Blues Brothers routine. Live music is featured seven nights a week. During the summer music festivals in Ottawa, many of the musicians and spectators gather here. 76 Murray St. ✆ **613/241-5123.**

107 Fourth Avenue   This Glebe wine bar has jazz every Wednesday evening. It's a small but friendly place with around three dozen wines by the glass or bottle. Light fare served. 107 Fourth Ave. ✆ **613/236-0040.**

PIANO BARS

Friday's Roast Beef House   Pianists entertain nightly. 150 Elgin St. ✆ **613/237-5353.**

Zoe's Lounge   Relax in Zoe's Lounge at the Fairmont Château Laurier Hotel and enjoy the sounds of a pianist from 5pm to 9pm weekdays. Live jazz on Saturday evenings 8pm to midnight. 1 Rideau St. in the Château Laurier Hotel. ✆ **613/241-1414.**

DANCE CLUBS & LOUNGES

Babylon   Billing itself as Ottawa's only live underground venue, Babylon features live reggae every Thursday and live local bands other nights of the week. Check out the website for the gig calendar. 317 Bank St. ✆ **613/594-0003.** www.babylonclub.ca.

Club MTL   A chic two-floor club featuring martinis and wine by the glass. House, world beat, soul, jazz, hip-hop — there's something different each evening, Wednesday through Sunday. 47–49 William St. ✆ **613/241-6314.**

The Collection & Bar 56   This martini lounge and dance club spins hip-hop, funk, rhythm & blues, soul, and house. Hip urban decor. Open nightly until 2am for drinks and music. 56 ByWard Market St. ✆ **613/562-1120.**

Inferno   Upstairs at 380 Elgin St., this club is packed five nights a week. Tuesday is the Acapulco Style Party — for those who like to party hot. 380 Elgin St. (corner of Gladstone). ✆ **613/234-0537.**

Mercury Lounge   Targeting a professional clientele, the prices are a little higher here and the crowd's a little older. It has been described as a 21st-century soul club. This is a place to dance or listen to the music as you sip martinis on red velvet couches. A mix of live bands and DJs. NuJazz is currently in demand, but you'll also hear electronica, funk, soul, Latin, and world rhythms. 56 ByWard Market Square (side door and upstairs). ℂ 613/789-5324.

Paraiso Latin Nightclub Both young and old flock here for the salsa, meringue, *bachata,* and Latin mixes. Free salsa dance classes on Fridays. Large dance floor and seating area. Free parking nearby. 300 Preston St. ℂ 613/236-1628.

3 The Bar Scene
BARS

ARC Lounge The lounge bar at ARC the.hotel is sleek, minimalist, and sophisticated. Try their signature martini, the Arctini. An upscale destination. 140 Slater St. in ARC the.hotel. ℂ 613/238-2888.

Eighteen In a historical building at 18 York St., this is a bar and restaurant. Martini madness on Saturdays. Friday features jazz and acid jazz; Saturday is retro soul. The 25-plus crowd dresses up rather than down. If you want to sample several wines from their extensive selection, order a cluster of four 2-ounce glasses. 18 York St. ℂ 613/684-0444.

Empire Grill Trendy and upscale, the Empire Grill has exciting cocktails and an extensive wine list. Outdoor patio, live jazz some nights, DJs after 10pm other nights. 47 Clarence St. ℂ 241-1343.

Social There's a bit of everything at this popular upscale evening destination. A fusion of French and Mediterranean cuisine is served in the restaurant. At night, enjoy jazz or blues. At weekends, a DJ revs up the music. 537 Sussex Dr. ℂ 613/789-7355.

PUBS

The Arrow & Loon This comfortable neighborhood watering hole in the Glebe is filled with regulars. Ontario and Quebec microbrews are featured. Try a draft sampler — four 5-ounce glasses of different locally crafted beers for C$5 (US$4). 99 Fifth Ave. ℂ 613/237-0448.

The Barley Mow Cask-conditioned ales and around 18 microbrews and imported beers on tap, plus an extensive selection of single-malt Scotch earns this pub a nod from beer and whiskey lovers. 1060 Bank St. ℂ 613/730-1279.

D'Arcy McGee's Irish Pub Housed in a heritage building at the corner of Sparks Street and Elgin Street, D'Arcy McGee's has an authentically Irish interior (it was actually designed and handcrafted in Ireland and imported). The crowd includes a smattering of politicians, civil servants, and tourists. Live Celtic, Maritime, and folk music. The patio has a great view over Confederation Square, with the Château Laurier in the background. 44 Sparks St. ℂ 613/230-4433.

Earl of Sussex Located right on the tourist track, the Earl of Sussex is an English-style pub, with wing-backed chairs, a fireplace, and a dartboard. The atmosphere is friendly and cozy, as tourists mix with regulars and business people. There are more than 30 beers on tap, including European and domestic. The sunny rear patio is very popular in warm weather. 431 Sussex Dr. ℂ 613/562-5544.

The Irish Village In the heart of the ByWard Market, four distinct pubs have come together to make a small "Irish Village"; all the pubs are Irish owned and operated. The first, the Heart & Crown, opened in 1992. A few years later the

For Beer Lovers

True beer connoisseurs always appreciate a pint of the best. Ottawa has dozens of British-style pubs and North American–type bars where you can sample brews from Britain, Ireland, Germany, Belgium, and, of course, Canada.

There are several local **microbreweries** to keep an eye out for in Ottawa-area restaurants and pubs. The **Scotch Irish Brewing Co.** in Fitzroy Harbour produces a British-style bitter called Session Ale and an Irish-style porter, Black Irish. **Heritage Brewing Ltd.** in Carleton Place brews Heritage Premium Lager and a traditional dark ale.

If you want to sample the homemade draught of a **brew pub,** here are a couple to try. The **Clocktower Brew Pub** at 575 Bank St. ⓒ **613/ 233-7849** features an ever-changing selection of seasonal brews, listed on a chalkboard menu. Two of the most popular are Bytown Brown, a heavy, dark beer to accompany a pub meal on a winter's night, and Indian Summer Ale, which is perfect in a pitcher on the large summer patio. **Master's Brew Pub & Brasserie,** at 330 Queen St., brews a variety of lagers and ales on site. Decor is Art Deco and they're generally open Monday to Friday, early to late, to serve local office workers and downtown hotel patrons. For more places to get a decent pint, check out the Pub listings in this chapter.

Snug Pub was added. The Snug Pub has a fireplace and cozy corners for small groups. Mother McGintey's and Roisin Dubh (The Black Rose) are the most recent additions. All have a good range of beer. Live Celtic music at Heart & Crown and Mother McGintey's several nights a week. Favorite pub fare is served, including fish'n'chips. 67 Clarence St. ⓒ **613/562-0674.**

Lieutenant's Pump   In the heart of the Elgin Street bar district, this large pub draws a big crowd. More than a dozen beers on tap, including Montreal microbrews. 361 Elgin St. ⓒ **613/238-2949.**

The Manx   This British-style pub has a mix of younger and older clientele. An impressive selection of Scotch — more than 50 single malts, plus 10 Irish whiskeys; the pub occasionally holds Scotch tastings. Provides wall space for local artists. 370 Elgin St. ⓒ **613/231-2070.**

Patty Boland's Irish Pub & Carvery   A spacious meeting place, with two floors of dark wood and brass. Pub fare available. Two fireplaces to warm your toes in winter, and two patios for summer sipping — one out front for people watching, and a quieter one at the back for conversation. 101 Clarence St. ⓒ **613/789-7822.**

Royal Oak   You'll bump into Royal Oaks all over town — downtown, east end, west end, the Glebe; there are ten in total. The original pub, dating from 1980, is at 318 Bank St., where the crowd tends to reflect whatever band is headlining at Barrymore's Music Hall across the street. The most recent addition is at 188 Bank St. The two-level patio of the Echo Drive location, near Pretoria Bridge, has a nice view over the canal. All locations have a good selection of British and Irish beers on draft. 318 Bank St. ⓒ **613/236-0190;** 221 Echo Dr. ⓒ **613/234-3700;** and eight other locations.

4 The Gay & Lesbian Scene

Social life and entertainment for the gay and lesbian community in Ottawa is clustered around Bank Street in the vicinity of Frank Street, Somerset Street W., and Lisgar Street. There are also a couple of venues in the ByWard Market district.

Centretown Pub   Located in a three-story Victorian house, this pub doesn't have a sign outside but you can identify it by the brown awning that covers the main walkway. It's comfortable and friendly and frequented by regulars, mostly men. It has been described as a "gay Cheers." 340 Somerset St. W. ✆ **613/594-0233**.

Icon   There is a multi-level dance bar. The main-level lounge has a bar and cafe tables, plus pool tables, video games, and a dance floor with a screen showing music videos. Wednesday is Karaoke night and Thursday is Bingo night. 366 Lisgar St., near Bank St. ✆ **613/235-4005**.

Lookout Bar   Upstairs at 41 York St. in the ByWard Market, this bar attracts a diverse crowd of gays, lesbians, and straights of all ages. The balcony is popular in the summer. On DJ nights, tables are moved back to make room for dancing. Afternoon social on weekends. 41 York St. (upstairs). ✆ **613/789-1624**.

Swizzles Bar & Grill   Events and entertainment for girlz and boyz include Karaoke nights, open-mic poetry and prose readings, all male go-go shows, and movie nights. Bar food served from lunch through to midnight. 246B Queen St. ✆ **613/232-4200**.

5 Film

If you love the silver screen, you'll have plenty of choices in Ottawa. Experience the latest in cinematic technology at the IMAX Theatre in the Canadian Museum of Civilization, cozy up at a budget family movie theater, or enjoy tiered seating and big sound at an urban monster megaplex.

HIGH-TECH CINEMA

IMAX Theatre   This amazing theater at the Canadian Museum of Civilization is the only one of its kind in the world. The technology of IMAX plus a giant dome gives you the feeling of being wrapped in sights and sounds. At seven stories high, the IMAX screen is amazing enough, but the real adventure begins when the 23m (75 ft.) hemispheric dome moves into place overhead once the audience is seated. Not all films use the entire screening system. This theater is busy, so buy your tickets in advance and plan to arrive 20 minutes before show time — latecomers will not be admitted. All ages are welcome. Canadian Museum of Civilization, 100 Laurier St., Gatineau. ✆ **819/776-7010** for show times. For tickets visit the museum box office or call Ticketmaster at ✆ **613/755-1111**.

REPERTORY CINEMAS

Bytowne Cinema   Ottawa's premier independent cinema has been screening independent and foreign films in this large, locally owned and operated theater for more than 50 years. Get real butter on your popcorn and settle down in the comfy chairs to enjoy the big screen and Dolby sound. Two to four movies are screened every day, with the lineup changing every few days. 325 Rideau St. ✆ **613/789-3456**. www.bytowne.ca.

Canadian Film Institute Cinema   The Canadian Film Institute presents a regular public program of contemporary, historical, and international cinema in the auditorium of the National Archives of Canada. Festivals and special events are held. If you have an interest or expertise in the art of cinematography, check out their calendar of events. All screenings at the Auditorium, Library and Archives Canada, 395 Wellington St. ✆ **613/232-6727**. www.cfi-icf.ca.

Mayfair Theatre   Screening a mixture of relatively recent releases and older films, the Mayfair changes its bill almost daily. Two films are run every night, and most evenings are two movies for the price of one. Pick up the monthly printed calendar at the theater, or look them up online. 1074 Bank St. ✆ **613/730-3403**. www.mayfair-movie.com.

Ottawa Family Cinema   Also known as Westend Family Cinema, this non-profit theater offers movies on the big screen with digital stereo sound, cartoons, and door prizes. A friendly, family atmosphere prevails, with special events and movie parties held throughout the season. Films include recent releases and older films that are suitable for family viewing. 710 Broadview Ave. ✆ **613/722-8218**. www.familycinema.org. Open Sat afternoons and every second Fri evening, Sept–May, except Christmas and Easter weekends.

MAINSTREAM NEW RELEASES

The city is well serviced by large multi-screen movie theaters. Ticket prices range from C$6–C$10 (US$5–US$8). For current listings and prices, check the *Ottawa Citizen* (the Friday edition has the most comprehensive arts and entertainment coverage). **Famous Players** has a movie hotline ✆ **613/688-8800** with showtimes for Rideau Centre (50 Rideau St.), Coliseum (in the west end, north of Bayshore Shopping Centre at 3090 Carling Ave.), and Silver City Gloucester Famous Players (2385 City Park Dr.; in the big-box complex at the corner of Blair and Ogilvie roads). South Keys **Cineplex Odeon** is in the south end (2214 Bank St. S. at Hunt Club Road; ✆ **613/736-1115**). World Exchange Plaza **Cineplex Odeon** (111 Albert St., 3rd Floor; ✆ **613/233-0209**) is in the heart of downtown and screens matinees daily.

AMC 24 Kanata is in the west end of the city (Highway 417 and Terry Fox Drive; ✆ **613/599-5500**). There's also Orleans Cinemas Cineplex Odeon (250 Centrum Blvd. in the Place d'Orléans shopping complex; ✆ **613/834-0666**).

6 Gaming

CASINO DU LAC-LEAMY

The extensive facilities of Casino du Lac-Leamy have continued to grow since the complex opened in 1996 on the shores of Lac Leamy (Leamy Lake). 1 boulevard du Casino, Gatineau (Hull sector), QC; ✆ **800/665-2274** or 819/772- 2100. Daily 9am to 4am. Admission restricted to persons aged 18 and over. Free admission, self-parking, and coat check.

Gaming Area   This huge entertainment and gaming destination can accommodate 6,500 visitors at a time. There are 2,557 gaming spaces, including 1,866 slot machines. Gaming tables number 64 and offer blackjack, roulette, baccarat, Pai Gow poker, mini baccarat, grand baccarat, Caribbean poker, poker grand prix, Sicbo, and craps. Additional gaming facilities include a Keno salon, electronic horse race track, and a high-limits gaming area and lounge with personalized service. The interior of the gaming area is vast. Thousands of tropical plants and the creative use of water features result in a unique atmosphere. The following customer services are free: self-parking, admission, and coat check. The Casino has been designed to accommodate guests with physical disabilities. Smoking lounges with high-performance ventilation systems are provided; smoking is prohibited in all other areas. Approximately two-thirds of the gaming area is nonsmoking. Dress code is in effect, but casual is okay — just make sure your blue jeans are neat and your running shoes aren't too scruffy. For more detail on the dress code, visit the website at www.casino-du-lac-leamy.com and click on "Practical Information."

Restaurant and Bar Services   Four dining areas and two bars are on-site. **Le Baccara** is an elegant fine-dining restaurant that has established a remarkable reputation for its cuisine. **Banco** offers a choice of buffet-style or a-la-carte dining. **La Fondue Royale** serves fondue from C$22 (US$18) per person, with live entertainment on Friday and Saturday evenings. For a quick snack, drop in to **Le Café**. A forest of tropical plants fills **Le 777 Bar**. Offering a selection of more than 70 imported beers, **La Marina** features a saltwater aquarium, an outside patio, and panoramic views over Lac de la Carrière, which has a 60m high (197 ft.) fountain as its focal point. Musical entertainment is provided in Le Baccara and La Marina in the evenings.

Theatre du Casino du Lac-Leamy   This state-of-the-art live performance theater opened in the fall of 2001. With 1,001 seats, including 10 places for wheelchairs, the theater has been designed so that all seats in the house are 25m (82 ft.) or closer to the stage, minimizing the distance between the audience and the performers. The space has been designed to give an impression of height and airiness despite the proximity of the seating to the stage. The theater has a separate entrance from the casino, so that audiences of all ages can enjoy performances. Theater and dinner packages available. To find out what shows are coming up, or to book a package or buy tickets, call the Casino du Lac-Leamy at ℂ **800/665-2274** or 819/772-2100. Tickets can also be purchased through Admission Network (ℂ **800/361-4595** or www.admission.com).

Hilton Lac-Leamy   The magnificent Hilton Lac-Leamy is a luxury hotel equipped with first-class facilities and amenities. It borders Lac Leamy and is connected to the Casino du Lac-Leamy. Call the hotel for information or reservations at ℂ **866/488-7888** or 819/790-6444, or visit online at www.lacleamy.hilton.com. See full listing details in chapter 4, "Where to Stay."

RIDEAU CARLETON RACEWAY & SLOTS

Less than a 10-minute drive south of the airport, this gaming complex features more than 1,200 slot machines and live harness racing. Facilities include a dining room, sports bar, outdoor patio, and three grandstand lounges. Take the Airport Parkway to Lester Road, travel east to Albion Road, and head south. You'll see Rideau Carleton Raceway & Slots on your left, between Leitrim Road and Mitch Owens Road. 4837 Albion Rd., Ottawa., ℂ **613/822-2211**. Daily 9am–3am. Free admission. Free parking. Admittance restricted to persons aged 19 and over.

Tips **Gambling Should Be Fun, Not Obsessive**

Many people enjoy playing games of chance for entertainment. But for a minority of people, gambling becomes a real problem and they find themselves unable to control the amount of money they spend. Information on dealing with a gambling problem can be obtained by calling ℂ **800/461-0140** in Quebec or ℂ **888/230-3505** in Ontario.

10

Exploring the Region

If you've read this far into the book, you already will have discovered there's enough to do in the city of Ottawa itself for more than one vacation. But I urge you to escape from the city during your stay and venture into the surrounding countryside. There is another side to Canada's capital, filled with scenic drives, picturesque towns and villages, summer and winter sports, artisans' studios, museums, and heritage buildings. In this chapter, you'll find some of the best daytrips to destinations within an hour or so's drive of Ottawa.

1 The Outaouais Region of Quebec

VISITOR INFORMATION

For visitor information on the Outaouais Region of Quebec, visit the **Association touristique de l'Outaouais,** 103 Laurier St., Hull, QC J8X 3V8 (✆ **800/265-7822** or 819/778-2222; fax 819/778-7758; www.outaouais-tourism.ca). The office is open mid-June to Labour Day (first Monday in September) Monday to Friday 8:30am to 8pm, Saturday to Sunday 9am to 6pm. The rest of the year, it's open Monday to Friday 8:30am to 5pm, weekends 9am to 4pm. The building is wheelchair accessible and there is free parking on the west side. The easiest way to reach the tourist office from Ottawa is to walk or drive across the Alexandra Bridge, which leads off Sussex Drive just east of the Parliament Buildings and west of the National Gallery. You'll see the office facing you as you come to the end of the bridge.

URBAN EXPERIENCES

While 2001 heralded a new beginning for the city of Ottawa as it experienced amalgamation of a dozen local municipalities, expanding its geographical area as well as its population, 2002 ushered in the new city of Gatineau. Comprising the cities of **Hull** and **Gatineau** plus the neighboring communities of **Aylmer, Buckingham,** and **Masson-Angers,** the new city has a population of almost 230,000. While visiting Quebec you may come across references to the various sectors, which have preserved their original names. Hence, an address in the old city of Hull is often referred to as being in Gatineau (Hull sector), or Gatineau (secteur de Hull).

GATINEAU (HULL SECTOR)

Hull was established in the early 1800s by Philemon Wright, an American Loyalist who shrewdly exploited the area's rich natural resources, primarily the forests of red and white pine. The forestry industry brought lumber camps and wood-processing factories to the region and attracted new residents — lumbermen, rafters, farmers, tradespeople, and merchants. Today, the pulp-and-paper mills of the Outaouais region still play an important role in the economy, with the federal government and the service industry as other major employers.

Tips   **Walk in the Steps of History**

If you want to walk in the steps of history, seek out the Indian Portage Trail at Little Chaudière Rapids in **Brébeuf Park.** To reach the park, take boulevard Alexandre-Taché, turn left onto rue Coallier, opposite the south entrance to Gatineau Park, then continue to **Brébeuf Park.** At the eastern end of the park, where the trail continues beside the river, you will find the old portage route that was used by First Nations peoples, fur traders, and explorers. A statue of Saint Jean de Brébeuf stands as a memorial to this 17th-century French missionary. Look for the rock steps used by the voyageurs as they transported their goods and equipment by land to circumvent the rapids.

Hull is renowned for its excellent French cuisine. Reservations are recommended to avoid disappointment. **Café Henry Burger** has been preparing fine French cuisine in elegant surroundings for its patrons since 1922. It's located across from the **Canadian Museum of Civilization** at 69 rue Laurier (✆ **819/777-5646**). **Café Jean Sebastian Bar** has a more casual atmosphere in which it serves its French, regional, and contemporary cuisine, including mussels, cassoulet, and filet mignon, at 49 rue St-Jacques (✆ **819/771-2934**). Dishes featuring an integration of French and Québécois cuisine, using local, seasonal produce, can be found at **Le Tartuffe,** at 133 rue Notre Dame (✆ **819/776-6424**). Housed in an old railway station, **Laurier sur Montcalm** is a small, well-established restaurant with a delicious menu. You'll find it at 199 rue Montcalm (✆ **819/775-5030**). See "On the Quebec Side" in chapter 5 for reviews of **L'Argoät,** 39A rue Laval ✆ **819/771-6170; Le 1908,** 70 promenade de Portage ✆ **819/770-1908;** and **Le Pied de Cochon**, 248 rue Montcalm ✆ **819/777-5808.**

On the shores of the Ottawa River next to the Canadian Museum of Civilization, **Jacques-Cartier Park** has beautiful pathways for strolling or cycling. The small stone house at the western end of the park was built by Philemon Wright, the founder of Hull, in the late 1830s. At the opposite end of the park you'll find an information booth, La Maison du Vélo, where you can obtain information on recreational pathways in the Outaouais region. Jacques-Cartier Park offers spectacular views of the Ottawa skyline. Annual events include Winterlude (Bal de Neige, *en français*) activities and a fireworks display on Canada Day. **Lake Leamy Ecological Park** (Parc du Lac-Leamy, *en français*) is bordered by Lake Leamy, the Gatineau River, and the Ottawa River. Vehicular access is via boulevard Fournier. The park offers a supervised beach, a refreshment pavilion, washrooms, and picnic tables. The **Casino du Lac-Leamy** is on the opposite shore of Lake Leamy. For park information, call ✆ **819/239-5000.**

Canadian Museum of Civilization   The striking architecture of the Canadian Museum of Civilization simply cannot be missed as you gaze from Ottawa across the Ottawa River to the Quebec shore. A short walk from Ottawa across the Alexandra Bridge will take you there, but you can also take a cab or drive if the weather is inclement. To explore the museum thoroughly you need a full day, particularly if you want to spend time in the Children's Museum and the Postal Museum, which are in the same building (there's no extra charge for these attractions), and take in an IMAX film (you *do* need separate tickets for the IMAX Theatre). For detailed information on the Museum of Civilization, see chapter 6, "What to See & Do."

100 Laurier St., Hull, QC. ✆ **800/555-5621** or 819/776-7000. www.civilization.ca. Admission C$10 (US$8) adults, C$6 (US$5) students, C$7 (US$6) seniors, C$4 (US$3.25) children 3–12, C$22 (US$18) family (4 members, max. 2 adults). Sun half price. Free every Thurs 4–9pm. Additional fee for IMAX Theatre. May 1–Thanksgiving (second Mon in Oct) daily 9am–6pm, Thurs until 9pm; July 1–Labour Day (first Mon in Sept) also open Fri until 9pm; Thanksgiving–Apr 30 Tues–Sun 9am–5pm, Thurs until 9pm. IMAX screenings do not always correspond with museum hours and extended evening hours do not apply to the Children's Museum, except between July 1 and Labour Day.

Casino du Lac-Leamy   The magnificent Casino du Lac-Leamy is picturesquely situated between Lac De la Carrière and Lac-Leamy. A sweeping tree-lined drive leads to ample parking in front of the main entrance. Once inside, you enter a different world. The enormous casino area boasts lofty ceilings, thousands of tropical plants, soothing waterfalls and reflecting pools, an abundance of natural cherrywood, and an ingenious catwalk suspended above the gaming area. Fifty gaming tables offer popular gambling games including blackjack, baccarat, roulette, Pai Gow poker, Let It Ride, and Caribbean stud poker. There's also a Keno lounge, Royal Ascot Electronic Track Horse Racing, and more than 1,800 slot machines. Admission is free, but restricted to persons ages 18 and over. Smoking is restricted to designated areas. There are four restaurants, including the award-winning fine-dining restaurant Le Baccara, and two bars. See Chapter 9, "Ottawa After Dark," for more information.

1 boulevard du Casino, Gatineau (Hull), QC. ✆ **800/665-2274** or 819/772-2100. www.casino-du-lac-leamy.com. Free admission. Admission restricted to persons 18 and over. Daily 9am–4am.

Ecomuseum (Ecomusée)   Don't be fooled by the apparent size of this museum, housed in a quaint historical building. Good things come in small packages, and this museum is a fine place to spend a couple of hours. A huge sphere representing the planet Earth greets you as you wind your way down a curved pathway to the main exhibits, which trace the origins of life on Earth up to the arrival of modern humans. There are plenty of authentic fossils on display. Interactive exhibits demonstrate the formation of continents, volcanoes, earthquakes, and magnetic fields. If you've ever wondered what an earthquake feels like, step into the high-tech simulator and experience two quakes — the larger one reaches 7.0 on the Richter scale. More than 5,000 insect specimens are displayed in the Insectarium and along the sides of the main corridor. Don't worry, they don't crawl or creep around. Marvel over spiders, beetles, moths, butterflies, and stick insects in myriad colors, forms, and sizes. Take a few minutes to watch the water clock in operation in the lobby.

170 Montcalm St., Hull, QC. ✆ **819/595-7790.** Admission C$5 (US$4) ages 16 and over, C$4 (US$3.25) students, seniors, and children 4 and over, C$13 (US$11) family (max. 4 members), Daily 10am–6pm.

GATINEAU (GATINEAU SECTOR)

The old city of **Gatineau,** across from Hull on the east side of the Gatineau River, was created in 1975 with the merger of seven smaller communities. Its population numbered around 105,000 until January 1, 2002, when a new city of Gatineau was established, which includes Hull, Aylmer, Buckingham, and Masson-Angers. One municipal government now serves almost 230,000 residents of the Outaouais region. Gatineau's Municipal Arts Centre features entertainment throughout the year. Every year on Labour Day weekend the **Gatineau Hot Air Balloon Festival** draws large crowds. **Rue Jacques-Cartier** has numerous sidewalk cafes that offer a great view of Ottawa and the Ottawa River. **Lac-Beauchamp Park** is a large urban park where you can swim, picnic, canoe, bike, skate, and cross-country ski. For park information call ✆ **819/669-2548.** For more information on

Exploring the Region

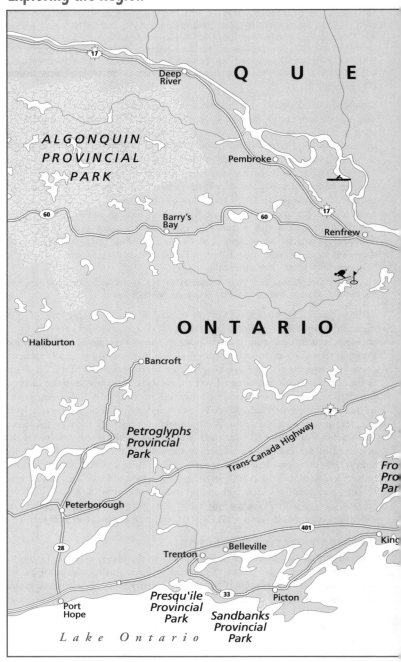

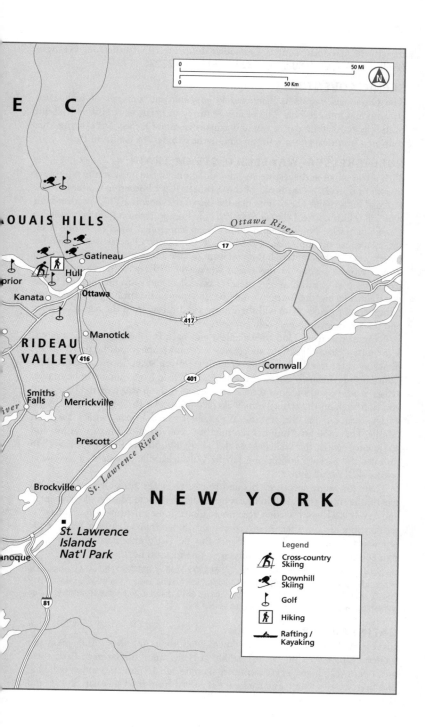

E C

0 ——————————— 50 Mi
0 ——————————— 50 Km
N

Ottawa River

17

OUAIS HILLS

Gatineau

Hull

prior

Kanata

Ottawa

417

Manotick

RIDEAU
VALLEY 416

Cornwall

Smiths
Falls   Merrickville

401

iver

Prescott

Brockville

St. Lawrence River

N E W   Y O R K

St. Lawrence
Islands
Nat'l Park

noque

81

Legend

Cross-country
Skiing

Downhill
Skiing

Golf

Hiking

Rafting /
Kayaking

the city of Gatineau, contact Outaouais Tourism, 103 Laurier St., Gatineau (Hull sector), QC ℭ **800/265-7822** or **819/778-2222.**

SCENIC ADVENTURES

The Outaouais Region is blanketed in majestic outcroppings of rock, clear streams, and forested hills. The beauty of the countryside is irresistible. Get out of the city bustle for a day or two and experience rural Quebec. Travel on a scenic tour on a historical steam train or explore the wonders of Gatineau Park.

HULL–CHELSEA–WAKEFIELD STEAM TRAIN

Take a trip on an authentic steam train along one of the most scenic rail routes in eastern Canada — the banks of the Gatineau River bordering Gatineau Park. Railroad buffs might like to note that the star of the show is a 1907 Swedish-built type 2-8-0 locomotive, believed to be the only European steam train operating on Canadian tracks. Nine Swedish-built climate-controlled coaches, dating from the 1940s, can accommodate a total of 528 passengers. One car is accessible for passengers with disabilities, but if you want to take advantage of this service, you should request seating in this coach when you make your reservation. Each coach has two washrooms and there's a snack bar and souvenir shop on board the train. During the journey, you'll be entertained by strolling minstrels and bilingual tour guides, who will share stories and music from the region's history and the steam locomotive's colorful past.

A round trip from Hull to Wakefield and back is 5 hours — the journey is 1$^1/_2$ hours in each direction, and there's a 2-hour stopover in the pretty village of Wakefield. After disembarking, watch the 93-ton steam locomotive pivot on Canada's only manually operated turntable. Wakefield has a number of boutiques, artists' studios, and outdoor terrace restaurants to help you pass the time until you hop back on the train. From Wakefield Memorial Park, in the heart of the village, you can see the historic Wakefield covered bridge, which has been rebuilt. The 1838 grist mill has recently been converted to a luxurious inn and conference center, the Wakefield Mill. Call ℭ 888/567-1838 or 819/459-1838 for rates and package information for the Wakefield Mill, or visit their website at www.wakefieldmill.com.

There are many special events and tourist packages available that include a trip on the steam train. Fall foliage tours, Sunday brunch, Mother's Day brunch, and family packages featuring accommodations, museum admissions, and sightseeing tours are on offer. A special sunset dinner train excursion features the renowned cuisine of Hull's Café Henry Burger. The dinner train can seat up to 356 guests, and musical entertainment is provided on board.

165 Deveault St., Gatineau (Hull sector), QC. ℭ **800/871-7246** or 819/778-7246. www.steamtrain.ca. Return ticket prices starting from C$39 (US$32) adult, C$36 (US$30) senior, C$35 (US$29) student, C$19 (US$16) child (3–12), C$99 (US$81) family (max. 2 adults and 2 children). Price varies according to season and package. Reservations required. May–Oct on various days.

GATINEAU PARK

Just a short 15-minute drive from downtown Ottawa lies a beautifully preserved wilderness park. Within the 361 sq. km (141 sq. miles) of **Gatineau Park,** there are 200km (125 miles) of cross-country ski trails and 165km (103 miles) of hiking and biking trails. The park's landscape is carved from the Canadian Shield, and the exposed rocks, dating back to the Precambrian Era, are among the oldest exposed rocks on Earth. More than 50 glacial lakes are scattered throughout the park. The forested areas consist mainly of maple and oak; spruce, white pine, and eastern hemlock cover only about 3% of the park's land. The large number of rare plant and animal species has stimulated many scientific research projects. Gatineau Park is open year-round and has something to offer in every season. Vehicle access fees are in effect in certain areas of the park during the peak summer period of mid-June to early September. Your first stop should be the **Visitor Centre,** at 33 Scott Rd., Chelsea, QC (*C* **800/465-1867** or 819/827-2020), open every day of the year. It's a great source for all kinds of park maps and information on special events and festivals. The knowledgeable and friendly staff are available to answer questions and help you to plan your visit. The village of Chelsea, lying roughly halfway between Hull and Wakefield and close to Gatineau Park's Visitor Centre, has several restaurants serving French cuisine. **L'Agaric** has a rustic setting close to the Gatineau Park entrance and is located at 254 Old Chelsea Rd. *C* **819/827-3030.** You'll find **L'Orée du Bois** at 15 Kingsmere Rd. *C* **819/827-0332.** You could also try **Les Fougères** at 783 Hwy. 105; call *C* **819/827-8942.**

WILDLIFE   Lakes in the park are home to **40 species of fish,** including trout, yellow perch, pike, and bass, which are all popular sport-fishing catches. Around 2,000 **white-tailed deer** also live in the park. They are most likely to be observed feeding in early morning or late afternoon, close to La Pêche Lake and Philippe Lake, or in open fields and alongside roads. In the far northwest corner of the park live one or two **timber wolf packs.** You are unlikely to see them because they avoid contact with humans, but you might be lucky enough to hear them howl. A wolf pack howls in a drawn-out, harmonious chorus, which is distinguishable from the short, high-pitched bark of a coyote pack. When you're on the trails, keep an eye out for **black bear** tracks on muddy sections of the trail and around **beaver** ponds. If you're unfamiliar with animal tracks, drop in to the Visitor Centre before your hike and ask the staff for information. Also watch for claw marks on the trunks of trees — black bears love to climb.

Along the Gatineau Parkway, there are numerous beaver ponds where you can observe these busy, furry creatures in action, especially at dawn and dusk. Other wildlife that make the park their home include the **bobcat, Canada lynx, wolverine, mink,** and **otter.** If you enjoy bird-watching, you're in for a treat. The waterways, fields, forests, wetlands, and rocky escarpments provide vital food and shelter for about **230 species of birds.** A brochure listing dozens of species and hints for when and where to observe the park's feathered friends is available from the Visitor Centre. **Grass snakes, turtles, frogs, toads, bull frogs, tree frogs, salamanders,** and **newts** are also native park inhabitants.

CAMPING

Gatineau Park has three campgrounds, each offering a different outdoors experience. Philippe Lake is the largest campground, with 250 wooded campsites. Sandy beaches, a convenience store, and plenty of water taps and washrooms

---

Tips   What Should I Do If I Meet a Bear?

Black bears make their home in Gatineau Park. If you happen to see a bear on a trail, calmly back away from it while maintaining visual contact. Make loud noises and keep your distance. Never try to feed a bear or approach it, as you may make the bear feel threatened. Keep well away from a mother and her cubs, and never position yourself between them. Never try to outrun, outswim, or outclimb a bear, since the animal may interpret your actions as a sign of weakness.

contribute to a comfortable vacation. If you don't mind fewer modern conveniences in exchange for being a little closer to the wilderness, try Taylor Lake, which offers rustic tent camping with only 33 sites, all close to the lake. If you want still more of a back-to-nature adventure, La Pêche Lake has canoe-in camping available at 35 individual sites in a dozen wooded areas around the lake. For all three sites, call ℂ **819/456-3016** to make campsite reservations. Prices range from C$20 (US$16) to C$24 (US$20). To arrange boat and mountain-bike rentals at Philippe Lake and La Pêche Lake, call ℂ **819/456-3016.** Note that alcoholic beverages are not allowed in the campgrounds or elsewhere in the park. Pets are not allowed in campgrounds, picnic areas, or on beaches, although dogs on a leash are permitted on hiking trails.

CANOEING

Glide along the peaceful waters of Gatineau Park's lakes in a canoe. Launch your own craft at the McCloskey Boat Launch on Meech Lake. Philippe Lake has a boat launch and **canoe, rowboat, kayak,** and **pedal boat rentals.** La Pêche Lake offers canoe and rowboat rentals in addition to a boat launch facility. Rental fees, which include two paddles and two lifejackets, are C$10 (US$8) per hour, C$30 (US$25) per day, or C$38 (US$31) per 24-hour period.

CYCLING/MOUNTAIN BIKING

Purchase a detailed trail map at the Visitor Centre to help you plan your route on the network of trails and paved bikeways in the park. The length and variety of **mountain-bike trails** are excellent. Trails are open from May 15 to November 30. The sport is restricted to 90km (56 miles) of designated trails to protect the natural environment; you may not use cross-country ski trails for winter biking. Mountain bikes are available for rental.

HIKING

There are 165km (103 miles) of **hiking trails** in the park, including about 90km (56 miles) of shared-use trails (walkers and mountain bikers), with the remainder set aside exclusively for hiking. Some of the shorter trails feature interpretation panels and are suitable for wheelchair and stroller access. If you are considering hiking one of the longer trails, make sure you are sufficiently prepared, with appropriate clothing, food, water, and sturdy, comfortable footwear. The Gatineau Visitor Centre has an excellent map available (1:25,000 scale) for C$5 (US$4); it is strongly recommended for hikers and mountain bikers.

If you enter the park at the south entrance, off boulevard Alexandre-Taché in Gatineau (Hull sector), the first short trail you'll find is **Des Fées Lake,** a 1.5 km (1-mile) trail around a small lake; the trail should take about an hour to walk. A little farther along the Gatineau Parkway, **Hickory Trail** is just under 1km

---

(*Tips* Looking for a Smooth Ride?

Because of its topography, the park's network of bike paths requires cyclists to be in good physical condition and experienced in cycling on challenging terrain. If you're looking for a leisurely cycle ride, you will find the relatively flat and smooth surface of the bikeways in the city of Ottawa easier and more enjoyable. You might also consider cycling in the park on Sunday mornings in the summer, when the main roadways are closed to motorized traffic.

Fun Fact   **Unique Waters**

A "meromictic" lake is an unusual body of water where there is no circulation between the different layers of water. It typically has a green color and is home to saltwater fish that have adapted to freshwater conditions. There are often sedimentary deposits dating back 10,000 years and prehistoric bacteria in its depths.

(0.5 mile) long, and takes about 20 minutes to walk. This trail is ideal if you need stroller or wheelchair access. A picnic area and interpretive panels provide diversion along the pathway.

As you drive deeper into the park, you'll pass **Pink Lake.** This site is exceptionally beautiful in the fall, when the many deciduous trees turn to red, orange, and yellow against a background of dark green firs. Pink Lake (it's green, by the way, not pink) is unusual because it is one of only a dozen or so meromictic lakes in Canada. Because there is no circulation between the different layers of water, the lake harbors prehistoric bacteria, 10,000-year-old sedimentary deposits, and saltwater fish that have adapted to fresh water. There is a 2.5km (1.7 mile) trail around the lake, which takes about 1¹/₂ hours to walk.

If you're looking for panoramic vistas, try one of the trails leading to the top of the **Eardley Escarpment.** A steep 2km (1.25 mile) path called **King Mountain Trail** rewards hikers with a wonderful view of the Ottawa Valley. Farther into the park, the **Champlain Trail,** 1.3km (0.9 mile) long, has interpretive panels explaining how the site has evolved since the time of the last glaciers. From the **Champlain Lookout,** the valley view sweeps majestically for many miles. To reach the picturesque **Luskville Falls Trail,** travel west on boulevard Alexandre-Taché past the main south entrance to Gatineau Park, and continue west on Highway 148 to Luskville. Follow signs for Luskville Falls, where you'll find a parking lot and picnic site. The 5km (3 mile) trail — a steep 300m (975 ft.) vertical rise from base to summit — leads to the top of the Eardley Escarpment, where you will be rewarded with a sweeping view of the Ottawa Valley.

SWIMMING

There are **five public beaches** with lifeguard supervision within the park, located at Philippe, Meech, and La Pêche lakes. The sandy beaches, which are all popular with families, are open mid-June to early September daily 10am to 6pm. Swimming is prohibited in the beach areas outside these times, and at all times elsewhere in the park.

WINTER IN THE PARK

Gatineau Park has lots to offer winter visitors. An extensive network of **cross-country ski trails** and special trails for **hiking, snowshoeing,** and **kick-sledding** will keep you active outdoors. Rent snowshoes at the Visitor Centre for C$5 (US$4) per hour or C$15 (US$12) per day. Cross-country ski equipment can be rented from a number of outfitters close to the main entrance of the park. See Chapter 7, "Active Ottawa," for details.

Gatineau Park has earned a reputation as one of the best ski-trail networks in North America because of its remarkable 200km (125 miles) of trails, which are well-maintained using the latest technology. Both classic Nordic-style cross-country skiing and the more energetic skate-skiing are accommodated. The park

---

Tips   Sleepovers in the Park

Skiers and snowshoers can experience the silence of nature in winter by spending the night in one of Gatineau Park's cabins located deep in the heart of the forest. Bunk beds and wood stoves are installed in each cabin. Reservations are required.

---

provides eight heated shelters. Ski patrollers travel the area, ready to assist skiers in difficulty. When you arrive at the park you can buy a day pass for the trails at any of the 16 parking lots that give direct access to the trails, or at the Visitor Centre. If you don't have a map, your first stop should be the Visitor Centre to buy the official winter trail map. An extremely accurate winter trail map has recently been produced using GIS technology, which includes contour lines, magnetic north orientation, and exact representation of the trails. Because skiing and weather conditions change frequently, Gatineau Park reviews and updates ski information three times daily. A ski-condition report can be obtained by calling ℂ **819/827-2020.** For **downhill skiing** and **snowboarding,** Camp Fortune ski resort ℂ **819/827/1717** is right in Gatineau Park. Lessons and equipment rental are available. See "The Great Outdoors," later in this chapter, for more information.

Mackenzie King Estate   The summer residence of William Lyon Mackenzie King, Canada's longest-serving prime minister, was bequeathed to the Canadian people upon his death in 1950. You can visit the restored cottages on the property and stroll through the gardens, which include formal flower beds, a hidden rock garden, and a collection of picturesque ruins. There is a tearoom on the premises serving light refreshments. The estate is open mid-May to mid-October, weekdays 11am to 5pm, weekends and holidays 10am to 6pm. Admission fee is C$8 (US$6.50) per car per day. For more information call ℂ **819/827-2020.**

SPECIAL EVENTS IN GATINEAU PARK

Other events may be scheduled in addition to the ones listed below, and dates may change from year to year. For more information, contact the **Gatineau Park Visitor Centre,** 33 Scott Rd., Chelsea, QC ℂ **819/827-2020.**

January

The park celebrates winter with Ski-Fest, a weekend ski festival, which includes ski lessons for beginners and activities for the whole family.

February

The annual Keskinada Loppet is Canada's largest cross-country skiing event. Races are offered for all ability levels and every member of the family — there's even a 2-km (1.25-mile) mini-Keski for children under age 12.

May

The Mackenzie King Estate opens for the summer season.

The Canadian Tulip Festival is celebrated at the Mackenzie King Estate. Sunday Bikedays begin for the season.

July

Canada Day celebrations take place at the Mackenzie King Estate.

The Mackenzie King Estate hosts their annual "Estate in Bloom" event.

Learn about conservation and the natural and historic heritage of Gatineau Park on Parks Day.

September/October

Fall Rhapsody, a celebration of nature's autumn colors, takes place in the park. Ride the Camp Fortune chairlift to view the fall colors, participate in orienteering events, or enjoy an autumn menu at the Mackenzie King Estate's tearoom.

2 The Rideau Valley

The **Rideau Valley** lies southwest of Ottawa, following the path of the **Rideau Canal.** The canal is actually a continuous chain of beautiful lakes, rivers, and canal cuts, stretching a distance of 202km (125 miles) between Ottawa and Kingston, and often described as the most scenic waterway in North America. The **Rideau Canal Waterway** has been designated a **National Historic Site** and is one of nine historical canals in Canada. Parks Canada has the responsibility of preserving and maintaining the canal's natural and historical features and providing a safe waterway for navigation. You can explore the region by boat; drive along the country roads that wind their way through the towns and villages along the waterway; or hike a portion of the **Rideau Trail,** a cleared and marked footpath about 300km (185 miles) long that meanders between Ottawa and Kingston. If you're interested in a bicycle tour, get in touch with **Rideau Lakes Cycling** at ℂ 888/804-4696 — they offer week-long tours from July through October.

RIDEAU CANAL AND LOCKS

The canal and locks that link the lakes and rivers of the **Rideau Valley** were constructed between 1826 and 1832 to provide a safe route for the military between Montreal and Kingston in the wake of the War of 1812. Colonel By, the British engineer in charge of the project, had the foresight to build the locks and canal large enough to permit commercial traffic to access the system, rather than building the canal solely for military use. As things turned out, the inhabitants of North America decided to live peaceably. The canal became a main transportation and trade route, and communities along the canal grew and thrived. With the introduction of railroads in the mid-19th century, the commercial traffic subsided and the canal gradually became a tourist destination owing to its beauty and tranquility. The locks have operated continuously since they first opened. See chapter 6, "What to See & Do," for more details on the canal and locks located within the city of Ottawa. To experience the canal outside Ottawa, try **Paul's Boat Lines.** They operate an **all-day cruise** that navigates seven lock systems between Ottawa and Long Island Marine at the village of Kars. Reservations are required; call ℂ 613/225-6781.

Rideau Canal Numbers

• Number of locks in the main channel	45
• Number of lockstations	24
• Length of canal (Ottawa–Kingston)	202km (125 miles)
• Length of man-made canal cuts	19km (12 miles)
• Minimum available water depth	1.5m (5 ft.)
• Size of locks	41m by 10 m (134 ft. by 33 ft.)
• Travel time, one-way	3 to 5 days

Fun Fact Watson's Mill

Watson's Mill is reputedly haunted. Ghostly sightings have been reported of a tall, fair-haired young woman, believed to be the wife of Joseph Currier, one of the original mill owners. During a visit to the mill in 1861, the young bride's long skirts were accidentally caught in a revolving turbine shaft. She was thrown against a nearby support pillar and died instantly.

MANOTICK

Manotick is a quiet village about 24km (15 miles) south of Ottawa on the banks of the **Rideau River.** The original settlement grew around a water-powered gristmill, now known as **Watson's Mill,** on the west side of the river. The village expanded around the original buildings, which date from the mid-1800s, and now includes residences on Long Island, a 3.5km (2 mile) long island in the river, and an area on the east side of the river. Dickinson Square, in the heart of the village, is a good spot for strolling and visiting local shops. Wander across the dam and feed the ducks on the millpond. **Watson's Mill** is open to visitors in the summer. Every second Sunday afternoon from June to October the mill swings into operation, grinding wheat to make flour. You can wander through the five-story historic stone building or take a guided tour. Call ✆ **613/692-2500** for information on opening hours and tour times. To get to Manotick from Ottawa, take Riverside Drive south to the village. To reach the mill, cross the bridge to the west bank of the river.

There are several places to eat in the village, ranging from tearooms to family-style restaurants and fast-food outlets on Mill Street, Main Street, John Street, and River Road. For a nice leisurely lunch — or if you fancy quaffing a brew by the river on a warm summer day — head south on River Road. About 7km (4.5 miles) south of Manotick you'll find **The Swan on the Rideau** (2730 River Rd. ✆ **613/692-4550**), a pub/restaurant on the east banks of the Rideau River. Have a quiet drink or enjoy a snack or meal — the menu lists steak, chicken, pasta, and seafood. The atmosphere is casual and friendly.

MERRICKVILLE

To reach **Merrickville,** continue south along the scenic route beside the **Rideau River** past **Manotick.** If you travel along the west bank of the river on County Road 13 you'll pass **Baxter Conservation Area,** where you can stop for a picnic, stroll, or swim. Continue on County Road 13 to County Road 5. Turn left toward Becketts Landing, passing **Rideau River Provincial Park** on your left, another pleasant spot to stretch and enjoy the outdoors. Just after the park, the road changes to County Road 2 and takes you straight to Merrickville. For a more direct, faster route from Ottawa, use Highway 416 south (exit 42 or 43). The picturesque village of Merrickville is a popular tourist destination, especially in the summer months when the streets are decorated with flowers. One of Canada's best preserved and restored 19th-century villages, Merrickville has more than 100 historical and heritage properties. The community was chosen as Ontario's most beautiful village in 1996 and as Canada's most beautiful village in 1998. Dozens of professional artists make their home in the vicinity of Merrickville, and their wares — ranging from paintings to leather crafts, wood carvings, blown glass, pottery, and other creations — are available in boutiques and shops in the village. The village, founded in 1793 by William Merrick, was originally a large industrial center on the Rideau River with a number of woolen mills, sawmills, and gristmills. The original blockhouse, overlooking the locks, is now a small museum. Several cafes and restaurants are dotted about the village. **The Baldachin Inn** (111 St. Lawrence St. © **613/269-4223**) offers comfortable rooms for an overnight stay in addition to a fine-dining restaurant and a British-style pub, in a historical building that dates from the 1860s. Farther south on St. Lawrence Street at number 317, you'll find the **Goose and Gridiron English Country Pub** © **613/269-2094.** Serving imported and domestic beer accompanied by English-style pub meals, this eatery does a smashing job of imitating the Brits. Try the steak and kidney pie with chips and peas. Overlooking the Rideau Canal at 118 Main St. E., **Sam Jakes Inn** (© **800/567-4667** or 613/269-3711) is a heritage limestone property. Rooms and suites are furnished and decorated in period style. There is a restaurant on-site serving breakfast, lunch, and dinner. Cozy fireplaces are lit in the winter and there's a garden patio for summer enjoyment. Packages are available for romantic getaways. Just west of the village is the **Rideau National Migratory Bird Sanctuary.**

SMITHS FALLS

The town of Smiths Falls, established in the mid-1800s, was built around the heart of the Rideau Canal. There are three small museums in town that chronicle the history of the canal, the railroads, and the pioneers who settled in this district. Check opening hours before visiting, since two of them are open by appointment only during the winter months. There's one other attraction that chocoholics will not let you drive by — the Hershey Chocolate Factory. To reach Smiths Falls, take County Road 43 west from Merrickville (exit 43 on Hwy. 416). An alternative route from Ottawa is to take Highway 417 west to Highway 7 west, then take Highway 15 south to Smiths Falls. Driving time is approximately 45 minutes.

Hershey Canada Chocolate Factory Tour   Kids and grown-ups will love this free tour of the Hershey plant, where you can watch thousands of chocolate bars take shape right before your eyes. The tour is actually a self-guided walk along an elevated enclosed gallery with windows, giving you a bird's-eye view of the factory floor. You can peer down into huge vats of melted chocolate, watch chocolate molds travel along conveyor belts to be filled with chocolate, see individual bars being wrapped and packed for shipping, and follow boxes as they move along the conveyor belt around the factory. At the end of the tour, where else could you possibly end up but in the middle of a shop crammed with Hershey products? You may snag a bargain, but prices are not necessarily discounted. Be prepared to elbow your way past customers loaded down with bulging bags of calories as they eagerly line up at the cash registers. If you wish, you can shop at the store without taking the tour. The factory is easy to find by road, since it's well signposted once you reach the town of Smiths Falls.

Hershey Canada Inc., 1 Hershey Dr., Smiths Falls, ON. © **613/283-3300.** www.hersheys.com. Free admission. Mon–Fri 9am–6pm, Sat 9am–5pm, Sun 10am–5pm. Closed on some holidays, so call before you go.

Smiths Falls Railway Museum   Railroad buffs will enjoy a visit to this museum, which is housed in a former Canadian Northern Railway Station built in 1914. Railway artifacts on display include express train and passenger train memorabilia, archives, track tools, and old photographs and prints. Kids will love the full-size steam and diesel locomotives, passenger coaches, and cabooses.

90 William St., Smiths Falls, ON. © **613/283-5696.** C\$5 (US\$4) adult, C\$3 (US\$2.50) senior/student, C\$2 (US\$1.65) child 3–11. Mid-May–end June Sat-Sun 10am–4:30pm; July 1 to first Monday in Sept daily 10am–4:30pm; early Sept–mid-Oct Sat–Sun 10am–4:30pm.

Rideau Canal Museum   This museum has many hands-on displays for visitors to explore. You can operate a working lock model or test your skill as a canal skipper as you maneuver a model boat. Climb up to the lookout to get a panoramic view of the Rideau Canal and the town of Smiths Falls. Artifacts and historical displays share five floors with high-tech touch-screen computers and laserdisc mini-theaters. A guided tour of the Smiths Falls Combined Locks is available daily June to August or by request. The outdoor walking tour is about an hour and includes the modern hydraulic lock system and the original three-lift manual system built by Lt.-Col. John By in 1829.

34 Beckwith St. S., Smiths Falls, ON. ℰ **613/284-0505.** Indoor exhibits: C$4 (US$3.30) adult, C$3.50 (US$2.85) senior, C$2.50 (US$2) child 7–18, free for children 6 and under. Outdoor visit to the locks has an additional fee of C$3 (US$2.50) adult, C$2 (US$1.65) senior and child. January–mid-May open by appointment, Mid-May–mid-Oct daily 10am–4:30pm; Oct–Dec Sat–Sun 10am–4:30pm, Mon–Fri open by appointment.

Heritage House Museum   Adjacent to the Rideau Canal, Old Slys Lockstation, and a Victorian landscaped picnic area, this house has been restored to the time of Confederation (1867). Seven period rooms are featured, reflecting the lifestyle of a wealthy mill owner. Special programs, tours, and events are scheduled throughout the year.

Old Slys Rd. (off Hwy. 43), Smiths Falls, ON. ℰ **613/283-8560.** C$4 (US$3) adult, C$3.50 (US$2.85) senior, C$2.50 (US$2) child 6–18. Jan 2–Apr 30 Mon–Fri 10:30am–4:30pm; May 1–Dec 21 daily 10:30am–4:30pm.

3 The Great Outdoors

Blessed with excess energy? Burn up the ski slopes, swing on the golf courses, or ride the white-water raft runs. Searching for a new experience? Bungee jump in a limestone quarry, descend into an underground antinuclear shelter, or go spelunking. The fun just never ends.

DOWN THE HILLS IN EVERY SEASON

Within an hour or so by road from Ottawa are many ski centers that cater to downhill skiers and snowboarders. Vertical rise at the ski hills near Ottawa is modest, ranging from 106 to 381m (350 to 1,250 ft.). The facilities and runs are certainly compact compared to those in major resort destinations like Mont Tremblant (about a 2-hour drive from Ottawa) and Mont Ste-Anne (about a 4-hour drive from Ottawa), but they have the advantage of being easily accessible, meaning you can even ski a half-day if that is all the time or energy you have on hand. Equipment rental, lessons, facilities for children, terrain parks, and challenging downhill runs — it's all here on a small scale and you can be home in time for supper. A number of resorts have expanded their facilities to include activities for all seasons. Waterparks have been included in this section. Golf courses are listed under "Along the Fairways" later in this chapter. Mountain biking and hiking are available at some resorts; call individual resorts for details. Cross-country skiing is listed in chapter 7, "Active Ottawa."

Calabogie Peaks   Reputed to have the highest vertical in Eastern Ontario (232 m; 760 ft.), this four-season resort on the shores of Calabogie Lake offers 22 downhill runs. The snowboarding terrain park has four 6.1m (20-ft.) rails and five boxes. New for 2005 is the addition of three tubing runs. Ice skating is available at the resort, and cross-country skiing, ice fishing, snowshoeing, and snowmobiling facilities are nearby. In the summer, you can swim, fish, canoe, windsurf, play tennis or beach volleyball, go mountain biking, or just lie on the beach. To get to Calabogie Peaks, travel on Highway 417 (the Queensway) west.

Approximately 8km (5 miles) past Arnprior, turn left onto Calabogie Road and continue to Calabogie Peaks Resort. Driving time just under one hour.

Calabogie Rd., near Arnprior, ON. ⓒ **800/669-4861** or 613/752-2720. www.calabogie.com.

Camp Fortune   In the heart of Gatineau Park, just 15 minutes from downtown Ottawa, Camp Fortune has 20 runs, a snowboarding park, and a designated children's area. This resort is served well with numerous lifts, including several quad chairs. Greatest vertical rise is 180 m (590 ft.). Camp Fortune's ski school and racing programs enjoy a good reputation. Mountain biking is offered in summer. A ski bus service is available from Ottawa; call the resort for details. To get to Camp Fortune, take Highway 5 north to exit 12, chemin Old Chelsea. Travel west on Meech Lake Road and turn left into Camp Fortune.

300 chemin Dunlop, Chelsea, QC. ⓒ **888/283-1717** or 819/827-1717. www.campfortune.com.

Edelweiss   With a vertical rise of 200m (656 ft.), Edelweiss offers 18 runs served by 4 lifts. The tubing park has 11 trails and one lift. A more than C$2-million (US$1.65-million) investment has been made for the 2004/2005 season, including a new quad chair, new beginner's run, and new lighting system for the trails. A ski bus runs on weekends and holidays; call the resort for details. In Edelweiss Valley, you can also swoosh down the hills in the summer months at Le Grand Splash Water Park. This family waterpark features five water slides, a children's pool, a lounge pool, and an enormous 15m (50 ft.) hot tub. Picnic areas and tennis courts are also on-site. To get to Edelweiss, take Highway 5 north to Route 105 toward Wakefield. Take Route 366 east (chemin Edelweiss) to the ski hill. It's about a half-hour drive from Ottawa.

540 chemin Edelweiss, Wakefield, QC. ⓒ **819/459-2328.** www.mssi.ca.

Mont Cascades   This resort, with a vertical rise of 160m (525 ft.), offers plenty of activities in winter and summer. For skiers and snowboarders, there are 6 lifts and 19 runs, with illuminated night skiing on 12 of those. Lessons and equipment rental are available. The six-slide waterpark has something for everyone. There's an area for kids under 121cm (4 ft.) tall, with water sprays, three small slides, and a wading pool. For older and braver kids, there's a tunnel slide, a four-lane racing slide, a large slide that several people can slip down together in a raft, and other innovative ways to get wet while having fun. When it's time to eat, visit the restaurant or bring your own lunch and munch at a picnic table in the shade. To get to Mont Cascades from Ottawa, take the Macdonald-Cartier Bridge to Hull, then take Highway 50 east. Take the first exit, which is boulevard Archambault. Turn right onto Highway 307. Turn left on chemin Mont Cascades, and proceed 7km (4.3 miles) to Mont Cascades. It's about a half-hour drive from Ottawa.

448 chemin Mont-Cascades, Cantley, QC. ⓒ **888/282-2722** or 819/827-0301. www.montcascades.ca.

Mont Ste-Marie   This resort has the highest vertical in the Outaouais region, at more than 366m (1,200 ft.). Two peaks and two high-speed chairlifts give beginners and experienced skiers a choice of 24 runs in total. The resort boasts one of the longest beginner trails in western Quebec and a terrain park filled with boxes, rails, and table tops. Rentals and lessons are available. To reach Mont Ste-Marie, take Highway 5 north through Hull and join Highway 105 north. Stay on 105 until you see the signs for Mont Ste-Marie, a driving time of about 1 hour from Ottawa. A ski bus operates from Ottawa; call for details.

76 chemin de la Montagne, RR#1, Lac Ste-Marie, QC. ⓒ **800/567-1256** or 819/467-5200. www.montstemarie.com.

Mount Pakenham West of Ottawa, Mount Pakenham offers downhill and cross-country skiing, snowboarding, and tubing. The vertical is a modest 91m (300 ft.), but families with young children and beginners will find this to be challenging enough. Pakenham is equipped with six lifts, including a quad and a new triple chair, and 10 alpine runs. There's a terrain park, and night skiing is available. To get to Mount Pakenham, take the Queensway (Hwy. 417) west past Kanata. The road will reduce to two lanes and become Highway 17. Turn left on Road 20 across a stone bridge, and turn left at the stop sign onto Road 29/Highway 15. Drive through the village of Pakenham. Turn right on McWatty Road to a T-junction. Turn right to Mount Pakenham. It's approximately 25 minutes' drive from the Corel Centre exit on Highway 417.

Pakenham, ON. ✆ **613/624-5290**. www.mountpakenham.com.

Ski Vorlage This resort, with a vertical rise of 152m (500 ft.), offers a choice of 15 runs including a terrain park, with 12 runs illuminated for night skiing. Try tubing — fly down the slope on an inflatable donut and get towed back up the hill. Ski Vorlage promotes itself as a family ski area and extends a special welcome to families and kids. Non-skiers might like to spend a couple of hours in the shops and restaurants of nearby Wakefield. Vorlage is about 25 minutes from Ottawa by car. Follow Highway 5 north to Highway 105 north and turn right into Wakefield. Turn onto Burnside Road and follow the signs to Vorlage.

65 Burnside Rd., Wakefield, QC. ✆ **877/867-5243** or 819/459-2301. www.skivorlage.com.

ALONG THE FAIRWAYS

There are literally dozens of golf courses within an hour's drive of Ottawa. A few suggestions are listed below, but there are many more excellent courses to visit. Check out www.ottawagolf.com or www.golfeogo.ca for a more comprehensive listing.

Amberwood Village Executive 9-hole, par 66 course in a quiet suburban setting about a half-hour from Ottawa. Take Highway 417 (Queensway) west; exit at the Carp Road/Stittsville exit. Turn left onto Carp Road for approximately 2km (1.25 miles). Turn left onto Hazeldean Road, then right onto Springbrook Drive until you reach Amberwood.

54 Springbrook Dr., Stittsville, ON. ✆ **613/836-2581**.

Calabogie Highlands Resort and Golf Club Rated in the top 50 golf courses in Ontario, this resort features an 18-hole championship course and a 9-hole lakeview course ideally suited for beginners. Accommodation available. Practice range, outdoor pool, and tennis. Take Highway 417 (Queensway) west past Arnprior. Turn left on Highway 508 to Calabogie (about 23km; 14 miles). Turn left onto Highway 511, then right onto Barryvale Road. About an hour's drive from Ottawa.

981 Barryvale Rd., Calabogie, ON ✆ **613/752-2171**.

Capital Golf Centre Situated in the south end of the city next to the Greenbelt, this 18-hole course is exclusively par 3, with the longest hole at 202 yards. The layout deliberately omits water and sand hazards as a benefit to beginning golfers, and it is an affordable place to learn and practice. More experienced golfers can play the course to sharpen up their short game. There's also a championship miniature golf course with holes ranging from 25 to 65 feet, and three practice ranges for all types of play — drives, short irons, bunkers, and chipping. Lessons available. Situated 2km (1.25 miles) south of Hunt Club Road on Bank Street.

3798 Bank St., Ottawa, ON. ✆ **613/521-2612**.

Champlain Golf Club   Just 10 minutes from downtown Ottawa, this 18-hole championship course was established in 1929. There's a great practice center here where all levels of players can improve their game. Facilities include a driving range, two chipping greens, three practice sand traps, and two putting greens. Lessons available. Pro shop and refreshments. Cross the Champlain Bridge over the Ottawa River to Gatineau (Hull sector) and turn left on Highway 148 (boul. Alexander Taché/chemin d'Aylmer). A mere 1.3km (0.8 mile) on your right you'll find the golf club.

1145 chemin d'Aylmer, Gatineau (Aylmer sector), QC. ℂ **819/777-0449.**

Château Cartier   A luxurious golf and conference resort, situated on 62 hectares (152 acres) on the north shore of the Ottawa River, Château Cartier is just a short drive from Ottawa. See chapter 4, "Where to Stay," for details on this beautiful property. Cross the Champlain Bridge over the Ottawa River to Gatineau and turn left on Highway 148 (boul. Alexander Taché/chemin d'Aylmer). The resort is a couple of minutes' drive on your left-hand side.

1170 chemin d'Aylmer, Gatineau (Aylmer sector) QC. ℂ **819/777-8870.**

Eagle Creek Golf Course   Eagle Creek public course is a challenging 18-hole championship course designed by U.S. Open winner Ken Venturi with the aim of rewarding precision over power. The course has been rated as one of the top ten courses in Ontario. The Eagle Creek Classic Tournament has been held for several years here as part of the Canadian Professional Golf Tour. The course has been a *Golf Digest* 4-Star award winner from 1996 to 2001. Take Highway 417 (Queensway) west and exit at March Road/Kanata/Eagleson Road. Travel north on March Road for about 8km (5 miles), then turn right onto Dunrobin Road for 10km (6 miles). Turn right onto Vances Sideroad for around 3km (2 miles). Turn left onto Greenland Road. About 1.5km (1 mile) along, turn left onto Ventor Boulevard. A few meters (yards) along here you'll find the club.

109 Royal Troon Lane, Dunrobin, ON. ℂ **613/832-0728.** www.eaglecreekgolf.ca.

The Marshes   Located in the heart of Silicon Valley North, the design of this public course is a Robert Trent Jones father-and-son collaboration. As you might expect from the name, water is a predominant feature of the landscape. Golf carts are equipped with color monitors that use GPS technology to give players distance statistics at every swing. The recently opened Brookstreet resort hotel overlooks the course. The course has been awarded platinum status by *GolfRank,* Canada's golf ranking magazine.

320 Terry Fox Dr., Ottawa, ON ℂ **613/271-3370.** www.marshesgolfclub.com.

Mont Cascades   One of the most scenic golf courses in the Ottawa area, this semi-private golf club has a mature championship course, clubhouse, and outdoor deck overlooking the Gatineau River and Gatineau Hills. To get to Mont Cascades from Ottawa, take the Macdonald-Cartier Bridge to Hull, then take Highway 50 east. Take the first exit, which is boulevard Archambault. Turn right onto Highway 307. Turn left on chemin Mont-Cascades, and proceed 7km (4.3 miles) to Mont Cascades. It's about a half-hour drive from Ottawa.

448 chemin Mont-Cascades, Cantley, QC. ℂ **819/459-2980.** www.golf.montcascades.com.

Mont Ste-Marie   This classic mountain course set in the rolling contours of the Gatineau Hills has a challenging layout. Driving range, power carts, locker room, golf boutique, and bar/restaurant are available at this public course. To reach Mont Ste-Marie, take Highway 5 north through Hull and join Highway

105 north. Stay on 105 until you see the signs for Mont Ste-Marie, a driving time of about 1 hour from Ottawa.

76 chemin de la Montagne, RR#1, Lac Ste-Marie, QC. **800/567-1256** or 819/467-3111. www.montstemarie.com.

Pine View Municipal Golf Course   Play a choice of two 18-hole courses here — one championship and one executive at this City of Ottawa–owned public golf course. Locals have voted this course a favorite in past years. Take Highway 417 (Queensway) east, and continue on Highway 174 when the highway splits in two (don't take 417 toward Montreal at exit 113). Exit Highway 174 at Blair Road. Turn left onto Blair Road for 400m (1,312 ft.) to the course.

1471 Blair Rd., Ottawa, ON. **613/746-4653.**

ON THE RIVER

One of the most popular white-water rafting and kayaking rivers in Canada, the Ottawa River has everything for the white-water enthusiast — dozens of islands, rapids, waterfalls, sandy beaches, and dramatic rock formations. It's even said that the water is warm (I can't confirm or deny that, but you're welcome to tackle the white water and find out for yourself). An hour or two northwest of Ottawa, a number of white-water tour operators have established businesses that allow novices and families to enjoy running the rapids just as much as experienced extreme-sports participants do. Keep a lookout for one of the newest thrills, riverboarding. Equipped with a board, wetsuit, lifejacket, helmet, and fins, riverboarders ride the rapids lying prone on their board. They read the direction of the current and point the board where they want to go using their arms as paddles and their flippers as rudders.

Esprit Rafting   Offering day trips and longer-stay outdoor adventure packages, Esprit Rafting operates on the Ottawa River about 1^1/2 hours by road from Ottawa; the company can arrange transportation between Ottawa and the rafting site. There's a wide range of adventure packages, including white-water rafting, white-water canoeing, white-water kayaking, and riverboarding. You can add horseback riding, mountain biking, or a bungee jump to your package. Esprit offers a great family white-water experience. In the morning, the family (children must be ages 7 or older) rafts together with the assistance of an experienced guide. In the afternoon, children under age 12 take part in supervised shore activities while parents and children over age 12 take a more adventurous trip through the rapids. The day trip meets at a rendezvous point along the highway; get directions when you call to make your reservation. Overnight accommodation can be arranged at Esprit's private 5-acre peninsula on the Upper Ottawa River, where camping facilities (tent and sleeping bag rental) and a hostel provide a place to sleep. There is a lodge serving meals, and activities include kayaking, canoeing, volleyball, and mountain biking.

800/596-7238 or 819/683-3641. www.espritrafting.com.

Owl Rafting   Owl Rafting operates on the Ottawa River near Forester's Falls, between Renfrew and Pembroke off Highway 17. Paddle your own course with a guide if you wish, and choose everything from chicken runs to a champion challenge. Two-person inflatable kayaks available. Owl Rafting also offers a half-day family float trip that takes you more than 6km (3.7 miles) along the river, through white water and calm pools. They return you to base on a gentle cruising raft (with chairs and a barbecue lunch on board). Passengers must weigh a minimum of 22kg (50 lb.) Trips run on weekdays, and lifejackets and helmets are provided. No paddling is required — just hold on and enjoy riding waves up to 1m (3 ft.) in height. Overnight accommodation (2 nights camping and 5 meals provided) is available. Reservations are required.

Summer: 40 Owl Lane, Forester's Falls, ON K0J 1V0. ✆ **613/646-2263.** Winter: 39 First Ave., Ottawa, ON K1S 2G1. ✆ **613/238-7238.** www.owl-mkc.ca.

River Run Whitewater Resort   River Run, just a 90-minute drive northwest of Ottawa, is a 56 hectare (137 acre) riverfront resort on the Ottawa River. Experiences range from gentle family rafting rides to aggressive sport-boat programs, and everyone on board gets involved — you get to paddle on this one. There's also a complete range of outdoor recreational activities at the resort. Packages with overnight accommodation (everything from camping to rustic cabins to luxury inn rooms) can be arranged, including raft'n'golf and raft'n'spa packages.

P.O. Box 179, Beachburg, ON K0J 1C0. ✆ **800/267-8504** or 613/646-2501. www.riverrunners.com.

Wilderness Tours   Wilderness Tours is a 266 hectare (650 acre) resort and adventure destination on the banks of the Ottawa River. Paddle a small, sporty six-person raft with a guide, or take a family raft trip geared toward families with children between the ages of 7 and 12. Raft trips include professional guides and a post-trip video and barbecue. A variety of vacation packages is available, for short and long stays. Packages include meals, scenic camping or cabin rental, use of the resort facilities, and a supervised children's program in the evenings.

P.O. Box 89, Beachburg, ON K0J 1C0. ✆ **800/267-9166** or 613/646-2291. www.wildernesstours.com.

OUT OF THE SKY

Great Canadian Bungee

Try to picture a majestic limestone quarry with 60m (200 ft.) high sides, surrounding a spring-fed lagoon of deepest aqua blue. Now, imagine your loved ones jumping off a platform suspended above the water, attached by a bungee cord, experiencing what is reputed to be the highest legal jump site in North America. You either love the idea or you hate it, but it's certainly an unusual spectacle. If you don't want to take part in the madness, come to enjoy the barbecue and picnic facilities, play and swim at the supervised beach area, rent a paddleboat or kayak, and be entertained by all those crazy dudes who are willing to pay up to C$100 (US$82) for the biggest adrenaline rush of all time. Note that there are no age restrictions, but jumpers must weigh at least 36kg (80 lb.). Recently another thrill was introduced at the site — the RIPRIDE. It's a 310m (1,015 ft.) cable slide that accelerates as you travel along its length, reaching a top speed of 100kmph (62 mph). You can ride tandem on the slide if the combined weight is between 36 and 109kg (80 and 240 lb.). Life will never be the same again.

Morrison's Quarry, Wakefield, QC. ✆ **877/828-8170** or 819/459-3714. www.bungee.ca.

LaFlèche Adventure (Aerial Park)

This recently constructed aerial adventure park — consisting of an impressive 82 bridges suspended from the tops of trees in the forests of the Laurentians — will thrill young and old. Wannabe Tarzans must be at least 1.35m (53 in.) tall for the two junior sections. The remaining four park sections are restricted to visitors with a minimum height of 1.5m (59 in.). The other major attraction here is the LaFlèche Caves, which are open all year around; see "Under the Ground" below for more details.

Route 307, Val-des-Monts, QC. ✆ **877/457-4033** or 819/457-4033. Package prices that include caverns, the aerial park, and winter snowshoeing range from C$32 (US$26) adult to C$90 (US$74) family (2 adults and 2 children). Call for admission fees to individual attractions. Reservations required. May–Aug daily; Sept–Apr Thurs–Sun.

UNDER THE GROUND

When you've explored air, land, and water, what do you do next? Go underground, of course.

Diefenbunker Cold War Museum   Visit an underground bunker built during the period of the Cold War and designed to shelter the Canadian government in the event of a nuclear attack. This is a rare opportunity to glimpse a somber and alarming period in recent world history, when precautions were taken against the threat of nuclear war. The huge 4-story bunker, buried deep under a farmer's field, is designed to house more than 500 people and enough supplies for a month. The guided walking tour takes about $1^1/_2$ hours. Many of the guides used to work in the Diefenbunker before it was decommissioned in 1994. During the tour you will see the blast tunnel and massive blast doors, the CBC radio studio, the Bank of Canada vault that was designed to hold Canada's gold reserves, the War Cabinet room, the decontamination unit, a detailed model of the bunker, a 1-megaton hydrogen "practice bomb," a reconstruction of a family fallout shelter, and lots more. To get to the Diefenbunker from Ottawa, follow Highway 417 (the Queensway) west, take the Carp–Stittsville exit, and bear right onto Carp Road. Travel about 8km (5 miles) into the village of Carp. Watch for signs on the left indicating the entrance to the Diefenbunker.

3911 Carp Rd., Carp, ON. ✆ **800/409-1965** or 613/839-0007. www.diefenbunker.ca. Admission C$14 (US$11) adults, C$12.50 (US$10) seniors and students, C$6 (US$5) children 6–17, free for children 5 and under. Guided tours begin in summer daily at 11am, noon, 1pm, 2pm, and 3pm; in fall, winter, and spring weekdays at 2pm and weekends at 11am, 1pm, and 2pm. Reservations recommended.

Laflèche Adventure (Caves)   Visit the white marble caverns at Laflèche Caves and explore the large network of domes, rooms, and tunnels that were carved into the rock by the pressure from water and ice during the last Ice Age. The general tour is suitable for all ages and takes about $1^1/_2$ hours. More adventurous souls can follow an experienced guide on a 3-hour tour of narrow spaces and galleries. The temperature inside the caves remains steady all year round, between 3 and 7°C (37–45°F). Wear sturdy walking shoes and warm clothing. Guides will provide you with hard hats and headlamps for both tours, as well as with the extra equipment needed for the caving adventure tour. Above ground, enjoy the snowshoeing trails in winter and picnic areas and nature trails in summer. An amazing aerial park with 82 bridges is open year round; see "Into the Sky," above. Reservations are required for cave tours. To reach Laflèche Caves, take Highway 50 north through Gatineau (Hull sector), exit on Highway 307 north, and travel to Val-des-Monts. It's about a half-hour drive from Ottawa.

Route 307, Val-des-Monts, QC. ✆ **877/457-4033** or 819/457-4033. Package prices that include caverns, the aerial park, and winter snowshoeing range from C$32 (US$26) adult to C$90 (US$74) family (2 adults and 2 children). Reservations required. May–Aug daily; Sept–Apr Thurs–Sun.

Appendix: Ottawa in Depth

Ottawa's transformation from wilderness to a camp for the builders of the Rideau Canal to Canada's capital spans a period of more than 200 years. The fascinating story of how this landscape of remarkable beauty encompassing Chaudière Falls, Rideau Falls, and the Gatineau River became today's clean, green, dynamic national capital has been condensed in the next few pages.

1 History 101

The heart of Ottawa's history is the grand Ottawa River, Canada's second longest river at more than 1,100km (700 miles). The river had been used as a major transportation route by Native peoples for thousands of years prior to the arrival of the first Europeans in the early 1600s. Anxious to expand the fur trade, which was the basis of New France's economy, French governors encouraged exploration of the interior of the continent but did not give priority to establishing new settlements. Consequently, although many French explorers and fur traders paddled and portaged past the site of the future city of Ottawa, almost 200 years went by before the first settlers arrived.

The French explorer Samuel de Champlain, who had sent two Frenchmen on missions up the Ottawa River prior to his arrival in 1613, is often considered to be the first white man to visit the vicinity of present-day Ottawa and Gatineau. Champlain recorded detailed descriptions of Rideau Falls, Chaudière Falls, and the Native peoples in his diary.

Settlements finally began to be established in the Ottawa Valley toward the end of the 18th century, but it was Philemon Wright, a prosperous farmer from Massachusetts, who saw potential in the district. In 1800 he persuaded five homesteading families to join him, his wife, and six children to establish the first community in the area. Wright chose the

Dateline

- **1610** Étienne Brûlé, by order of French explorer Samuel de Champlain, becomes the first white man to travel through the future site of Ottawa.
- **1613** Champlain records detailed descriptions of the Chaudière Falls and Rideau Falls while traveling up the Ottawa River.
- **1600s** to **1900s** A large number of trading canoes travel up and down the Ottawa River, trading goods for furs.
- **1763** The first Treaty of Paris ends French rule in Canada, and land is granted to the British.
- **1800** A Massachusetts farmer, Philemon Wright, establishes the first non-Native settlement in the area on the north side of the Ottawa River. Wrightsville, now known as Gatineau (Hull Sector), Quebec, grows and prospers along with the expanding lumber trade.
- **1812** The War of 1812 between the United States and England, which employed Canada as a battleground, sparks British military leaders to search for a more secure route between Montreal and Lake Ontario, to protect against a possible future invasion by the Americans.
- **1822** The first steamboat to travel up the Ottawa River, *Union of the Ottawa*, makes its inaugural journey.
- **1826** Lieutenant-Colonel John By arrives on the south shore of the Ottawa River to oversee the construction of the Rideau Canal, a 202km (125 mile) waterway between Lake Ontario and the Ottawa River, designed to provide

continues

north shore of the Ottawa River, and within 20 years Wrightsville became a thriving village of more than 700 residents. Wright's plan was to make the community self-sufficient, and with five mills, four stores, three schools, two hotels, two distilleries, a brewery, and agricultural endeavors, it seems he succeeded.

Wright was searching for additional income to boost the local economy, and timber was the obvious choice for an export commodity because of its quality and abundance. Wright established markets for the local lumber in Quebec and England, and the wood was transported down the Ottawa River.

At this time, 20 years after Wright's arrival, the south side of the Ottawa River was still covered in dense bush and swampland and sparsely populated by settlers. What sparked the establishment of a larger community on the south side of the Ottawa River was the need — following the War of 1812 — for a more secure transportation route than the St. Lawrence River between Kingston and Montreal. It was the British, who by that time were governors of Upper and Lower Canada and therefore had the responsibility of defending the territory, who were pushing for a back door between Montreal and Lake Ontario as a security precaution in the event of an American invasion. They were unable to find any interested parties to share the cost of construction of a canal to link Lake Ontario with the Ottawa River. As a result, the canal project ended up as a costly operation for the British, but the advantage was that they had control over the building of the canal and its attendant settlement.

In 1826, Lieutenant-Colonel John By was assigned to oversee the construction of the Rideau Canal. By the end of that year, hundreds of people had arrived at the canal site in preparation for its construction. In the spring of

a safe transportation route between Kingston and Montreal.

- **1827** A settlement, population 1,000, is established on the south side of the Ottawa River and named Bytown.
- **1841** Work begins on Notre-Dame Cathedral Basilica on Sussex Drive.
- **1848** Population 6,000.
- **1855** Bytown becomes a city called Ottawa.
- **1857** Queen Victoria chooses Ottawa as the capital of the British Provinces of Upper and Lower Canada, ahead of Montreal, Toronto, Kingston, and Quebec City.
- **1860** Queen Victoria's son Edward, Prince of Wales, visits Ottawa and becomes the first member of the Royal Family to visit North America.
- **1866** The Parliament Buildings, modeled on the British Houses of Parliament, are completed.
- 1866 The University of Ottawa is founded.
- **1867** With Confederation, Ottawa becomes the capital of the new Dominion of Canada. Population now 18,000.
- **1870** The capital's first streetcar service, Ottawa City Passenger Railway, begins operation.
- **1873** The grounds of Parliament Hill are laid out by Calvert Vaux, a landscape architect who also designed New York's Central Park.
- **1874** The city's municipal water supply is established.
- **1877** A new city hall is constructed of limestone on Elgin Street.
- **1879** Cartier Square Drill Hall, the oldest armory in Canada still in use, is built.
- **1880** A group of 26 prominent Canadian artists decides to found a National Gallery. The gallery has many temporary homes in the years to come.
- **1888** Lansdowne Park fairgrounds are built on what was then the outskirts of town.
- **1891** The region's first strike takes place, as 2,400 millworkers walk out in protest at wage cuts.
- **1899** The Ottawa Improvement Commission (ancestor of today's

continues

the following year, the settlement was named Bytown.

The first buildings to be constructed were an engineering office and a commissariat, sited at the foot of the canal. At the head of the canal on the east side, civilian barracks were built in what would soon become known as "Lower Town." This area was an almost impenetrable swamp choked with cedars. As most of the land was uninhabitable, land purchasers were encouraged to buy or lease plots of land on the west side of the canal, then known as "Upper Town."

The canal works yard was located in Lower Town, and as it expanded settlers found it necessary to drain the surrounding swampland in order to free up more land. Most of the new inhabitants of Lower Town were Irish and French laborers, thereby establishing a predominantly Roman Catholic community; some of the poorest Irish immigrants lived in shanties along the edge of the canal construction site.

Upper Town, which was not as densely populated, attracted more affluent and better-educated settlers, predominantly English and Scottish Protestants. The 202km (125 mile) Rideau Canal was completed in 1832. It was an enormous feat, all the more admirable for the fact that no fewer than 45 locks were constructed, manned by 24 lockstations; the locks allowed boats to ascend and descend the spine of the Precambrian Shield, an ancient rock formation that covers much of northern Canada and part of New York State. The highest point on the Rideau Waterway is Upper Rideau Lake. At one end of the lake, water flows down to Lake Ontario, dropping a distance of 50m (164 ft.) in total. At the other end, water flows in the opposite direction down to the Ottawa River, dropping a distance of 83m (273 ft.), ending in the 30m (98 ft.) high Rideau Falls.

National Capital Commission, aka NCC) is created to oversee city planning.

- 1901 The Alexandra Railway Bridge opens; its construction was at the forefront of engineering in its day.
- 1908 The Royal Canadian Mint is established as a branch of the British Royal Mint.
- 1911 Population 87,000.
- 1914 World War I begins.
- 1916 A devastating fire sweeps the Parliament Buildings — only the Parliamentary Library is saved. The Parliament Buildings must be almost completely rebuilt.
- 1916 The National Research Council is founded in Ottawa.
- 1927 A carillon of 53 bells is rung for the first time in the Peace Tower.
- 1930s The Great Depression; thousands are out of work.
- 1938 The federal government purchases the first lands of what is now Gatineau Park following pressure from local citizens to protect the wilderness.
- 1939 World War II begins.
- 1941 Population 155,000.
- 1945 Queen Juliana of the Netherlands presents a gift of thousands of tulip bulbs to the city in appreciation of Canada's granting a safe haven to the Dutch Royal Family during World War II.
- 1965 Canada gains its own flag, and it is raised for the first time on the top of the Peace Tower on February 15.
- 1967 Then–prime minister Lester B. Pearson lights the Centennial Flame on Parliament Hill to commemorate 100 years of Confederation.
- 1969 The National Arts Centre, with its distinctive series of repeating triangles and hexagons, opens.
- 1971 Population 302,000.
- 1970s The NCC constructs the first section of recreational pathway, marking the beginning of the "greening" of the city.
- 1980s The growth of Ottawa's tech industry continues to strengthen and Silicon Valley North takes hold.
- 1988 A permanent location for the National Gallery of Canada opens at 380 Sussex Drive. Canadian architect

continues

The canal never did fulfill its original purpose as a military transportation route, but for many years it operated as a commercial waterway before adopting its present recreational role for boaters and tourists.

Following the completion of the canal, Bytown evolved into a merchant-based community, supporting the growing timber trade by providing retail shops and services. Most of the supplies for the lumber camps up and down the Ottawa River were purchased in Bytown. Taverns, gaming houses, and brothels sprang up in response to demands from the rough, boisterous lumber workers. Street brawls were common, with racial and religious tensions running high, especially when fueled by drink. As the timber trade continued to flourish, lawlessness and violence prevailed.

The native white pine, and to a lesser degree red pine and oak, were much in demand by the British for shipbuilding during the mid–19th century. As a result of interference by Napoleon, Great Britain's supply of timber from the Baltic countries was halted, and for a time the British began to purchase a large amount of timber from Canada. However, by 1842 Britain was able to obtain timber from the Baltic countries as it had in the past, and the timber trade in the Ottawa area began to decline.

The local lumber industry was launched into a new era of prosperity with the arrival of several American entrepreneurs in the early 1850s. These men established sawmills to supply sawn lumber to the United States. Around the same time, a branch railway was built between Bytown and Prescott to serve as a link with the main line between Montreal and Toronto. Although the railway turned out to be a financial disaster, its presence was an important influence in the choice of a capital city.

Moshe Safdie creates a marvelous glass, steel, and concrete structure.

- **1989** The outstanding Canadian Museum of Civilization opens in Hull, now part of the city of Gatineau.
- **1992** Ottawa's National Hockey League team, the Ottawa Senators, is reborn.
- **1990s** Ottawa's high-tech industry explodes, bringing new jobs to the district and indirectly causing traffic congestion and a housing shortage.
- **1999** Population 324,000 in the city, but surrounding communities continue to experience rapid population growth
- **2000** Hull's Jacques-Cartier Park is designated "Mile 0" of the new Trans Canada Trail, a multi-use trail that will eventually stretch from coast to coast.
- 2001 Canada and the World Pavilion opens, an exhibit to celebrate Canadian success stories around the world.
- **2001** A new city of Ottawa is born, as 12 local municipal governments are amalgamated to create one new municipality of Ottawa. Population of the new city is 800,000.
- **2001** High-tech stocks begin to slide and Silicon Valley North, Ottawa's high-tech community, feels the pinch.
- **2002** Following in Ottawa's expansion footsteps, the new City of Gatineau is created from five former municipalities — Aylmer, Buckingham, Gatineau, Hull, and Masson-Angers, with a combined population of 229,000.
- **2002** Ottawa re-enters the Canadian Football League after a six-year absence with a new team named the Ottawa Renegades.
- **2003** The new Ottawa airport passenger terminal building (PTB) opens in October, six months early, on budget and without the help of government subsidies.
- **2005** Ottawa celebrates its 150th anniversary as a city. On January 1, 1855, the town of Bytown became the City of Ottawa.
- **2005** The new Canadian War Museum, featuring 4,200 sq. m. (45,000 sq. ft.) of exhibition space, opens on LeBreton Flats, about 2km (1.25 miles) west of Parliament Hill.

As Bytown marched toward the future, it received a change in both name and status. On New Year's Day, 1855, Bytown became a city called Ottawa. It was time to move forward and put the community's sordid reputation of the past behind. The citizens were excited at the prospect of being considered a contender for the title of capital of the Province of Canada.

There was such bitter debate on the issue of a suitable location for the seat of government that Parliament finally asked Queen Victoria to select the city. Montreal, Quebec, Kingston, and Toronto were Ottawa's rivals and worthy contenders. Factors in Ottawa's favor were its geographical position on the border of Upper and Lower Canada and its origins as a mixed English- and French-speaking settlement, in addition to the presence of the Rideau Canal and the new railway link. Queen Victoria duly appointed Ottawa as the capital of the Province of Canada in 1857. In the years immediately following the announcement, Ottawa enjoyed a period of strong growth. Within six years, several hundred stone buildings were erected and the population grew by 50%, reaching 14,000 by 1863. Wellington Street and Bank Street were lined with shops, medical facilities were improved with two hospitals serving the city, and a police commission was established. There were dramatic increases in the commercial and professional classes as well as in the number of industrial workers.

The construction of the government buildings took more than five years to complete. At the end of 1865 about 350 civil servants from Quebec City transferred to the new buildings. By the time Ottawa had a mere 18 months' experience as capital of the Province of Canada, it took on the much larger role of capital of the new Dominion of Canada.

On July 1, 1867, there was a great celebration on Parliament Hill. The day was declared a public holiday. Viscount Monck was sworn in as Governor General of the Dominion of Canada at 10am, followed by a march-past of the troops. In the evening, revelers lit bonfires and watched a fireworks display. Since that first Dominion Day, Canadians have celebrated July 1 (now known as Canada Day) on Parliament Hill.

In the second half of the 19th century, Ottawa faced a number of conflicts: the lumber industry versus the government as economic influences; Catholics versus Protestants in terms of religious practices, culture, and education; and immigrants versus Canadian-born citizens, which often reflected differences in social class.

Despite the challenges of a growing city, growth in public and private enterprises surged ahead. A municipal water supply and electricity supply were established, and public transportation was improved with the installment of electric streetcars to replace horse-drawn trams. Many of Ottawa's recreational clubs were founded in the latter half of the 19th century. The Ottawa Field Naturalists Club, Rowing Club, Curling Club, Cricket Club, Tennis Club, Aquatic Club, and Golf Club all originated in the 1800s.

The urban landscape altered with the years. The Parliament Buildings dominated the skyline, while numerous mills crowded around Chaudière Falls. Stone and brick commercial and residential properties abounded in Upper Town, while Lower Town was marked by the twin spires of the Basilica and the more modest wooden houses of the inhabitants of the Market district.

In the spring of 1900, a major fire swept through Hull and across the river to the Chaudière area of Ottawa. Seven people died, 15,000 became homeless, and more than 3,000 buildings were destroyed. The cities recovered, thanks mainly to a relief fund and the resilience and strength of the citizens.

At the turn of the last century, Ottawa's prosperity could be attributed to three major factors: the lumber industry, which was able to produce 500 million board-feet of lumber annually by harnessing the power of Chaudière Falls; growth of the civil service; and the trade generated by the railways. Downtown Ottawa was a maze of tracks: four rail systems with nine different lines. In 1912, the imposing Union Station with its domed ceiling and huge stone pillars opened on the east bank of the Rideau Canal, bordered by Rideau Street. The same year, one of Ottawa's most famous landmarks opened — the Château Laurier, which sits directly opposite the Union Station building (now used as a convention center). Built of granite and sandstone in a Loire Valley Renaissance style similar to that of the Château Frontenac Hotel in Quebec City, the building is topped with a copper roof, echoing the structure of the adjacent Parliament Buildings. Also in 1912, the Victoria Memorial Museum, now known as the Canadian Museum of Nature, was completed. Three hundred Scottish stone masons contributed their expertise to the intricately designed turreted stonework of the museum.

In 1916, fire destroyed the Centre Block of the Parliament Buildings. Only the Parliamentary Library was saved, due to the actions of a quick-thinking employee who closed the steel fire doors against the advancing flames. The height of the drama occurred when the huge bell in the clock tower crashed to the ground on the last stroke of midnight.

Rebuilding began a few months afterward, and the new Centre Block, similar in appearance to the original, was completed six years later. The central tower, named the Peace Tower, contains a memorial chamber dedicated to Canada's war dead, a 27.3m (91 ft.) belfry with a carillon of 53 bells, a four-faced clock, and an observation deck. Rising from the peak of the roof of the Peace Tower is a 10.5m (35 ft.) bronze flag mast proudly flying the Canadian flag.

Ottawa, along with the rest of the world, suffered and survived two World Wars, but by the end of World War II, the city was a far cry from the beautiful green capital of today. Rail lines choked the city. More than 100 trains, with their associated smoke and soot, thundered into Ottawa every day, and there were no fewer than 150 level crossings within city limits.

Much of the credit for the establishment of Ottawa's physical beauty goes to Jacques Grüber, a French urban planner, and then–prime minister William Lyon Mackenzie King. Prior to World War II, in the late 1930s, King had invited Grüber to Ottawa, initially as an advisor to plan the War Memorial and Confederation Square. World War II interrupted these plans, but following the war Grüber returned to Ottawa and prepared a report with recommendations for extensive urban renewal. The report outlined several major proposed changes to the urban landscape.

One of the most significant was the establishment of a wide swath of greenbelt around the city. Grüber also recommended eliminating slum areas, creating parks and pathways, purchasing land in Quebec to further enhance Gatineau Park, and removing or relocating railway lines.

To implement Grüber's plan, the National Capital District was enlarged to 2,900km (1,800 miles), encompassing 72 municipalities in Ontario and Quebec, and the Federal District Commission (the official agency of capital planning) was restructured and renamed the National Capital Commission and given a full-time chairman.

Removing the vast network of railway lines dramatically changed the face of Ottawa. In their place, sweeping scenic drives were created for vehicular traffic, and pathways for walkers and cyclists were built alongside the waterways, lined with grass verges, shrubbery, and flower beds. To manage high volumes of through traffic, the multi-lane Queensway (Hwy. 417) was built on an old railway bed. Completed in 1965, the Queensway stretches for more than 50km (31 miles) from the city of Kanata in the west to the town of Orleans in the east.

In the mid-1900s, the number of diplomatic missions with embassies in Ottawa grew at an enormous pace. There are now more than 100 countries represented in Canada's capital, contributing vitality and diversity to the city's cultural and social life.

Throughout the 1970s, bilingualism became commonplace in the capital. The federal government adopted two official languages, and civil servants who could speak both English and French found themselves at a distinct advantage in the workplace. This move toward a bilingual population helped to break down the class barriers in the city. Added to this improved relationship between the two major cultures in Ottawa was the growth of immigrant populations, primarily German, Italian, Jewish, Lebanese, and Asian.

The presence of blue-collar workers dwindled in the years after the war, replaced by office workers to support the growing federal government and civil service. A second economic influence began to appear by the 1960s — one that was to become a major player in the region. The high-tech industry, with its emphasis on electronics and communications, thrived in Ottawa. The National Research Council, Communications Research Council, the two universities, and private companies such as Bell Northern Research were rich sources of research material and a highly skilled workforce. Demand for electronic equipment was increasing, and a ready customer, the federal government, was right on the doorstep. Other major markets, including Toronto, Montreal, the eastern seaboard of the United States, and Europe, were also within grasp.

The 1980s were characterized by the tech boom, when the more entrepreneurial of the research scientists began to start up their own companies. Ottawa became known as Silicon Valley North and millions of dollars changed hands in the hot world of the tech sector in the 1990s. Despite a recent slump and massive local layoffs in the industry, Ottawa's high-tech is here to stay. The injection of young, irreverent techies has brought new life to a city that was settling into a middle-income, middle-class snooze.

In all of this, the part played by the humble tourist must not be overlooked. Tourism is a major industry in Canada's capital city. Ottawa's natural beauty, its museums, attractions, and historic buildings, and its many festivals and colorful ceremonies all draw millions of visitors each year, many of them Canadian.

As Ottawa shapes its future in the new millennium, it continues to wrestle with the challenge of its dual role as a city and a capital. The formation of the new city of Ottawa in 2001, an amalgamation of 12 local municipal governments, has perhaps made this challenge easier to manage. With the new city of Gatineau in 2002, also formed from several local municipalities, an opportunity exists for both cities to join with the National Capital Commission to plan for the growth of the entire region to the benefit of all.

Index

See also Accomodations and Restaurant indexes, below.